Trevor Royle was born in India and his early childhood was spent in Malaysia. Brought up and educated in Scotland, he is a well-known writer and broadcaster with a special interest in the history and literature of war and imperialism, and is defence and foreign affairs specialist of the *Scotland on Sunday* newspaper. His recent books include literary criticism, *The Macmillan Companion to Scottish Literature*; biography, *The Kitchener Enigma*; and military history, *The Best Years of Their Lives*, a widely-acclaimed history of post-war National Service.

He lives in Edinburgh and is married with three sons.

'Royle proves himself to be a writer able to cope not only with military history but with a complex and introverted man who felt it his duty to hide his true nature' *The Scotsman*

'A rattling good yarn . . . Trevor Royle deserves our thanks' *Daily Telegraph*

'Royle's biography is a useful portrait of an individual born into imperial grandeur who witnessed and participated in its speedy collapse' *Scotland on Sunday*

Glubb Pasha

Trevor Royle

An *Abacus* Book

First published in Great Britain in 1992 by Little, Brown and Company
This edition published by Abacus 1993

A CIP catalogue record for this book is available from the British Library.

ISBN 0 349 10344 5

Typeset by Leaper & Gard Ltd, Bristol, England
Printed in England by Clays Ltd, St Ives plc

Abacus
A Division of
Little, Brown and Company (UK) Limited
165 Great Dover Street
London SE1 4YA

Contents

List of Photographs

List of Maps

Preface

The name of Glubb Pasha has been familiar to me since childhood; indeed, as an eleven-year-old boy in March 1956 I well remember the shock caused by his sensational dismissal by King Hussein of Jordan. At the time it was headline news and it remained a controversial subject for some time thereafter. In those days it was not the custom for important British subjects to be treated in such peremptory fashion by other countries and the treatment meted out to Glubb was a tremendous blow to Britain's prestige.

Later I read his books and took pleasure from the story of his service with the Bedouin people of what used to be known as Arabia: there was a resonance in his desert-song-chaps-round-the-campfire prose which had a great appeal in the 1950s when foreign travel was still a novelty. Not that such descriptions were in any way alien – my mother's family had lived in India since the nineteenth century and my childhood in Malaya and Scotland had been spiced with Indian words and phrases – but Glubb's account was entirely different, for it seemed to belong to a long-lost romantic age.

There were other connections. My father, a military engineer in the Indian Army, had served in Iraq and Syria when Glubb's Arab Legion won its spurs in battle; and I myself spent some time in the northern Saudi Arabian desert in December 1990 before the beginning of the war to oust Iraqi forces from Kuwait. In the constantly changing landscapes and weather conditions of the desert, Glubb's descriptions of his own time amongst the tribesmen came vividly to life. Whatever else he achieved – and he accomplished a great deal during his long life – Glubb knew how to write about scenery and places and the people who inhabited them.

During the land battle in February 1991, the UN coalition forces fought over some of the ground which Glubb's Desert Patrol had defended for Iraq during the late 1920s and the names on the campaign maps were a reminder of the largely forgotten Ikhwan wars between the tribes of southern Iraq and the Nejd, the country which was to become Saudi Arabia. And there was one other personal link – I had already written a biography of Kitchener of Khartoum, another of those great imperial servants who served British interests in the Middle East and was fascinated by the history and traditions of the Arab people.

Kitchener wrote little about his experiences, but Glubb in his time recorded a great deal in notes, reports, letters and diaries, both about his political and military ideology and about his lifelong love affair with the Arabs. Less revealingly, he also wrote about his own life in the first two books about his service with the Arab Legion and in an autobiography published in 1983. Later, while Grubb was still alive, his friend Major-General James Lunt wrote a biography, also entitled *Glubb Pasha*. As a battalion commander in the Arab Legion, General Lunt knew his subject well and the result was an affectionate portrait of the man and his career.

However, the book I have written is neither an official biography of a man who lived an exciting life amongst the Bedouin people of the desert, nor is it an account of a Christian soldier's time in the service of empire – although both elements play their part. Rather it is a political biography of a man who is rightly regarded as a key player in Britain's diplomatic initiatives in the Middle East between the 1920s and the mid-1950s. Throughout that period Glubb was the prop on which British policy stood or fell: so long as he remained in command of the Arab Legion and had the ear of the Hashemite Royal Family of Jordan, the British had a strong bulwark against the encroaching tide of Arab nationalism and Zionist expansionism, especially after the Second World War when Glubb was responsible for many of the political initiatives which have made the region what it is today.

There is, of course, Glubb the private man too, but he preferred to keep his prominent public self quite separate from the quiet life he led with his wife and family. Although he wrote voluminously about his career in the Middle East – and was also an accomplished interpreter of Arab history – he rarely introduced his private self into his writing, except by way of family anecdotes. This trait does not make him any less interesting than those who lead their lives under the full glare of personal publicity, but it does make him different in a world in which the revelation of intimate details is frequently regarded as a public right. Nonetheless, through the smoke-screen he laid to deter the inquisitive it is possible to discern this extraordinarily varied man – the Christian who understood the tenets of Islam, the man of God who was also a man of action, and the retiring family man who was also a loyal servant to the British government and to the Hashemite Royal Family of Jordan.

Glubb's books are long out of print (as is James Lunt's biography) and they are long out-of-date as modern reference works. However, the release of official documents dealing with the period 1946–56 has made much clearer the direction of British foreign policy in the Middle East as successive governments attempted to steer a path between the conflicting needs of the Jordanians, the Israelis and the Palestinians made homeless by the first Arab–Israeli war of 1948. In many of the documents Glubb's name features prominently and his own reports on the political situation were taken seriously by the Foreign Office in London. Like several other British administrators in the Middle East at that time, Glubb was pro-Arab, in that he admired the Bedouin people and owed his loyalty to King Abdullah of Jordan, but he also acknowledged the existence of Israel and had several Israeli friends. Being a good servant of Britain, though, he would have preferred a compromise which would have allowed Arab and Jew to live together in harmony.

A word about the presentation of the book. In addition to finding its own way through the minefield of Middle Eastern politics, any study of the Arab world has to address the question of Arab orthography because there is no consistent tradition of Arab transliteration. For example, Glubb in his day would talk about, and official documents would record, 'Trans-Jordan' or 'the Amir Abdulla' whereas modern usage prefers 'Transjordan' and 'the Emir Abdullah'. Government papers would also discuss 'the Nejed' ('Nejd') or 'Ibn Sauod' ('Ibn Saud'). I have therefore retained the older styles when quoting official documents but in my own text and commentary I have employed the modern-day spellings.

Trevor Royle
Edinburgh, December 1991

Acknowledgements

This book could never have been written without the active support of the Glubb family and I was fortunate enough to receive nothing but kindly help and encouragement from them throughout the project. I am particularly indebted to Rosemary, Lady Glubb, both for her guidance and care on the one hand, and for her kindness and hospitality on the other. Not only did she patiently and painstakingly consider all my many queries but she also went out of her way to be helpful with the loan of documents and photographs.

I was also in the happy position of having an enthusiastic ally in her daughter Naomi who provided me with several illuminating insights into her father's life and work. She and Lady Glubb both read the book in manuscript form and made many useful suggestions and corrections although I must stress that any remaining errors are my responsibility alone.

During his lifetime Jack Glubb wrote many thousands of words. As well as publishing twenty-two books he kept a regular diary and was a veritable magpie with his own private papers. After his death the bulk of his collection was donated to the archives of the Middle East Centre at St Antony's College, Oxford, where they were loosely catalogued by Gillian Grant. During the course of several invigorating visits to the library I received much valuable assistance from the Centre's director Derek Hopwood, librarian Diane Ring and archivist Floresca Karanasou.

At an early stage in my research Colonel Robert Melville

was kind enough to take an interest and he gave me much practical advice about the work of the Arab Legion in the post-war years. As Glubb's liaison officer in London he was well placed to observe the political relationship between Britain and Jordan and Glubb's role in shaping it. Wing Commander Jock Dalgleish helped enormously by letting me see his privately produced memoirs and by talking to me about his service in Jordan. Other former officers of the Arab Legion who helped me come to a better understanding of Glubb were Nigel Bromage, James Lunt (the author of an earlier biography about Glubb), John Salmon and Robert Young. They all have my thanks.

Family friends of the Glubbs who helped in similar fashion include Geoffrey Barlow and Molly White who was kind enough to provide me with a written memoir of her time as Glubb's secretary in Jordan. Lady Glubb also gave me a copy of Canon Donald Carter's thought-provoking funeral address.

Through the good offices of John Bowes, secretary of the Cheltonian Society, I received many useful insights into Glubb's education at Cheltenham. He was also kind enough to present me with a copy of M.C. Morgan's spirited history of the college.

I was in the happy position of receiving much helpful advice and encouragement from friends and colleagues. Lawrence James, mould-breaking biographer of Lawrence of Arabia, offered some keen insights into the Anglo-Arab world of the 1920s, as did Alexander Maitland friend and biographer of Dame Freya Stark. Others who helped in different ways include Dr Alan Bell of Rhodes House Library Oxford, Dr Sheila Brock of the Royal Museums of Scotland and Major Ken Lewis, assistant regimental adjutant Welsh Guards.

During the Gulf crisis and war of 1990–1 Andrew Jaspan, editor of *Scotland on Sunday*, encouraged me to write for his newspaper about the political and military issues: I am grateful to him and to his deputy Brian Groom for much ready support. (Not forgetting Christopher Irvine, my colleague in the 'bunker' during those memorable days.)

Captain Peter Voute, Royal Navy, made arrangements for me to visit the region and I acknowledge with thanks both his help and the hospitality I received from Lieutenant-Colonel John Sharples and the officers and men of The Royal Scots Dragoon Guards and Lieutenant-Colonel Rory Clayton and the officers and men of 40 Field Regiment Royal Artillery (The Lowland Gunners).

For help in locating documents and photographs I wish to thank the staffs of the Imperial War Museum, London; the National Library of Scotland, Edinburgh; and the Public Record Office, Kew. Crown copyright material in the Public Record Offfice is reproduced by permission of the Controller of Her Majesty's Stationery Office. Extracts from the *Middle East: British Military Personnel* archive are reproduced by permission of the Director of the Imperial War Museum.

The maps were drawn by Sir John Bagot Glubb and were first published in *War in the Desert*, *The Story of the Arab Legion* and *A Soldier with the Arabs*.

For financial assistance in researching the background to Glubb's life and career I gratefully acknowledge the generous help given to me by Douglas Blyth and the trustees of the Hélène Heroys Foundation.

Others whose help cannot remain unacknowledged include my good friend John Bright-Holmes who edited the manuscript with his customary care and precision; my agent Gloria Ferris who was a tower of strength throughout the project; and my publisher Alan Samson who never complained about having to wait somewhat longer than expected for the final manuscript.

Prologue

Like many other British imperial servants of his generation, John Bagot Glubb spent his life in two different worlds. There was the England of his birth, the late Victorian and Edwardian years in which his childhood was spent; half a century later he was to return to his native country, by then a changed place, to live out his life in rural Sussex. Then there was the world in which he saw his years of service to Britain's imperial cause, the countries of the Middle East which had sprung into being in the aftermath of the collapse of the Ottoman Empire and the Allied victory in the First World War. Both worlds were to influence the man he became, a soldier who was also on the side of the poor and the dispossessed, a committed Christian who admired the tenets of Islam, a man of action who believed that it was possible to interpret Western ways to Arab minds.

Glubb was born in 1897, a few months before the sonorous celebrations mounted for Queen Victoria's Diamond Jubilee. This was the high-water mark of a century which had seen Britain increase her imperial holdings to become the richest and most powerful nation on earth. With her battleships, armies, colonies and the money to finance them, Britain appeared to be an unassailable power which could confidently face the rest of the world from the splendour of her fortress isolation. British commercial and financial supremacy was an acknowledged fact and seemingly in every part of the globe British adventurers were either building railways and canals,

1

or opening up virgin jungles, or investing in new industries, or revenging wrongs committed against them, or putting native states in their place, or grandly ruling the waves.

It was known, in self-conscious imitation of the rule of Rome, as the Pax Britannica but this new imperialism was not just a commercial or administrative concept; it had also become adopted as a creed. The governance of empire was a sacred duty which had been given in trust. Quite simply it amounted to an insistence that it was civilised Britain's pre-ordained role to bring light where there was once darkness, to rule the poor, the oppressed and the non-whites for their own sakes and to bring wealth and order to the underprivileged of the world. It allied itself to an aura of manliness which for the late Victorian male was to become the apotheosis of empire: the young district officer riding the desert plains of Sudan, the planter in Ceylon, the Guides' officer keeping vigil on the North-West Frontier of India, the railway engineer in Uganda, the miner reaping the earth's riches in Borneo or South Africa, or the explorer almost anywhere: all those characteristic types added up to an imperial ideal and fuelled a generation's imagination.

It was a self-satisfied age – arrogant, smug and mettlesome – and the mood found its greatest expression in the celebrations laid on for the commemoration of Queen Victoria's Diamond Jubilee in London on 22 June 1897. Its centrepiece was the largest military parade ever seen in London, some 50,000 men strong, and, as the soldiers marched their colourful way to a service of thanksgiving outside St Paul's Cathedral, it seemed to the cheering crowds that here was assembled the pomp and power of an empire destined to stay in being for decades to come. There were colourful squadrons of lancers from India, mounted carabiniers from Natal, bush-whacking troopers from New South Wales, Canadian high-landers and a bewildering, even bizarre, mixture of men in uniform from the more exotic corners of the empire – British Guiana, Cyprus, Malaya, Borneo and Hong Kong. Small wonder that even *The Times* was to break from its normally sober tones to claim that Britain possessed 'the mightiest and most beneficial empire ever known in the annals of mankind'.

The mood would have affected the Glubb family, middle class and typical of the period, a family which had given loyal service to the army and the empire. They had served as soldiers in India during the nineteenth century and in 1897 Frederic Manley Glubb, John's father, was a serving officer in the Royal Engineers whose career would take him to the rank of major-general, a knighthood and illustrious service in both the Boer and the First World Wars. On his mother's side John Glubb's background was Anglo-Irish, that curious relic of Britain's historic links with Ireland, all horses, wit and gently decaying country houses. The atmosphere at home was patriotic, loyal and confident. God was in his heaven and, no doubt, supporting British interests. At sea the ships of the Royal Navy protected the nation's holdings from the jealousies of European rivals and in the Sudan, making his inexorable way to Khartoum, was a man who was the very epitome of British imperial pluck, Major-General Horatio Herbert Kitchener, a soldier who came from a similar background to the Glubbs.

The class into which Glubb himself was born also schooled its sons in the imperial ideal of service and duty. The great Victorian English public schools had been founded for that very purpose and educational institutions like Clifton, Malvern, Wellington, Marlborough, and Cheltenham – John Glubb's school – set standards of physical and mental discipline which were designed to last a man throughout his life. With a diet of games, classics and the Christian religion they inculcated such important Victorian concepts as the stiff upper lip, a sense of fair play, the importance of maintaining appearances, and adherence to an unbending moral code. What they engineered was a product built for public service, men who possessed great physical courage and who were imbued with such manly virtues as a sense of good form and honour.

3

It was into such a background that John Glubb was born and, even though its aura of invulnerability was to be destroyed by the First World War, its echoes were to remain with him throughout his life. Unlike his forebears who had seen service in India, and his father who had spent some time in Mauritius, young Glubb was to find fulfilment in the Biblical lands of the Middle East, in countries – such as Iraq and Jordan – which did not even exist as states when he was a schoolboy.

In fact, the term 'Middle East' was not even in common usage at the time. Glubb knew the area as the 'Near East' which included much of the Balkans, or 'the Levant', the eastern Mediterranean areas of Syria, Palestine, Lebanon and the Sinai peninsula. However, after the First World War the term Middle East was used more often to encompass both those areas and, as conceived by Glubb's generation, it consisted of present-day Egypt, Israel, Lebanon, Syria, Jordan, Iraq, Iran, Turkey, Soviet Central Asia, Afghanistan and the Arab states of the Arabian peninsula. It was into that world that John Bagot Glubb arrived as an imperial policeman in Iraq and then as a soldier and statesman in Transjordan, which became the Hashemite Kingdom of Jordan in 1946. He served both countries faithfully and enjoyed a love affair with the Arab world which lasted a lifetime.

It was a comfortable arrangement, for the Anglo-Arabs were perhaps the most relaxed and happiest of Britain's great imperial servants. Not only did they admire and like the Bedouins, they also saw in their quiet reserve and unobtrusive arrogance some of the virtues of the English gentleman. Glubb was one of the most distinguished of the Anglo-Arabs and, as Glubb Pasha – the title came from that given to a provincial governor or high official of the Ottoman Empire – he was to become the very personification of Britain's obligations to the Arabs of the Middle East, a second, and perhaps greater, Lawrence of Arabia.

Little did those Anglo-Arabs know, though, that their imperial enterprise would be so short-lived, that all the boundary fixing, all the special creation of League of Nations' mandates and all the political and military support of the early 1920s would ultimately count for so little. The signs were hopeful in 1922, but the Middle East had already been set on the course which would put the region on the rack at the end of the twentieth century – the endless wars between Israel and her neighbours, the battling between rival religious factions in Lebanon, the upsurge of Arab nationalism leading to assassination and massacre, not just in the lands of the Middle East and Central Asia but also in other further-flung parts of the world, the tragedy of the Palestinian refugees in the Israeli-occupied territories and the conflicting sects of Islam, from Iran in the Shi'ite world to the Wahhabi faith in Saudi Arabia and the Muslim Brotherhood in Syria, Egypt and elsewhere in the Sunni world.

In August 1990 the shadow cast by the artificial creation of boundaries and the partition of tribal areas led indirectly to Saddam Hussein, the peasant dictator of Iraq, invading and claiming the small but wealthy neighbour state of Kuwait. Six months later, in January 1991, the armies of the United Nations' coalition went to war to protect the rights of one of its member states, a country whose boundaries had been fixed in 1921, as part of the British and French carve-up of the Middle East.

Glubb's story is part of that muddled imperial process.

1

A Boyish Education

John Bagot Glubb was born on 16 April 1897 in the Lancashire garrison town of Preston. His father, then Major Frederic Manley Glubb, was himself the son of a soldier and for the previous twenty-two years had served in the Corps of Royal Engineers, the 'sappers'. The Glubbs were a solid, unprepossessing middle-class family, never rich, whose antecedents lay in the English west country, the counties of Devon and Cornwall. His mother, Frances Letitia, belonged to an altogether more glamorous family and to an easily recognised social group in Victorian Britain: the Anglo-Irish gentry. With their easy manners and interest in country matters they had been great servants of empire and, like the Prussian Junkers in Germany, the Anglo-Irish families had provided the British Army with some of its finest soldiers – including Field Marshals Wolseley, Roberts, Kitchener and French.

The name 'Glubb' does not feature in any of the major dictionaries of British surnames and a glance at the telephone directories proves that holders of the name are few and far between. There is a sizeable clan of Glubbs in New Zealand, formed from nineteenth-century immigrants, but as John Bagot Glubb noted in his old age, 'the Glubbs in England have always been few in number, often consisting of only four or five persons'.[1] At the time, 1983, he had been told that his name might be Gaelic in origin, a corruption of *bog* meaning damp or soft, although he was also prepared to admit that the

7

real decipherment might be lost in antiquity.

One thing was certain: from their very beginnings the Glubbs were a noted military family. Their coat-of-arms is 'gules a water bouget argent' and their crest 'a demi-lion rampant azure seme of byzants'. Water bougets were the goatskins of water carried across the shoulders and they were used by European knights during the Crusades. As the crest was only awarded to the knights of the Fourth Crusade who looted Constantinople in 1203, it is reasonable to suppose that the Glubbs had emerged as a notable family by the end of the twelfth century. The first Glubb to be recorded in history, though, was one Henry Glubb, Member of Parliament for Okehampton in Devon in 1313 during the reign of King Edward II. He came from a farming family who owned land near Tavistock and it was from him that Glubb traced his ancestry.

The Devon Glubbs were typical of their class, lesser landed gentry who loved rural life. They farmed the land and served as justices of the peace; hunting and field sports were their leisure pastimes – by the thirteenth century English country gentlemen were notorious throughout Europe for their devotion to their horses and dogs – and they tended to intermarry with other local landed families. A recurring name in the Glubb family tree is that of the neighbouring family of Glanville who came originally from Normandy. Rarely wealthy and never poor, the various branches of the Devon Glubbs regarded their manors as home and lived in the certain knowledge that son would follow son in line of succession. Younger sons went into the Church or law and it was from one of these lines that John Bagot Glubb was descended.

His great-grandfather, John Matthew Glubb, was the youngest son of Peter Goodman Glubb, a lawyer, who had settled at Liskeard in Cornwall; he was the common ancestor of the Cornwall and Sussex branches to which Glubb belonged. John's grandmother was a Cunningham, a near relation of the Scottish Earls of Glencairn. Family tradition has it that these Cunninghams were 'out' with the Jacobites during the 1715 rebellion but this seems unlikely as the 12th Earl of Glencairn was at that time a firm supporter of Scotland's union with England. John Matthew Glubb had been educated at Exeter College, Oxford, and graduated in 1814. Thereafter Rector of St Petrox, Dartmouth, he was later transferred to Shermanbury in Sussex where he died in 1871. His wife was Mary James Lyne of Little Petherick in Cornwall; by coincidence Peter's brother John married Mary's sister Christian in the same year, 1815.

The Cornish branch continued by Peter and Christian became extinct in the 1920s but the Sussex branch begun by John and Mary flourished. A first son, Orlando Manley, was born in 1827 and a second, also John Matthew, in 1837; both were sent out to India to become officers in the Bengal Army of the East India Company. Orlando was commissioned as an ensign in the 37th Bengal Light Infantry in 1847.

A young man who joined the army of the East India Company had little hope of seeing his family again once he had left for India and so it proved in Orlando's case – having survived the Mutiny of 1857 he died of cholera in Meerut in 1861. Indeed, the annual returns of the Bengal Army in the first quarter of the nineteenth century show that only 201 officers retired on pension while 1,243 were killed on active service or died of cholera and other diseases.[2] Nonetheless, competition to enter the service of the East India Company was keen and the directors could afford to pick and choose. The brighter boys went into the commercial side of the operation and became skilled merchants and administrators while the more adventurous became officers in one of the three armies operated by the company in Bengal, Bombay and Madras.

For them there was ample opportunity to see action and although battles were often one-sided affairs, warfare and its accompanying casualties also brought the promise of promotion. Moreover, service in India meant that a young man could live well for no great expense, an important consideration for a family of modest means like the Glubbs. The one

9

drawback was the lack of leave. Both the Glubb boys could not expect to be given furlough until they had completed at least fifteen years of service and even then they would be expected to pay their own and their family's passage home. If the officer were married, as Orlando was, then leave became even more expensive as he would have to find the fares for his wife and any family.

Orlando, John Glubb's grandfather, married Frances Letitia Kelly in Calcutta on 2 October 1856; she was the eldest daughter of Captain John Kelly who was serving in India with the Royal Irish Fusiliers (87th Foot). Thus began the Glubbs' first connection with an Irish family – the Kellys came from New Park in County Longford and the grandfather, also a John Kelly, had served with Wellington in the Peninsular War. Unlike the later Victorian soldiers who discouraged marriage below the rank of major, the officers of the Bengal Army were not discriminated against if they took a wife. Orlando Glubb was just under thirty when he married but his military career had not been without danger. He had served in the 2nd Sikh War of 1848–49 which had resulted in the annexation of the Punjab, and he had seen action in both the major battles of Chillianwallah and Gujrat. During the Mutiny his regiment was disbanded because it took part in the revolt against the British, but it was always Orlando's proud boast that his company alone refused to open fire on its British officers. According to John Glubb, 'His wife, my grandmother, who was looking on from the window of their quarter in the barracks, used to tell how he drew his sword and stood in front of the armoury, or possibly the ammunition store. Presumably he was personally popular with the men. A few scattered shots were fired at him, but he stood his ground. Eventually the men marched off to join the mutineers at Delhi, leaving him, sword drawn, at the door of the armoury.'[3]

After the Mutiny Orlando became an administrator, becoming firstly Cantonment Chief Magistrate in Allahabad and then Military Secretary in the North-West Frontier

Province. His final job was District Superintendent of Police in Meerut and it was there that he died on 27 June 1861. His brother John had different luck: he, too, escaped the Mutiny and the massacres in Delhi and later became a captain in the Bengal Staff Corps. Illness prevented further promotion and he resigned his commission in 1866 to live in retirement in Bedford. Following the family tradition his son, also called John Matthew, went to Exeter College, Oxford, and, like his grandfather, entered the Church.

Orlando's death meant that his wife had little option but to quit India and return home to Britain. For a decade she stayed with her father-in-law at Shermanbury, but when he died in 1871 she bought a small cottage and lived out her life at Cowfold in Sussex. Like many other Victorian widows of her class, she wore mourning clothes for the rest of her life. She died in 1904 and her grandson John Glubb always remembered her 'peculiarly sweet face and gentle smile'. Two children had been born to her while she was in India – Frederic Manley on 19 August 1857 and Louisa Fanny on 18 November 1858. Shortage of funds meant that her son had to pay his way through school by working hard – after prep school in Brighton he won a scholarship to Wellington College and in due course passed third into the Royal Military Academy, Woolwich.

Frederic Manley Glubb was commissioned into the Corps of Royal Engineers on 25 January 1877 and, after leaving the School of Military Engineering at Chatham, he was posted to Portsmouth and then to the Curragh in Ireland. During the late Victorian period a regular soldier had a one-in-two chance of serving abroad. The army was around 212,000 men strong and of these 72,000 were stationed in India and a further 32,000 in the various colonial possessions which required military garrisons. In 1879, Frederic Glubb was posted to Bermuda which was considered to be one of the better stations due to its climate and its proximity to North America. Taking advantage of the latter, Frederic Glubb used his first leave in 1882 to visit America and Canada. There he

11

spent much of his time on the Atlantic seaboard – he paid a visit to the American military academy at West Point – but, as his diary records, he also took the opportunity to visit the real 'wild west'.

11th August. Early in the morning we arrived at the end of our journey, twelve miles from Billings, just across the Yellowstone [river]. Here we stayed a few hours and then returned eastwards. We stopped a short time at the towns we passed on the way, among them Glendire and Miles City. They are both new towns, not yet settled down to wheat growing and honest industry, but full of desperadoes and villains of every nationality, who retire before the advance of civilisation. We stopped at Fort Keogh, near Miles City, and were kindly received by the officers stationed there. Nearby was an encampment of friendly Cheyenne Indians, to the chief of whom, Yellowhorse, we were introduced.[4]

The letters and diaries from that period reveal Frederic Glubb as a lively young man with an inquiring mind, much given to pranks and high jinks and, if required, much hard drinking. (His advice on the avoidance of nervousness during amateur theatricals was unequivocal – 'drink a glass of port behind the scenes before every act'.) It is also easy to believe that his Irish charm and boyish good looks made him a popular figure both in the mess and in civilian society.

From an early age, too, he was a good horseman and as a young officer he threw himself into equestrian activities with great gusto. After the Bermuda posting he was transferred with the 15th Field Company, Royal Engineers, to Malta and it was there that his interests became something of an obsession. Because he lacked the funds to keep decent mounts he devoted himself to buying unpromising or difficult horses which he then trained for his own use. At other times he rode his brother officers' horses in steeplechases, his slight figure giving him the ideal frame for an amateur jockey. By 1886 he was honorary secretary of the Malta Gymkhana and was a respected figure in military equestrian circles. This love of horses he passed on to his son.

A turning-point in Frederic Glubb's life was his posting in 1887 to the Curragh, Britain's principal military base in Ireland. A large grassy plain to the west of Dublin in County Kildare, the Curragh offered Glubb the chance to take up hunting, another lifelong interest, and it also introduced him to polite Anglo-Irish society. Within two years of his posting he had met and married Frances Letitia Bagot, the daughter of a Dublin barrister whose country seat was at Carranure in County Roscommon. By then he was a captain in the 12th Field Company, Royal Engineers, and was in charge of works at Athlone in the centre of Ireland. Immediately after their wedding, though, the Glubbs sailed for Hong Kong where they remained for three years. 'My father still rode in the garrison races,' remembered John Glubb later, 'and my mother lived the usual life of a garrison overseas, playing tennis or leaving visiting cards on the families of the other officers.'[5]

The Bagots were one of Ireland's oldest Anglo-Norman families whose ancestors had crossed over in 1169 as part of the invasion force mounted by Richard Fitzherbert de Clare, Earl of Pembroke, and better known to history as 'Strongbow'. In the subsequent Norman settlements of Ireland the Bagots were granted land in County Limerick with their seat at Bagotstown Castle. Like most other Norman families they were assimilated into Irish life becoming, as the saying has it, more Irish than the Irish. (Another branch remained in England with their seat in Staffordshire.) Originally, the Bagots had crossed to England in 1066 and their name appears on the Battle Abbey Roll of knights who fought with William at the Battle of Hastings.

Frances Letitia Glubb was the perfect foil to Frederic Glubb. She could match him in wit and charm and enjoyed the round of social activities which were an integral part of army life. Even in her old age – she lived into her nineties –

13

she could still sparkle with a sense of enjoyment and gaiety which was the envy of others. John Glubb's wife, Rosemary, remembers her mother-in-law keeping the family amused and entertained with unlikely, but highly enjoyable, stories of Irish rural life, the passing of the years never diminishing her powers of recall. It was not all froth, though: she had to demonstrate a good deal of fortitude and independence in her marriage, because in the years to come her husband was to be absent on active service and she was often left alone to be responsible for her children's welfare and education – Gwenda May was born on 1 June 1894 and John Bagot three years later.

Those separations did cause problems. In later life Glubb admitted that his father's long absences allowed him to give full rein to his own emotions and, as a result, he fell victim to outbursts of bad temper. In his mature years Glubb rarely spoke a harsh word but, like other potentially volatile men, he had by then learned to keep his feelings in check. It was not always so. Once as a child, while staying with family friends in Norfolk, Glubb reacted to a sharp word from his mother by throwing one of his shoes at an engraving and smashing it. This 'violent fit of temper' as he described it was followed by shame and penitence and by fresh promises to keep his temper under firmer control.

For all that he recalled kicking against his mother's attempts to bring him up properly, Glubb was very attached to her and throughout their lives they enjoyed a close and loving relationship. He also believed that he was in some way responsible for the gynaecological difficulties suffered by her during his birth. 'Unwittingly I had inflicted constant pain on her,' he recalled. 'Something had gone wrong when I was born in that little house in Preston, and ever afterwards, if she were tired, she would suffer from acute abdominal pains.'[6] In spite of those continuing problems, though, she still had a full life and her intellectual curiosity led her to master French, German and Italian and she was a regular visitor to those three countries. From his mother Glubb inherited much of the gaiety and sense of fun which, paradoxically, he preferred to keep hidden, except in the company of family or close friends. From his father, often a remote figure, came the ideals of duty and discipline. It could be said that Glubb's mother nurtured the 'heart' or the emotional side of John Glubb ('Jack' to his family), while from his father he inherited the 'mind' or intellectual side of his character. The split between the two, often a conflict, was to become a noticeable feature of Glubb's psychological make-up in later life.

By the time of their son's birth, the Glubbs had been in England for four years, first in Preston and then in Portsmouth where they had a house at Netley on Southampton Water. It was then that war broke out between the British and the Boer rebels in South Africa. 'My soldiers are in ecstasies,' wrote Lord Lansdowne from the War Office to Joseph Chamberlain, the Colonial Secretary, on hearing the news of the declaration of war on 12 October 1899. That early rapture, though, was to give way to dismay by the year's end as the British Army was humbled in the field by smaller and more mobile Boer forces. By the beginning of 1900 it was obvious that a larger army would be required and the British began to move more men to South Africa under the command of Roberts and Kitchener.

Every officer in the army was keen to be in on the act as war offered the opportunity to test themselves against their peacetime training. As professional soldiers they wanted to know how their men and equipment would stand up to combat and there was a curiosity, too, about battle itself. 'The desire of soldiers to serve in wars cannot be attributed, as is sometimes done, to mere bloodthirstiness,' argued John Glubb in the family history he wrote towards the end of his life. 'It is perhaps more like the feeling of a young surgeon, for example, who having completed his training, is assigned to an administrative post.'[7] More to the point, perhaps, war provided the chance to engage in fighting, battles meant casualties and casualties meant promotion. At the time of the outbreak of war Frederic Glubb had just been promoted to the rank of major and like other officers in that position he realised that the next two promotions to lieutenant-colonel and colonel would be vital for his future in the army.

Having 'fretted and fumed at Netley', Frederic Glubb received his marching orders in February 1900 and sailed for South Africa on board the troopship SS *Goorkha*. On his arrival at Cape Town on 21 March he took over command of the 17th Field Company, Royal Engineers, which had been badly mauled during the Battle of Spion Kop. As part of General Buller's field force Glubb and his men took part in the advance from Natal into the Transvaal which included the skirmishes at Laing's Nek and Botha's Pass. Although these operations helped to bring to a close the war of set-piece battles, the guerilla stage of the war was destined to last until early 1903. An unforced injury – he fell from his horse and broke an ankle – brought Glubb home before then, in 1901, but the war had served its purpose. He had seen action, he had been promoted to lieutenant-colonel and for his services in South Africa he had been awarded the Distinguished Service Order.

There was to be little respite for the Glubb family with the return to peacetime soldiering. In 1903 Glubb was posted to the Crown Colony of Mauritius to command the Royal Engineers' detachment there. Once a French possession – it had been transferred to Britain in 1815 – Mauritius offered an ideal climate and outstanding scenery. The Glubbs lived up-country at Vacoa and Jack Glubb, by then a lively six-year-old, was to remember the exotic plants and trees and the profusion of sugar-cane fields which had been planted by the French settlers. It was in Mauritius that he was taught French by his French governess, demonstrating at that early age a precocious ability to pick up foreign languages as easily as his mother did. Like other youngsters reared in the tropics Glubb came to regard that part of his childhood spent in Mauritius as a period in paradise. Here perhaps he was not too far off the mark, as one of his father's predecessors, Gordon of Khartoum, used to argue that the Garden of Eden lay further to the north, in the island of Praslin, part of the Seychelles group.

Three years later, in 1906, the Glubbs returned to Britain, travelling through South Africa and continuing aboard the Union Castle liner SS *Armadale Castle*. Frederic Glubb had been posted to Aldershot, the British Army's principal training base in southern England and it was there that he introduced his son to the pleasures of horse riding. The regiments of the Brigade of Guards were trained at Aldershot in the Marlborough Lines and the sights and sounds of their ceremonial and operational duties were to have a lasting effect on the young boy: 'It was during these years that I acquired two dedications, which were both to play a considerable part in my life – my devotion to soldiers and to horses.'[8]

The idyll was rudely shattered. In 1909, having completed three years as a lieutenant-colonel, Frederic Glubb was placed on half-pay, the army's solution for retaining promising officers for whom no suitable appointment could be found. For well-to-do officers the hardships were slight as the move involved a period away from the army which could be used for travel or leisure. Glubb, though, had no private means and going on half-pay created difficulties for him and his family. The only solution, one taken by many another officer in his position, was to move to Switzerland, then one of the least expensive countries in Europe. The English had other reasons for liking the place. With its mild climate and its preponderance of spas, Switzerland had attracted a large colony of expatriate English settlers during the Victorian and Edwardian periods; and to make them feel at home the Swiss had thrown up gaunt villas and hotels in the commonest English styles. The country also boasted a number of English private schools and young Glubb was educated at one of them, the Institution Sillig at Bellerive on the shores of Lake Geneva. Here he learned to row and to ski, a sport, for the British at least, still in its infancy.

The enforced period of exile lasted for eighteen months and came to an end when the War Office recalled Colonel

Glubb to take up the post of Chief Engineer with Northern Command in York. There they lived in a house called Fairmount Lodge which stood opposite the racecourse; it was during this period of his boyhood that Glubb extended his knowledge of horsemanship to include hunting. As his father was entitled to two mounts one of them was given to Jack Glubb – a grey Arab pony which he called 'Jumbo'. One day was to stick in the boy's memory, 2 January 1911: whilst riding with the York and Ainsty Foxhounds he was in at the kill and was blooded by an enthusiastic huntsman – the boy's face was smeared with the blood of the dead fox. The mask was also presented to him and after it was stuffed and mounted it became a prized possession.

This was one of the happiest periods in Glubb's life, partly because the family remained together and his father was employed in a senior position, and partly because he was involved in all manner of things to do with horses. Indeed Glubb's written memories of his early boyhood have a literary quality that stands comparison with Siegfried Sasson's *Memoirs of a Fox-hunting Man*. Although Glubb followed the traditional English middle-class route of prep school followed by public school, it was always the holidays that stuck in his mind. In 1911 his father was transferred to Southern Command at Salisbury where the hunting country was not as testing as in Yorkshire. Nonetheless it was a countryside which bewitched the young Glubb. Here he is at the end of a day's hunting, having braved a daring jump over a high oak fence:

About a mile further on as we topped a rise, we came in sight of hounds, crying and jostling round the huntsman, who was holding the dead fox in his hands. 'Who-hoop!' he cried. 'Who-hoop!' as he threw the carcass into the air to be caught and torn by the hounds. There were only five horsemen up. The huntsman and one whip, and three other men. Another galloped up not far behind me. Soon my father appeared on old Joe, who was blowing hard and wagging his tail. He had come up the next valley and through a gate in the wire, without seeing our oak rails. 'Who-hoop!' said Jummy [Jumbo] and I in our hearts. 'We did teach them a lesson. What a day! Forty-five minutes at full speed without a check, jumping all the way and a flight of oak rails at the end!'[9]

Glubb could just as easily have been Siegfried Sassoon's alter ego, young George Sherston out with the Packlestone Hunt.

While his father was serving at York, Jack Glubb was sent to Stancliffe Hall school at Matlock in Derbyshire. It was an unpretentious establishment whose sole purpose was to get its boys into public school and its headmaster judged his success rate by academic achievement. In Glubb he had a ready pupil who worked hard for the scholarship which was required to help pay his way through school – in 1901 the *Cornhill Magazine* advised that an annual income of £800, more than a colonel's basic pay, was necessary to support two boys at public school. Great was the joy, therefore which greeted the news that Glubb had won an open scholarship worth £70 to Cheltenham College – a sum sufficient to pay all the fees. Throughout his life Glubb remained justly proud that he had contributed to the cost of his education and had not been a financial burden on his parents.

Cheltenham was an interesting choice of school – his father had been educated at Wellington, the country's leading officer-producing school, but by the end of the nineteenth century its primacy was under threat from schools like Clifton and Cheltenham. Gwenda, three years older than Jack, had already made a connection with the spa town by attending Cheltenham Ladies College where she had taken great pride in her mother's side of the family and always described herself as Irish. 'Well, if your family has lived in Ireland since the thirteenth century,' she would tell friends, 'I assume you can call yourself Irish even if we did come over with the Plantagenets!' She was also one of the first women drivers – self-taught in the family car of a schoolfriend – and she passed on the skill to Jack. Although their father was, first and foremost, a horseman he always encouraged his children to experiment and in Gwenda's case her enthusiasm led to a career when she became one of Britain's most prominent post-war racing-car drivers.

Glubb arrived at Cheltenham College in September 1911, the seventieth anniversary of its foundation. It had been established in 1841 to provide a decent means of schooling for the sons of the gentry who had come to live in the thriving Gloucestershire town. From the outset it provided boarding facilities and within a short time its reputation for getting its boys into the armed forces and Oxford and Cambridge had attracted entrants from all over the country. The opening of the Cheltenham–Swindon line by the Great Western Railway provided a further incentive to middle-class families who wanted their sons to enjoy the kind of public-school education which had been made so popular by Thomas Arnold at Rugby. What this amounted to was a thorough grounding in elementary subjects, an emphasis on the classics, a reverence for the tenets of Christianity and, later, a glorification of sport. Moreover Arnold, who had a constitutional dislike of young children, encouraged his prefects to develop and maintain a code of discipline under-pinned by his own sermons and strict religious doctrines. Although the system had obvious limitations it was embraced enthusiastically by the Victorian middle classes and Rugby spawned a number of imitations of which Cheltenham was one.

By the time that Glubb arrived at Cheltenham many of the more extreme elements of the Arnoldian doctrine, such as the beatings and the high moral tone of the Christian teachings, had disappeared, but the college was still run on fairly rigorous lines. There was a classical side which prepared boys for entry into the universities and the prestigious Indian Civil Service, and a military side whose sole purpose was to get boys into the army's military academies at Sandhurst and Woolwich. In this, Cheltenham was extremely successful:

between 1890 and 1912 the average annual number of entrants into the Royal Military Academy, Woolwich, was fifteen and it was reckoned a bad year in which Cheltenham did not gain most of the top places in the list. Their only rivals during that period were Wellington and Clifton. To achieve those impressive results the boys on the military side were given a stolid, if repetitive, curriculum which included Classics, English, History, Geography, French, Mathematics, Chemistry and Drawing, with the emphasis being placed on learning by rote.

As a scholarship boy Glubb was expected to do well and he admitted later in life that he never had any difficulty coping with the academic side of school life. In particular, he excelled at French, one of the few subjects, according to the college history, which Cheltenham taught only moderately well. Here Glubb had an edge because he had learned French as a little boy in Mauritius and had mastered it at school in Switzerland. His mother, too, encouraged him to read French literature – Pascal's *Pensées* were an early favourite, as much for their religious content as their literary worth – and French was often spoken at home, for Gwenda, too, was a gifted linguist. The ease with which he picked up a foreign language stood Glubb in good stead when he went to the Middle East in the 1920s – he picked up colloquial Arabic and quickly became sufficiently proficient to read and write the language. He also insisted that every British officer under his command should be able to speak basic Arabic.

Although the missionary fervour of Cheltenham's founding fathers had largely disappeared from the curriculum, religion and the Church were still an important part of college life in Glubb's day. Matins and Evensong were compulsory and for those boys, like Glubb, who had been confirmed, there was Holy Communion each Sunday. For them, chapel became a real focus of school life and Glubb always insisted that he took pleasure in the majestic statuary at the centre of the reredos – a triumphant Christ on the Cross, with the Virgin Mary and St John on either side. (Cheltenham repaid

21

the debt in 1991 when a memorial tablet in Glubb's memory was unveiled in the chapel.)

Scripture lessons, too, were compulsory throughout the school, right up to the Upper Sixth, and most boys were able to recite portions of the Bible by heart. Here, too, Lady Glubb's influence was felt, for she was given to sending her son revivalist religious tracts with titles like *Words of Comfort and Consolation* and Brother Lawrence's *Practice in the Presence of God.* Although these were undoubtedly embarrassing – Glubb admitted that he could only read them while hiding in the lavatories – he always dutifully thanked his mother for sending them. According to Maurice Bowra, a contemporary, Glubb was a reserved and high-minded boy who escaped the bullying his religious tracts might have inspired by simply keeping out of trouble.

Where Glubb did experience problems was in Cheltenham's exaggerated respect for games which were compulsory for all boys. Sport, especially rugby football and cricket, were taken extremely seriously, for not only were they considered healthy and manly but they were also held to be an important part of a boy's moral education. Athleticism was something of a cult which found its highest expression in the sporting rivalry between the houses, and boys who were good at games were heroes to their fellows. Glubb was not of that number. Being small of stature and light of weight he did not shine on the football field – then as now rugby football was a decidedly physical sport demanding strength and speed – and he did not greatly care for cricket. 'During my years at Christowe she was Cock House and won practically all the interhouse Pots,' he wrote sadly in later life. 'This had nothing to do with me. I was limited to second teams in everything.'[10] Being in a house team carried enormous prestige and it was an entrenched belief – often wrong as it turned out – that boys who got their colours for sport would evolve into natural leaders, especially in time of war. Games also promoted devotion to the house and as one of Glubb's near-contemporaries noted in a sentimental note to the college magazine, loyalty was merely another kind of patriotism and was therefore to be encouraged. To him, and no doubt to many others of that generation, the pattern was clear enough – loyalty to the house, to the school, to the country and to the empire; in that order.

Curiously, the emphasis on sport, though all-pervasive, did not breed the kind of bullying often associated with the promotion of sporting hearties. Though Glubb might have been considered a natural target, he was never a victim and in his notes on his schooldays he also mentions that the absence of harassment coincided with a less rigorous attitude towards corporal punishment. The principal of the day, Canon Reginald Waterfield, 'rarely caned anyone'. Academic achievement was not frowned upon – the college also had a good record in Oxford and Cambridge scholarships – and boys spent much of their time swotting in the richly named 'sweatrooms' of their respective houses.

Although in 1982 Glubb provided the Cheltenham College magazine with some notes about his education, he was never one to place too great an importance on his schooldays. He liked the college because it gave him a robust education which helped to pave the way for his entry to Woolwich but he never felt the nostalgia shared by so many others of his generation. The rituals (walking to chapel arm-in-arm, two or three boys together), the uniform (mortar boards in winter and straw hats in summer) and the anthems ('Carmen pridie ferias canendum'*) all left little impression on him, and he avoided the kind of sentimentality which, forty years on, made schooldays seem better and more golden than they really were. The most lasting impact Cheltenham left on him was a distaste for crude swearing. According to Maurice Bowra, swearing was endemic at Cheltenham before the First World War and something of a scandal: 'topics of conversation being few, most boys talked smut of which in fact they knew very little and on which they were boring and

---

*'A song to be sung on the day before the holidays'

23

repetitive.'[11] Swearing, like sport it seemed, was considered to be manly.

Reserved, slightly aloof to the point of shyness and yet entirely self-contained, Glubb also avoided the type of sentimental friendships which were frequently part of the Victorian and Edwardian public-school education. These were rarely homo-erotic; rather they were what might be called romantic attachments, close but usually sexless.* Absence of female company was one reason for their prevalence, the distant family another, but the hot-house monastic atmosphere of the boarding school with its emphasis on achievement and the cultivation of a high moral tone made such friendships unavoidable. As most Cheltonians were bound for service in the forces or in the empire, both of which implied an absence of women and the creation of an all-male solidarity, close masculine friendships at school were merely a foretaste of the life that lay ahead and were encouraged by the masters. As a soldier and a servant of empire Glubb was to spend much of his life in relative social isolation but he never seems to have yearned for close male friendships. Instead, he preferred the companionship of his parents and, when at home in York during the school holidays, he spent most of his spare time with his father indulging their shared interest in riding and hunting.

The one area of school life which Glubb did enjoy and which left an impression on him was his service in the Cheltenham College rifle corps. It had been formed in 1862 during a nationwide craze for establishing volunteer rifle corps based on civilian organisations including the public schools

---

*Maurice Bowra relates in his autobiography *Memories*: 'Early in my time I was sent for and Hyett [his housemaster] read out, with painful embarrassment to himself and to me, a pamphlet about the love life of flowers. In itself it was highly entertaining, but it had nothing to do with anything I knew about, and I was unable to see why he had read it.'

and universities, but for much of its early history Cheltenham's corps was little more than a shooting club whose efficiency may be gauged by this report of its participation in the annual Public Schools Field Day of 1901.

> We took a long and expensive journey to Aldershot, marched to battle with an imperfect idea of what was expected of us, ultimately got into the firing line and blazed away merrily at anything or anybody, or nothing, retreated and blazed again; then marched back to the station for lunch and had a needlessly long wait before entraining.[12]

All that changed in 1909 when the corps was transformed into a quasi-military operation which was fully integrated into the school's curriculum. A new commanding officer, Captain R. F. Pearson of The Buffs (East Kent Regiment), was appointed and during Glubb's time at Cheltenham 400 of the college's 460 boys served in the corps. Training took place once a week, there were two field days a year – more military in intention than those of previous years – and exercises on Salisbury Plain. As was the case in other public schools, there was a serious military reason for the corps' existence: as part of Haldane's reforms of the army, from June 1908 school rifle corps were to be regarded as a junior officer training corps, part of the country's territorial reserve force. Many senior soldiers and public figures supported the move because they believed that war in Europe was a probability – Field Marshal Lord Roberts was the most outspoken on this count – and that Britain should prepare herself by raising strong and well-trained volunteer reserve forces for home-defence duties. The corps of the country's leading public schools, they believed, would provide the army with a much needed supply of junior leaders in time of war. Old Cheltonians paid for that concept between 1914 and 1918 – there are 697 names on the college's roll of honour.

Glubb liked the Officers Training Corps (OTC) with its field days and summer camps – the exercises in 1912 were

25

held on Dartmoor – but they were not the reason he turned to the army for a career. Long before entering Cheltenham he had decided to follow his father into the Corps of Royal Engineers by way of the Royal Military Academy at Woolwich. His father's gentle prodding during their never-to-beforgotten days out with the horses had been one spur, but the underlying reason, surely, was that the army was the only life he had known. It had been bred into him.

The decision to aim for the Engineers had been easily made. Not only was it his father's corps but it was almost tailor-made for a family with the Glubbs' limited finances. Then, as now, the Royal Engineers was considered a *corps d'élite* within the British Army and in Glubb's day it was generally understood to attract the more intelligent type of officer who, unlike his compatriots in the cavalry, foot guards and most line-infantry regiments, did not possess a private income. Engineers had been an integral part of the army in Britain since the fifteenth century when they had been responsible to a Board of Ordnance for the Control of the King's Works and Ordnances. In 1716 an officer corps of engineers was established to command the Corps of Sappers and Miners, an arrangement which lasted until 1787 when the Corps of Royal Engineers received a Royal Warrant. In 1855 the Board of Ordnance was abolished and the Royal Engineers and the Royal Artillery came under the control of the army's commander-in-chief. Within the army the Royal Engineers, or 'sappers', had the reputation of being 'mad, married and Methodist' although Glubb only possessed the second of those attributes.

To gain entry into such an élite formation, potential officers had to score good marks in the Woolwich entrance examination and thereby win a high place on the entrance list. It was a powerful incentive for Glubb's military career might have floundered at an early stage if he only secured a middling grade. And it was a test of some complexity. Eight subjects were obligatory – English, English History, Geography, French or German, Elementary Mathematics (arithmetic), Intermediate Mathematics, Physics, Chemistry; and one subject was optional, a choice of German or French, Latin, Greek or Higher Mathematics, depending on what had been taken in the first group. A total of 14,000 marks could be scored overall but to scrape through the candidate had to gain at least 33 per cent in all subjects except Elementary Mathematics where the pass mark was 75 per cent. The emphasis in the arts subjects was on the British imperial role and a standard question from the history papers of the pre-war period concerned itself with a subject familiar to Victorian minds: 'What is meant by the Eastern Question and how came Britain to be interested in it?' Overall, though, the army was looking for clear thinkers who could communicate logically and precisely. The general introduction to the examination left no candidate in any doubt about what was expected of him: 'Irrelevance will be regarded as the most serious fault in an essay but incoherence, obscurity, needless repetition, diffuseness will also be regarded as grave defects. Bad grammar, the incorrect use of words and phrases, and serious errors in punctuation will be heavily punished.'

Today the examination would be regarded as a rigorous test of general knowledge in a wide range of subjects and Glubb was well prepared for it, having been firmly tutored by the masters on Cheltenham's military side. Under the direction of, firstly, W.B. Baker and, in his final year, J.W. Mercer, Glubb enjoyed tuition from some first-rate teachers including W.G. Borchardt who was the author of a well-known series of English school mathematical text books. 'The teaching staff were an amazing mixture of all sorts of idiosyncrasies,' remembered one of Glubb's contemporaries. 'Some seemed to us definitely too old, and one sometimes wondered whether keeping order was considered more important than teaching a subject.' He added that, for the most part, the teaching was outstanding, especially on the military side, although like schools anywhere Cheltenham had its share of eccentrics amongst the staff, all of whom attracted unenviable nicknames.

27

College's success in sending boys into the Army was largely attributed to Mr Baker who was for some reason known as 'Scab'. I began in what I think was the 4th form with 'Boozer' Bennett. I don't suppose Mr Bennett ever touched a drop, but the alliteration was too tempting. I think it must have been the 5th form which was taken by 'The Bun' (C.E. Youngman). He used to be particularly angry if anyone hummed a tune in class and as a result the drill was for someone at the back to start humming. 'The Bun' would stride down the room to see who it was. When he got halfway the boy at the back would stop and someone up at the front would begin. 'The Bun' would stop and glare all around like a bull in the arena.[13]

By the time Glubb came to sit the Woolwich entrance examination Britain was at war with Germany and like most of the senior boys who served with him in the corps, Glubb's first inclination was to enlist immediately. In fact, so many boys left to join the armed forces in the autumn of 1914 that by the year's end Cheltenham was forced to close one of its boarding houses. Within a few months, though, it was noticeable that more boys were being entered on the military side, presumably because their parents wanted them to be better prepared for the inevitability of military service. 'As regards the 1914 war,' said Glubb later, 'we looked on it much as an exciting football match against the Germans, our only fear being that it would be over before we could get into it.'[14]

That sense of enthusiastic schoolboyish conviction gave the early weeks of the war an unreal quality, creating a feeling that war was a glorious adventure and that man had been transformed and liberated from the doldrums of a humdrum existence. The sentiment finds its truest expression in Rupert Brooke's poem 'Peace', and in Herbert Asquith's equally emotionally charged poem 'The Volunteer', but it struck a chord too in the actions of ordinary people who felt ennobled by the exhilaration of war. Chivalry, self-sacrifice and heroism were the watchwords of those first weeks and there were few who did not respond to their call.

And yet there was little reason for such jingoistic fervour. There was no immediate danger of invasion and very few civilian lives were at risk. There was little love for the French whose country Britain seemed to be defending, and the intricacies of Balkan politics were as unfamiliar to the British public as the other side of the moon. Nor was the British Army a popular institution and the British retained a healthy contempt for the huge conscript armies of the European nations. If the country ever had to go to war, the fighting could be left to the Royal Navy and to the small professional volunteer army – in 1914 the British Expeditionary Force, earmarked for active service in western Europe, numbered 120,000 men. But despite those beliefs, many of them deeply rooted in the nation's consciousness, the menfolk of Britain clamoured to offer their services to the war effort throughout the remaining months of 1914 and well into the following year.

On 6 August the government authorised an increase to the army of 500,000 men and the first recruiting posters appeared in the streets the following day announcing: 'An addition of 100,000 men to His Majesty's Regular Army is immediately necessary in the present grave National Emergency. Lord Kitchener is confident that this appeal will be at once responded to by all those who have the safety of our Empire at heart.' By the end of the year 1,186,000 men had volunteered and, on one day in August, 35,000 men joined up, as many as had been recruited during the whole of 1913.

Lord Kitchener's famous appeal for volunteers, a sense of patriotism and a fear that they might miss out on a glorious adventure were the main reasons for the men of 1914 flocking to join the colours, but there were other impulses. War had not come as a bolt from the blue. German rearmament and continuing unrest in the Balkans and the Near East, plus the formation of the major power blocs, had alerted the informed to the possibility of conflict, a prospect which the Liberals had sought to avoid by appeasement. Now that the policy had failed it was the turn of the younger men to

29

put a stop to the arms race and to end international aggression: for those idealists the war in 1914 would be a war to end wars. There was, too, a sense of honour that, if Britain were to remain a first-class power, a world leader worthy of the right to control its empire, then the only way to uphold that privilege was to fight.

Glubb would not have been human had he remained untouched by the prevailing mood. Several of Glubb's schoolfriends had already enlisted and from his diary it is painfully obvious that he wanted to follow them. Without further ado he asked for his father's permission to leave Cheltenham so that he could enlist in the infantry: 'When the war broke out, I was in camp with the Cheltenham College Officers' Training Corps. I wished to run away and enlist in the Rifle Brigade, for everyone expected the war to be over in three months, but my father dissuaded me.'[15]

After the camp had broken up Glubb made his way home to Salisbury as best he could and all along the route he found scenes of mobilisation which fired his thoughts towards deeds of derring-do. Trains full of troops waited in stations where reservists and Territorials were lining up to make their way to distant parts of the country. The next day, Glubb's patriotism was stirred again by the sight of a Territorial battalion marching off to war behind a military band. 'People on the pavements cheered and called "Good luck!"' he remembered. 'A white-haired old man standing beside me, held his hat raised above his head until the whole battalion had passed. Tears ran down his face. Perhaps he was an old soldier, a veteran of past campaigns.'[16]

For Glubb's father it was a difficult decision. As a soldier he well understood his son's enthusiasm and he had already received himself a wartime appointment as Chief Engineer to III Corps in France. Also, he could not confide in his wife as she had gone on holiday to Austria and he was deeply concerned about her whereabouts. With the whole of Europe in turmoil communications were well-nigh impossible and he had had no word from her for several days. Fortunately she was a sensible woman with a strong practical streak and after a difficult journey across Europe, often in crowded troop trains, she had managed to catch the last passenger ferry from Calais to Dover. With his mother back at home and the family temporarily reunited Glubb saw reason and promised to wait for the Woolwich examinations so that he could go to war as a trained soldier. His father also expected him to look after his mother during those early months of the war when, like many other army families, there would be a good deal of disruption to their private lives. The house in Salisbury was closed and a week later Glubb drove his father to Southampton where III Corps was embarking for France.

> I felt that mixture of fear and the ache of bereavement, which precedes a long parting. Our home in Salisbury was to be broken up and my mother would live in a hotel. My father sat sewing a button on to his field uniform and checking over his kit. What agony he felt in his heart after saying goodbye to my mother and leaving his home, I do not know. He was a man who never showed his emotions, though he was sensitive and felt deeply.[17]

In that respect Glubb was very much his father's son; for although he often felt deeply about people and worried incessantly about life's problems, it was noticeable in later life how he preferred to keep his personal feelings firmly in check.

Later that year, in the autumn, came the gratifying news that Glubb had not only passed into Woolwich but, to the surprise of everyone who thought him too quiet and reserved, he came second, one place better than his father forty years earlier. Although the general had just been involved in operations during the Battle of the Marne, he still found time to praise his son's achievement and to remind him of the standards expected of an officer and a gentleman:

> My dear old boy,
>   You will know how proud I was when I heard the news

31

of your having passed into The Shop second. You are very nearly a commissioned officer and a man now, dear old boy. See that you are also a gentleman, a simple honest English gentleman – you cannot be anything better whatever you are. Never lower your standards, old boy. And remember that now you are a man, work is no longer 'beastly swot' but preparation for your duties as an officer.[18]

The vocabulary used by Glubb's father is telling – simple, honest, gentlemanly – and its sentiments are very typical of the spirit of the age. By upbringing, education and now career father and son were joined together in a mysterious fraternity which placed great importance on such values as duty, honour, respect and altruistic patriotism. For the older soldier these were concepts which had been tried and tested in good times and bad throughout his service career. Even for young Glubb – he had only just passed his seventeenth birthday – they were not just idle words; they were deeply ingrained in his conscious mind. At Cheltenham he had been schooled in the heady tradition of the Greek and Roman classics and listened avidly to stories from The Iliad and The Odyssey in which heroes met a swift and painless oblivion. Ideals like companionship, courage and self-sacrifice were integral parts of that ethos, to which had been added the heartier teachings of a muscular Christianity. Reinforced by the pre-eminence of games, the self-importance of the school corps and a mystical belief, preached by more than one housemaster, that the public schools were the last bastions of chivalry, it was a heady brew. For impressionable young men who had been raised in such a hothouse atmosphere, there could be no holding back, and like many others of his generation who came from similar backgrounds Glubb firmly believed that the supreme test was upon him.

'I was passionately desirous,' he wrote sixty years later, 'to play a part in this glorious crusade, the last war, I believed, which would ever be fought in history.'[19]

2

A Subaltern's War

Glubb arrived at the Royal Military Academy, Woolwich, at the beginning of October 1914 to begin training as an officer cadet of the Corps of Royal Engineers. The academy had been founded by Royal Warrant on 30 April 1774 as the cadet training establishment for army officers commissioned into the Artillery, the Engineers and, later, the Signals. Known to generations of soldiers as 'The Shop', Woolwich was a tough down-to-earth institution whose commandant in Glubb's day, Major-General W.F. Cleave, RA, demanded high standards of learning and discipline. The academy produced fine soldiers too – other notable alumni of Woolwich included Gordon, Kitchener, Ironside and Alanbrooke.

Before the First World War the course at Woolwich lasted two years and provided a broadly based grounding in the theoretical aspects of gunnery and military engineering. There was, too, a certain public-school atmosphere in the place with an emphasis on games, ragging, spit and polish, and a delight in practical jokes. Indeed most of the cadets were ex-public schoolboys, the 1914 list being dominated by Cheltenham, Wellington, Clifton, Marlborough, Winchester and Charterhouse. (The Royal Military College at Sandhurst trained cadets for the infantry and cavalry but the majority of its intake, although public-school educated, had usually been 'crammed' for the entrance examinations.) In addition to the military training there was an introduction to the mysteries of mess life with its paraphernalia of customs, traditions and uniforms.

Although Glubb was never overawed by any of the rituals fostered by the army, one aspect of training to become an officer did excite him – horsemanship. His early childhood experiences and training stood him in good stead at Woolwich where every cadet had to endure the riding course directed by the Chief Riding Master, Captain Dann. A soldier of the old school, he was merciless in his treatment of officer cadets who could not ride, and, as Glubb remembered, woe betide anyone who fell off his horse. When asked by the Commandant what he thought of the officer cadets, Dann always gave the dusty response: 'Guts, sir. They've no G-U-T-S. Yes, gentlemen, no guts.'[1] Fortunately for him, Glubb managed to avoid the perils of not sitting properly, making his horse show its teeth or, worst of all, falling off after a jump.

Other rituals included the early morning cold bath, whatever the weather, and the ancient custom of 'toshing', a typically British piece of tomfoolery designed to keep boys in their place. Anyone caught speaking out of turn, boasting or showing signs of pomposity would be chased by a pack of cane-wielding cadets and, once caught, the victim would be forced to make a speech explaining the error of his ways. Then he would be given a sound thrashing and tossed into the lake:

> No great injury was ever done to the victims, as far as my experience went. It was the fear of being toshed which was so alarming. I was once in my room on a dark winter evening when I heard the distant baying of the pack. The noise grew louder and louder, it stopped outside the building, it began to ascend the stairs. In a few seconds, a deafening pandemonium was raging outside the door of my room. For several moments, my heart stood still. Then the screaming torrent went on up the stairs to the floor above. The victim taken was in the room immediately above

mine. There is something terrifying in an excited crowd which inspires more fear than shells or bullets. I have been involved in various battles since those days, but I doubt if I have ever again been so frightened.[2]

For good or ill, noted Glubb in later life, the system produced men who had explored or conquered a great part of the world in the previous century. He was just relieved that some of Woolwich's wilder customs had been shelved with the coming of the war: the Shop which Glubb knew was certainly very different from the more relaxed institution of the peacetime years. For all cadets the course was now reduced to six months; games were hardly played; drill and 'bull' were increased; only purely military subjects were taught and the passing-out examination was replaced by continuous testing. Other changes reflected the urgency of the times. Fees were abolished and the age-limit was increased to twenty-five so that the Army Council could nominate suitable older candidates from the universities. With a training day that lasted from 6 a.m. until 10 p.m., the main thrust of the revised course was to train officers as quickly as possible and to place them with formations already serving with the British Expeditionary Force in France. (By 1916 the folly of force-feeding the cadets was recognised when examinations were reintroduced and the course extended to twelve months.)

The intense atmosphere at Woolwich neither depressed nor worried Glubb. Not being a great enthusiast for rugger, he hardly missed the daily outings to the sports fields or the leisure hours which would have been spent on the racquets courts. Indeed, as he admitted later, the military routines learnt at Woolwich during the early part of the war were to stand him in good stead on active service. It was no use being a star wing three-quarter on the Western Front where the first necessity was to adapt as quickly as possible to the conditions of front-line service in the trenches. For that reason the Commandant refused to be starry-eyed about the war: he and his staff of mainly older officers were determined that their young men should have the best possible preparation for the cut and thrust of modern warfare. This was in some contrast to the training given to infantry cadets at Sandhurst where there was little schooling in the infantry tactics necessary for the monstrous war of attrition which had come to the Western Front in France and Flanders by the end of 1914. For far too long, young officers continued to be taught the principles of open warfare while the battlefields were rapidly littered by obstacles which made such combat impossible.

Glubb completed his course at Woolwich and was duly commissioned on 20 April 1915, four days after his eighteenth birthday. Under normal circumstances he would then have proceeded to his first posting but at that stage in the war the War Office had a ruling that no soldier could go on active service until he had reached the age of eighteen years and six months. (As casualties grew in 1916, this order was withdrawn.) Instead, he had to spend the summer at the Royal Engineers' depot at Chatham, kicking his heels and worrying lest the war might come to an end before he was old enough to cross over to France – 'Every day I passed in England seemed like a year.'[3]

He need not have worried. By the end of 1914 stalemate had come to the Western Front and fortress warfare had returned to replace the mobile warfare preached by Napoleon, Grant and Lee. After the first Battle of Ypres, in November 1914, which denied the German Army access to the Channel ports, a complex line of trenches soon stretched from the North Sea to the Swiss frontier. For the remainder of the war these lines would be advanced up to fifteen miles in either direction but never broken on any large scale: the strategy on both sides was devoted to penetrating the defensive barriers that had been developed. In such an uncompromising arena the engineers of every army would play a decisive role.

By long-standing tradition it fell to the sappers to make battle possible for the infantry and cavalry. They constructed the defensive positions which protected their own men whilst they were under attack, and when the assault was taken to the enemy their role was to prepare the ground by demolishing obstacles, building bridges and clearing the roads. Most of their work was done in dangerous conditions under heavy fire in open positions.

Glubb received his marching orders at Aldershot and on 25 November 1915 he crossed over to France from Southampton, noting somewhat wistfully in his diary that the transport was the *Hantonia*: 'two years before, I had crossed to France in the same ship with Dad and Mum when we went to spend a summer holiday in Normandy.'[4] Glubb was to keep a diary throughout the war, although it was not published in book form as *Into Battle* until 1978 after he had found it again in a box of old papers. The diary was written in Glubb's neat, flowing hand in a series of school-type exercise books and it is very much a young man's realistic commentary on the war he experienced in France and Flanders. Scarcely a day is omitted and, like most good diarists, Glubb tried to make a note of everything that happened to him and his men: no matter how difficult the conditions, and defying his own exhaustion, he tried to record his observations on a regular basis.

The unit to which Glubb had been posted was the 7th Field Company, Royal Engineers, known to its officers and men as the 'Shiny Seventh'. (An engineer field company consisted of around six officers and 220 non-commissioned officers and men plus a number of horses for riding, pack and draught purposes. It was divided into four sections and a company headquarters.) At the outbreak of war Glubb's company had been stationed at Shorncliffe as part of 4th Division under Eastern Command and it had crossed over to France with the British Expeditionary Force on 23 August 1914. Eight months later it was transferred to the 50th (Northumbrian) Division, a Territorial Army formation which had crossed over to France on 16 April 1915. It was to remain with them until the end of the war.

When Glubb joined the 7th Field Company it was

stationed at Armentières where the officers had their billets in the Rue Jules Bleu. Some idea of the work being undertaken by them at that time can be found in their war diary's summary for November 1915:

> Throughout this period the company was working at repairing the subsidiary line N[orth] of River Lys, at erecting machine-gun emplacements in this area. And at erecting the divisional winter quarters: by this time most of the huts for the men were finished, and the chief work in hand was the erecting of bathing establishments, each consisting of 5 large huts – at Steenwercke, Outtersteene, Strazeele.[5]

At the time the field company was not in the front line which in the Ypres–Armentières sector stretched for twelve miles, over the River Lys and through Ploegsteert, Messines and Wytschaete. Its main distinguishing feature was the notorious Ypres Salient, the flat, curved defensive line to the east of the city which had been created by the fighting around Ypres in November 1914 and May 1915. During the later stages of the fighting the salient had been reduced in size to three miles across and five miles deep. As an area of strategic importance to both sides – Ypres stood astride the Menin Road and Yser Canal – it had been fiercely contested and Glubb noted what a ghastly environment it was for the men who served there:

> All the destroyed villages in the Ypres Salient are full of horrors, with dead men and animals barely covered with earth, lying about everywhere.
> Every shattered fragment of a house is full of filth, old clothes, rags and bedding, left behind by the original inhabitants when they fled, and since used for sleeping on or torn up to dress wounds. Everything is soaked with rain, blood and dirt. Strewn around are thousands of half-empty jam or bully-beef tins, the contents putrefying, together

with remains of rations, scraps of bone and meat. There is no living thing visible but rats, big brown rats, who themselves are often mangy, and who barely trouble to get out of your way.[6]

Glubb's field company had moved up to the village of Vlarmertinghe within the salient on 13 December in order to begin repair work on the trenches held by 9th (Scottish) Division. This was to be a familiar pattern of service for Glubb during the next three years of war: periods of active service spent in frequently dangerous front-line positions, followed by some respite in the rear areas. Although the trench warfare of the First World War has become the classic motif for that conflict, it should not be thought that soldiers spent their entire existence in the kind of front-line location commemorated by artists and writers after the war. Glubb's unit, for example, spent time in three different types of posting: in the front line and support trenches (generally known as 'the front'); in billets behind the front line; and in rest camps to the rear, well behind the main combat areas. Like most units they spent at least a fortnight at the front or in billets, followed by up to a week in rest areas. For most men, though, the lasting memory was the curious mixture of fear and comradeship that they found in the front-line positions.

The British Army had a basic trench system, developed by the sappers, which rarely varied, whatever the local conditions. This consisted of three lines of trenches – front, support and rear – usually built in a zigzag pattern as a defensive precaution against enfilading and shell-fire. Communication trenches linked them and the defensive positions were protected by thick curtains of barbed wire. Officers lived in dug-outs which were hewn into the ground and built up with wooden supports and sand-bags to provide basic living accommodation and administrative quarters. In the better trenches the men lived in dug-outs, too, but all too often they were required to dig their own basic accommodation ('funk holes') in the sides of the trench system. Trenches varied in quality according to the prevailing local conditions: in the Ypres Salient they were not particularly good as the ground was fought over so many times and the positions frequently changed hands. The men of the Northumberland Fusiliers, one of the infantry elements in 50th Division, had nothing but praise, though, for the entrenchment work carried out by the sappers of 7th Field Company. As E.W. Cotton wrote in *Tommy Goes to War*:

At Neuve Eglise and Armentières the trenches were splendid: they had been in existence for nearly a year, were very thick and deep, had lateral trenches running the whole length in the rear, plenty of dug-outs, and good communication trenches which made it possible to leave during the day and return to the billets in the town. The trenches had trench boards to walk on, fire platforms to stand on, drains and sumps with pumps, shelters for lookouts with rifle racks, rubbish shoots, gas alarms, rifle batteries, loop-holes, periscopes, etc., and war could be carried on in a comparatively safe manner.[7]

Praise of that sort was all very well but, as Glubb noted during his first days at the front, enemy artillery fire made repair work extremely difficult: 'all serious work is impossible in the short intervals between strafes'.

While he was working in the trenches with his sappers, Glubb had his first experience of coming under enemy bombardment from the dreaded German 'whizz-bangs' – 'This name is given to the field artillery, which fires bursts of high-velocity shells into our trenches at intervals. They come in violent tornadoes suddenly, *whizz-whizz-whizz-bang-bang-bang-whizz-bang-whizz-bang!*'[8] The barrage continued intermittently for forty-eight hours and caused considerable damage and casualties as 50th Division moved up to the front to take over the positions held by 9th Division.

Although statisticians have proved that it took over a

thousand rounds of ammunition to kill one man and that artillery barrages produced few casualties for all their sound and fury, shell and mortar fire still counted for some 60 per cent of the casualties on the Western Front. The effects of an exploding shell in or near the front-line trenches could be frighteningly unpredictable. If luck were on their side, the soldiers might only be covered by mud and debris thrown up by the exploding shells. The less fortunate would be killed, their bodies ripped apart by shrapnel or jagged shell casings. Even a low-velocity shell could cause damage and shell-splinter wounds often turned gangrenous when foreign matter was ripped into the broken tissue. Sometimes there might be no external damage at all – internal organs would have been ruptured by the concussive effects of the blast – but as Glubb found out, only days into his war, the most feared were the shells that did physical damage:

We were standing in the front-line trench, when a whizz-bang burst in the middle of the group. Obviously sniping. They obviously saw Colonel Jeffrey [6th Durham Light Infantry], who is a very tall man.

The shell killed three men instantly. I heard someone say, 'Are you hit, sir?' and Colonel Jeffreys answer, 'I am afraid I am.' Symons, my own O.C., was lying on the floor of the trench with a wound in his thigh. I ran down the trench to get stretcher-bearers, and had Symons carried to the dressing station in Maple Copse. Poor old man! We shall not get such a good O.C. again, I am afraid.

The Boches have been whizz-banging for two days, and the dressing station, a dugout in Maple Copse, was crammed with wounded. The doctor dressed Symons' wound, which seemed to be a nasty one. One poor devil there had had his arm taken clean off at the shoulder by a direct hit from a whizz-bang. He was talking cheerfully. 'Those bloody guns haven't stopped for forty-eight hours,' he said.[9]

In fact, as Glubb was to discover later, the real misery of being under heavy artillery fire was the oppressive anticipation of what would happen next. Men became accustomed to recognising the different sounds made by the enemy's gunfire. There was a whizz-bang-crump of the medium-field artillery. Shells from a distant heavy gun sounded like an approaching express train, field guns cracked like a bang on the head, mortars set off a hideous moaning sound: all were a source of terror to the men in the trenches and it was not uncommon for even the most hardened soldiers to buckle under the strain.

During the course of that late December bombardment of the Ypres Salient Glubb received his first war wound when his left big toe was smashed by a piece of shrapnel. Keen to stay at his post he might have been, but the fragments of broken bone could have led to gangrene and Glubb was evacuated for treatment at No. 12 Casualty Clearing Station at Hazebrouck near Cassel, the headquarters of 2nd Army. Hearing of his son's plight, General Glubb had sent a car to collect him. When Glubb arrived at the hospital he was helped by an RAMC orderly and duly tipped him sixpence: only later did he discover that the elderly corporal was the Earl of Crawford and Balcarres, the Premier Earl of Scotland. 'Being too old to get a commission, he enlisted in the RAMC,' noted Glubb, in his diary, 'and so got out to France. I don't suppose I shall ever again have the chance to give a sixpenny tip to an earl.'[10]

While Glubb was in hospital his field company set about repairing the damaged trench system at Zillebeke Street and in Gourock Road which lay in Sanctuary Wood. It was not until 25 January 1916, a month after his injury, that he returned to the front, to find his men in rear billets near Vlamertinghe. Due to the absence of Symons and the wound suffered by his replacement, Captain Atkinson, Glubb found himself in temporary charge of the field company until the end of February – not an unusual situation in positions which were under continuous enemy fire.

One of the biggest problems facing the British forces in the Ypres Salient was that the Germans had captured the only high ground and were able to control and direct accurate artillery fire on to the opposite line. Whenever Glubb and his sappers were working on the trench systems, German fire interrupted their labours and caused casualties. On 15 February Glubb was wounded again, on this occasion by another piece of shrapnel which grazed his head and sent him back to hospital near Cassel. The bad weather – heavy rain and snow – brought with it another problem: illness amongst the men. The outbreak merits only a bare mention in the 7th Field Company war diary but in a unit of only some 200 men, any absence from illnesses – pneumonia, heavy colds, trench foot and the like – created problems for the rest of the company.

A good deal of sickness was present in the back billets, this being due partly to the ground being waterlogged and consequent dampness and the barn accommodation in-different. It was noticeable that there was little sickness with the advanced sections at Zillebeke.[11]

Small wonder that Glubb noted somewhat wryly in his own diary a few days later that 'Sappers are never allowed to rest'.

Throughout the winter and spring months of 1915–16 the pattern of Glubb's life in the trenches rarely varied while his company was stationed in the Ypres Salient. The war diary of 7th Field Company makes matter-of-fact mention of high casualties, all of which were dutifully recorded in an annex to the main narrative. Glubb wrote about them, too, for when-ever sappers were in the line they were killed by shell or small-arms fire while undertaking the necessary tasks of repairing trenches, building tramway or surveying new defen-sive positions, all of which fell to 7th Field Company during those interminably long winter months.

From the evidence of his early diary entries and letters it is difficult to discover what Glubb made of the constant round of death and wounds which surrounded him when he was in the front line. In March 1916 he observed in a curiously neutral and muted way that one of the most interesting sights in the vicinity of the 'Bluff' was a corpse caught in a climbing position – 'By some miracle, he remained in the same identical position. Except for the green colour of his face and hand, one would never have believed that he was dead.'[12] The Bluff was a spoil heap created by the earlier construction of the Yser–Comines canal: held by the enemy, along with the neighbouring Hill 60, it was one of the raised features which gave the Germans a tactical advantage, and it was much feared by the British troops in the salient.

On the other hand, Glubb could find time in September 1916 to comment on the absolute otherness of death, an emotion he experienced while looking at casualties near High Wood during the Battle of the Somme. This is one of the most revealing and most moving descriptions amongst the literature of the First World War, for it gives a truthful account of the war as it was for the front-line soldier:

The area is thickly dotted with specks of black and grey, lying motionless on the ground. When you approach, the black patches rise into a thick buzzing swarm of bluebottles, revealing underneath a bundle of torn and dirty grey or khaki rags, from which protrude a naked shin bone, the skeleton of a human hand, or a human face, dark grey in colour, with black eye holes and an open mouth, showing a line of white snarling teeth, the only touch of white left. When you have passed on again a few yards, the bluebottles settle again, and quickly the bundle looks as if covered by some black fur. The shell-holes contain every debris of battle, rifles, helmets, gas-masks, shovels and picks, sticking up out of the mud at all angles.

One cannot see these ragged and putrid bundles of what once were men without thinking of what they were – their cheerfulness, their courage, their idealism, their love for their dear ones at home. Man is such a marvellous, incredible mixture of soul and nerves and intellect, of bravery, heroism and love – it *cannot* be that it all ends in a bundle of rags covered with flies. These parcels of matter seem to me proof of immortality. This cannot be the end of so much.[13]

In a religiously minded young man like Glubb such moments of introspective reverie are hardly remarkable. What is noteworthy is that he expressed his thoughts in his diary at the time. For most of his war service he seems to have been keener to keep his true feelings submerged; afraid, no doubt, that were he to express them, he would be undone. Like many other men of his generation Glubb seems to have betrayed little apprehension about the possibility of being killed. (This does not mean that he never knew fear: he did, and confided it to his diary on several occasions.) But like other young men, he believed that war was a young man's affair and when a man is young he believes that nothing is impossible and that he will live forever.

He was also painfully aware of the lot of the men under his command and worried about their comfort and safety. When Glubb first arrived at the front his inexperience had led him to charge a man with cowardice during an artillery barrage: his superior officer had tactfully ignored the outburst and Glubb soon came to understand the narrow dividing line between fear and courage. Like others in the company he was mightily relieved when a middle-aged sergeant, showing signs of battle fatigue, was ordered to return to the rear areas. There were many other small acts of kindness: a drunk sapper was concealed in a pontoon to prevent him being arrested during a route march; in his diaries Glubb constantly deprecated the offensive spirit insisted upon by the British high command as it caused unnecessary casualties on the quiet sectors of the front line; he also worried about enjoying comfortable quarters while his men shivered in makeshift billets; and there were unlooked-for moments when he experienced a deep feeling of togetherness and comradeship with his men. For Glubb, this was the true meaning of

Christianity: the rejection of self and the dedication to the service of others. As he wrote in his diary on 14 January 1917:

> An infantry party, their waterproof sheets glistening on their shoulders, and the drops of rain trembling round the edges of their helmets, slops past with shovels in their hands. They flounder through the mud or try to jump from stone to stone in the ruins, grunting and grumbling in the most abusive language to themselves. Their legs and thighs are encased in sand bags as is the winter custom. They disappear into Gunpit Road and once again there is dampness and silence, except for the flapping piece of curtain and the distant booms.
>
> Suddenly I feel my whole self overwhelmed by waves of deep and intense joy, which it is impossible to describe. Never before had I experienced such a feeling of deep interior joy, so that I could hardly contain myself. I sat for what must have been several minutes, filled with the passionate joy of Heaven itself – then the feeling slowly faded away.
>
> I remembered how St Francis of Assisi once said that perfect joy lay in being cold, hungry, exhausted and repulsed from the doors of every house at which one knocked. It was the depths of cold, misery, weariness and exhaustion of that day in Martinpuich, which had produced in me those waves of spiritual joy. I had given everything to do my duty and had held nothing back.[14]

The experience came to Glubb whilst he and his men had been building a new tramway near Martinpuich, below High Wood on the Somme. The weather was foul and Glubb admitted that no words of his could evoke the 'the dreariness and hopeless desolation of the scene', but despite the grim surroundings he felt at ease with himself, as if life had narrowed itself down to this one vital sensation. Later in life he was to feel again that same fierce sense of joy amongst his Bedouin soldiers in the desert places of the Middle East.

The unaffected comradeship of men in front-line positions is a well-documented feature of the First World War – and indeed of most other wars. Group cohesion, or loyalty to the unit, was an important factor in maintaining morale and was therefore greatly encouraged. Men lived and worked together in close proximity, often in dangerous positions; they shared one another's rations, let their friends read their letters when the mail failed to arrived and looked after the weaker members of the group. Often they would say that the army offered them closer friendships than they had ever experienced in civilian life and that their mates were dearer to them than their families. Glubb not only frequently remarked on this phenomenon but noticed too that the sense of affection was extended to the horses which pulled the wagons and even to the pieces of equipment themselves. Whenever possible the wagons would be washed down in rivers and then recoated with wagon oil; the harnesses would be cleaned and polished and the loads would be carefully tied down. Not without a little pride he claimed that his company looked fitter and smarter than a passing French battalion whom they met on the road to Foucaucourt on 14 February 1917. Whilst the British sappers marched past at attention Glubb was amused to note that the French officer 'delivered some sort of exhortation to his men, but with no visible effect. They were straggling along, roughly in file, but with no two men in step, some were riding on their cooker, and ones or twos were straggling along behind the column.' Given his unconcealed delight in their abilities it is hardly surprising that whenever Glubb was on leave or absent through injury, his constant worry was to return to the well-ordered world of his company where life had reduced itself to an easily understood code of brotherly behaviour.

Not that he was entirely self-sufficient. His father provided a much-needed prop, occasionally sending over a staff car for a brief respite at 2nd Army headquarters at Cassel and generally keeping an eye on his son's whereabouts. There was the animal pleasure of riding Min, his liver-chestnut cob, and like all soldiers Glubb derived strength from his mother's letters. She wrote to him regularly and affectionately and in return he kept up a lively correspondence which managed to give her some idea of what he was doing whilst shielding her from any mention of the harsher aspect of life on the Western Front.

My own dear Mum,

Thanks so much for the parcels which were as usual very welcome, and consisted of dates, socks, Camembert and tea tablets. I also received the beautiful muffler you sent and I have used in this cold weather.

It is a good deal warmer this evening and may be a thaw at last. Fancy Aunty saying my breeches smelt of stale tobacco. I am sure they didn't, at any rate I never noticed it. No, I don't smoke now. Anyhow I wouldn't smoke with my legs and make my breeks smell of smoke!

Yes, I do get the gurgly grunts stopped in the gramophone although I am afraid your optimistic remark about my getting leave soon is rather premature.

We are living back in a civilised part of the world far from the madding crowd and are only reminded of the war by an occasional Boche plane. We are having a *recherché* dinner tonight to celebrate our sojourn in civilised Europe.

The weather has been warmer lately yet beautifully fine. This evening is absolutely perfect. The sun has just set and there is not a breath of wind. The sky is still quite blue overhead, then gradually paler towards the horizon, then a very, very light greeny yellow, merging into the palest yellow, orange red and on the horizon misty grey. I love the pale yellow part, it gives an idea of infinity. Everything is so perfectly still and quiet, that the perfect peace of it seems to enter into one's whole soul.

Now I have to trot round to the office. One never gets away from an office of sorts, even commanding a field company, which I am doing at present as McQ [Glubb's

CO] is off doing a course of instruction.
    Goodbye Darling and much love,
Jack.[15]

At this time – March 1917 – Glubb and his company were in reserve at Morcourt where they were being trained to build bridges with pontoons – 'a thing which had not been done in years'. This was in preparation for the forthcoming Allied Spring Offensive at Arras. In those quieter moments Glubb was able to devote more time to his correspondence with his mother; at other times when he was in the front line or where the conditions were difficult, he would always apologise for writing 'a poor letter'.

For his mother, living alone in rented rooms opposite South Kensington Underground station in London, the letters from her husband and son were virtually the only contact she had with them during the war years, for home leave was never generously granted. Even worse, she was not to see her daughter Gwenda for most of the war. Showing the same independence for which she had been renowned at Cheltenham Ladies College, Gwenda had joined the Scottish Women's Hospitals at the outbreak of the war and saw service with them in Russia and the Balkans. Founded in August 1914 by Dr Elsie Inglis, one of Edinburgh's first and most famous women medical graduates, the Scottish Women's Hospitals proved to be one of the great volunteer medical services of the First World War and was justly renowned for its work on the Eastern Front. Altogether fourteen fully equipped hospitals were raised and, as well as attracting female nurses and doctors, they also needed volunteers. Because she was an experienced driver, Gwenda was employed to drive motor ambulances, often under difficult and dangerous conditions. Her worst memory of the war, though, was the long train journey to the Crimea which took several weeks because they had to stop every twenty miles or so to chop wood for the engine's boiler. For her work with the Scottish Women's Hospital Gwenda was awarded the

Cross of St George and St Stanislav by the Romanian government after the war.

Due to the difficulties of communication with the Balkans, Gwenda could only maintain a fitful correspondence with her mother – although like Jack she was a conscientious correspondent – and for long periods she was perforce out of touch completely. Indeed, when she returned in 1918, family legend has it that Lady Glubb, as she now was, merely looked up from her weeding and said, 'Oh, there you are, Gwenda. We've been wondering what you've been up to all this time!' With her daughter absent and usually uncontactable, Lady Glubb bent her energies to providing her husband and son with comforts and Jack Glubb was not slow to request that she should include useful items like razors and batteries. As was the custom in the mess the officers pooled luxuries like cake, cheese and drink. Sometimes their dinners could be jolly affairs, as he noted in his diary on 11 February 1917:

We rested for three days in Méricourt. Baker and I had a red-letter day, riding into Corbie for tea. The blasé inhabitants of England can form no idea of the childish joy of a day of festivity in a real town with shops and women. There is no such joy for those who live in civilisation! There are many French officers in Corbie, and also the 8th (regular) Division, a very smart one. They played Retreat through the streets in great style. It is curious that the French, with so long a history of military glory, have no *panache* like this any longer.

Rimbod [the company translator] also went in on a push-bicycle, and we did some exciting shopping, a football, a primus stove and such like. I longed to go into the shops and buy everything! What a wonderful day!

On our last night before re-joining the division, I got up a little dinner of farewell to the Tramway officers of B Echelon, profiting by the absence of McQueen, who does not approve of such frivolities. The ever-ready, cheerful Rimbod excelled himself and went shopping in Bray. The result was excellent.

MENU

Soup

Roast Beef. Vegetables

Crème de Marrons (tinned)

Whipped cream and bottled cherries

Savoury – Toasted cheese

Champagne

Coffee

Port wine

Crème de menthe

I proposed the health of the Tramway officers, which was drunk with cheers. Good replied with an amusing speech, all delivered with the solemnity of a judge. Finally, a couple of tunes on the mess gramophone and 'Auld Lang Syne'. A most convivial evening.[16]

McQueen was, in fact, a great source of strength to the men under his command. A middle-aged Scots Presbyterian, he must have seemed ancient to the younger officers like Glubb, but he earned their respect by his dedication to the task in hand. Although Glubb admitted later that he, himself, was 'often a trial to McQueen, for I was no more than an adolescent, and was inclined to be arrogant and to think that I knew everything', he also realised that his commanding officer only had his men's best interests at heart. A typical McQueen action was his decision to get rid of the mess's much-prized gramophone – mentioned by Glubb in his letters home – before the Battle of Arras: in his book anything smacking of levity was out of the question before a major action. Glubb resented the decision at the time because the gramophone provided much innocent pleasure but, in later years, he came to realise that the successful battlefield commander often has to make unpopular decisions. In that respect, McQueen had a considerable influence on Glubb's future military career, as Glubb described:

... the most delicate lesson to acquire was how to be intimate without being familiar. The commander must face more danger and hardship than his men; he may be united to them by a profound affection and comradeship, yet he must never be just one of them. Part of this delicate matter of leadership may depend on social behaviour. An officer should never swear, tell vulgar jokes or behave in an undignified manner.[17]

There is a conundrum here. Glubb enjoyed the intimacy of the officers' mess, and he took great pleasure from being in the company of the men he commanded, but when he was away from them, in an alien environment, he quickly became tongue-tied and shy. With his father at headquarters there were few difficulties but, bidden to dine at brigade headquarters amongst unfamiliar faces – not an uncommon experience – he felt distinctly uncomfortable. Those who knew Glubb well in later life, like James Lunt,* noticed that this was an enduring characteristic. Whilst Glubb enjoyed the intimacy of small groups of men, especially those whom he knew well, he could appear reserved, even awkward in larger company.

After spending his first nine months of war in Flanders, mainly on the Ypres Salient, Glubb was sent home on leave in April 1916. Two days after arriving home he developed severe abdominal pains which turned out to be appendicitis and he was rushed into the Army Hospital at Millbank for emergency surgery. Granted sick leave, he was not passed fit until August by which time the Battle of the Somme, the Allies' summer offensive over an eighteen-mile front, had already begun. Although the British had suffered 58,000 casualties on the first day of the battle, 1 July, there had been

---

*Major-General James Lunt commanded a Bedouin regiment of the Arab Legion, and published the first biography of Glubb in 1984.

some gains in the southern sector and Field-Marshal Haig, the British Commander-in-Chief, was preparing for a new assault on a different front south-west of Bapaume. This was planned for mid-September. Glubb was therefore anxious to be back with his company for this 'big push' – by then 50th Division was part of General Sir Henry Rawlinson's 4th Army which had broken the German line at Bazentin Ridge during the surprise night attack on 13/14 July.

Once again the sappers were being used to repair the front-line trenches but they were also being trained for an assault role, following the infantry to construct defensive positions behind the advancing attack. The theory was that these would provide defences in the event of a German counter-attack but, as Glubb noted, the heavy artillery barrages made this difficult and dangerous work. It was during this period of preparation for the forthcoming battle, in positions behind Mametz Wood, that Glubb had his first sight of the new British weapons of war, the tanks which saw action in the Flers–Courcelette offensive of 15 September 1916.

This afternoon was to me one of the rare occasions when the war has been dramatic and exciting. I was quite thrilled watching the long streams of troops and wagons pouring up the Mametz road. Then, all of a sudden, I heard a strange noise, accompanied by shouts and cheers, and saw the most extraordinary-looking vehicles approaching, with men sitting on them cheering. They were a kind of armoured car on caterpillars and each towed a sort of perambulator behind it. They are said to be new assault wagons, called tanks. I don't know if the Germans knew about them, but the secret has been very well kept on our side. None of us had any idea of their existence.[18]

The world's first tank had been developed earlier in the year when a prototype lozenge-shaped vehicle on tractor tracks had been built for testing by the British Army. Its success per-suaded the high command to order 100 similar vehicles (later increased to 150) which, it was hoped, would help to solve the familiar problems of trench war – the trenches themselves, the machine-gun positions and the forests of barbed wire, all of which hindered the advancing infantry. Although the unsuitable terrain of much of the Western Front encouraged scepticism about the tank's future role, Haig was sufficiently encouraged to order a further 1,000 tanks towards the end of 1916. The name 'tank' was designated for security reasons during their development, but Glubb's description – 'a sort of armoured car on caterpillars' – is more accurate.

Thirty-six tanks were employed during the Flers–Courcelette offensive but lack of experience about their correct deployment, and also being few in number, meant they were not entirely effective. At High Wood they got stuck in the difficult ground – consisting of felled trees, craters, mounds of broken earth, all recently fought over – and at one point during the assault the tanks opened fire on the men of 47th Division, having mistaken them for Germans. Nonetheless, some gains were made in the centre of the line and there was a successful advance over the heavily defended Thiepval ridge, which prompted thoughts of a British breakthrough along the Somme front. Then the weather changed for the worse and days of heavy rain turned the ground into a morass of mud; the advance faltered and the Germans were able to bring up reserves. By October the battle had been reduced to fruitless assaults on the German lines, and the onset of vile winter weather brought the Battle of the Somme to an end in the dying months of the year, 1916. (Although Glubb, like many other junior officers, thought that the offensive had failed abjectly – 'casualties enormous' – the British attack had in fact inflicted permanent damage on the German Army.)

During the later stages of the battle Glubb's company was involved in the construction of tramlines to carry ammunition between High Wood and Martinpuich, another dangerous task as the ridge was on open ground in full view of the enemy's guns. The sappers were shelled constantly and, to add to their discomfort, they had to bring up their supplies through tracks which Glubb described as being more porridge or thick lentil soup than mud:

> We spent about three hours, slopping up and down in the mud, rain and inky darkness, collecting a few men, getting a few loads off, then moving another wagon on a bit, then getting hold of some more men (the others having meanwhile disappeared). It was impossible to see the shell holes in the dark and I constantly trod into one full of water up to my thighs, or else I fell forward on all fours in the mud.
>
> Eventually we got away. Heaven knows how! Luckily we were not shelled, as all the traffic and horses were wedged together chock-a-block. Heaven knows what would have happened. I several times nearly sat down and wept from sheer exhaustion and despair. Thus is a typical night on service, darkness, wet and hopeless confusion – but one gets out somehow before dawn.[19]

Respite came at Christmas when his father once more sent for him to spend a brief leave at Cassel. Once there Glubb could not help but notice the sharp contrast between the convivial little town full of brightly lit shops patronised by smartly dressed women, and the conditions at the front. There were, too, the pleasures of a clean bed, fresh clothes, a canter before breakfast and the delight of hearing birds singing. Those moments out of the war were precious intervals for Glubb but they also unsettled him. Not only did he feel privileged to enjoy them but he was also aware that the leave granted to his own men was miserly – a mere seven days which began officially the moment the serviceman arrived at the mainline station nearest to his home. After the Battle of the Somme, men simply went home in their mudcaked uniforms, so desperate were they to savour every moment of their time away from the front.

Back in the line at the beginning of 1917 Glubb used his diary to record his impressions of battlefield life during the bleak months of winter. He was at pains to describe in minute detail the cold weather and the hardships endured by the men; but never was he self-pitying. He wrote dispassionately about beginning every freezing day with a mug of scalding tea, a piece of greasy bacon and a slice of bread which tasted cold in the mouth, like ice cream. Men struggled through the mud to get to the tramline positions where they worked in slow motion – 'agony for the hands and feet'. Then there was the ever-present danger of shell-fire and one near miss while Glubb was using a latrine – 'a horrid place to be killed', he noted laconically. Day in, day out there was paperwork to be completed, for, whatever the state of the battle, the British Army insisted on maintaining its administrative procedures:

> After tea, I repaired to my little hut, to compose the work tables for the next day, together with lists of stores to be drawn, indents, orders for transport and other routine affairs. Then I would adjourn to the company office to wade through more trays of administrative routine and sign company orders. Those who have never taken part in wars imagine them to be full of fears, danger and excitement. In reality, such things are comparatively rare interludes.
>
> More than anything else, war is work – day and night, wet and dry, cold or hot, monotonous, backaching work. Next to work comes discomfort, especially to be always cold and wet – at least when the war is in France and Belgium. These characteristics apply as much to the infantry as to gunners and sappers. Every now and again, infantry may be involved in an attack and suffer intense danger and heavy casualties. But, year in year out, infantry also spend most of their time working, repairing their trenches, carrying up rations, stores and ammunition, mending roads to allow their horsed transport to come up, and endless monotonous cold, wet and backaching fatigues.[20]

Nonetheless, for all these daily dangers and discomforts,

Glubb's account of his service on the Western Front resounds with a fierce sense of commitment and singlemindedness. It was at this stage of the war, too, that he experienced that mystical sense of joy on the road to Martinpuich.

Fortunately, the periods of winter discomfort in the front line were always finite and in February the company was pulled out into reserve billets at Albert in preparation for the first Spring Offensive of 1917. At the beginning of March they moved again, this time into the III Corps reserve area at Morcourt on the Somme, a village 'full of colours, brown and red tiled roofs, often coated with the most brilliant green moss, and the walls of the cottages painted in white, yellow or pink'. The battle for which they were preparing was the Arras offensive which was timed to start on 9 April. By then 7th Field Company, as part of 50th Division had joined XVIII Corps commanded by a thrusting Guards' officer, General Sir Ivor Maxse: its purpose was to be part of a 'corps of pursuit' which, along with the cavalry, would exploit the expected British breakthrough on a narrow front east of Arras.

Hopes were high that this would be the decisive campaign of the war, one that would create a gap in the German line and pave the way for the break-out into Belgium. 'Gentlemen, you know all about trench warfare, of course,' Maxse had told his senior officers. 'Well, forget it! It's finished! Put it out of your minds! We don't want it any more!' Unfortunately, bold though Maxse's plan was, it foundered, largely because the Germans had become aware of British intentions and had reinforced their line and reserve areas. The 'corps of pursuit' was also expected to advance through a front which was so narrow that it quickly became a bottleneck. Glubb remembered that Arras was so tightly packed with troops from just about every division in the Corps that the lingering impression was of 'a dreary retreat-from-Moscow-the-remnants-of-an-army'. The weather, too, was bad. In spite of some early successes – the Canadians took Vimy Ridge and the German first-line defences were breached – there was no break-through. At the end of May the fighting petered out after the

British had lost 150,000 men in a costly battle of attrition.

As a result the much-vaunted 'corps of pursuit' was abandoned and 50th Division went back into the line at Wancourt where 7th Field Company was given the task of repairing bridges. During this phase of the war Glubb's company suffered 30 per cent casualties and, although he had become more or less hardened to violent death, Glubb was greatly upset by the high losses. One death, in particular, unmanned him – the death of Second-Lieutenant Littlewood, a popular officer who was killed by a shell blast on 12 July. Glubb had just received news of his promotion to full lieutenant and had bought six bottles of champagne for celebrations in the mess when the news of Littlewood's death came though:

> I was sitting in the company office (a tarpaulin on a framework of poles) after getting a note to say that Littlewood was found dead, when Rimbod came in with the bottles of champagne. I could only say, 'Oh, he's dead', and then could stand it no longer. I ran out of the office and over the downs behind, for fear that anyone should see me in tears. He was buried at midday next day, in the little cemetery of Neuville-Vitasse, close to Chaplin [another 7th Field Company casualty].
>
> As he was a Roman Catholic, Father Evans came up to read the service, the greater part of which was in Latin. Nevertheless, I could not stop the tears, when that body, so gallant and so young, was let down by the ropes into its grave.[21]

For Glubb it had been a terrible blow. Not only had he liked Littlewood – 'he seemed so young, so fresh, so gay and so natural' – but he had also led by example, refusing to show any fear in front of his men while they were under fire. This was the acme of personal leadership as far as Glubb was concerned, but it was very much the attitude of a younger man. In the weeks before the Battle of Arras Glubb had noticed that McQueen would take cover once shells started falling nearby, and argued later that it was bad soldiering for an officer to expose himself unnecessarily. Although Glubb admired his Commanding Officer and stood somewhat in awe of him, he rather despised this behaviour, sensible though it was. 'Personally, apart from the question whether such measures are any good,' he wrote, 'I hugely admire a man who doesn't give a damn for them, and I believe this has a very great moral effect. Even if you are not leading your troops at the time, someone will probably see you, and you always have your orderly with you, who soon lets the boys know if you seem to have the wind up.'[22] That attitude almost cut short this own life later in the summer when he failed to take cover while supplies were being moved under enemy fire between Henin and St Martin-sur-Cojeul.

It was an avoidable accident. Throughout August Glubb's company had been working on the right-hand sector of the divisional line which had a 'bad reputation' for coming under heavy enemy artillery fire. The narrow roads and lanes in the vicinity had been badly broken up by shell-fire and there were few passing places in the over-congested up and down routes. As a result, whenever Glubb had to move equipment up to the line, his wagons got stuck in lengthy queues. On the evening of 21 August Glubb set out to the dump at Henin to oversee the unloading of stores but when he discovered that his own wagons were not there, he went back to St Martin-sur-Cojeul 'which consisted of a sea of untidy mounds of broken bricks covered by grass'. Some German four-inch shells were already falling in the vicinity but Glubb refused to take cover because he was in full view of his men.

While he was talking to a soldier called Gowans he became aware of a distant whining sound followed by a huge explosion which buffeted him from his horse on to the ground. Dazed, he set off at a run towards the nearby village of Henin. It took some seconds before he realised that he had been hit in the face. The first shock was that he had been hit at all – it was like getting a violent blow from a cricket bat or a kick from a lively horse. Then came the pain followed quickly by the fear that he had been hit in the head – the face has a good blood supply and he was bleeding copiously. Fortunately, the traffic man – a kind of policeman – had seen the incident and he pulled Glubb into a dressing-station further down the road where he was treated by an RAMC orderly. It was then that Glubb had the first inkling of what had happened to him – 'I could feel something long lying loosely in my left cheek, as though I had a chicken bone in my mouth. It was in reality half my jaw, which had been broken off, teeth and all, and was floating about in my mouth.'[23]

Quite apart from the horror of knowing that a piece of shell shrapnel had so severely fractured his left mandible that it had become detached, Glubb was in severe pain because a large number of nerve endings and facial ligaments had been ruptured. Iodine was poured into the wound which was dressed with a simple field dressing and his broken jaw was braced with a barrel bandage. Head wounds were especially feared due to the dangers of secondary infection; before anti-biotics became common the most common preventive was the insertion of a drain into the wound thus allowing septic matter to escape. Glubb was lucky in this respect – before dressing the wound the orderly had inserted a rubber tube before sending his shocked patient to a doctor who lived in a dug-out at the far end of the village.

From there Glubb became part of a well-rehearsed sequence which withdrew the wounded from the front line to the rear areas. The first stop was a casualty clearing station, a military hospital in miniature, behind the line where his wound was dressed again and he was prepared for the surgery which would remove debris and set the compound fracture. Here the surgeons worked under great pressure, operating on dreadful injuries, amputating limbs, cleaning deep wounds and cutting away damaged tissue: all executed under trying conditions. It was here, too, that the doctors made the decision whether to send the wounded man to a base hospital or back to England.

The prognosis for Glubb was not good. Head wounds counted for a higher proportion of deaths in the field than any other wound – according to a War Office survey conducted in 1917 there were 47 per cent such casualties from a sample of 12,000 wounded men – and as Glubb became aware during his time at 20th Casualty Clearing Station at Ficheux, his wound was far from clean.

> I remained half alive for several days, lying still all day only semi-conscious. I asked for a book to read but found I could not read it. I had apparently nearly swallowed my tongue during the operation and, to prevent this, they had pierced my tongue and threaded a wire through it with a wooden rod on the end of it. This was extremely uncomfortable. A good deal of discharge came from my mouth, and I was very miserable, with my pillow always covered with blood and slime. I was later told that I looked very bad, with my mouth dragged down, discharging and filthy, and with my head and neck all bandages.[24]

A few days after the operation Glubb's father visited him and within a week it was decided to send him back to England by hospital train. The absence of suitable antibiotics meant that his wound continued to suppurate and when he got back to London Glubb was unpleasantly aware of a smell like "foul drains' near his face. This was one of the worst aspects of treating badly wounded men during the First World War, the lingering smell of gangrene in the wards of the base hospitals and clearing stations. Like many other badly wounded men, though, Glubb felt strangely detached from his predicament and it was only when he became aware of the other wounded soldiers that he 'realised vividly now that the real horrors of war were to be seen in the hospitals, not on the battlefield'.

At Waterloo Station the hospital train was met by the usual crowd of well-wishers, sightseers and relatives. Some soldiers felt diminished by the attention and regarded the onlookers as ghouls intent on a vicarious experience. Not so Glubb:

In the lighted streets, children ran after the car cheering, and some stopped and looked back to wave their hands. I made quite a triumphal entry into old London, and, in my exhaustion, the tears rolled down my cheeks. It was with a sudden wave of emotion that I realised that England cared. This had never occurred to me before. In France, we slogged along in good times and bad, supported only by our feeling of comradeship for one another. Now I knew that Britain's heart was in the war, down to the smallest details.[25]

From Waterloo the ambulance took Glubb to 3rd London General Hospital at Wandsworth, his home for that next two months until he was transferred to a hospital in Sidcup, Kent, which dealt with face injuries. There his teeth were extracted to prevent the risk of further infection – most soldiers at the front suffered from pyorrhea due to inadequate dental hygiene – and the still-broken compound fracture of his lower jaw was cemented to his upper jaw, the upper jaw acting as splint.

Because his jaw had been so badly shattered there was still a possibility of grafting fresh bone on to the mandible to make good the damage. The surgeons were keen to remake Glubb's face in this way but he would have none of it, preferring to keep what little remained of his jaw. It took some time for the bone to heal but when it had done so Glubb was physically transformed. In place of the fresh-faced, rather jowly young man there was a new Jack Glubb with a receding and faintly aristocratic chin. This new feature, far from weakening his appearance, gave him a determined yet graceful expression and earned for him the nickname by which he came to be known by the Bedouin people: *Abu Hunaik*, or Father of the Little Jaw.

In January 1918 Glubb was well enough to be discharged from hospital and, after a short convalescence with his mother in Torquay, he returned to live with her in London – Gwenda was still in southern Russia. Having recovered from a dreadful injury it would have been entirely natural had Glubb sought a 'cushy' job away from the dangers of the front line. His father, though, who was in a position to pull strings, wanted his son to become a staff officer with the Chief Engineer of a Corps. Not only would that keep him out of the line and in comparative safety, but it would also be valuable to a young officer's future career. It was a tempting offer, one which any young man might be glad to accept, 'but sentiment and affection for my comrades overcame interest, and I wrote refusing, saying that I would soon go up the line again with the boys'.

For his mother especially this was a bitter blow. The injury to her son had alarmed her and she was already looking forward to the post-war world when her husband would retire and her son would be safely ensconced in a military career. But Glubb's decision was the first hint to his family that his two years in the front line had changed him. From being an obedient and biddable boy he had turned into a young man with a mind of his own. As an acting company commander he had experienced war at the sharp end. He had demonstrated leadership qualities and learned to make decisions; he had witnessed death and destruction; he had come to love the comradeship offered by the fraternity of men in his company: in short, he had been forced to grow up quickly. He felt he was his own man, and he wanted to have control of his own destiny.

Having rejected the possibility of a staff job, Glubb bombarded the Adjutant-General's office with requests to go back to the front and was rewarded in June when he was passed fit by a medical board. On 11 July 1918 he was given command of a draft and crossed over to France to rejoin his beloved 7th Field Company. The fact that he had been awarded the Military Cross helped – this was for his courage under fire during the Battle of Arras and gazetted while he was at Sidcup – but the War Office was always anxious to return experienced reconditioned officers to the front. One reason was patriotic – it was felt that officers should be keen to return to the fight; another was practical – the more experienced the officer, the less likely he was to be killed during his first days at the front.

By this time the war was in its final stages and the most obvious change noticed by Glubb on his arrival in France was the large number of American soldiers who seemed bigger and fitter than their British counterparts. During this stage of the war Glubb's company was back in the line with 50th Division in their old stamping ground between Arras and the Somme in preparation for the Allied push eastwards. Their task was rebuilding bridges and clearing roads, making good the shattered battlefields for the final Allied offensive which began on 27 September. The British contribution was the attack on the line towards Cambrai and St Quentin. It was this war of movement, together with the Franco-American offensive in the Meuse–Argonne area which led to the Germans seeking an armistice in October and November.

The German Army was on its heels and, like many other soldiers who were part of the breakthrough, Glubb regretted that there would be triumphant pursuit of the enemy back into Germany. He felt almost disappointed when the war came to an end on 11 November 1918:

Alas, the war is over, at the moment when it was beginning to be exciting and enjoyable, after all these years. At first we got orders to rub up, inspect boots and clothing and get ready with a view to a triumphal march into Germany. But soon that hope was destroyed also.[26]

The Field Company's war diary was even more impersonal. It simply read: 'Cleared roads part of Mauberges-Avesnes and Mont Douplers-sur-Poteries with 3 Coy's infantry. Completed bridge at F13.90.25. Worked in La Savate crater.'[27] The war was over and, as one old NCO remarked to Glubb, it was time for the army to get back to 'some real soldiering'. But what, to Glubb, did real soldiering mean?

3

To the Deserts Wild

Shortly after the Armistice on 11 November 1918 Jack Glubb and his father made a brief sightseeing tour of the Belgian towns which had been occupied by the Germans during the war. After the hardships and discomfort of the front line, the two soldiers were surprised to find places like Bruges and Ghent untouched by the war and the shops full of good things to eat. 'Apparently things are not too expensive for the population,' wrote Glubb in a letter to his mother, 'the people all looking fat and happy and *extremely* smartly dressed.' As he also noted, being an island might have saved Britain from invasion, but the German blockade had also led to food shortages and rationing. Both men feared that the Allied decision to allow the Germans to surrender would have unhappy results: General Glubb had entered Cologne with the Headquarters Staff of the British 2nd Army and had been disgusted to discover German officers proclaiming that they had been 'stabbed in the back' by the politicians. As Jack Glubb noted in later life, 'wars never end wars. Every war, on the contrary, gives rise to more wars and more violence, hatred and revenge.'[1]

Glubb's observation was made with the benefit of hindsight. At the time the wish uppermost in the majority of soldiers' minds was to get home and put the memory of fighting behind them. The great military machines created by Britain to fight the war was slowly dismantled and thousands of men went back to civilian life, often to unemployment and hardship, leaving behind the professional soldiers of the British Army. As a career officer, Glubb could look forward to the kind of life which his father had led before the war. Britain still had her empire, the garrisons overseas had to be filled and there were still small wars to be fought and disturbances to be put down in places east of Suez. With his interests in field sports and hunting – the officer's traditional leisure activities – Glubb should have been happy but he was not. 'So much hardship, so much courage, so much comradeship, so much heroism – and now such overwhelming glory,' he wrote after returning from France in February 1919. 'I am only twenty-one, but I feel that the crisis of my life is past. Anything which happens to me after this can be no more than an anti-climax!'[2]

By this time Glubb was back at the Royal Engineers' depot at Chatham, attending a 'supplementary course' designed to put young officers on a peacetime footing and prepare them for their futures as regimental soldiers. Time hung heavy on his hands and he found himself bridling against the routine of bull and drill and the formality of training and mess life. Having taken part in a war that had been increasingly complex, with the introduction of new weapons and new tactics, Glubb felt that peacetime soldiering would be boring. Nor was his mood lightened by spending a leave with his parents at San Mamette on Lake Lugano during the summer of 1919. After the years of fighting and hardship, the peace and beauty of the Italian countryside was a balm to his senses, but the scenic grandeur also made him uneasy. He realised that there was a world for him yet to discover and that he was now mature enough to explore it from outside the confines of army life. At the end of the holiday he went back to Chatham knowing that he did not want to take up peacetime soldiering. His salvation came in a War Office circular which requested the services of 350 officers to serve in Mesopotamia, then in the grip of a tribal rebellion.

Glubb had already toyed with the idea of seeking a transfer to the Indian Army – after all, his grandfather had served in it – but had been told that there was a waiting list for the three great engineer regiments, Queen Victoria's Own Sappers and Miners, King George's Own Bengal Sappers and Miners and the Royal Bombay Sappers and Miners. However, the same stricture did not hold true for the Mesopotamian postings which were done on a first-come-first-served basis: there was no interview and within a few weeks of applying Glubb received a War Office letter appointing him for the period of the emergency. Here was the adventure he had been seeking. The Middle East was unknown territory; for, unlike many other army officers who had seen service with Allenby or T.E. Lawrence in Palestine during the First World War, Glubb felt no attraction for the charms of Arabia and, as he admitted when he arrived in Mesopotamia, he knew nothing about its history or culture. All that changed later, of course, but when he lodged his application with the War Office, he was merely indulging his craving for doing something different. When asked about his decision many years later in an interview for the Imperial War Museum's Middle East archive, he confirmed that it had been taken on the spur of the moment: 'I had no interest and no contact, it was just a method of release. Or rather we'll say also perhaps a desire for further adventures – I was very young.'[3]

When John Glubb was born the Middle East was still largely controlled by the long-established Ottoman Empire but, in truth, by the beginning of the First World War, the government of the Porte* was a rickety affair, dominated by sloth and undermined by vanity and corruption. Traditionally Britain had supported Turkish primacy – one good reason being that the Sultan claimed to be a Caliph of the Faithful, the spiritual leader of the world's Muslims, seventy million of whom lived in British India – but she herself was not without interests in the area. Most of Britain's oil supplies came from

---

*Sublime Porte, the court or government of the Ottoman Empire.

the Persian Gulf, the Suez Canal was under British control, she had substantial commercial and diplomatic interests between the Mediterranean and the Gulf, and had governed Egypt since 1882. To complete the guardianship of the strategically vital route to India, Aden, too, was under British control, coming under the suzerainty of the Government of Bombay. Even the names were evocative and half-familiar to the British. The places of the Holy Land were known from the Bible, and from school atlases came the amorphous boundaries of the Ottoman Empire. 'Syria' included modern Syria, Lebanon, Jordan and Israel; 'Arabia' was the Arabian Peninsula; 'Mesopotamia' lay between the rivers Tigris and Euphrates; and to the east lay unknown Afghanistan where the 'Great Game' had been played out with Russia. In one form or another, Britain had substantial interests in the Middle East and more forward-looking imperialists like Kitchener and Curzon daydreamed about the establishment of a British dominion there, with Baghdad as its capital.

The outbreak of the First World War brought the situation into sharper focus. At first the British cabinet hoped that Turkey might be dissuaded from entering the war, though it had long been known that the Germans had built up a powerful sphere of influence at the Porte. There was a belief, too, that even if Turkey were to side with Germany the Ottoman forces could do little harm and that the military threat to British interests was negligible. Lord Kitchener, the British Agent in Cairo, did not subscribe to this view. Like many others of his generation who had served the British Empire in India and the Near East he feared for the safety of the Suez Canal and warned that it might be attacked by Turkey. His solution was a pre-emptive strike against Turkey, a move he continued to advocate after war was declared in August 1914, by which time he held the politically powerful appointment of Secretary of State for War. To carry out an attack quickly and decisively Britain would not only need large armed forces but also powerful and committed allies who were also enemies of the Turks. Fortuitously, Kitchener had been concerned for some years about the increased German influence in the Ottoman Empire and was aware that, in the event of war, Britain might be isolated in the Middle East. He had, therefore, already sown the seeds of a compact between the British and the Hashemites, the noblest of the Arab desert families who trace their descent from the prophet Muhammad.

In the spring of 1914 he entered into informal discussions in Cairo with the Emir Abdullah ibn Hussein, the second son of Hussein ibn Ali, head of the House of Hashim and Grand Sharif of Mecca. Little is known about what passed between the two men although it seems likely that Abdullah sought assurances of support from Britain should the Porte ever act against Hashemite interests. At the time Kitchener was non-committal but after war had been declared with Germany he encouraged British officials in Cairo to begin fresh negoti-ations with the Sharif. Kitchener hoped that the Arab tribes could be of service to Britain by remaining neutral in return for Allied pledges to ensure Arabian independence after the war. However, the Turkish decision to enter the war on Germany's side and their call for a *jihad*, or holy war, against the infidel quickened the pace of the British discussions with the House of Hashim. From the intelligence agency in Cairo known as the Arab Bureau, British officials began the task of hatching a plot with Hussein; firstly to encourage him to ignore the call to join a holy war, in which they were successful, and secondly – a longer-term intention – to bring about an Arab revolt against Ottoman rule in the Middle East.

It was a muddled and not entirely honourable progress. The Hashemites had no love for the Turks – Hussein had spent some time in Constantinople as a political prisoner – and they harboured ambitions to create, and then head, an independent and united Arab kingdom. This would be no easy task as the Arabs were not a united political group with a single spokesman – other notable leaders with their own points of view included Ibn Raschid, Abdul-Aziz Ibn Saud in southern Arabia and Sayydi al-Idrissi in the Yemen. Nevertheless, the Hashemites as guardians of the Holy Cities of Islam enjoyed considerable religious and temporal influence, enough to raise a revolt in their own region, the Hejaz. All they required was backing from a powerful ally and this they found in the British who agreed to supply arms, money and men as well as the promise of political support after the war to fulfil Hussein's dream of self-rule. The trouble was that the pledges were vague and disingenuous and couched in a language which avoided any definite commitments. There was no official compact, merely a succession of courteous letters exchanged between the British High Commissioner in Cairo, Sir Henry MacMahon and Sharif Hussein: in time, the MacMahon Letters, as they came to be known, were not worth the paper on which they had been so carefully written.

By mid-1916 the conspiracy was ready to break. In an attempt to reach the eastern coast of the Red Sea a Turkish force moved south into Arabia along with German troops who wanted to create a link with their country's possessions in East Africa. This gave Hussein the impetus to go into action and thus began the Arab Revolt, a movement partly political, partly religious and partly romantic. To Hussein and his followers it represented their best bet to make a bid for pan-Arab power, but to the British it was a timely intervention by a useful ally in their war against the Turks. The promises made so easily to Hussein would never be kept once the war was over for not only did the British find the Sharif a little tiresome – he was much given to intrigue – but they had also entered into secret talks with their European allies about the creation of spheres of influence in the Middle East. The talks did not mention the creation of an independent Arab kingdom under Hussein.

The evidence for these talks was released by the Bolsheviks in 1917 in a big to discredit Russia's former allies. Known as the Sykes–Picot agreement, after the authors Sir Mark Sykes and Georges Picot, the treaty laid plans for the division of the

Arab lands of the Ottoman Empire into British and French spheres of influence. The newly created countries would be held under the mandate of the newly established League of Nations until such time as they were able to govern themselves. The area divided up by the French and the British was the so-called 'Arab Rectangle' of present-day Syria, Israel, Lebanon, Jordan and Iraq. France was given control of Lebanon and coastal Syria with rights of suzerainty over the northern area around the important towns of Damascus, Aleppo and Mosul. Britain received control of Iraq and the ports of Haifa and Acre and suzerainty over the southern area from Aqaba to Kirkuk. Palestine would come under international administration and the Arabs would only be offered full independence in the lands of the Arabian peninsula. No mention was made of Hussein's dream of a united Arab kingdom. It was a confused situation full of contradictions from which Britain emerged with little credit, although a mitigating factor was the need to appease a powerful ally, France, and to reduce French suspicions of British intentions in the Middle East. Even the specialist agencies were not agreed on what should be done: the India Office and the Government of India, for example, were opposed to any deal with Hussein and would have preferred a treaty with Ibn Saud in southern Arabia.

For Hussein it was a poor pay-off for his family's part in a successful military initiative against the Turks. Although the Arab Revolt has been hopelessly romanticised by the role played by Colonel T.E. Lawrence, it was nonetheless a solid achievement. Led by Feisal, Hussein's eldest son, Arab irregular soldiers won a number of easy victories which encouraged the British to advance across Sinai to El Arish. Palestine was the next goal and 1917 saw an escalation of guerrilla warfare on the desert flank of the British advance with the result that Turkish forces were tied down guarding the strategically valuable rail links. At the same time another Hashemite force, commanded by Abdullah, attacked the Turks in the desert and threatened Medina. That same year

71

Allenby assumed command of the British forces in Palestine and the campaign entered a new and more determined phase. Increased funds and more modern weapons were given to Feisal's army which provided much needed tactical support for Allenby's forces during the march on Damascus in the summer of 1918. Everywhere in the Middle East, it seemed, the Hashemites had been triumphant and their stock was high.

This situation did not last. Feisal represented his father at the ensuing Paris peace conference but his pleas for the creation of the Hashemite-governed Arab kingdom were politely disregarded. Instead the victors set about carving up the Middle East into spheres of interest roughly along the lines that Sykes and Picot had directed. France was awarded the mandate in Syria and Lebanon and the British were allowed to establish mandatory governments in Mesopotamia and in Palestine which included the territory on both sides of the River Jordan. Under the terms of the Palestine mandate, which was an international obligation, Britain had also included the Balfour Declaration of November 1917, Britain's wartime pledge of support for the creation of a Jewish national homeland in Palestine. The region contained a 90 per cent Arab majority but at the time of the promise Britain had been anxious to receive, and to continue receiving, Jewish money and support for the Allied war effort. (In fairness, it was not just a matter of good business: Balfour, the British Foreign Secretary, was as much moved by his reverence for the Old Testament as he was concerned with the *realpolitik* of empire.)

The treaty arrangements and boundary fixing got off to the worst of starts for the whole of the Middle East was still unsettled. There were anti-British riots in Egypt in 1919 and in the following year Arab nationalists rose against the Anglo-Indian administration which had been established in Mesopotamia at the end of the war. In Syria, having proclaimed himself king in Damascus, Feisal was ousted by the French and returned to the Hejaz to lick his wounds. British officials in Palestine soon found that the task of controlling the warring tribal factions was beyond them, and they were further discomfited by the arrival of a Zionist commission intent on protecting Jewish interests. Fighting also broke out between Bedouin tribesmen and newly arrived Zionist settlers in Upper Galilee, a grim foretaste of the troubles still to come. The French, too, were under fire from Arab nationalists and the Soviets, weakened by war and revolution, faced ugly riots in their central Asian provinces of Georgia, Armenia and Azerbaijan. Even in Turkey, defeated in war, there was anti-British agitation, but the countries to the south of Asia Minor, in the Middle East proper, were the real object of Britain's immediate post-war concern.

Mesopotamia, a country some 500 miles long and 300 miles wide, was still designated Occupied Enemy Territory and large areas of it were racked by conflicts between warring tribes. For years they had fought against each other and against the constraints of Ottoman rule. During the war many of them had been granted liberal subsidies to continue the fight against the Turks in order to protect Britain's lines of communications along the Tigris and Euphrates as an Anglo-Indian force made its way into the Mesopotamian provinces. The move was instigated to protect British oil supplies in the Gulf and to safeguard the overland route to India but it was quickly seized upon as a chance to gain an easy victory over the Turks. Despite the experience and undoubted leadership qualities of its commander, General Sir Charles Townshend, the campaign soon ran into difficulties. Cut off and surrounded at Kut-al-Imara, Townshend was forced to surrender and the Government of India, responsible for the planning, was forced to think again. A new commander, Major-General Sir Stanley Maude, was appointed and his new broom cleared the way for a successful campaign into the Mesopotamian provinces. By March 1917 Kut had been recaptured, Baghdad had fallen and Mesopotamia was in British hands. Maude's success prompted the government in London to determine what form of government should be installed in the provinces, but for the time being the area remained under the rule of the Government of India.

Britain had several reasons for wanting to hold on to the Mesopotamian provinces in the post-war carve-up of the Ottoman Empire. The first was strategic. The area could provide vital staging posts in the chain of air bases that would eventually link Egypt with India. Although these would have a strong commercial bias, they would also have a military value for reinforcing British garrisons in the Middle East. It was also essential to retain the port of Basra for the protection of the Gulf, traditionally a sphere of British influence.

The second reason was economic. Mesopotamia held the key for guarding the oil fields in south-west Persia. It was also believed that oil might be discovered in Mesopotamia itself; as indeed it was in 1927. A third and less tangible reason was prestige. Britain had spent £200 million winning the war in Mesopotamia and the armed forces had lost 100,000 casualties: it was considered essential, therefore, to demonstrate to the Arab world that Turkey had been beaten and that Britain had won the war. Allied to this concerned was a belief that the possible creation of an anti-British Muslim power bloc in the Middle East could destabilise the Muslim population in India. (The Muslim League, representing Muslim nationalist opinion, had been founded in 1906.)

The trouble was that, although Britain wanted a strong and friendly government in Mesopotamia, the planners in London, headed by Lord Curzon, the Foreign Secretary, were not sure how to proceed, and little thought had been given to the local conditions or to the wishes of the people who came from different racial and religious backgrounds. The majority were Shi'ite Muslims who were centuries-old rivals of the Sunni Muslims; there was a large Jewish community in Baghdad and a substantial group of Christians in the area of Mosul which included many Nestorian-Chaldean refugees from Turkey. While the British subsidies continued during the war there had been relatively few problems: these came into focus when the British-Indian administration attempted to raise revenue from taxation. A further potential cause of trouble came from the demands of the Arab nationalists who dreamed of an independent Arab country and whose hopes had been fanned by the success of Sharif Hussein's British-inspired Arab Revolt on the other side of the Arabian peninsula.

When peace came in 1918, Mesopotamia was nominally under the control of Captain Arnold Wilson of the Indian Political Service which had temporary jurisdiction over the area. With his experience of Hindu–Muslim rivalries in India, he feared that the fractured nature of Arab society in the provinces would make all-Iraqi unity difficult. He feared, too, that his political superiors would not understand the local conditions. What the politicians in London regarded as unnecessary communal strife and habitual disorder amongst lawless tribes, he saw as a major religious and political problem. As he reported to London in 1919, the country's two million Shi'ite Muslims would hardly accept dominance by the Sunni minority, yet Britain still insisted on a plan which would encourage the formation of a Sunni government. Not for the first time in Britain's history, politicians were bent on forming boundaries and settling types of government which were repugnant to the local population. As a good servant of the Government of India, Wilson favoured a period of direct rule until the country was ready for self-government.

His assistant Gertrude Bell, the noted Arabist, did not see it that way. She supported the creation of a protectorate, arguing that the people of Mesopotamia, having supported Britain during the war, wanted to remain within the British sphere of influence. (Along with the subsidies, British political agents had held out the blandishment of Egypt's wealth and influence as an example of what could happen to Mesopotamia in the future – provided that it, too, became a protectorate.) From her Arab intellectual friends Gertrude Bell also understood the strength of nationalist opinion and was alive to the necessity of honouring promises made during

75

the war. But like other imperialists of the time she believed that Britain knew best and that a policy of paternalism was required during any period of transition.

For all that her opinions differed from Wilson's, neither of them believed that Arab unrest would erupt into violence. When the trouble came in 1920 it shocked the Government of India, still responsible for the administration, and extra troops were sent into the country. It began with the assassination of political officers in the districts and by June the country – now known as Iraq – was in open revolt following an attempt to levy taxes. It was then that the War Office appealed for 350 regular officers to serve in Iraq for the duration of the trouble.

The notice was issued as Glubb's course at Chatham came to an end. He applied and was accepted: the decision marked the beginning of Jack Glubb's life-long love affair with the Arab world.

The news that their son intended to serve abroad in an unspecified capacity greatly alarmed Glubb's parents. His father had retired from the army in April 1919 having been knighted the previous year, and like most military fathers whose sons follow them into the services, he was interested to see what his son would do next. He was also ambitious for him and believed that his son's career should be consolidated in a peacetime field company before embarking on adventures in strange parts of the world. Although it was not unusual for a young officer to volunteer to serve abroad in a colonial station, most were infantry or cavalry officers who were often attracted by the higher rates of pay and lower expenses. General Glubb now argued that a sapper had to collect professional qualifications and experience and that these could only be achieved through service in one of the regiments of the Royal Engineers. But his arguments were to no avail: Jack Glubb had made his choice and refused to go back on it.

That there was friction between father and son over the

decision can be seen in a revealing diary note which Glubb wrote shortly after his arrival in Iraq at the end of September 1920:

> The relations between fathers and children are one of the perpetual great tragedies of life. The devotion of the old, the carelessness of the young. The agonised way in which the former sees the only joy of his life yearning only to leave him, without a thought or a comprehension of how all the light of the old man's life proceeds from the young; the selfish concentration with which the latter looks only at the world and his future without even a word of sympathy for the old heart which he breaks by a departure which he makes all the more bitter by the joy with which he conscientiously strikes wound after wound into the old soul who is too weak to allow his son to depart without a protest.[4]

It was like the childhood episode in which he smashed the engraving, delighting firstly in his savage outburst and then feeling bitter remorse. Although he realised that he was a disappointment to his father, his heart told him that there was no other way, that to continue as a peacetime UK-based officer would only lead to monotony and stupefaction.

Glubb also realised that he was causing grief to his mother. By then she was happily making a new home at Pembury, near Tunbridge Wells in Kent, and was looking forward to a settled time with her family. For her husband there would be an active life in the county community and involvement in field sports; for herself there would be time to read and long summer holidays spent travelling in Europe. Her daughter Gwenda, too, had returned home and even though she had chosen a somewhat unorthodox career, at least she was living not too far away – at the Brooklands racing circuit near Weybridge in Surrey. In fact, Gwenda was destined to be perhaps the most unconventional Glubb of all. Using her wartime experience as an ambulance driver to good effect she started racing motorcycles and in November 1921 became the first woman to race 1,000 miles at the rate of 190 miles a day: the machine she used was called a 'Ne'er-a-car' which resembled a modern scooter. From these she turned to racing cars and quickly gained a reputation as a fast and skilful driver of the famous Morgan three-wheeler. Her marriage to Douglas Hawkes, a racing driver who drove in the Indianapolis 500 of 1926, only increased her fascination with motor racing and in the 1930s the couple settled in France at the Montelhéry circuit outside Paris. There she drove a Derby Special at 145.94 miles per hour to set a lap record which was never broken and she achieved the same feat at Brooklands in 1925 when she drove the same vehicle at 135.95 mph.

When asked why she took such risks Gwenda always replied that she dreaded death and that motor-racing was the one way of life which helped her to come to terms with her fears. It was an attitude which Lady Glubb respected as both women shared a certain devil-may-care attitude to life and were much given to whimsy and story-telling. Perhaps, too, Lady Glubb saw something of herself in Gwenda – both were strong personalities who liked to dominate proceedings – but she wanted something different for her son. In her mind's eye she saw Jack's career progressing steadily without the threat of war to compromise it. Now he was throwing all that bright promise in her face by opting for service overseas without any hope of leave for at least five years. No sooner had her son embarked in 'a small and extremely ancient vessel, called appropriately SS *Vita*, for she seemed to have lived forever', than she had sent off a telegram begging him to change his mind. It caught up with Glubb when the ship called at Malta and caused him great distress.

Indeed, at that stage of his journey Glubb might well have wondered if he had made the right decision. The *Vita* was an elderly troopship, well past her prime, slow, uncomfortable and unsuitable for sailing through equatorial waters in midsummer with all 350 volunteers on board, and the voyage out to Bombay was an enervating experience. There was a further delay in the Indian port when the volunteer officers were forced to wait for another ship to take them up the Persian Gulf to Basra, at that time of the year languishing in a stifling autumnal heat. 'Throughout most of the summer life is made reasonable in Basra by a daily cool northerly breeze which, however, ceases in the autumn, making the flaming heat extremely trying. This was before the days of electric fans or of air-conditioning and constituted my first introduction to real heat.' Somewhat wryly, Glubb also noted that the weather was known as the 'date-ripener', excellent for the local harvest but hard going for the city's inhabitants.[5]

Although the tribal fighting had almost come to an end it was still too dangerous to travel up country to Baghdad by rail; instead, the volunteers were despatched on barges pulled by tugs for the long journey up the River Tigris. It was a slow and laborious process enlivened only by the odd day's shooting, at which Glubb excelled. As a child he had been found to have a weak right eye and to compensate for this his father had purchased for him a special shotgun with a curved stock which allowed him to place the butt in his right shoulder and to aim with his left eye. As happens so often in sporting company, unassuming ability brings it own rewards and Glubb's prowess during the first day's shooting quickly made him 'the lion of the party, surrounded by a group of such exalted personages as majors and captains'.[6]

Because the rebels had used the insurrection as an opportunity to smash up anything belonging to the administration, there was a good deal of work to be done on repairing public works. Many of the worst excesses had been committed against the intricate canal system in the area below Baghdad where the Tigris is joined by the River Duyala. Regulators and sluices built by the Irrigation Department had been badly damaged and these had to be repaired both to control the flow of water needed for the local farmers and also to prevent the rivers from flooding in spring when they were swollen by the melting snows of the Persian mountains. Being an engineer, albeit a half-trained one, Glubb was in great demand

79

and he was posted to this relatively remote area where a detachment of Indian coolies was employed on repairing damage to the irrigation works. Accompanying them was a company of riflemen drawn from the 99th (Deccan) Infantry, Indian Army, whose task was to guard the working parties from possible attack by dissident tribesmen.

It was a curious existence at Diyala, informed both by a pioneering spirit and by a passing sense of imperial duty. Glubb's major task was the bridging of the river, no easy matter as materials were in short supply and improvisation had to be the order of the day. Fortunately he overcame the problem by finding an elderly ferry boat which was then attached to a length of strong wire with pulleys on both banks. In that way it could be hauled back and forth across the waters without too much difficulty. The posting at Diyala also gave Glubb his first experience of another colonial phenomenon – the soldier who has lost himself and his sense of self-respect in a hot climate far away from home. Sharing their makeshift mess was an elderly quartermaster from the Gloucestershire Regiment who would settle down each evening with a bottle of whisky and drink himself into oblivion. So upset was Glubb by this behaviour that he reported the matter to headquarters in Baghdad and the old soldier was quietly recalled and sent back to Britain.

A few months later, in April 1921, Glubb was transferred from this lonely camp to Ramadi on the Euphrates, up river from Baghdad, where he was put in charge of constructing a pontoon bridge over the flood waters of the mighty river. Glubb's only previous experience was a lecture at Chatham on the construction of the Forth railway bridge: at Ramadi a somewhat different technique would have to be employed! Luckily for him, he had an easy-going gang of Arab workmen at his disposal and they introduced him to the ancient technique of daubing the pontoon boats with pitch in the biblical manner (Noah's ark and Moses' cradle). From them, too, he picked up enough colloquial Arabic to understand their motives and their sense of humour. To his delight, Glubb found that he enjoyed their company and he was soon making forays on horseback into the local communities, further extending his knowledge of the local society and its customs. As he admitted later, the warm and simple hospitality he encountered on those rounds first enamoured him of the Arab world and in his heart of hearts he realised that for him there could never be any return to life on the barrack square.

Although Glubb was unaware of them at the time, political steps were being taken elsewhere which would settle the future of Iraq – and of his own long-term role in the country's development. The rebellion of 1920 had convinced the British government that it could not rule over such a disparately formed country by force alone. It cost £2.7 million a month to maintain the British and Indian armed forces in the area and critics of this high expenditure claimed that it was akin to pouring water into the desert's wastes. Nonetheless, Britain needed to see the creation of a strong Iraq which would be responsible for internal security under indirect British supervision. A provisional government had been created in Baghdad in November 1920 with a Council of State headed by a moderate nationalist, Abd Al-Rahman Al-Gaylani, but each member had to be approved by the British High Commissioner Sir Percy Cox, formerly of the Indian Political Service. For all its shortcomings it was a first step towards creating an indirect form of rule which would keep Britain in control while yielding some concessions to the nationalists. Cox – 'Kokkus' to the Arabs – was, incidentally, well used to such a system. When he had been British agent in Muscat before the 1914 war he virtually ran the country.

The future of Iraq – and the rest of Britain's interests in the Arab world – was discussed further at the Cairo conference convened in March 1921 by Winston Churchill as Colonial Secretary, with T.E. Lawrence as his adviser on Arab affairs. Basically, a Hashemite solution was adopted, thus honouring in some measure the promises made by Britain to Sharif Hussein during the war. Feisal, Hussein's eldest son and Britain's ally during the Arab revolt, was offered the throne of Iraq, although measures were taken to make it appear that the offer came from the people themselves. Thus, in one stroke, a country containing a mixed population of Kurds, Sunni and Shi'ite Muslims, Jews and Christians was put under the control of an Arab prince. In the terms of a mandate from the League of Nations Iraq looked like an independent country but it would remain firmly under British supervision. To the west in Transjordan Feisal's brother Abdullah was established as a temporary ruler with British support: in time this would become a new Arab country east of the River Jordan. West of the river was Palestine which was designated a Jewish homeland, also under a mandate from the League of Nations. The Persian Gulf emirates were also included in the agreement – they became 'Protected States' in treaty with Britain and Egypt was allowed to become independent, although still under British influence, in 1922.

With the fixing of new boundaries and the creation of new governments Churchill's solution had a neat and statesman-like appearance. None of the new countries could be claimed as colonies and they appeared to be, if not fully independent, then at least in control of their own destinies. The format contented those American politicians who distrusted Britain's imperial ambitions in the Middle East and it also appealed to the British public who increasingly viewed imperial adventuring as a costly drain on the country's resources. And yet, for all that Britain seemed to have stopped short of colonising the Middle East, by 1922 she had become the paramount power in the area. Feisal and Abdullah owed their positions to Britain and for years to come rulers would be dependent on the army of political and military advisers who would virtually control Iraq and Transjordan. That Britain was able to do this without incurring huge expenditure on the defence of the region depended largely on a new strategic concept – 'Air Control'.

*

Air Control was the creation of the founding father of the Royal Air Force, Huge Montague Trenchard, a Royal Scots Fusilier who had served in the Boer War before taking up flying and subsequently joining the Royal Flying Corps. During the First World War he had commanded the British air forces in France and at the war's end he was a persistent advocate of the creation of an independent air force. Although strategic bombing had been developed by 1918 and the fledgling RAF had achieved complete control of the skies over France, senior officers were still sceptical about the new arm of service and many believed that it should be scrapped or divided and passed to the control of the army and navy.

Trenchard, one of the great visionaries of air power, insisted that his new force could be gainfully employed independently in support of the land and sea forces and that it could also take on a role in the policing of the empire. Air Control, as Trenchard's theory came to be known, was offered as a substitute for land power in the more remote areas of the British Empire where communications and usable roads were few and far between.

In theory, the tactics were simple but effective. Bomber aircraft, supported by armoured cars on the ground, would be deployed to flush out rebellious tribesmen. By attacking them from the air the bombers would cow the enemy into submission while the ground-based troops would be used to make arrests and to mop up. Speed, unpredictability and terror would be the keys to its success. Trenchard also pointed out that it was a relatively humane method – the bombs then in use were small enough to cause minor casualties, yet terrifying enough to create alarm and despondency in the target areas. It was a kind of inverted blockade, he argued, for the bomb attacks would disrupt the tribes' economic structure by keeping villagers away from their harvests and nomads from their cattle.

Above all, Air Control was cheap. In 1919 the RAF had already suppressed the rising of the 'Mad Mullah' in Somaliland at a cost of only £77,000 and similar RAF operations in

Kurdistan had checked Turkish irregular forces with the loss of only one British soldier killed and fourteen wounded. Trenchard estimated that a policy of Air Control in Iraq would cost £8 million as opposed the £20 million estimated by the War Office for the employment of soldiers in defensive operations. Colonel T.E. Lawrence, who had witnessed the effect of Turkish air attacks on Arab tribesmen during the war, was an advocate of Trenchard's theories and he was able to convince Churchill, already an enthusiastic supporter, of the usefulness of such tactics in Iraq and Transjordan. An integral part of Churchll's Cairo doctrine, therefore, was the creation in Iraq of a chain of air bases which would allow the RAF 'to operate in every part of the protectorate and to enforce control, now here, now there, without the need of maintaining long lines of communication eating up troops and money'.[7]

It was revolutionary strategy – it was cheap to operate and suited the spirit of the times. There would be no large expensive bases to maintain and the lives of British soldiers would not be put at risk. Both were important considerations in British politics in the years following the war. The concept that the far-flung British Empire would shrink under the wings of modern aircraft appealed to the young visionaries in the air force. Only the army was unhappy about the implementation of the policy. Not only did some officers believe that the army's traditional role in the policing of the Empire was being eroded by a handful of machines and men, but they also doubted if Air Control would ever work. Direction finding was still in its infancy, air-to-ground communications were primitive and the desert was a large and lonely place. According to Field Marshal Sir Henry Wilson, a wartime Chief of Staff who was assassinated by Irish Republican terrorists in 1922, Trenchard's scheme amounted to the RAF 'appearing from God knows where, dropping their bombs on God knows what, and going off again, God knows where'.

When the first British aircraft arrived in Iraq, Wilson's fears seemed at first to have been realised. Five squadrons of

De Havilland DH9A bombers and Snipe fighters* had been assigned to the local air headquarters at Baghdad and the aircrews believed that they could take off after breakfast, complete their mission and be back at base in time for lunch. However, they soon realised that, from the air, most villages and the surrounding desert area looked alike and that the existing maps were rudimentary and virtually useless for plotting routes. Moreover, the recent disturbances meant that several tribes had moved out of their traditional areas, making existing boundaries redundant. 'How was the ordinary RAF pilot to distinguish the friendly from the hostile?' asked Glubb. 'This problem suddenly threatened to make the whole plan of Air Control impractible.'

The Air Staff in Baghdad decided to appoint a small number of Special Service Officers (SSOs) who would be assigned individually to a district and ordered to get to know its topographical and demographic characteristics. In the event of tribal unrest they would then be able to guide in the aircraft, either by making arrangements on the ground – the preferred method was a system of marks in the sand – or by flying as an observer in the leading aircraft. In short, they were intelligence officers responsible for getting to know local conditions and understanding the subtle shifts in the political affiliations of the local tribes. Altogether, eleven SSOs were appointed and their duties were defined in a 'most secret' memorandum prepared by the Air HQ in Baghdad.

The main object of the Special Service Officer system of

---

*The squadrons deployed in Iraq were numbers 1, 8, 30, 45 and 84. The De Havilland DH9A bomber had been developed in 1918 and remained in service until 1931. Known as a 'ninak', it carried a crew of two, had a top speed of 114 mph and was armed with a Vickers gun forward and a Lewis gun aft. It had a 450 lb bombload. The Sopwith Snipe was the RAF's successor to the successful Camel fighter of the First World War.

intelligence is the provision of information to Air Head-quarters from a source entirely independent of the intelligence organization at the disposal of the civil authorities. Whereas information supplied by the civil authorities may be biased by an Iraq Government point of view, the information obtained and forwarded by the Special Service Officer is free from any such influences. The civil authorities obtain their information from police and junior government officials while the Special Service Officer obtains what is required by personal investigation or through agents in close touch with local conditions.[8]

Under those top-secret conditions such appointments required tact, patience, discipline and the ability to work alone far down the chain of command. The principal requirement, though, was the ability to speak Arabic and to have a basic understanding of the ways of the desert peoples.

Not surprisingly perhaps, the Air Staff could find few suitable candidates from within the ranks of the Royal Air Force. Pilots had joined the service to fly aircraft, engineers to service them: few wanted to surrender their technological careers for a dubious and ill-defined job in the desert. It was then that Glubb's 'intense interest' in the country was recalled and he was summoned from Ramadi to Baghdad to be interviewed. The proposal was that he should be seconded to the RAF as an SSO – Glubb accepted the offer on one condition, that it would only be on attachment as he still considered himself a Royal Engineer.

His reasons for taking the job were fairly obvious. He was still young and adventurous and he had come to love the country and its people – the post required him to live and work amongst the kind of Arab tribesmen who had so captivated him whilst building the pontoon bridge at Ramadi. A more pragmatic reason was the gradual withdrawal of the British Army from Iraq which would have meant, sooner or later, Glubb returning to regimental soldiering. So it was the chance of a lifetime – he called it the culmination of all his schoolboy dreams of adventure in strange places – and in April 1922, still wearing the khaki uniform of a sapper officer, he became the RAF's intelligence officer in the district of Muntifiq which included the strategic air base at Nasiriya. Before he departed, the civilian workers under his command presented him with a specially printed letter of farewell and congratulation which was read out to him slowly and precisely by the Indian foreman who had been brought up in the ways of the Raj.

It is a well-known fact that the highest criterion is demanded by His Majesty's Government, especially since the Great War, in making appointments to the Political Department.

In selecting you for a Political Appointment, it shows how highly your services have been appreciated by His Majesty's Government. May we humbly add, Sir, that the honour is a well-deserved one owing to your hard work and high sense of duty, tempered with justice and mercy; it is a pride to your staff to know that they have served under such a high officer.[9]

Glubb kept the statement carefully amongst his papers: its sentiments may seem alien to the modern mind, but like the letter he received from his father on entering Woolwich, it was an expression of the lifetime of service that lay ahead of him.

Muntifiq, the area to which Glubb had been posted, contained large tracts of desert in the southern region which marched with Nejd, or Central Arabia, which was controlled by Abdul-Aziz Ibn Saud, a long-standing ally of the British. To the east lay the frontier with the tiny independent emirate of Kuwait. The dominant feature of Muntifiq, though, was the middle section of the River Euphrates which splits into several streams below Nasiriya, an area of marshland and hidden channels. Eventually the Euphrates is reunited in a large expanse of water known as the Hammar Lake which lies

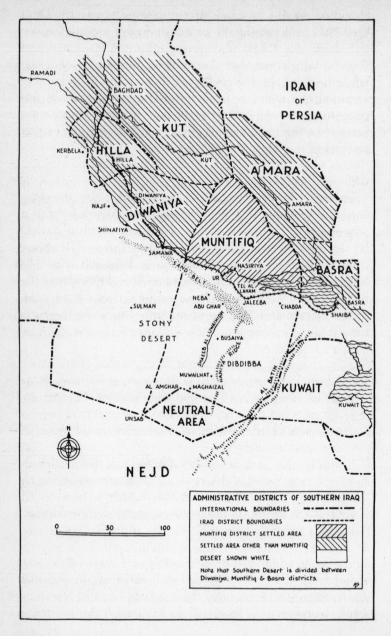

ADMINISTRATIVE DISTRICTS OF SOUTHERN IRAQ
INTERNATIONAL BOUNDARIES
IRAQ DISTRICT BOUNDARIES
MUNTIFIQ DISTRICT SETTLED AREA
SETTLED AREA OTHER THAN MUNTIFIQ
DESERT SHOWN WHITE
Note that Southern Desert is divided between
Diwaniya, Muntifiq & Basra districts.

between Suq and the confluence with the River Tigris. This is the land of the marshmen, or marsh Arabs, a motley collection of hostile tribes who were constantly at each others' throats. Little more than desperadoes they were beyond the law and prided themselves on their ability to kill and destroy seemingly without pity or mercy. For all those failings, like other European visitors to the region – Wilfred Thesiger and Gavin Maxwell, for example – Glubb was captivated by their easy ways – 'the marshmen used perhaps to be the most ruffianly blackguards, but they all had a humorous twinkle in their eyes.'[10]

During this period Glubb made several forays into their domain, travelling in a *mashhof*, the marshmen's long pole-powered canoe, into the muddy islands and sandbanks which lay all around the edges of Hammar Lake. The going, through the thick reeds, was difficult and the sun beat down from a hot sky; the habitations were little more than filthy hovels but Glubb was fascinated and he carried his memories of the marshmen of the lower Euphrates with affection into his old age:

> Wild, bearded, paddling about all day naked in his canoe, unscrupulous, hot-headed, courageous, little more moral than an animal, but jovial, undignified, confessing, and laughing at his own worst enormities – he is far from being so repulsive a savage as a list of his crimes would cause the uninitiated to believe.
>
> Many a pleasant day he has afforded me, pushing blindly in a canoe through the reeds, gliding silently down the mirror-like canals between the date groves, filled in the morning with the cooing of doves, or paddling ankle deep in the wavering ricefields.[11]

Much as he admired the marshmen's easy ways Glubb soon realised that they were regarded with contempt by the other Arab tribes. It was not until eight months later, in December 1922, when he was promoted in his British Army rank of captain to the Jezira desert region, that he came into contact with an altogether different group of people, the Bedouin tribes of the Shammar and Dhafeer. As Glubb admitted in later life, this was an important juncture, the moment when he fell under the spell of these haughty and fiercely independent desert folk.

Glubb had been moved into the area – known as the Dulaim Division, with its headquarters at Ramadi – because of the increased international tension between Britain and Turkey over the possession of the *vilayet* (province) of Mosul which was considered to be part of Iraq. Large deposits of oil were being discovered, and were soon to be exploited in a region which the neighbouring Turks thought to be theirs by right. With few land forces in Iraq Britain feared that the Turks might take the opportunity to invade Mosul and use it as a base for marching down the valley of the Euphrates, just as Xenophon and the ten thousand had done twenty-three centuries earlier. Should that happen, the main opposition would be provided by the aircraft of the RAF and the police and militia of the local 'desert forces'.

Despite warnings from London, Turkish forces made a number of serious infiltrations into Kurdistan along the border with Mosul and tension remained high in the area until 1924 when the question of the *vilayet* was passed to the League of Nations. (In August 1925 it was agreed that Mosul should remain part of Iraq.) Throughout the period of stand-off between the two sides RAF bombers prove their worth by making several decisive strikes against Turkish lines of communication. These raids also showed the local tribes that Britain was serious about protecting Mosul and dissuaded them from making local attacks. On the ground, the newly appointed SSOs also came to the fore by providing valuable intelligence: Glubb himself thought that there was little chance of an all-out Turkish attack and that the main danger came from the tribal irregulars who would follow the side likely to be successful. That he was little impressed by Turkish bluster can be seen in the tenor of his intelligence reports which he sent from Ramadi to Baghdad in the first months of 1923:

> The story of Ajaimi Pasha being about to invade Iraq at the head of a Turkish army can hardly be said to strike terror as it has been reliably reported once a week for two years that he is about to do so.[12]

Left largely to his own devices, Glubb believed that his best course of action was to familiarise himself with the people of the division and, hopefully, to win their trust. He purchased an Arab stallion which he called 'Al Feel', or 'the Elephant', on account of its size and girth, and thus equipped he set out on his first travels in the desert accompanied only by his servant Ali al Yunis and a Shammar orphan called Ambarak.

Although in later life Glubb was inclined to make light of his travels and refused to consider them as 'expeditions' similar to those undertaken by Great Arabian travellers like Charles M. Doughty or Colonel Gerald Leachman, his journeyings were never without incident. The maps of the area were usually primitive or inaccurate, water holes could easily be missed or might have dried up, and beyond the culti-vated strips the desert was a sprawling waste, peopled by tribes who were often a law unto themselves. Nonetheless, by the middle of the year Glubb had been confident enough to have wandered as far as the Syrian border, crossing tracts of desert and staying overnight with the villagers and tribesmen he met on the way. It was his introduction to the hospitality of the Bedouin people, an open-handedness which brooked no refusal of shelter to the desert traveller. No matter how small the encampment or how impoverished its inhabitants, room would be found for Glubb and his party, a meal of hot rice and mutton would be cooked and coffee would be specially ground for the traditional drink of welcome. Then, under a starlit sky, the men would eat and talk together. 'Finally we rose and, walking out a few yards into the desert, I lay down, rolled in my cloak, to sleep,' remembered Glubb of one such experience. 'I lay looking up at the bright stars. My mind was full of new experiences. Although these people were, in some ways, so addicted to violence and bloodshed, although there were lice in their clothes and they ate with their hands, there was something about them which attracted me. Was it just simplicity – an utter lack of sophistication?'[13]

Like other European travellers who had explored the Arabian deserts Glubb fell in love with the place for its clear air, the long gallops over the sand and the friendship and loyalty of the Bedouin people. And, as he made clear in his diary, like them too he realised that the desert was not a lunar landscape but a place of variety and continuous fascination, a land of 'wild attraction':

The desert areas included in the Kingdom of Iraq do not by any means resemble the wastes of rolling sand dunes usually represented in the desert scenes of popular fancy. The Iraq deserts may perhaps generally speaking be more aptly described as rolling downs, rising in some areas to heights of a thousand or more feet above sea level and intersected here and there by cliffs and wadis or by outcrops of rocks.

While it is true that in summer and autumn the surface of these downs becomes brown and scorched, yet in winter and spring they are clothed with grass, while the valleys and hollows are often gay with wild flowers, poppies, corn-flowers, marguerites and innumerable other varieties. At all seasons of the year the more level spaces are covered with drought-resisting shrubs which provide grazing for camels and burn with an incense-like fragrance peculiar to them.

While lack of water in the late summer compels the majority of the tribes to descend to the banks of the Euphrates or the Tigris, yet in winter and spring the desert supports a considerable population. The goat-hair tents of the nomadic tribes spread far and wide over the rolling steppes and great herds of camels and sheep graze round the groups of tents from which rise homely curls of smoke to reproduce scenes of pastoral peace so dear to the ancient poets.[14]

By then Glubb had begun to immerse himself in the literature of the great Arabian explorers and his diaries in the 1920s owe much to the heroic style of Doughty's *Arabia Deserta* which T.E. Lawrence believed to be 'a book not like other books' in the annals of travel literature. A receipt amongst Glubb's papers shows that he had arranged for the famous 1921 reprint, introduced by Lawrence, to be sent out to him from London. He had also read Richard Burton (who reached Mecca and Medina in 1853) and W.E. Palgrave (the first to reach Ha'il and Riyadh); and from his own period Glubb was well aware of the adventures of Captain H.W. Shakespear, Gertrude Bell, Bertram Thomas and H. St John Philby. Described by his son Kim as the 'Greatest of Arabian Explorers', Philby met Glubb in Amman in March 1924. 'I am not surprised that we have no prestige in the country after seeing the tourist hordes in Jerusalem,' wrote Glubb to him later. 'I feel quite ashamed of going about dressed in European clothes.'[15] At that stage in his life, like Lawrence, Glubb preferred wearing Arab dress on duty, although, unlike him, he always changed into uniform when not in the desert.

It would be fair to say that even at that early stage in his career Glubb, like Philby and the others, had committed himself to the Arab world and considered himself in some small measure to be more Arab than the Arabs. It was not an unusual stance for a young man in one of the outposts of empire; District Officers operating in the more remote areas of India tended to take fierce delight and pride in the company of the people they served and were considered to have become 'jungly' when they returned to the civilising influence of the club and cantonment. British colonels from the shires spoke with pride of their 'little Gurkhas' or 'stalwart Sikhs' and affected to despise the argumentative lawyers and middle-class *babus* who clamoured noisily for independence. Indeed, their preference was for the martial races, Pathans or Punjabi Muslims, people who were loyal and trustworthy and whose demeanour seemed to mirror British virtues.

Glubb liked the desert tribesmen for similar reasons – but there was a great difference between the men who served British India and those, smaller in number, who lived and worked to further British interests in the Middle East. Whereas the British community in India was relatively large and well organised, with a plethora of clubs, messes and hill stations to provide an almost idealised version of English life, the same outposts in Iraq were few and far between. There was an organised social life in Baghdad with receptions, dinners and bridge parties, but elsewhere in the country life could be raw and primitive. Never at ease in urban society anyway, Glubb was content to spend much of his time in the desert areas where the extremes were greater, and as a consequence, the companionship more committed. As he noted at the time, he felt that in the desert he had tasted the salt of life and that its savour would never leave him:

On first making his debut in Iraq the newcomer frequently gazes from near the Euphrates shore, over to the west across the great desert, hundreds of miles beyond which lie Damascus, Jerusalem, Mecca and the Central Arabian kingdom of Nejd, with its martial prince Ibn Saud and Muslim puritan fanatic soldiers. This first romantic glow perhaps to some extent wears off after a succession of long weary rides in flaming sun. Returning from each, he swears never again to break his back and split his head in these long glaring days in the saddle; but a month of ease and town life fills the true wanderer once more with impatience to be up and inflict on himself once more the same torments.[16]

It was not just the desert which had him in its thrall: he

was also captivated by the Bedouin people who inhabited it. So much has been written about these nomadic tribesmen that they stand in danger of being viewed in the same artificial and romantic light that surrounds the Scottish Highland clans. Just as Sir Walter Scott and other novelists, and diarists, including Queen Victoria, helped to foster the tartan-clad myths of sentimental Jacobitism and Highland chivalry during the nineteenth century, so too have Anglo-Arabs like Lawrence and Bell glamorised the desert dwellers. They saw the Bedouin people as a warrior race that maintained high standards of chivalry and courtesy, that disdained luxury yet was generous and hospitable, that regarded courage and personal honour as supreme virtues and despised meanness, cowardice and soft living. It was natural for Englishmen schooled in the classics and Arthurian literature to see such people as the true heirs of Saladin and to admire them for the apparent simplicity of the rules that governed their lives. Besides, as James Morris has pointed out, the Bedouin tribes seemed almost to be English public schoolboys translated into another, yet still familiar, idiom: 'With his patrician style and his picturesque appearance, his great flocks of goats and camels, his taste for coffee and beautiful boys, his blend of arrogance and hospitality, his love of pedigree, his fighting ability and what would later be called his *machismo*, the Bedouin was every Englishman's idea of nature's gentleman.'[17]

For a time, too, Glubb was similarly impressed and he wrote a number of highly charged descriptions of the sheer animal pleasure of riding across the desert in the company of his Arab guides and bodyguards. As he often admitted, he felt more at home with them and could relax in a way that he never could in the company of his fellow countrymen. Here, beyond the reach of artificial civilising influences, life could be clean and uncomplicated.

The Bedouin, as their habit is when travelling free across their own broad deserts, become as boisterous as schoolboys. Salih and Mohd al Ruba'an racing ahead of the party neck and neck burst into a wild song, the rhythms of which were tuned to the trotting of the camels. Anxious not to be outdone, and infected moreover myself by the clearness and brightness of the morning, I put my own camel to its best pace, and raced beside them till a rocky wadi across our path brought us back to a walk. Mohd Ruba'an produced a handful of dates, covered with hair and dust, from his saddlebag and tendering me half proceeded to devour the remainder as he rode. 'May God curse all the food which I eat not on the back of my camel,' he shouted, quoting a Bedouin poem. Thus, between the mouthfuls of dates, he continued, still shouting at the top of his voice. 'Ya, Sahib, the Bedu is never happy except on the back of his camel! Riding camels are birds. No distance is too far to them. They are the ships of the desert!'[18]

In time Glubb was to modify that early romantic view of the Bedouin people, but he was never to shift far from the solid basis of affection he felt for them. In a lecture delivered to the Royal Central Asian Society on 25 November 1936, Glubb discussed at length the concept of 'Arab Chivalry' and emphasised the Bedouins' generous and self-effacing conduct which he believed was 'a distinctive but practical everyday system of life and government, just as [is] democracy or communism'. Although he admired many characteristics of their society Glubb warned his audience that they should divest their minds of any romantic associations normally connected with the words 'chivalry' and 'knights'. The Bedouin warrior, he explained, had nothing whatsoever to do with Chaucer's 'parfit gentil knyght'. Instead, his experiences told him that the Bedouin lived their lives according to an uncodified yet elaborate set of rules which he summarised as: seeking glory in war by the performance of individual deeds of bravery, the worship of women, fantastic generosity and hospitality, an illogical preference for whimsy and a haughty disregard for possessing valuable objects.

The opposite of these virtues were a number of faults which Glubb numbered as boasting and jealousy, the neglect of the public interest in pursuit of personal glory and an improvident outlook on life. In other words, Glubb admired the Bedouin people neither for the artificial glamour of the black tents in which they lived nor for the swirling clothes of their traditional dress nor their delight in war – all elements which had won Lawrence's heart – but for the ordinary rules of courtesy and courage which governed their day-to-day lives. He also realised that to be accepted by such a people was high praise indeed and in his diary he frequently remarked on the humility he felt whenever the tribesmen showed him any mark of respect or honour.

Above all, Glubb warned against treating the Arabs as fractious children: he had been much taken by a remark made by a Bedouin sheikh, Auda al Hasan, who said that he could never understand the English. One day they might be cool and officious, often to the point of rudeness; then they would make up for their behaviour with a display of justice and fair play. The trouble was that most Arabs never knew which type of behaviour to expect. In other words, argued Glubb, the British bred suspicion by surrounding themselves with an imperial and mysterious aloofness and then compounded the error by refusing to acknowledge the Arabs' own code of honour. This understanding of the fickle relationship between the two people was to stand him in good stead in the years to come.

In addition to getting to know the Bedouin peoples of the Iraqi deserts Glubb also had an important intelligence role to perform and it is an indication of his single-minded approach that he never allowed his sense of duty to be blinded by any romantic notions. He understood perfectly well that the tribes had a well-understood set of rules which governed their warfare and petty-skirmishing. Although inter-tribal fighting was a recurring feature of life in the desert, casualties were few and the principal aim seemed to be the capture of loot, sometimes for material gain, at others for symbolic victory. As

Glubb noted in his diary, such warfare was often little more than a sport which added colour and excitement to Bedouin life. In the summer of 1923 that theory was put to the test.

After eight months at Ramadi Glubb had been transferred back to the Muntifiq Division where the main source of local excitement in the early years of the mandate had been the unruly behaviour of the Beni Huchaim tribes. They had played a dominant role in the anti-government disturbances of 1920 and were still a force to be reckoned with – intelligence reports suggested that an infantry division would be needed to subjugate them. By 1923 there were no signs of further trouble from them but the government of Iraq was fearful for the safety of the Baghdad–Basra railway and it was decided to make an example of the Beni Huchaim whose tribesmen had often threatened to attack these important lines of communication. For the first time in many years it was decided to levy taxes from them, a move that caused a lot of ill-feeling. A force of Iraqi militia was sent to collect the payments but it was easily driven off. Subsequent expeditions met the same reception and the sight of the routed government officials only added to the resolve of the rebel sheikhs. Such a position could hardly be tolerated and as the ground forces could achieve little, it was decided to test the tactics of Air Control. Two sections of the Beni Huchaim were earmarked for punitive action – the Barkat and the Sufran, both of whom lived in the more remote part of Samawa, far from the main lines of communication.

At first, Air Headquarters in Baghdad was convinced that a short, sharp operation would settle the problem, but an inspection of the rudimentary maps of the area dampened their enthusiasm. These had been produced during the war but had been made on such a large scale that they were virtually useless. Pilots on reconnaissance flights over the area also reported they were unable to identify any distinguishing features, far less recognise the settlements they were supposed to attack. Accordingly, as SSO for the district, Glubb was ordered to devise and produce a series of target maps for use by the attacking aircraft. As bombing procedures were still in their infancy, Glubb was forced to fall back on improvisation.

A first flight over the area in a DH9A confirmed that the pilots would require something more sophisticated than the existing maps: even from a slow-moving bomber flying at low altitudes it was difficult to make any sense of the terrain which appeared from the air to be a 'fawn-coloured plain intersected by so many canals and by winding irrigation ditches'. The only solution would be to traverse the ground by horseback in order to survey the land and meet the tribes who lived there. The local *qaimaqam*, or governor, was horrified by Glubb's proposal as the local Barkat and Sufran tribes refused to allow government representatives to enter their territory. Undeterred, Glubb set out into the desert wearing an Arab cloak over his army uniform so that his appearance could be disguised from a distance. His only companion was his servant, Ali al Yunis.

For days on end throughout September and October 1923 his routine would be the same. He would set out at first light into the desert, charting the positions of the main settlements as well as the natural features, and at night he would accept the simple hospitality of the tribesmen. Their friendship alone suggested that this was not a dangerous area and from them he began to understand some of the difficulties faced by nomadic peoples when they are organised and regimented by the government. The Sufran tribe was so poor that it had no funds to pay taxes, having given up any attempts to cultivate their land, and the Barkat were little more than threadbare beggars. He also reported that there were serious water shortages due to the fact that irrigation channels had been diverted by Sha'lan Abu Chon, the most powerful sheikh in the area against whom they were powerless. 'It is a regrettable fact that Government at the moment presents itself to their minds as a kind of absentee landlord which never concerns itself with them except periodically to demand revenues,' reported Glubb to Baghdad on 18 November.

Knowing that he was guilty of accepting the sheikh's hospitality while plotting to attack their people, Glubb felt that he had to speak openly about his mission. 'I candidly told than that I was preparing the map to be used for the bombing, and that I myself would have to be in the leading aircraft.'[19] The sheikhs seemed unruffled by these disclosures and allowed Glubb to continue his survey unhindered – perhaps they did not fully understand what he meant or believed it would never be fulfilled. Besides, it was a longstanding Bedouin obligation to offer care and protection to any guest, be they friend or be they foe.

As well as manufacturing the target maps – a task made easier by his engineer training – Glubb had to turn his mind to their application for aerial bombardment. Because the targets had to be pinpointed from the air, he had to make several sorties by aircraft to make sure that all the targets were positively identified. This was no easy task. The DH9A had an open cockpit and in the observer's seat Glubb was obliged to stand up and lean out of the aircraft wearing helmet and goggles while the pilot circled each target. In that position he had to make notes and sketches, all the while trying to ignore the scream of the slipstream and the ever-changing roar of the 400-bhp engine. Some sorties lasted five hours, pushing the aircraft and its crew to the limits of their endurance. In between flights Glubb made regular trips to Baghdad for consultations with the air staff; by mid-November they had enough confidence to put Glubb's plans into operation.

The first step was to drop leaflets on the Barkat and Sufran warning them that they would be attacked unless they reported to the *qaimaqam* at Samawa and make arrangements for the payment of taxes. Hardly surprisingly, given their previous intransigence, the tribes ignored the request and the Air Staff ordered the attack to begin on 30 November. The tactics were kept simple: these involved the maximum use of force on the target areas, or what is known in modern military parlance as 'power projection'. The bombers of 8 Squadron were to lead the attack from Samawa while the second wave was entrusted to 30 Squadron operating out of Hinaidi. Defensive support for the bombers was provided by the Sopwith Snipe fighters of 1 Squadron. In keeping with his position as intelligence officer, Glubb was obliged to fly in the leading aircraft of 8 Squadron.

Before the raid each pilot had been provided with specially photographed copies of Glubb's maps. On them they found that each target had a number and that each number had been assigned to an individual aircraft. The raid began at dawn and Glubb's aircraft was detailed to attack target number 14, the war tower of the sheikh of the Barkat who had been his host only a few nights previously. Glubb had mixed feelings about his role but, once the raid began, he had no time to allow his conscience to rule his emotions. As the aircraft approached the target the pilot had to struggle to swing it round so that it was facing up wind during the first bombing run. From the observer's seat Glubb leaned over the right-hand side to look through the primitive bomb-sight and as the target came into view he pulled on the toggles releasing the large 550-pound bomb. It was the first time that such a weapon had been used by that type of aircraft. 'Suddenly the aircraft shot up into the air as the big bomb came off it. I turned quickly and looked over the side towards the rear. I could still see the huge bomb going down and down until I lost sight of it. I glanced up quickly to see the other machines of our formation coming in over their targets. Then I looked down again, just in time to see a great fountain of smoke and dust shoot up into the air on Target 14.'[20]

The bombing missions against the tribal areas lasted for two days and as all the objectives had been hit the attack was deemed effective. To his horror, though, Glubb discovered that 144 people had been killed and many more injured. Immediately he sent off a report noting his regret that there had been so many casualties and suggesting that in future air control should not be used to frighten people into paying taxes. Instead, he added sardonically it might make sense to discuss their grievances with them before bombing them into submission. The reckoning came later. While walking through the bazaar of Samawa during the afternoon of 1 December Glubb came face to face with the leaders of the Barkat and Sufran tribes. They had come in as ordered and had agreed to pay their taxes. To Glubb's surprise and shame they bore him no ill-will – before the aircraft appeared they had abandoned their homes and taken cover in the nearby desert. Over a hundred of their people had not been so lucky.

Their subsequent behaviour was equally surprising. When the adviser to the Ministry of the Interior, Kinahan Cornwallis, arrived in Samawa to address the tribes of the Beni Huchaim, he admonished the sheikhs and ordered them to hand over their weapons – a terrible reprisal for such a warlike people. Meekly, the sheikhs agreed to the order and drifted back to the desert where they promptly vanished. Much to Glubb's delight the tribesmen held on to their weapons – a vital symbol of manhood – and melted away from their homes. Although Glubb spent several fruitless weeks searching for them he could find no trace of the tribes but during those patrols one more lesson was learned. It was a point of honour amongst the Bedouin never to give up their arms or to surrender a fugitive who was under their care and protection. Somewhere out in the desert, Glubb knew, the Barkat and Sufran people were waiting their opportunity to return to their homes once the government forces had moved out of the area.

Although the operation had offended Glubb's sensibilities it had proved the efficiency of Air Control as a means of policing the tribal areas cheaply and with little loss of life to the government forces. The Air Staff in Baghdad was well pleased by the success and Glubb's name was singled out for praise. 'By means of his map,' wrote Sir John Salmond, the Air Officer Commanding (AOC), 'it was possible and even simple to ensure that any bombing which took place was concentrated without error on any particular village or villagers which might be selected.'[21] Nonetheless, he was more circumspect when the report was sent back to London.

102

Appended to it was a suggestion that casualties should be glossed over and that 'certain paragraphs should not be sent out without further consideration'. Due to this reluctance to give the incident any publicity and to cover up aspects of it, Glubb did not receive the decoration for which he had been recommended, but the report at least ensured that his name was noticed in high places. When a new threat appeared in the desert Glubb was once again asked to play a key role in providing the necessary intelligence for Air Control. These were for operations in a long and intermittent war against the Ikhwan raiders from Ibn Saud's neighbouring kingdom of the Nejd.

4

Sowing the Wind

One of the earliest lessons which Jack Glubb had learned after arriving in the Middle East was that his European view of history differed in most respects from the Arab version. Whereas Cheltenham had given him a solid grounding in British imperial history and a brief introduction to ancient civilisations through the writings of the Bible, Herodotus, Thucydides and Livy, he knew next to nothing about the lives of Cyrus, Sargon or Nebuchadnezzar. Still less did he know anything about Islamic religion and culture, its different sects, customs and dynasties. The Babylonian and Assyrian periods were but echoes from dusty text books and the resonance of names like Sennacherib or Genghis Khan owed more to high romance than to any historical reality. This was not unusual in a young man who had been brought up in the early years of this century with an Anglocentric view of the world, but it was an impressive and endearing habit of the handful who served in the remote areas of the British Empire that they took the trouble to learn the languages, customs and history of the people amongst whom the lived. This was especially true of those who served in India and the Middle East.

In time Glubb was to become the foremost Anglo-Arab of his generation, an imperial servant who understood the different facets of the Arab mind and a scholar whose books offer a concise introduction to the history and culture of the Middle East. While writing those books in his retirement

Glubb always claimed that the learning process had begun as soon as he set foot in Iraq. A key moment, he claimed, was the realisation that the Old Testament contained an accurate description of Bedouin life in Genesis 18. According to Glubb, the story of Abraham offering hospitality to the strangers could have been repeated amongst any of the desert people with whom he lived between 1924 and 1925. Throughout that period he was busy gleaning facts and storing up knowledge that would stand him in good stead in his day-to-day dealings with the peoples who lived along the frontier between Iraq and the Nejd. More to the point perhaps, he quickly became aware of the more recent history which had created Iraq and of Britain's not altogether honourable dealings with the Arab peoples. It was, he said, as if Britain were an old rooster flapping and cackling round a farmyard to keep in order the numerous Arab chicks she had brought into being.

There was much to the conceit. Iraq had been created as an accident of war and, later, its frontiers had been framed in a half-hearted and almost absent-minded way. The architect was Sir Percy Cox, the High Commissioner to Iraq, who summoned the representatives of King Feisal and Ibn Saud, his neighbour to the south, to a port called Uqair in the Hasa. Both sides made extravagant claims. The Iraqis declared that their authority ran south into the Nejd to a point twelve miles south of Riyadh and that the frontier should be drawn from Yanbu on the Red Sea to Qatar on the Persian Gulf. Ibn Saud replied by claiming that his kingdom should have the Euphrates as its northern border. Fearing that neither side would give any ground, Cox lost his patience and started drawing the lines on the map of the Middle East which are today the frontiers between Iraq and Saudi Arabia and Iraq and Kuwait. Ibn Saud was greatly angered by Cox's delineation and was only slightly mollified by a subsequent agreement to give him territory claimed by the Sheikh of Kuwait, Ahmad Al Sabah, who was not even present at the conference or allowed to express any point of view. As a buffer between the states Cox also invented a neutral territory south of the Stony Desert, separating the tribal peoples who owed their allegiance to Feisal or Ibn Saud. The agreement was signed in November 1922 and appended to the Treaty of Muhammarah which had been signed between the two kingdoms in the previous year. As Glubb noted, for the first time in history the deserts of Arabia had been divided by frontiers marked on maps.

At the time British officials hoped that the policy of divide and rule would put a stop to the tribal warfare which had disfigured the region for centuries. They were to be sadly disappointed. Ibn Saud accepted the protocols drawn up by Cox at the Uqair conference but returned to his capital of Riyadh determined to increase the size and authority of the kingdom of the Nejd. In the summer of 1920 he had defeated his rival to the north, Ibn Rasheed, and by capturing his capital of Ha'il had extended his frontier up to that imposed by Cox. To the west lay the kingdom of the Hejaz, ruled over by Sharif Hussein whose sons were now pre-eminent in Iraq and Transjordan. This was their reward for supporting the British during the Arab Revolt but to Ibn Saud it appeared that a conspiracy had been formed against him and his authority in Central Arabia.

From his point of view there was much to fuel those fears for he, too, had received seemingly unequivocal support from Britain. During the early part of the 1914–18 war, at Britain's behest, he had led his tribesmen against Ibn Rasheed who had thrown in his lot with the Ottoman Empire. Also, for some years, he had received patronage and arms from the Government of India who supported his claims to be a power in Central Arabia and a possible leader of a revolt against Turkish rule. The executor of this policy was Captain William Henry Shakespear of the Indian Political Service who had used much of his time as Political Agent in Kuwait to build up a close and confidential friendship with Ibn Saud. Shakespear's death at the inconclusive Battle of Jarab in January 1915 meant that Ibn Saud only took a minor part in the rest of the war but in the post-war years he was not without political supporters in the British camp. The most influential of these was H. St John Philby who argued that instead of supporting the Hashemites Britain would do better to put its weight behind Ibn Saud. Absurdly, Britain continued to sustain both leaders even though by 1922 they were bitter rivals in Central Arabia.

In his pursuit of maintaining and reinforcing his power in the region Ibn Saud had come to rely heavily on his army of shock troops – for so they appeared to their enemies – all of whom were members of the puritanical Wahhabi faith. Strict Muslim fundamentalists who eschewed alcohol, tobacco and other worldly vanities, the adherents were uncompromising zealots with a religious passion for battle which Lawrence had likened to Cromwell's Ironsides. Their prophet was Muhammad Ibn Abdul Wahhab, an eighteenth-century religious leader whose family had intermarried with the House of Saud to produce a fierce and warlike religious faith. It was Ibn Saud's genius in 1912 that turned a revival of Wahhabi fundamentalism to the service of his own ambitions. Those who embraced this strict religious life were known as the Ikhwan, or Brethren, and one of their principal aims was the forcible conversion of the rest of the Arab world to their own faith. These were the people who would raid the newly formed Iraqi border with an energy and aggression which the agrarian communities could not withstand.

As Glubb discovered, when he was appointed SSO, Ikhwan Defence, the Wahhabi warriors raided at will over a terrain which they knew well after years of fighting:

During his long years of war with Ibn Rasheed, Abdul-Aziz Ibn Saud had evolved a system of Ikhwan strategy against which the Iraqi shepherds were helpless. The Wahhabi tribes were able each to concentrate raiding parties composed of some three or four thousand camelmen. These they would hold back in readiness until their spies had located a suitable target. Then, one evening before sunset, they would set out, march all night covering perhaps seventy miles and surprise their victims in a wild charge at dawn. . . . The factor which added such a peculiar poignancy to these raids was massacre. The Ikhwan killed all males in cold blood, even small boys or male babies in arms. Women were not killed and the survivors of these raids consisted only of a weeping and wailing crowd of exhausted women and girls, who had probably straggled back on foot in panic flight over a hundred miles of desert.[1]

Such zeal made them fanatical warriors, so that when Ibn Saud proclaimed himself their leader he had at his disposal a highly committed and disciplined army. The trouble was that, having utilised them to consolidate his position in Central Arabia, he had difficulty keeping them in check as the occasion demanded. Glubb was quick to note that Ibn Saud was caught in the classic dilemma of those who use extremes to further their ambitions. His Wahhabi warriors had tasted victory over the followers of Ibn Rasheed; now they wanted to extend their influence into Iraq and 'were totally unprepared to halt at a political frontier which someone had drawn on a map'.[2]

Glubb was right. The Ikhwan did not acknowledge the boundaries drawn up between the two countries or the diamond-shaped neutral zone with its wells and grazing grounds. To them the desert was open and uncontained and they navigated its caravan routes in the same way that a sailor would the oceans. Besides, the essential dynamism of their religious fundamentalism was evangelism: they had a religious mission to fulfil and to the north, as they saw it, were peoples waiting to be converted. Not that they harboured any love for them. On the contrary, the Ikhwan despised all things Hashemite, regarding their followers as the ungodly in the pay of the British.

To worsen matters, Ibn Saud was uncommitted in his approach to containing the Ikhwan. Not only had they served him well in the past, but they had 60,000 men in arms and, if crossed, they could be a troublesome internal enemy. Moreover, after years of exhorting them to fight his battles for him, Ibn Saud now had to preach a more peaceful policy, one that went against the Ikhwan concept of holy war. He did his best to keep both his fellow countrymen and his Iraqi neighbours happy, it is true, but to the British his attitude seemed highly equivocal. One part of his mind told him that as a ruler with pretensions to create a modern Arab state he should curb the activities of his Ikhwan tribesmen, but the other half reminded him that, as Feisal was a British-supported threat, there might be little harm in turning a blind eye to the occasional raid into Iraqi territory. The latter belief may have been reinforced in 1924 when the British ceased their subsidies to the Nejd as part of their post-war economies in the Middle East.

Ibn Saud was certainly no fool. Although it was the custom in Baghdad to ridicule him for his delight in war and his many wives, he was, as Glubb realised, a shrewd and capable leader. Alone amongst the British officials who had dealings with him, Glubb could understand that Ibn Saud was walking a tightrope and that if he tried to quash the Ikhwan's activities he stood in grave danger of being deposed. 'When Ibn Saud has said in the past "I cannot control my tribes and I warn you that they may raid," he has always really meant, "I do not intend to try to control my tribes and I warn you that they may raid." '[13] Notes of that tenor punctuate Glubb's diaries between 1925 and 1929 when the Ikhwan raids were at their height.

That Glubb had managed to pick up personally so much essential information about recent events and personalities of Iraq, the Nejd and Transjordan owed everything to his restless nomadic nature which made light of the difficulties involved in desert travelling. These were, after all, the years before Iraq and Saudi Arabia were served by modern roads or even reliable maps. In March 1924, before his appointment as SSO, Ikhwan Defence, he used up two months of leave to ride the desert route to Transjordan, a

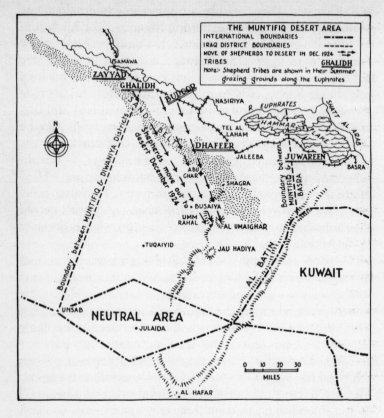

journey fraught with danger as the Ruwalla tribe was not always keen to find Europeans in its territory. When he arrived in the country Glubb had sought an audience with the emir, Abdullah, who was in his winter quarters at Shuneh. It was an auspicious meeting, made more memorable when Sharif Hussein, Abdullah's father, told Glubb that his desert adventures had made him a Bedouin. *Wallahi hadha Bedawi!* It was on this journey that Glubb had met Philby to whom he later wrote expressing his contempt for the tourist hordes he met in Jerusalem and Jericho. 'I hope when we meet again,' he ended his letter, 'the star of our prestige may be more in the ascendant that it is at present.'[4]

The forays into the desert continued when Glubb returned to Nasiriya to discover that the Ikhwan had been raiding along the Iraqi frontier and terrifying the largely peaceful sheep-rearing tribes. These were very different from the Bedouin who tended to despise such a regulated and bucolic life. During the summer months the shepherds lived along the banks of the Euphrates but in winter when the desert hills were covered with grass and the valleys had a plentiful water supply, they moved south into an area of desert some 30,000 square miles in area. Here they were scattered and helpless and it was in this wilderness that Glubb had been asked to evolve a system of defence to protect them. The first step was to live amongst them and to regain their confidence, for the shepherd tribes – and Bedouin tribes like the Dhafeer who had also been raided by the Ikhwan – were convinced that Ibn Saud was still supported by British subsidies as he had been throughout the war.

Glubb understood and sympathised with the tribes' point of view. From 1922 to 1926 the Iraqi government had ignored what was happening on the desert frontier with the Nejd. One reason was that they were obsessed by the fear of being drawn into the unnecessary military commitments which would be required to police the region adequately. Another was that few politicians understood the extent of the problem and believed that, in any case, desert tribes had no place in a modern Arab country. The frontier was about 350 miles long and much of it was at least 100 miles away from the nearest settlements containing government posts or police stations. During the grazing season the whole area was dotted with temporary camps which appeared one day and disappeared the next; hence the difficulty of gaining sufficiently detailed intelligence reports. In one of his gloomy reports to Baghdad after he had come across evidence of a raid, Glubb wrote, 'In these circumstances it was easy for a small party of fifteen or twenty men to slip across the frontier from one of these camps and steal some camels without the Government hearing about it.'[5]

In addition to suggesting that greater use be made of camel patrols, Glubb also recommended that armed or armoured cars be used for desert reconnaissance. These were long-nosed Rolls-Royce vehicles of civilian design equipped with crystal radio sets and machine-guns – antiquated they might appear in comparison to modern armoured cars but they were more than a match for tribesmen riding horses or camels. In answer to his request a section of armoured cars arrived in the southern desert shortly before Christmas 1924 but, to Glubb's disgust, they did not venture near the frontier and their crews maintained standards of discipline that seemed inappropriate for desert reconnaissance patrols. The last straw was their decision to withdraw to Baghdad in time for Christmas, at the very time when Glubb's intelligence reports suggested the raids would commence. In despair Glubb despatched what he would later call a 'disrespectful' report to Air Headquarters in Baghdad in which he 'compared the operation to sending the fire brigade for a drive around the town and then allowing all the men to go on holiday for Christmas, on the grounds that there were no houses on fire at the moment'.[6]

Not unnaturally, the tone of his signal was resented by his superiors. A confidential report on Glubb suggested that he had become too emotionally involved with the desert people in his area and that he had allowed his judgement to be clouded by that bond of friendship. Stuck in the desert, with only the tribesmen as his companions, he could not put his fears and suspicions into a proper perspective. (This was believed to be a common failing amongst colonial officers who worked in remote areas.) It was also believed that as an army officer Glubb did not always understand the tactical importance of aircraft and was more likely to employ a military solution to the problem of raiding.[7] Despite their incomplete success in the Barkat and Sufran punitive expeditions, there was still a school of thought in the RAF that Air Control could be best carried out purely by aircraft with minimal ground support.

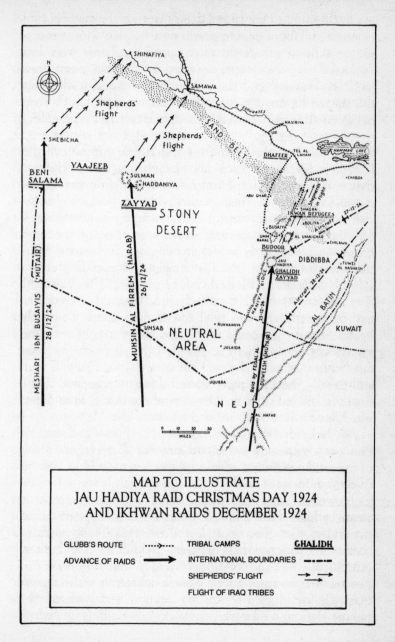

MAP TO ILLUSTRATE
JAU HADIYA RAID CHRISTMAS DAY 1924
AND IKHWAN RAIDS DECEMBER 1924

GLUBB'S ROUTE	TRIBAL CAMPS **GHALIDH**
ADVANCE OF RAIDS	INTERNATIONAL BOUNDARIES
	SHEPHERDS' FLIGHT
	FLIGHT OF IRAQ TRIBES

On Christmas Day 1924 Glubb's worst fears were realised when he and four Bedouin guards were helpless witnesses of a savage Ikhwan attack on a group of shepherds who had wandered into the desert, attracted by the lush green grass which had sprung up in the wake of heavy rain. Knowing that the shepherds stood in danger of being raided, Glubb rode out in an attempt to persuade them to return to the comparative safety of the land along the Baghdad–Basra railway line. He was too late. As he and his bodyguards approached the Haniya Ridge, near a place called Jau Hadiya, or Gift Hollow, they encountered a scene which Glubb would never forget – crowds of shepherds, their families and their flocks fleeing for their lives across the desert. Behind them, to the south, was a long line of raiders, some of whom were carrying the large green war banners of the Mutair tribe, one of the most fanatical of the Ikhwan. As the stragglers streamed through Glubb's little party, they cried out in terror, 'The Duweesh! The Ikhwan! O Ali, Thy protection! O Husain! O God save us!' Because Glubb and his Bedouin bodyguards were only lightly armed they could hardly engage in a fight with the raiders but he was loath to abandon the shepherds to their fate. Instead of making good their escape – their camels were still fresh – the little party slowed down to the pace of the fugitives and led them to the safety of the belt of sand dunes which lay to the north, below the railway line.

As darkness fell Glubb borrowed a horse and with a Bedouin companion set off to ride the forty miles to the nearest railway station at Jaleeba where he would be able to transmit a message to the RAF in Baghdad. It was a terrible journey over rough and rocky terrain and the going was made worse by high winds and heavy rain which so disoriented the two riders that they soon lost their way. Glubb and his companion took what shelter they could in a desert hollow, only to discover the following morning that they were but two miles from the station. Almost collapsing with exhaustion, Glubb staggered into the station and ordered the railway clerk to send a message to Baghdad calling up aircraft to pursue the Ikhwan raiders. However, it was Boxing Day and it was not until the afternoon that a ninak of 84 Squadron arrived at Jaleeba to take Glubb back to the squadron headquarters at Shaiba, a delay which left him angry and impotent.

The following day, in clear weather, Glubb led a flight of three bombers to the scene of the massacre near the Haniya Ridge and from there it was easy to follow the raiders' line of retreat to the frontier. Within a few minutes the war party was sighted driving the captured flocks back towards the Nejd. Although the tribesmen made an easy target for the aircrafts' bombs, Glubb was disappointed to see the raiders making good their escape. What was needed, he reasoned, was the section of armoured cars which had returned to Baghdad for Christmas – they could have followed up the attack on the ground and recovered the stolen flocks. As if echoing the confidential report made by his superiors, Glubb decided that henceforth his services would be at the disposal of the Iraqi tribes in their struggle against a vicious enemy.

My experience on Christmas Day, 1924, had stirred me deeply. The terror of the women in their flight, the anguish depicted in the faces of the children, the miserable donkeys laden with the few pathetic possessions of the shepherd families – all these and much else had both aroused my compassion and made me boil with indignation that such misery could be inflicted on human beings who relied for their protection on the government of which I was a servant. With youthful passion, I vowed that I would devote all my energies to put an end to such abomination.[8]

The massacre of the shepherds finally proved to the Iraqi government that steps would have to be taken to put a stop to inter-tribal raiding. As a first initiative a new base was established near the old Ottoman fort at Abu Ghar which lay some thirty miles out in the desert. An airstrip was constructed and a radio transmitter was installed. This was to be Glubb's home for the next twelve months.

Because Glubb had recommended that troops were necessary for ground operations against the Ikhwan raiders to mop up after the bombers had done their work, a company of infantry drawn from the Iraqi Army was despatched to the old fort. At first it was thought in Baghdad that the garrison would be temporary because of the difficulties· involved in supplying them. Glubb thought otherwise. He borrowed a Ford van in Jaleeba and forged a route over the sand dunes and gravelly sand of the desert: now there could be no arguments about moving men and supplies between the railway line and the forty at Abu Ghar.

Once he had established himself there, Glubb pitched his camp a quarter of a mile away from the fort, thus symbolically creating a distance between himself and the uniformed government soldiers who were still distrusted by the Iraqi desert tribes. It also allowed him to gather intelligence in an unostentatious way: within a few weeks his little camp was recognised as a social centre where hospitality was freely given and gossip willingly exchanged. Following the Bedouin custom, Glubb set up a guest tent where he could entertain travellers and his three Bedu retainers ensured that coffee was always ready to be served and that the camp fire was always burning.

It was the beginning of the most romantic period in Glubb's life. By keeping open house he encouraged desert travellers to visit him and to tell him what they knew of conditions along the frontier. Coffee, dark and strong, would be poured into little cups; the fire would be stoked up and a simple meal of unleavened bread, rice and mutton would be cooked. Then, beneath the night sky, Glubb would gently cross-question his guest, obeying the subtle rituals of Arab conversation which demand that information should always be teased out and never requested. Slowly but surely Glubb built up a network of relationships with the sheikhs whose tribes were under threat from the Ikhwan raiders. It was a strange fellowship. Glubb admitted that the majority of the tribesmen were simple and unsophisticated, that their lives were committed to plunder and self-interest and that their religion and customs were very different from his own English High Church view of life. And yet, for all those disparities Glubb found that he felt at home with the Bedouin in a way that he had not experienced since living with his sappers on the Western Front. As his reputation in the southern desert gathered strength, the rumours started that perhaps Abu Hunaik was as great a man as Urans, or Lawrence of Arabia, another Englishman who found fellowship and friendship amongst the desert peoples.

Glubb's main task at Abu Ghar was reconnaissance. He used a Ford car to visit the tribes in the locality, gathering information about their peregrinations and passing on warnings about the movements of hostile tribes on the other side of the border. At other times he flew as an observer in one of the three aircraft stationed at Samawa – one of the RAF pilots, Guy Moore, had become a particular friend. He was the intelligence officer in the neighbouring Diwaniya district. Although the work was routine, not every flight was uneventful. On one occasion Glubb's ninak landed in a narrow, rocky wadi so that he could interrogate the local shepherds. When it took off again the under-carriage was shattered by the rocky ground and it was only the pilot's skill which prevented a serious accident when they returned to Abu Ghar. 'It was one of those occasions when you have no time to be afraid,' remembered Glubb, 'but your heart seems to cease beating when the danger is already past.' For his work as SSO Ikhwan Defence, Glubb was awarded the OBE in 1925.

The excitement and the pleasure which Glubb experienced during this period of service were certainly helped by the prevailing political situation. During the course of 1925 cross-border raiding came to a virtual standstill because the attention of the Ikhwan tribes had been engaged elsewhere, on the Nejd's western border with the Hejaz. Long irritated by Hussein's autocratic rule, and angered by his decision to prevent the people of the Nejd making pilgrimages to the holy places, Ibn Saud decided to take military action against him. In September 1924, 3,000 Ikhwan troops, led by Sultan Bijad Ibn Humaid and Khaled Ibn Luwai, captured Hussein's summer capital of Taif, forcing the old king to abdicate in favour of his son Ali. Urged on by his Ikhwan commanders, and encouraged by their success, Ibn Saud stepped up the raids on the Hejaz and within a year Ali had decided to follow the course taken by his father. By January 1926 Ibn Saud was master of the Hejaz and ruler of most of southern Arabia.

Ibn Saud now felt confident enough to move the Ikhwan warriors back to the Nejd and to ban them from further raiding. He also entered into a treaty with Iraq which both sides hoped would put an end to the warring in the desert. Known as the Bahra Agreement, it was signed on 1 November 1925, and by its terms Ibn Saud and Feisal agreed to prevent their tribes from raiding and promised not to encourage them to change their allegiance. This had been a long-standing source of aggravation and Ibn Saud was anxious to keep the frontier tribes of the Nejd within his suzerainty. It was, of course, only a stop-gap solution, for the passionate righteousness of the Ikhwan knew no bounds and they were anxious to continue their holy war against the infidel. Their leaders also realised that the movement was doomed if its members did not have an excuse to convert unbelievers and to massacre those who refused to undergo such proselytisation. Not for the first time in their history the Ikhwan tribes threw up a leadership equal to the moment – Feisal al Duweesh of the Mutair tribe, Dhidan Ibn Hithlain of the Ajman from the Hasa province, and Sultan Bijad Ibn Humaid of the Utaibah. For the next three years, between 1927 and 1930, they were to form a painful thorn in the flesh of the British administration in Iraq.

Glubb called this period of peace 'the year of the tent' because most of his time was spent in the desert amongst the shepherd tribes of the Dhafeer, the Budoor and the Juwareen. There his white tent quickly became accepted as the symbol of government and a sure sign that the tribes would be offered protection from the dreaded Ikhwan. However, once the danger of raids had diminished, Glubb's one concern was that he would be pulled out of the desert and placed in a dreary administrative job in Baghdad. His fears were not without foundation, for the Iraqi government was worried about the increasingly high costs of maintaining the defence of the southern desert, but in the event it was the British Army that was to be the agent of Glubb's next transformation. Early in the summer of 1926 he received a letter from the War Office ordering him to return to Chatham and to resume his career in the Royal Engineers. He had been on loan to the Royal Air Force for a little over the normal five-year period and the army was now anxious to make use of his services.

It was a devastating, though nonetheless expected, blow which presented Glubb with a predicament. To go home to England – as his parents hoped he would – meant a return to the kind of regimental soldiering he had gone to Iraq to avoid. To stay in Iraq as a civilian offered only an uncertain future, for Britain's treaty relationship with Iraq was due to end in 1928.

The deadlock was broken by Kinahan Cornwallis, the British adviser to the Ministry of the Interior, offering him a ten-year contract as a civilian administrative inspector, or political officer in Iraqi local government. In practice the contract was hardly worth the paper on which it was written, but Glubb grabbed it eagerly. In November 1926 he resigned his eleven-year-old commission in the Royal Engineers and took up the post of administrative inspector in the Diwaniya Division in the Middle Euphrates. As he admitted later, from the point of view of a world career it was a rash decision, but he was still young enough to take the risk (he was twenty-nine) and it allowed him to stay in the lands and with the people he had come to love.

Although Iraq was a British mandate under the League of

Nations, a separate treaty had also been signed in October 1922. Under its terms King Feisal had agreed to be guided in international and financial affairs by British advisers and Britain was permitted to station armed forces in Iraq. A separate secret military agreement was concluded in 1924 which gave Britain other privileges including the command of Anglo-Iraqi forces, the right to inspect Iraqi forces and the ability to raise local militia forces. This agreement expired in December 1928 but the Iraqi government now refused to sign any new treaty unless Britain surrendered the right to control Iraqi forces. It was not an unreasonable request, as the British had been running down its own forces as part of the defence economies in the Middle East. By 1927 expenditure on the defence forces in Iraq had dropped from the £20 million spent in 1922 to a modest £2,107,000. Moreover, there were only four battalions of infantry, one support and maintenance company, eight RAF squadrons and three companies of armed cars.[9] The Air Staff in London believed that these figures could be cut even further if the infantry battalions were returned to India and the defence strategy made completely dependent on Air Control. Despite Glubb's intemperate pleadings for the deployment of more ground forces, Sir John Salmond, the Air Officer Commanding in Iraq, still believed that his bombers provided the best solution to the problem of internal security.

During the whole period under review, a main factor in the pacification of the country has been the Royal Air Force. By prompt demonstrations on the first sign of trouble carried out over any area affected, however distant, tribal insubordination has been calmed before it could grow dangerous, and there has been immense saving of blood and treasure to the British and Iraqi governments. In earlier times punitive columns would have had to struggle towards their objectives across deserts or through difficult defiles, compelled by the necessity of their preparations and marches to give time to their opponents to gain strength. But now, almost before the would-be rebel has formulated his plans, the droning of the aeroplane is heard overhead and in the majority of cases their mere appearance is enough.[10]

Encouraging though those words were to the Colonial Office in London, while the Iraqis refused to renegotiate the treaty, Britain had no sanction for stationing its 'droning' aeroplanes in the country. In an attempt to retrieve the position Britain began to hold out promises that it would recommend Iraq for admittance to the League of Nations before the agreed date of 1932. In July 1927 Sir Henry Dobbs, who had replaced Cox as High Commissioner, was able to promise Feisal that Britain would increase the pace of change, 'if all goes well in the interval and the present rate of progress is maintained'. Dobbs had served in the Mesopotamian expeditionary force in 1915 and knew the country well: he was also a gifted administrator but a man of uncertain temper who was known to throw objects at members of his staff after they had made unforced errors. Nonetheless, he was a shrewd observer of Iraqi political life and played a key role in directing and regulating British political initiatives in the country.

Dobbs also understood both the character of King Feisal and the nature of the predicaments he faced. In confidential memoranda to the Colonial Office he frequently railed against the level of corruption in the king's court, elevation of favourites and the ever-present whiff of scandal, but he also had a firm grip of the local religious and political difficulties under which Feisal was forced to operate.[11] In a divided society like Iraq, made up of so many different groupings, the king had to steer a course between advocating independence and maintaining close relations with Britain, the mandatory authority.

This was especially true of his country's defence policy. Feisal recognised that an independent Iraqi state required an army under his own control and to gain that objective he became an insistent advocate of conscription. Dobbs was lukewarm about the idea, partly because he feared that the creation of a large regular army would endanger Britain's position, and partly because he knew from his local intelligence sources that the majority Shi'ite population would be opposed to it. Conscription to them meant a return to the old days of Ottoman rule and religious leaders feared that the officer corps would be predominantly Sunni, thus reinforcing the commonly held belief that Feisal's government was an instrument of Sunni rule propped up by the British. This was closely connected to a growing concern amongst the Shi'ite tribes of the southern desert that little was being done to halt the Ikhwan raids because the British did not want to sever good relations with Ibn Saud. The more dogmatic Shi'ite nationalists put the case more strongly: they argued that Britain was happy to see the Ikhwan raids continuing because the necessity of deploying aircraft made Feisal dependent on Britain for protection.

There was some truth to their assertions. In his confidential notes for a briefing with members of the Parliamentary Army and Air Committees, Sir Christopher Bullock, Assistant (later Permanent) Secretary, Air Ministry, made it clear that although political considerations were necessary to promote the idea of a strong and independent Iraqi Army, the reality of the local situation meant that Britain's long-term interests were better served by Air Control. Citing a recent attack by Kurds on an Iraqi transport train in which the ground troops had fled from the scene, he pointed out that the situation had only been retrieved by RAF bombers. The implication was clear: by all means pay lip service to the idea of establishing an independent force in Iraq, but for the time being the peace would have to be kept by British aircraft. He went on:

Had not the Royal Air Force immediately come into play there would undoubtedly have been a very serious reverse, and as it is the Royal Air Force has now had to undertake the major role in the operations which are at this moment proceeding [against the Ikhwan]. Only the Royal Air Force could have intervened *in time*; a battalion or two of British infantry would no doubt equally have restored the situation. But, even if they had been available at Baghdad, they would have arrived days too late. A heavy demand had been made on the squadrons concerned who, whilst the Iraqi Army were recovering from the initial shock, had to keep up constant patrol and stave off further attempted attacks by the enemy, which the Iraq Army would have been in no condition to withstand, whilst simultaneously they have had to fly up supplies of food and ammunition to parties of Iraqi troops which had been cut off. A single one of our large troop carriers dropped ten tons of supplies – rations for 500 men for 10 days – in the space of 48 hours.

This episode has served to underline yet again in the eyes of all concerned the fact that the Air Force has been the *primary* instrument for maintaining order in Iraq, although I repeat with emphasis, no one wishes to minimise the indispensable subsidiary work which has been performed by the various ground forces which have been so admirably organised under British Army officers.[12]

The British in Iraq found themselves in something of a cleft stick, Bullock's praise for the 'indispensable subsidiary work' of the Iraqi armed forces notwithstanding. While the Colonial Office was anxious to keep its expenditure in Iraq to a minimum, and to promote Iraq's membership of League of Nations, they still wished to maintain Britain's strategic interests in that part of the Middle East. One part of the solution to this problem had been introduction of a system of government known as dyarchy, or dual control, which had been first adopted in India in 1919. Under its terms matters such as public works, education, irrigation and local government were transferred to an Indian minister while other strategic topics like the police, land rents and prisons were reserved for administration by a British official. Dyarchy was supposed to

123

control the growing nationalist dissent in India and to channel it into a constructive use of power. Like any other initiative aimed at winning the support of moderate political opinion it was in fact a means of prolonging, with apparent Indian consent, the long-standing imperial relationship. One Indian Civil Service (ICS) officer, Philip Mason, regarded dyarchy as an unworkable compromise and described it as 'the technical term for handing over the steering wheel and retaining control of the accelerator, the gear-lever and the brake'.[13]

In spite of those drawbacks the system, in its crazily zigzag way, worked in many of the Indian provinces largely because the Indian ministers and their British advisers had good working relationships, based on long years of trust and mutual understanding. It only stuttered when the District Officer tried his best to retain his own power or the local Indian politicians conspired to chip away at his authority. Unfortunately, that kind of point-scoring more often than not became the norm when dyarchy was introduced in Iraq. This was principally due to the fact that there was no political tradition of co-operation between the Iraqi officials and their British advisers, whereas in India these had been nurtured over several generations. The other difficulty was that most of the local Iraqi officials were Sunnis who had been educated in the autocratic Ottoman system of government.

When Glubb arrived in Diwaniya to take over the post of British Administrative Inspector he soon realised that dyarchy was not working for both these reasons. Lateef Beg, the local mutasarrif, or governor, was a Sunni and a former Turkish Army officer who had accustomed himself after long usage to solve problems by the application of Ottoman law. As Glubb noted, this greatly favoured the landowners and was often implemented by much favourism and bribery. Lateef Beg was also a nationalist who had taken part in the 1920 revolt and the whole tenor of his attitude towards Glubb was obstructive. For example, during the collection of land rents, which under dyarchy remained a British responsibility, the mutasarrif continued on several occasions to protect local nationalist interests, leaving Glubb unhappy and frustrated. After discovering that Lateef had once more interfered in the collection of rents from a local nationalist sheikh, Glubb noted wearily in his diary:

> I cannot help liking him, but I always feel that he is susceptible to influence. He has never had a chance here in Diwaniya. The politicians in Baghdad keep writing to him to work administrative ramps to help their political supporters. If he does so, I protest. If he does not, he is abused by his political friends in Baghdad. If his ramps are made public, he is obliged to cancel them and feels that he has lost prestige. Yet I still like him. If it were not for the politics, we should be happy together.[14]

What Glubb failed to understand, of course, was that Lateef Beg was a committed Iraqi nationalist whose main concern was the granting of independence to his country. In such circumstances, the principle which Glubb held to be all-important – service to the community and the protection of the downtrodden – was but an obstacle in the path of Lateef's long-term goal. Later Glubb was to say that his experiences in Diwaniya as an Administrative Inspector, working under the intractable conditions of dyarchy, gave him an 'intense aversion' to politics. Perhaps that was the way he liked to view himself fifty years after the event, as a simple and uncomplicated soldier, but it is a contradiction of the facts. He may or may not have liked Lateef Beg, mainly because he was pawn in the party political game, but Glubb himself worked hard for the Iraqi government during that period at Diwaniya. The name of Captain Glubb appears on numerous official minutes and memoranda, mainly concerned with the defence of the Iraqi–Nejd frontier, and just as he had done during the previous year he bombarded Baghdad with ideas. 'The penetration of the Iraqi desert is a great progressive step,' he noted in June 1927, 'such has not been undertaken in Arabia for 800 years.' He was proving himself an adept political animal and his immediate boss Kinahan Cornwallis encouraged him to keep up his high output to the Ministry of the Interior.

Of course, being an independent man, Glubb continued to spend as much time as possible in the remoter areas of the division, speaking to the nomad tribes, but he did not neglect the long-term aim of evolving a plan which would provide them with better protection from attack by raiders. All the time he was adding to his understanding of Bedouin tactics and passing on that knowledge to others further up the chain of command. Most British military men in Arabia during that period believed that Bedouin tactics were simple: one tribe attacked another, defeated it and looted it, and then retreated quickly out of reach of retribution. That was the received wisdom and in the early stages of his researches, Glubb also inclined to that view as a memorandum of his to Dobbs makes clear:

> Bedouin war is like war in the air, the best defence is to hit back harder. The Bedouins will acquiesce in suffering sudden flights, retirements and raids if they in turn can inflict similar losses.[15]

However, as his discussions with tribal leaders continued, Glubb reached a fresh understanding of desert tactics, one based on attack from defence. To be sure, the Bedouin art of war depended above all on surprise, speed of attack and equally rapid retreat, but it needed a defensive aspect too. All too often, though, as Glubb discovered, defensive tactics were despised by most Bedouin leaders because they were thought to be adopted only by the weaker side. Creating suitable defensive positions in the desert also produced problems due to the lack of suitable ground and materials and to the need to defend flocks of sheep or herds of camels. It was possible to pitch tents in closely knit circles but this was only feasible if an attack were imminent and even then only for short periods as the accompanying flocks had to be guarded. Besides, such a defensive formation offended Bedouin sensibilities and it had not been used for many years.

Realising that the desert frontier tribes would always be at risk from sudden attack, Glubb bent his energies to the evolution of a defensive scheme which would provide them with the necessary cover. The construction of forts or armed camps was one solution. These would not be used by the Bedouin themselves as they were always on the move, but, equipped with wireless sets and garrisoned by troops or armed policemen, they would provide useful defensive positions in time of attack. (At other times they would be a focal point for intelligence gathering and a statement of the government's intention to protect the frontier.) Also, if they were to be adopted with any success, they would not be purely defensive: what was required were tactics which would allow the static defenders to surprise the raiders with well-planned counter-attacks. Glubb understood that this form of warfare was easier to control because it was largely static; he also recognised that the defending side would require superior strength and resources if it were to repulse attacks and mount strong counter-offensives. In the southern desert areas such a policy required two main ingredients: forts and armoured cars. In a fresh report to Dobbs, dated 15 January 1927, Glubb argued that the defence of the desert should be regarded by the government as a firm obligation and that it should consist of:

1. Police car patrols.
2. The construction of bases in the desert as a sign of government stability.
3. The establishment of settlements in the desert for trade and as centres of civilisation. This would prove to the world that Iraq was interested in the peaceful settlement of the desert.[16]

Glubb had put down a marker which he wanted to be noticed. The first response came from Cornwallis who replied that the Ministry of the Interior was interested but that any move would have to wait for the renegotiation of the Anglo-Iraqi military treaty. Meanwhile the papers would be passed to Air HQ for their comments, but back came the dusty response from the new commanding officer, Air Vice-Marshal Sir Edward Ellington, that he could not sanction the increased use of ground transport: 'Much of the country in the area of operations is quite unsuitable for the tactical handling of the present type of armoured car.' The question of building fortified police stations was given consideration but no action was taken.[17]

It was then, during the winter of 1926-7, that events elsewhere began to conspire to bring Glubb back to the desert. During that period Ibn Saud had established himself as a powerful ruler but the new position had brought fresh problems. His prolonged absence in the Hejaz had caused disquiet as his government had always been centralised on his person and the Ikhwan leaders felt that they were being ignored. They also believed that Ibn Saud's new power and the increased funds which permitted him to purchase modern weapons would one day be turned against them. While the kingdom was small and self-contained the Wahhabi leaders had been pre-eminent: they had enjoyed influential support and also the large shares of loot and subsidies handed out by Ibn Saud. The conquest of the Hejaz, however, had brought large numbers of other tribes under Ibn Saud's sway, including chiefs with as powerful followings as the Ikhwan leaders. Many of these were hereditary and bitter enemies of the Ikhwan but because Ibn Saud had to win their loyalty and friendship he invariably alienated the more intransigent Ikhwan leaders.

The most authoritative of these was Feisal al Duwish of the Mutair tribe which stood against any government interference in the desert, be it inspired by Riyadh or Baghdad. He was Ibn Saud's finest general and his tribe was renowned across the Arabian deserts for their black camels which charged, riderless, ahead of the main army before any attack.

His allies were Dhidan Ibn Hithlain and Sultan Ibn Bijad Ibn Humaid who led, respectively, the Ajman and Utaibah tribes.

At the beginning of 1927 Ibn Saud convened a conference of Ikhwan leaders who were encouraged to air their grievances. Principal amongst these was the religious shame they felt at the incursion into the deserts of Iraqi shepherd tribes protected by infidel aircraft and armoured cars. They demanded that these be removed, by force if necessary, and that Ibn Saud use his authority to force Iraq to pull out of its defences of the southern desert. Rather cleverly, Ibn Saud refused to remove his own weapons and wirelesses, themselves objects of Ikhwan wrath, but agreed to put pressure on Baghdad to remove British aircraft from the area. This was a concession which cost him nothing. A holy war was also demanded but the call was rejected by Ibn Saud. In response Feisal al Duwish started a rumour that the king had sold out to the infidels and had himself invited the British into the desert to help him put down the Ikhwan. 'If this is not so,' they said, 'let him join us in a jihad against the infidels. If he does not do so it will be proof that he is himself in secret relations to bring them into Nejd.'[18] Not surprisingly perhaps, the conference reached a compromise with Ibn Saud promising to put the Ikhwan case to the British in Baghdad while they themselves began making preparations for raiding the infidel to the north.

As it turned out, though, the first attacks had already come from within Iraq. During the autumn of 1926 the Iraqi government had issued an edict banning inter-tribal raiding but in defiance of it a Shammar war party from northern Iraq carried out an audacious raid in Kuwait. To do this they had crossed the Euphrates in the Mosul province and had then travelled down a long line of wells in the desert west of the river. The raid was not particularly spectacular, although the friendly state of Kuwait suffered the indignity of losing a large number of camels, but it did bring home to the Ministry of the Interior the absolute necessity of policing the western and southern deserts.

The other failure during the Shammar raid was the lack of intelligence. Although the rebel raiding party had been attacked eventually by RAF bombers, it had taken five days for the news of the raid to get through to Baghdad. Had there been armed police posts in the desert, based on the wells and equipped with wireless transmitters, these could have provided rapid intelligence and denied the use of the wells to the raiders. Glubb's recommendations were remembered and in February 1927 a police post was established at the strategically important well at Busaiya, south of Glubb's original base at Abu Ghar and within striking distance of the frontier. Within the year permission was granted to fortify the camp with a small blockhouse and walled defences. Glubb's ideas were now being put into practice but, ironically, the post at Busaiya and the changing political situation in the Nejd were to lead to an increased level of tension, and eventually to the outbreak of a fierce frontier war.

5

War on the Frontier

It has often been pointed out that small armed insurrections account for a high proportion of wars and that the presence of superior forces equipped with powerful weapons has done little to prevent them breaking out. The history of warfare is littered with examples of fanatical groups, often poorly armed and indifferently led, taking on and holding down large regular forces. All too often, such conflicts, though lacking cohesion and direction, can be major irritants which drain national exchequers and cause much misery and hardship amongst the people over whose land the fighting takes place. Another feature of warfare of this kind is its relationship to politics. While it may be said that all wars are fought to achieve political goals, here the insurgents, and the forces which attempt to contain the insurrection, take unusual steps to influence the people round to their point of view. In modern military parlance these are known as low-intensity wars and attempts to bring them to a successful conclusion are dominated by counter-insurgency operations which require both a military and a political contribution. The warfare on the Iraq–Nejd frontier which broke out at the end of 1927 was just such a conflict.

As happens in most wars the fighting was prompted by a simple flashpoint, although the underlying reasons for the conflict were deep-rooted and complicated. In this case the initial flare-up was started by the construction of the armed police post at Busaiya. In September 1927 twelve workmen

131

were sent to the well to build a block-house and rudimentary fortifications to provide a permanent base for the seven policemen who would use it. As the entire operation cost less than £100 it was not regarded by the Iraqi government as a major defence commitment; rather it was considered to be a signal of intent and a useful desert listening post based on a strategically important well. It was also believed that because Busaiya was at least eighty miles away from the Nejd border and well within Iraqi territory it would not cause any offence to Ibn Saud. In this the authorities were greatly mistaken.

On 24 October Ibn Saud wrote to Dobbs protesting about the 'fort', claiming that its construction was a breach of Article 3 of the Uqair protocol attached to the 1922 Treaty of Muhammarah. This clause mutually agreed that neither country would 'use the watering places and wells situated in the vicinity of the border for any military purpose, such as building forts on them, and not to concentrate troops in their vicinity'.

Ibn Saud had several reason for making a complaint. The first was genuine enough. To him a police station was a fort under another name and he could see no difference between soldiers and armed policemen in uniform as both represented the authority of Iraq. In addition, he lacked detailed maps to show him the distance between Busaiya and the frontier. Besides, any distance would have been bad enough: the main reason for Ibn Saud's protest was that he was under considerable pressure from the Ikhwan to make vigorous complaint about the Iraqi incursions into the desert. In turn they hoped to embroil him in a holy war because with Ibn Saud on their side the Ikhwan leaders did not fear a conflict with Iraq.

There was one other reason for Ibn Saud's hostility towards the construction of the base at Busaiya – he feared that it might be the thin edge of a British wedge which would threaten his country's internal security. To him, Busaiya was but the first stage in the construction of a railway from Baghdad to Ha'il. Not only would this be a direct route into his new kingdom, but Ibn Saud feared that it might be used in the future by pilgrims from Soviet Central Asia and that their arrival in the Nejd would spread Bolshevism and revolutionary unrest amongst his people. This was not an idle fear. The Soviet Union had been the first world power to recognise Ibn Saud as king of Hejaz-Nejd in 1927, hoping to secure trade agreements with the new country. However, the diplomatic manouevre came to naught and Ibn Saud, fearful of encouraging communism, ordered a total trade embargo against the Soviet Union in the following year.

Dobbs replied to the king's complaint with a courteous note pointing out that the Uqair protocol had not been breached and that the Busaiya project was an internal Iraqi security matter. At that time he still believed that Ibn Saud had control of his Ikhwan commanders and that the Nejd leader was merely going through the diplomatic motions to placate them. Dobbs was anxious not to provoke any hostilities in the area as he knew that the Turkish Petroleum Company (later the Iraq Petroleum Company) had plans to construct oil pipelines and a railway in the southern desert. The Ikhwan response was made on the night of 5/6 November 1927 when a raiding party of around fifty Mutair tribesmen attacked Busaiya and slaughtered the workmen and their defenders, with the exception of one policeman who was left for dead. It was a well-organised and premeditated attack made from a base deep within the Nejd and it was the signal for a series of murderous raids all along the frontier. Three weeks later some 400 Mutair raided deep into Kuwaiti territory and a Duweesh war party raided and looted the Shammar between Unsab and Jumaima on the western border. The attacks brought an immediate response from Dobbs:

His Majesty's Government have learnt with amazement of this unprovoked attack [against Busaiya] which they feel convinced cannot have been authorised by Your Majesty, but for which Your Majesty cannot divest Yourself of responsibility. They have instructed me to inform Your Majesty that they must look to Your Majesty to serve

133

immediate and rigorous punishment on those responsible, full compensation for the families of the killed and for the wounded men, and an assurance that adequate measures have been taken to prevent further raids into Iraq territory.[1]

At the same time he ordered Air Headquarters to make fresh provision for the defence of the frontier, no easy matter as many of the experienced pilots who had served in the previous emergency had returned to Britain on the completion of their two-year tour of duty. As their replacements had little experience of desert conditions the whole learning process had to begin again. As a first step a section of armoured cars was sent to Busaiya to guard the police reinforcements and the new team of workers who had arrived to make good the damage caused by the Mutair raiders. RAF reconnaissance flights were stepped up and on 14 December Dobbs signed an order giving permission for aircraft to pursue raiders over the border, a decision that intensified the war of words between himself and Ibn Saud, who wrote:

It has reached me that some aeroplanes from Iraq fly over our territories and over our tribes, some of them landing in the midst of our lands and taking off again; also that motor cars run through the neutral areas and on the extremities of our borders. Your Excellency is aware that the most important object of our concern is the maintenance of good relations between our two governments and that we loathe all that may result in the disturbance of peace. Aeroplanes in flying and motor cars in running fly over a desert that abhors such flying and running. Therefore I am fearful lest they should come up against some fellow who knows nothing about them, and I request that you will issue orders to officials and non-officials [sic] to avoid routes running through our borders, for their own safety and for the safety of the friendly relations between the two parties against possible disturbance which we neither wish, nor approve of.[2]

The sequence of raid and counter-attack, followed by diplomatic protest and counter-complaint rapidly escalated as the year of 1927 came to a close. It had all the ingredients of a low-intensity war. The Ikhwan operated from bases deep within the Nejd where they enjoyed the security of Ibn Saud's desert spaces – even if they had not won their leader's approval for their activities. They also believed that the ferocity of their attacks would convince the Iraqi tribes to join them in their 'crusade' against the infidel – a feature of the tribal warfare had been the notorious fickleness of the tribes' allegiance to Feisal and Ibn Saud. For their part the Iraqi authorities and their British advisers had to evolve tactics which would defeat the Ikhwan raiders and protect the desert tribes against further depredations. This would require the provision of a dedicated defence force in the area while a diplomatic offensive was started to encourage Ibn Saud to use his influence over the rebel Ikhwan leaders.

The RAF's first step was to locate its forward operational base at Ur of the Chaldees, twelve miles south-west of Nasiriya. Nine aircraft of 55 Squadron were despatched to the landing strip at Busaiya to reinforce the armoured cars and police garrison. To the west, an armed police post was constructed at Sulman and it was occupied by a company of infantry drawn from the Iraqi Army, nine DH9As of 84 Squadron and two sections of armoured cars. The remaining aircraft of both squadrons were held in reserve at Shaiba. Having fixed their defensive lines the RAF then ordered all the shepherd tribes to retire behind them, thus creating a *cordon sanitaire* on the Iraqi side of the border. This belt was widened on 11 January 1928 when RAF aircraft flew over the Nejd dropping leaflets which ordered the tribes to retire seventy miles from the border on pain of being attacked from the air.

Feisal al Duweesh and the Mutair tribe have, contrary to the orders of His Majesty the King of Nejd, made war upon the tribes of Iraq. As punishment for this offence, the

135

British and Iraq Governments hereby order that all Nejd tribes must retreat to a distance of four days' march from the Iraq frontier. Any persons who disobey this order will be liable to be attacked from the air without further warning.[3]

It was believed that the evacuation of the frontier areas would enable pilots to identify raiding parties and to distinguish between friend and foe. If the frontier and the immediate vicinity became a 'no-go area' then any party discovered in it would be considered hostile and therefore liable to be attacked. Sensible though the idea was, it failed in practice because the Nejd tribes either ignored the leaflets or failed to understand them. (They were written in English and Arabic.) A further complication was provided by the Nejd Shammar tribe who lived in the region and who were known to be loyal to Ibn Saud. When they were accidentally attacked in January they decided to change sides and throw in their lot with Iraq, thereby breaking one of the unwritten protocols of border warfare. As for the Mutair, the real culprits responsible for the first and the most vicious raid, they were not affected by the RAF's tactics as they lived further to the south, seemingly out of range of the bombers. At the end of February the *cordon sanitaire* was abandoned in favour of a more offensive policy.

The first move was to attempt to make an example of the Mutair. Although some tribesman had been located and bombed following a daring raid into Kuwait on 27 January, the limited range and light bomb loads of the pursuing aircraft meant that the Mutair and their looted flocks were able to escape relatively unscathed to their home base of Lusafa in the Nejd. This was well beyond the range of the bombers, being at least 400 miles away from Shaiba. Nonetheless, a solution was found on 23 February when a convoy of armoured cars and trucks carrying petrol across the border and headed for Al Hafar at the southern end of the Al Batin depression. They were followed by twelve DH9As and three Vickers Victoria heavy bombers, newly arrived from Britain. That night the aircraft landed and refuelled; the following day at first light they set off again to bomb the Mutair camp at Lusafa. Though hazardous – RAF planes had already been shot down that month by Ikhwan rifle fire – the operation was a complete success and it pointed the way to future close co-operation between air and ground forces, the policy advocated by Glubb.

In response to RAF requests, Cornwallis released Glubb from his post at Diwaniya and transferred him to the frontier on 2 March 1928 with the imposing title of Administrative Inspector, Southern Desert. Glubb was still a civilian and the newly created post carried no specific responsibilities other than to lend assistance to the authorities in coping with the increasingly ferocious attacks from over the border. The nationalist Iraqi newspaper *Al Istiqlal* immediately guessed the reasons for the appointment: Glubb was to be responsible for Anglo-Iraqi intelligence operations along the frontier, just as he had been two years earlier. Although the writer did not approve of the presence of British 'spies' in the desert, he did not deny Glubb's qualities:

> Mr Glubb has no fixed headquarters that may define the limits of his office and no instructions have yet been published to explain his duties and thus gather an idea as to the degree of his responsibility. One thing is however known; that he is all in all; he is the refuge to which the nomads fly; he is the shield behind which they seek safety and he is the commander and the prohibitor. It is sufficient to pronounce his name when all will fall down to their knees and to tell them that here comes Abu Hunaik and they will begin to tremble and then freeze as if thunder struck.[4]

The newspaper *Al Taqaddam* claimed that Glubb was a British spymaster who 'lives on dry barley bread and the water of the rain pools and rests neither day nor night'. The writer's use of hyperbole suggested further that Glubb was something a superman, another of the breed that had produced Lawrence, Leachman and Shakespear and, even allowing for the anti-British tenor of the piece, there is something in the writer's claims. The year 1927 had not been a particularly good one for Anglo-Iraqi relations. The conscription question still hung over the proposed extension of the military agreement and both sides faced stalemate. Feisal favoured the introduction of conscription but he also realised that he needed the RAF to protect both his throne and his kingdom; he knew that this is what the British wanted as well. Dobbs was aware of the king's feelings on the subject, and, although opposed to conscription, he was coming round to the idea that Iraq would have to be allowed to introduce it but only on condition that Britain did not help in any way. This view was contested by Cornwallis who was closer to the tribes than any other senior British official: he believed that the introduction of conscription would be a disaster as it would encourage the tribesmen to settle old scores whilst in uniform. To complicate matters further, Feisal had been left with the impression that Britain would sponsor Iraq for membership of the League of Nations in 1928.

Before Glubb went to the southern desert he was briefed by Cornwallis on the touchy political situation and warned that he would have to evolve defensive plans which would not insinuate Britain further into Iraq's domestic policies. He was to assist the RAF in the furtherance of their air control operations, working in conjunction with the local SSO, but he was to bear in mind that every military or quasi-military decision would have a political application. In other words, Glubb was to work on a policy whereby the security operations would be closely bound into a co-ordinated campaign which took into account political, economic and cultural factors.

When Glubb arrived at Busaiya early in March 1928 he found a fair degree of chaos. The area was full of service personnel from the RAF and the Iraqi Army but, as he admitted, because there was no administration, there was nothing for him to inspect. The weather, too, had been bad, with high winds and violent storms which had prevented the squadrons from launching reconnaissance patrols. Although the raid on the Mutair had given the aircrews a much-needed fillip, the pilots still complained that their patrols yielded little because they disliked the experience of flying over long stretches of the featureless desert. If they came across raiding parties or camps, as they often did, the tribesmen usually scattered in panic but there was no way of knowing whether or not they were friendly. It was also frustrating when news came through of an Ikhwan raid and it was too late to pursue them. What was needed was accurate forward intelligence but, as Glubb discovered, two things prevented its collection. First, the RAF doubted if they could gather information themselves as their armoured cars were incapable of operating deep into the desert without full logistical support; and, second, they were unwilling to rely on news brought in by friendly local tribes. Even their decision to create a *cordon sanitaire* along the frontier seemed to indicate that they viewed the local shepherd and Bedouin tribes as obstacles instead of useful allies. It was then that Glubb dreamed up the idea of a 'desert patrol' which would overcome both obstacles. Because its members would be Bedouin tribesmen who were accustomed to desert conditions and because they would be under the command of a British officer – Glubb – their intelligence would be trusted. In other words, Glubb wanted to harness the abilities and energies of the tribesmen and turn them into armed and mobile scouts in the service of the Iraqi government.

They were to be known as the Southern Desert Camel Corps, a sonorous title for what was, in reality, a small and tight-knit irregular militia drawn from the friendly Iraqi tribes on the frontier. Glubb claimed that it was important to give them a pseudo-military standing as this would provide his men with a focus and a reason for serving their country. He told the first seventy camel-men, all personally chosen, that their task would be the defence of the desert camps occupied by the shepherd tribes. To enable them to do this they would be provided with horses, camels and vehicles equipped with machine-guns; the latter would be deployed as the main fire-power in the event of an Ikhwan attack. Their main task, though, would be scouting and in that role they would be able to provide the RAF with detailed intelligence about the movement of hostile tribes. This was the ground support which Glubb had always recommended. In his notebook he summed up the tasks that the Southern Desert Camel Corps would tackle:

1. Collection and transmission of intelligence from the desert posts.
2. Marshalling of the Iraqi tribes in areas most suitable for grazing.
3. Maintenance of a secret service along the border.
4. Inspiring and directing the Iraqi tribes themselves to fight off attacks by raiders.[5]

The first response to Glubb's ideas was positive. Cornwallis agreed that mobility for the patrols was of prime importance and he persuaded the Ministry of the Interior to allocate funds for the purchase of suitable vehicles. To Glubb's astonishment an official was sent into the bazaar in Baghdad and in one day he purchased three Chevrolet one-ton trucks, three Chevrolet vans, one Ford one-ton truck, and one Ford van.

The next step was the arming of the vehicles. Most of the men carried their own rifles but Glubb was adamant that the trucks should be equipped with Vickers machine-guns and modern wireless sets. In a note to the Ministry he explained what a dangerous activity patrolling in the desert was, and that the men had to be armed and trained in the use of modern weapons. Glubb was convinced that only by training his force professionally would it be of any use to the RAF and Iraqi Army. His 'Note on the Southern Desert Force' went into considerable detail to bolster his main argument:

Life in the desert is a continuous guerrilla warfare. It can never be quite certain that one will not chance upon an enemy. It is true that in the greater part of the Iraq desert law and order now prevails. Still, if men are not trained to take tactical precautions on all occasions they become slack and forget them when necessary. A force weak in numbers and depending on cars and machine-guns should take precautions against surprise [attacks]. If caught unawares in a narrow wadi or at night with unloaded guns, a force of three or four cars may be overwhelmed by fifteen or twenty men, although in daylight, on open ground, or if prepared, they might engage a thousand men with success.

To give his little force the best possible chance in all operational circumstances, Glubb suggested adoption of the following ground rules:

1. Camp defence – park cars wheel to wheel with guns dug in beside them.
2. On the move – guns should be half-loaded and free from dust. Never halt in a wadi or on bad ground.
3. Car drill – perfect car manouevring by flag drill.
4. Practise machine-gun firing from cars – firing the gun should be as much an everyday event to a machine-gunner as eating his dinner.[6]

Well argued Glubb's memorandum might have been but it did not meet with the approval of the senior officers at Air Headquarters in Baghdad. They were wary of arming the tribesmen for fear that their modern weapons could fall into the hands of the Ikhwan and be used against RAF aircraft. Moreover, they still believed that the frontier should be a no-go area. In some desperation Glubb enlisted the help of Cornwallis who had become an enthusiastic supporter of his Administrative Inspector's proposals. 'I hope you will excuse this tale of woe,' wrote Glubb from Busaiya, 'but there is no use saying nothing when things seem to be going wrong.'[7]

Glubb was particularly vexed by the RAF's opposition to the supply of machine-guns as he knew that the absence of such weapons would be a serious drawback to his patrols. Armed only with rifles, they could hardly be expected to approach a large and potentially hostile force. The provision of automatic weapons would give them a decided advantage and the confidence needed for taking on the Ikhwan. In response to the RAF's fears about the weapons falling into the wrong hands, Glubb replied that his men were loyal and trustworthy and that in any case a few determined rounds from a Vickers gun would see off lightly armed raiders. Eventually, after six months of wrangling, Dobbs gave permission for the establishment and equipping of Glubb's little army. In September 1928 it joined the Iraqi order of battle with the following complement:

70 camel men
30 machine-gunners in trucks
8 miscellaneous vehicles, 2 armed with Vickers guns
4 new Ford trucks with Vickers guns
2 wireless vans (to be equipped)

It was also agreed that Glubb should be allowed to draw funds for 'secret service' work and 24,000 rupees was allotted for this purpose in 1928–9 – the money was to be used primarily for paying Bedouin tribesmen in exchange for intelligence information. The one drawback to the force's establishment was that the vehicles were not yet fitted with wireless transmitters and that it would take a further year before they could be supplied. As Glubb told Cornwallis, he was now obliged to patrol 25,000 square miles of desert without any modern means of communication. Nonetheless, his force was now up and running and, as he noted in his diary, he was determined to disprove the old Arab maxim that the Bedouin could never be organised into a disciplined military force.

The delay in supplying and equipping Glubb's force meant that five valuable summer months had slipped by without any opportunity to introduce the training schedules outlined in the original memorandum. During that time, though, Glubb had been kept busy enough by other matters, both political and diplomatic. As Iraq's principal desert expert he had been attached to the mission which went to Jeddah to negotiate the Ikhwan problem with Ibn Saud. Its leader was the noted Arabist and former head of the Arab Bureau, Sir Gilbert Clayton, who was due to succeed Dobbs as High Commissioner in Iraq. He was accompanied by his Arab expert, Guy Moore, Glubb's old friend from Samawa days.

Glubb travelled to Jeddah with Cornwallis. Their first stop was Cairo where they stayed overnight at Shepheard's Hotel, one of the great imperial watering holes. After several months in the desert Glubb was not particularly impressed by this sudden transposition to a modern environment. 'Cornwallis and I left Baghdad by air on 21 April 1928, reaching Cairo the same day,' he wrote in a note for an intended autobiography. 'We had drinks in the evening on the terrace of Shepheard's Hotel. With the Pharisaic arrogance of youth I noted in my diary that the hotel was full of women indecently dressed and of noisy American tourists.'[8] It would not be the first or the last time in Glubb's life that he was reminded of the old adage that while you can take the man out of the desert, you cannot take the desert out of the man.

He found the conference at Jeddah equally disconcerting. Having been joined by Clayton and Moore from London, the little party travelled from Port Said to Port Sudan and then onwards to Jeddah on board the Royal Navy sloop HMS *Dahlia*. They arrived on 2 May 1928 but were kept waiting almost a week before they saw Ibn Saud, time enough to savour the cosmopolitan atmosphere of this busy Red Sea port and to enjoy the lavish hospitality which had been prepared for them. Not without some dismay, Glubb noted that whisky and tobacco were freely available to them and at the banquet to mark the beginning of the conference the European representatives were expected to wear evening dress.

The consequent talks were weary and protracted with both sides splitting hairs on tribal boundaries and the legality of each country's jurisdiction over the desert areas. The real stumbling block, though, was the attitude taken by Ibn Saud who was caught between a desire to keep on good terms with the British and a need to placate and control his Ikhwan subjects. On 17 May Glubb summed up Ibn Saud's distrust in a revealing note which also explained the cultural gulf yawning between the European negotiators and the Arab leader.

> I have rarely been so miserable as in the last two days. Yesterday we again met Ibn Saud. His manner was much changed since our first meetings, and he seemed depressed and bitter. To Clayton he said – 'When the English first came to Iraq, I congratulated my people. They were surprised and asked me why. I had always abused the Turks as unbelievers, they said, yet here were people who were even worse, because they were not Muslims at all. I told them that we have despaired of the English and their hair-splitting. At Uqair I understood from Cokus [Sir Percy Cox] that the protocol meant no forts in the desert. Now you say that the wording of the agreement does not mean that. How do I know? I am a Bedouin and that was what Cokus told me and I trusted him.'[9]

The king's speech, although pathetic, seemed sincere enough to Glubb who was greatly embarrassed by Clayton's vague response which spoke of friendship in high-flown poetic terms. Rightly as it turned out, Glubb also noted that unless both parties reached a mutually acceptable settlement, raiding would begin again in earnest before the year was out.

Although no definite decisions about the Ikhwan problem were reached at Jeddah, Ibn Saud's independence was guaranteed and some adjustments were made to the frontier. The British party returned to Baghdad at the end of May with Glubb feeling depressed yet curiously certain about what the future would bring. He had met and greatly admired Ibn Saud who seemed to him to spring from the same mould as Charlemagne or William the Conqueror. This was not just flattery, for Glubb had reached a subtle understanding of the king's problems and, alone of the Iraqi party, seemed to realise that Ibn Saud faced a serious internal rebellion if he opposed the Ikhwan. It was the old story of west–east relations, thought Glubb. Ibn Saud's feeling for diplomacy told him that his position was best served by friendship with the British and that this meant opposition to the Ikhwan. On the other hand, his pride and ambition for the Arab people urged him to approve of age-old and traditional desert raiding. This the British could not understand. What Glubb feared most of all, though, was an all-out war between Iraq and the Nejd. If that were to happen, he reasoned, then the British might be tempted to pull out of Iraq precipitately and Ibn Saud's rule would be challenged by the Ikhwan leaders. These fears had provided much of the impetus to create the Southern Desert Camel Corps which he hoped would be instrumental in keeping hostilities localised in the frontier area.

To meet a renewed Ikhwan threat Glubb decided to instruct his men in the theory of counter-attack from a firm and integrated system of defence. His armed car patrols would provide a picket in advance of the grazing flocks and the shepherd tribes and thereby provide a first line of defence. In the event of an attack they would intercept the Ikhwan raiding parties before they reached the grazing areas – Glubb considered that the speed and mobility of his vehicles, plus their superior firepower, would be more than a match for lightly armed camelmen. If his men were forced back to defend a camp they would unload their machine-guns and form a tight central redoubt in the midst of the tents. (Glubb also instructed the shepherds to pitch their tents closely together so that the guy ropes would hinder the attacking camelmen.)

As soon as his men received their weapons Glubb began

145

instructing them in the tactical deployment of machine-guns, teaching them to exploit fields of fire and to manoeuvre their cars into sound positions. Orders were given by simple flag signals which the gunners and the drivers were taught to recognise. Above all, though, Glubb had to instil in his men the absolute need to strip and clean their weapons constantly and to ensure that the cars were efficiently serviced. This was no easy matter amongst a group of men whose only previous experience of mobile warfare had been confined to the Lee-Enfield rifle and the mark-one camel. Throughout the last quarter of 1928 Glubb spent most of his time with his men in the southern desert patrolling the outer reaches of the Iraq-Nejd frontier, offering them help and encouragement. It was much needed, for although the Ministry of the Interior had acted speedily to provide the vehicles, the lack of spare parts was a continuing problem. As Glubb complained to Cornwallis during the summer, of the eight vehicles at his disposal only four or five were serviceable at any one time:

> The trouble is chiefly, I think, that people don't understand our work. For instance, there are now Scout cars at Jahama about forty miles from the greater part of the Mutair. The cars carry eight rifles and no W/T [wireless transmitters]. I have just slept four nights with them there, and it wasn't much fun. We have to change our position at dusk to avoid being surprised at night and lying awake all night with a loaded rifle in one's hands isn't very amusing.[10]

The other recurring problem at this time came from the British government in London. Glubb believed in the enforcement of integrated tactics whereby his armed car patrols would operate in concert with reconnaissance flights. With the large amount of money at his disposal he had built up an efficient espionage system which provided him with detailed information about Ikhwan intentions. This intelligence was then passed to forward headquarters at Ur and patrols were then sent out into the areas where raids were expected. To Glubb's relief the system worked well and, although some pilots were sceptical about their role, they soon came to understand that the presence of their aircraft was a powerful deterrent. Then, in December 1928, without prior warning, the British government ruled that RAF patrols were not to fly within twenty miles of the border, thus negating the efficiency of Glubb's tactics.

Two arguments were put forward to justify the decision. First, Britain wanted to appease Ibn Saud after the relative failure of the Jeddah conference; and, second, some politicians had become increasingly sensitive to charges in the press that air control was an inhumane method of policing rebel tribes. Critics remembered the high casualties suffered during the attack on the Barket and Sufran camps: although ample warning had been given, they argued, the tribes had still kept together and women and children had suffered during the attack. (There was some evidence that the tribesmen would always use their families as an 'insurance policy' or 'human shield' in order to deter attacks from the air. Pilots who had been shot down and captured were also thought to have been used in this way.) So strong was this feeling that, after questions had been asked in the House of Lords, Sir Christopher Bullock of the Air Ministry felt obliged to brief members of the Parliamentary Army and Air Committee on the efficiency of the tactics:

I may add that there is nothing more inhumane in dropping bombs on a frontier village than in subjecting it to indirect howitzer fire – which latter, I remember, was actually happening at one time when it was being urged that air action was to be deprecated on humanitarian grounds. I was reading only the other day a description by the great African administrator, Sir Harry Johnston, of some operations he had to undertake in Central Africa where his ground expedition was accompanied by mountain guns. He makes regretful mention of the casualties to women and children inevitably inflicted by the bombardments which he had no option but to undertake. Indeed very often ground operations will entail far heavier casualities to non-combatants in the primitive countries at issue than bombardment from the air, for the simple reason that, as I have mentioned, notice is normally given so that inhabitants can evacuate their villages for the time being. This will often not be practicable if a village is invested by ground troops and defended by the enemy.[11]

For all that the policy was continued, largely because the Committee accepted Bullock's reassuring words about the importance of giving the targets prior warning, the government nonetheless believed that all air operations in Iraq should be handled with kid gloves and that, where possible, grievances and disputes should be discussed before force was used. To Glubb in the desert, the politicians' arguments seemed to miss the point. He believed that Ibn Saud would only survive as the ruler of the Nejd if the Ikhwan attacks were localised and, remembering the casualties of the 1924 bombings, he insisted that aircraft were best deployed in the deterrent role and should only attack as a last resort. To do that satisfactorily, more and not fewer patrols were needed but Air Headquarters in Baghdad replied that flights would only be sent out to intercept specific objectives, that is, potential raiding parties. However, there was one improvement to Glubb's lot when the Iraqi Army agreed to second a motor machine-gun company to the desert force – this provided him with the wireless sets which were so badly needed.

Two events during the winter of 1928–9 served to change local attitudes to frontier defence. Shortly before Christmas 1928 one of Glubb's agents arrived exhausted at the desert force encampment at Mughaizal, north of the neutral area. He brought news of an Ikhwan raiding party heading towards the grazing at Jumaimai on the western frontier. It was led by Ibn Ashwan, a minor sheikh of the Mutair tribe, who was taking advantage of the desert force's concentration 150 miles away to attack the unprotected shepherd tribes. The spy reckoned it would take the Mutair camelmen three days to swing south past Uqubba before heading undetected in a north-westerly direction towards the masonry cistern and campsite at Jumaimai.

Because he knew that his desert force could not intercept the raiders in time, Glubb sent a signal to the RAF at Busaiya requesting an armed patrol to fly over the area on 18 and 19 December. Three DH9As, with Glubb flying in the leading aircraft as observer, took off at once and by mid-morning they had located the grazing flocks and shepherd encampment at Jumaimai. Glubb ordered the pilot to land the aircraft on a nearby gravel strip so that he could interrogate the shepherds and warn them about the impending raid. In the past, to comply with RAF operational orders, Glubb would have ordered the shepherds out of the area, but this time he was determined to take the battle to the Ikhwan.

His plan was simple. The shepherds were told to continue as if nothing happened, to light their campfires and prepare their evening meals. 'The raiders will probably have scouts out to watch for your fires and make certain you are still in position,' Glubb told them. 'Then when it is quite dark, pack up and go for your lives and don't stop walking till you get to Sulman.'[12] Glubb not only hoped that the Ikhwan would fall into the trap, he realised that if they found the camp deserted they would linger awhile in order to collect loot, thus giving the RAF time to mount an attack against them. In other words, Glubb's tactics would force the Mutair to do what he wanted them to do.

The following day Glubb's flight took off again from Busaiya, fully armed and loaded with bombs. Once again they flew over the camp which was by then surrounded by around 100 camels but, disconcertingly, there was no sign of human life. Although Glubb guessed that the Mutair raiding party had arrived and was in possession of the camp, he had to make absolutely certain before ordering an attack. Lower

149

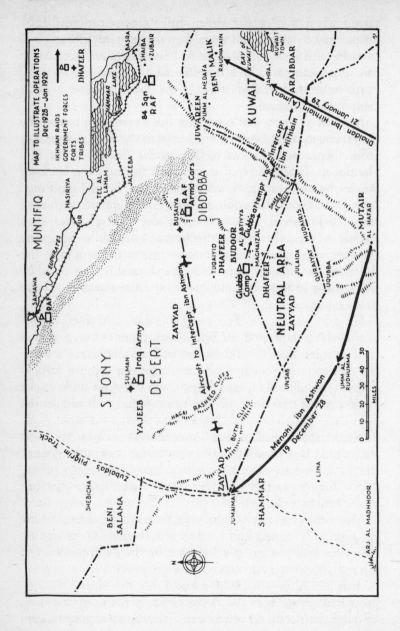

and lower flew Glubb's bomber until at just below 500 feet he could make out the riding saddles on the camel's backs. 'It was Ibn Ashwan and no mistake. I tapped the pilot on the shoulder again and gave him the thumbs up sign. Then, to make quite certain, I sat down in the cockpit and wrote on a slip of paper – "Raiders. Shoot." '[13]

As the Vickers guns opened fire the camp below the aircraft became a hive of terrified activity. Men dashed out from beneath the cover of the camels – where they had hidden in order to avoid detection from the air – and did their utmost to escape from the bullets and bombs. This time the scale of the retribution did not trouble Glubb. Here were no harmless tax-evaders but a ruthless raiding party which would have slaughtered the unarmed shepherds. The little victory also showed that Glubb's tactics worked, that the combination of air power and ground patrols, supported by accurate intelligence, could control the Ikhwan raids. Glubb was suitably satisfied:

> The defeat of Ibn Ashwan's raid produced a profound moral effect on the Ikhwan, exactly at the moment when they were preparing their grand offensive against Iraq. If we had missed the raiders and they had returned home laden with plunder, and driving flocks of sheep before them, the outcome of the season's operations might have been different. If the Ikhwan, exhilarated by this first success, had simultaneously raided Iraq at several different places, we could not have been everywhere at once. Some of the raiders would have been successful. Had they returned in triumph from raiding the 'infidel' Iraqis, more Nejd tribes would have joined them, Ibn Saud might have been overwhelmed and American companies might never – or not for many years – have secured a concession to prospect for oil in Arabia.[14]

However, it was now that further restrictions were placed on RAF flights near the frontier and the sudden disappearance of the aircraft encouraged the powerful Duweesh to muster the Ikhwan for one last attempt to attack and overwhelm Iraq.

The first stage of the confrontation ended in humiliation for Glubb's desert force. On 21 January 1929 Ibn Hithlain and the Ajman fell on a large party of Beni Malik shepherds who had been tempted by the rich grazing to move their flocks into Kuwaiti territory. Once again Glubbs's intelligence network had provided information about the forthcoming attack and his force moved up to the frontier to intervene. A signal had also been sent to Shaiba requesting support from 84 Squadron – Glubb hoped that the bombers would force the Ikhwan to flee, thus allowing his ground force to recover the loot and pick off the stragglers. It was all in vain. Because the Beni Malik were in Kuwaiti territory, Glubb's forces were not allowed to cross the frontier; moreover the order preventing the RAF from entering Kuwaiti air space was still in force. In desperation Glubb sent a series of urgent signals to Baghdad requesting permission to engage the Ikhwan in Kuwait. Back came a negative response with a rejoinder that the request was being passed on to the Colonial Office in London for their advice. It took three days before permission was given for Glubb's forces to cross into Kuwait, but by then it was too late: the Ikhwan had slaughtered the shepherds and had then driven the vast flocks of sheep and camels over the border into the Nejd. All that Glubb's force found was the familiar evidence of massacre.

It is not difficult to understand the rage and frustration which Glubb felt at that moment. For the past two years he had promoted the tactics of combined air and ground operations and had proved their efficiency at Jumaimai, yet within the space of a month his policy had been overruled by political decisions made at a high level in London. He knew, too, that the Ikhwan leaders would interpret the decision as a British withdrawal and that the sudden absence of air patrols would encourage them to make further raids into Iraqi territory. If the defeat of Ibn Ashwan had chastened them, albeit

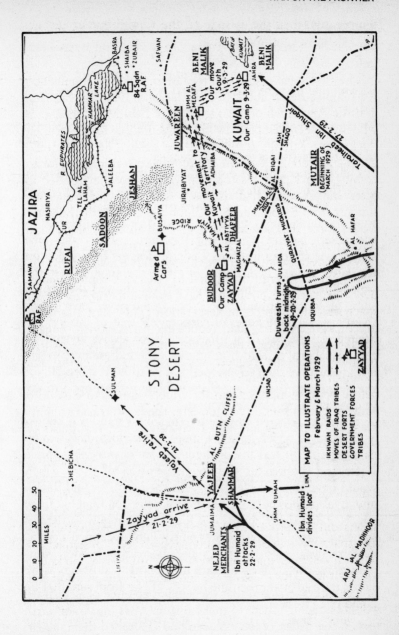

MAP TO ILLUSTRATE OPERATIONS
February & March 1929

IKHWAN RAIDS
MOVES OF IRAQ TRIBES
DESERT FORTS
GOVERNMENT FORCES
TRIBES

ZAYYAD

153

temporarily, then the episode on the Kuwait border encouraged them to continue raiding.

Sure enough, on 15 February 1929 one of Glubb's most reliable spies arrived at Mughaizal with news of a huge Ikhwan raiding party heading towards the frontier. One part, led by Ibn Humaid, would attack the wells at Jumaimai while the main raiding party of Duweesh would attack Glubb's forces at their desert encampment. '*Yebghik ent*,' the spy said to Glubb. 'He wants to get you yourself.'

Quickly checking the dispositions on the map, Glubb reckoned that he had three days in which to retreat towards Busaiya where the RAF armoured cars and a flight of aircraft were stationed, or to prepare a forward defensive position in the desert behind which the shepherd tribes could take shelter. After consulting the Bedouin leaders he decided on the latter course of action. Now was the time to test the capabilities of his Camel Corps: if they showed they could stand up to the Ikhwan raiders they would never have to fear them again. Glubb believed passionately that in this kind of limited warfare the Iraqi tribes could not always depend on the availability of British armoured cars and aircraft; in the long term they themselves would have to be responsible for the defence of their own territory. Here was an opportunity to do something positive about it.

The place selected by Glubb to make his stand was known as Al Abtiyya which lay a few miles to the north of his camp at Mughaizal. It had the dual advantages of providing ample water and grazing for the conglomeration of tribes which would have to assemble there with their families and flocks, and it also allowed an open field of fire for Glubb's force which still had the services of four machine-gun carriers of the Iraqi Army. More to the point, Glubb reckoned that Al Abtiyya was over twenty miles from the border, thus permitting the RAF to operate in support – although as he noted in his diary at the time he was still far from sure that he could rely on their help.

Glubb chose his tactics to suit both the forces at his

disposal and the topographical features of the ground. His order of battle consisted of the four Iraqi vehicles, seven armed cars, forty men of the Southern Desert Camel Corps and the tribesmen of the Zayyad and Dhafeer whom he had equipped with rifles. At Al Abtiyya the ground fell away towards the south and at the top of the slope Glubb fashioned a redoubt and ordered is men to dig in. Trenches were hurriedly constructed, complete with firesteps and emplacements for the machine-guns which had been unloaded from the cars. The flanks were also covered by machine-guns to enfilade an attacking enemy and to provide the lightly armed tribesmen with added protection. Glubb ordered the Zayyad to take up position on the right and the Dhafeer on the left. The remaining camelmen and drivers would be used to patrol the ground between Al Abtiyya and the frontier and to give advance warning of a forthcoming attack.

Having deployed his forces, Glubb sent a signal to the RAF at Busaiya confirming his intention and requesting the support of the armoured-car company and a flight of bombers. He confirmed that the ground, being a mixture of firm sand and gravel, was suitable for the deployment of both. It was an ideal position for the kind of defensive tactics which Glubb hoped would blunt even the most determined Ikhwan raid. Within a few hours, though, the RAF signalled that there would be no air or ground support and that in the event of attack he should fall back on Busaiya.

Sadly the authorities in Baghdad regarded Glubb's desert stand in a less than heroic light. To them the concentration of tribesmen at Al Abtiyya constituted an armed camp within the vicinity of the border, a military deployment forbidden by Article 3 of the Uqair protocol. Besides, in the minds of some traditionalists, there was something about Glubb's force which smacked too much of the private army. There were still people in Baghdad, like Dobbs and Cornwallis, who remembered Lawrence's exploits during the Arab Revolt and the exaggerated claims he had made subsequently for the guerrilla tactics of 'tip and run'. In the years following the end of the war many people serving in the Middle East also held to the view that Lawrence was little more than a bounder. His espousal by the American publicist Lowell Thomas and his tireless self-promotion in flowing Arab dress suggested to them that Lawrence was more of an exhibitionist than a forthright military man. As a recent biographer has pointed out, at that time Lawrence's 'cleverness, eccentricity and flamboyance were naturally distasteful to those with much to be modest about'.[15] Although Glubb had stopped wearing Arab dress − he contented himself with a simple civilian khaki suit − he was closely associated with the Bedouin tribesmen whose cause he had espoused with an intensity which reminded his superiors of Lawrence. In the increasingly urbane and cosmopolitan atmosphere of Baghdad, where Iraqi politics were dominated by a new class of town-bred Arab intellectuals, the Bedouin tribesmen seemed to be an anachronism from another age, primitive people who had no place in a modern society.

The British officers at Air Headquarters were also wary of Glubb's activities. Not only did they consider him trouble-some and disrespectful, but they also believed he had 'gone native' and was guilty of establishing a private army for an un-important side-show with the sole aim of winning personal glory.

To Glubb in the desert, though, awaiting the Ikhwan attack, the reasons for his presence had been reduced to the simplicity of a group of men face to face with their own destiny. In his diary he acknowledged the vastness of the desolation around him as being beyond reason, but he added the rejoinder that his position had nothing whatsoever to do with an easy exist-entialism. The Covenanters, facing the overwhelming super-iority of Claverhouse, or Monmouth at Sedgemoor would have recognised what he meant when he noted later:

That morning the vast emptiness of the desert seemed to be more than ordinarily full of meaning. It made the silly fussiness of civilisation seem trivial. These tribesmen lived such simple lives, confined to so few elemental things.

Their possessions were camels, sheep and a tent. Their food flour, rice and dates. Their clothes a shirt and a cloak. They were daily confronted by life and death, plain and undisguised. No wonder that such conditions bred in them the simplest of religions – one God, Almighty, Conquering, Merciful. The desert indeed had the same effect on me. Yet here was I, probably about to have my throat cut by men who had been affected by the desert, much as I had been affected. They would cut my throat in the name of their religion. But no – that was not really true. Wahhabism had started as a simple return to religion, but now it had degenerated into murder and loot.

All the world, I thought, was like that. Men began with a great idea, but it would then be captured and utilized by the powers of evil, and would soon be transformed into greed and cruelty.[16]

It was an image of himself and his role which Glubb liked to present in later years, of the clear-eyed Englishman at the head of a small but chivalrous band of brothers about to confront impossible odds. At the time he really did believe it; his notebooks and diaries reveal a strength of feeling about the desert and the Bedouin people that is almost mystical in its intensity.

Although Glubb might have romanticised his position he was, in fact, in a dangerous predicament. His little force was outnumbered and, despite being armed with machine-guns, had few reserves. Moreover, the refusal of the RAF to lend air support meant that he would be quickly isolated should the Duweesh attack in force. Retreat was out of the question, too, because behind his defensive lines at Al Abtiyya were the teeming hordes of women, children and flocks whom he was supposed to be protecting.

For two days Glubb's patrols ventured out into the desert, setting off at dawn and returning at sundown. Each time they came back Glubb feared the worse but each time the camelmen brought back only news of a deserted frontier. By

20 February the danger had passed and Glubb ordered his men to stand down as news arrived of a huge Duweesh force retiring back across the frontier into the Nejd. 'They had a spy with us,' remembered Glubb later, 'and he nipped across to them and told them the night before they were going to attack that we were all prepared and were very warlike and all dug in and all fixed up ... so the raiders called it off and we won a bloodless victory.'[17] For the first time in nine years a determined Bedouin stand had prevented the Ikhwan from raiding into Iraqi territory. No great battle had been fought but a notable victory had been won and after Al Abtiyya Glubb's name was known to everyone who lived on the Iraqi side of the desert. When Glubb reported to Dobbs he conceded that he had taken on the Ikhwan and defeated them at their own game:

> So successful were these measures that, once they had been inaugurated, no large-scale Wahhabi raid succeeded in crossing the Iraq border, although several forces, each 2,000 or 3,000 strong, remained for considerable periods on the frontier area, seeking some objective which offered a reasonable chance of success.[18]

It was not the end of the campaign against the Ikhwan, for in the following days Glubb's force had to deal with a subsidiary attack on Jumaimai, but it was the beginning of the end of border raiding. Frustrated by their failure to win easy victories in Iraq, and disconcerted by Glubb's show of strength, Ibn Bijad and Feisal al Duweesh turned on the peaceful Wahhabi tribes in the Hasa, now under the aegis of Ibn Saud. Realising that this attack constituted a threat to his authority, Ibn Saud raised a powerful new army, equipped with British armoured cars and machine-guns. At the end of March he defeated the rebel Ikhwan tribes at Sibilla, not far from the spot where his friend Captain Shakespear had been killed fifteen years earlier: it was the last major battle fought between Bedouin forces in Arabia.

Ibn Saud's victory at Sibilla broke the back of the Ikhwan rebellion which nonetheless continued intermittently into the winter months. A combination of military force and political bargaining had to be used during these latter stages of the conflict in order to bring it to a satisfactory conclusion. The new Air Officer, Air Vice-Marshal Sir Charles Burnett, visited Glubb's forces in the desert after Al Abtiyya and, having appraised the situation, promised to offer full air and ground support along the frontier. The Iraqi–Nejd border was effectively sealed and on the diplomatic front the British promised Ibn Saud that Ikhwan raiders would not be offered sanctuary in Iraq. In September 1929 the British extended their military protection to Kuwait, thus cutting off the last remaining base available to the Ikhwan leaders. By then the Colonial Office fully supported the view that the continued stability of Ibn Saud's kingdom depended on the defeat of the Ikhwan rebellion and that British and Iraqi forces should co-operate in this aim. The way was now open for a rapprochement between Ibn Saud and Feisal and an end to the war on the frontier.

The final peace treaty between the two countries was signed on 22 February 1930 on board a Royal Navy sloop, HMS *Lupin*, which was anchored out of sight of land in the bay of Kuwait. Glubb attended the conference as Iraq's desert expert, in the company of Cornwallis, the new High Commissioner Sir Francis Humpherys, and Air Vice-Marshal Sir Robert Brooke-Popham. Once the treaty had been signed an official photograph was taken of the delegates, with a stern-looking Feisal and bespectacled Ibn Saud sitting in the front row. Next to them sits Humpherys in formal diplomatic uniform and at the back stands Glubb in morning dress. The former sapper captain had come a long way in ten years from building pontoon bridges over the Tigris to adding his voice to imperial policy-making.

The agreement formally brought an end to tribal raiding on the Iraqi–Nejd frontier, each ruler promising to bring the tribes under control and to make good the losses sustained by the shepherd tribes – although as Glubb noted this latter clause was a pious hope which was never fulfilled. He also noticed that the demands of protocol often stretched to the ridiculous. Neither ruler would address the other as 'king', necessitating the substitution of 'my dear brother'; and in order to maintain the rules of precedence it had to be explained to Feisal, who was forced to board last, that this honour was reserved in the Royal Navy for the most important person visiting a ship. Nonetheless, the treaty was binding and the Ikhwan would no longer terrorise the peaceful tribes living in the southern desert areas of Iraq. Although Glubb did not recognise it at the time, he was witness to the end of an era. As he wrote in 1960:

> These thirty years have witnessed the complete transformation of the greater part of Arabia. The invasion of the desert by aircraft and mechanical vehicles (an invasion for which we unknowingly paved the way) have reduced to impotence the wild tribes which formerly terrorised their settled neighbours. American oil-fields are generously sprinkled over the desert and the sons of the Ikhwan warriors of yesterday are fain to work as labourers or mechanics in their once inviolate deserts. Soon all the battles and massacres, the glory, the terror and the gallantry, will be but vague memories of a past age.[19]

One reason why the British were so anxious to settle the frontier dispute was that the League of Nations mandate in Iraq was due to end in 1932 and they wanted to finalise their future political and military connections with the country. The last infantry battalion – drawn from the Indian Army – had left Iraq in November 1928 and Britain's future commitment to the defence of the newly independent country was to be entrusted to the Royal Air Force. By then, too, plans had been finalised to increase the size of the Iraqi ground forces to 12,000 and these would include an expanded Camel Corps as frontier guards. (It was also agreed to start training an independent Iraqi air force.) The details were formulated in a treaty of friendship which was signed on 30 June 1930; Iraq would become independent but Britain's strategic and economic interests in the country would be safeguarded. However, a further condition was the reduction of British officials in Iraq by 60 per cent. As Glubb had feared when he signed his contract four years earlier, he was now out of a job. 'I'd burned my boats,' he remembered later. 'I'd given up my army commission for a piece of paper which was worthless.'[20]

It was then that once more luck came to his aid. During the spring of 1930 his Camel Corps had been deployed in the Syrian Desert which Glubb discovered was as lawless a place as the southern desert had been prior to his arrival. Using the same tactics which had served him so well – the use of local spies to provide intelligence, and the rapid deployment of his armed cars and camelmen – Glubb put a stop to raiding by the troublesome Ruwalla tribe. At one stage during the operations his armed car patrol was given permission to pursue nomadic raiders into Transjordan in order to retrieve loot. This action was another stepping stone in Glubb's life. On 28 March 1930 he arrived in Amman where he received an enthusiastic and hospitable welcome from the Emir Abdullah, made auspicious by the Transjordanian leader's invitation to Glubb to parade his mobile force for an official inspection. Desert raiding was endemic in Transjordan: in Glubb's force the government believed that they had found an answer to the problem. Just as one door closed in Glubb's life, therefore, another opened; for no sooner was his contract in Iraq cancelled than he received a fresh one from the government of Transjordan.

Glubb left Iraq with a high reputation. From King Feisal he received the coveted Order of Rafidain but in the long term it was the confidential report on his service that was to have the greater significance on his future career. This was entrusted to Dobbs, who understood the importance of the service which Glubb had given to Iraq. At a time when Britain was anxious to maintain its oil interests in the Middle East and had, therefore, a vested interest in keeping the area free from internal strife – he argued – Glubb was a useful ally to have in the service of a country like Transjordan.

> He gained what I should think must be an unparalleled knowledge of Bedouin language, thoughts and customs and drew to himself the affectionate admiration of the whole desert. By incredible exertions, activities and hardships, he pacified the border between Iraq and Nejd, settled feuds, prevented raids, dug and restored wells and initiated a far-seeing policy of weaning the tribes from their nomadic habits by giving security to the Desert and making cultivation possible there. He is a man of boundless energy and enthusiasm, with an acute and exploring mind and he would be an acquisition to any Service or Administration. It would be great misfortune if the Empire were to fail to make use of his special Gifts and Experience.[21]

Other tributes spoke of Glubb's integrity and of his complete understanding of the desert and its people. Humpherys noted in a secret despatch to London that these attributes had been gratefully acknowledge by Ibn Saud during the *Lupin* conference two months earlier. The one sour note came from Air Headquarters in Baghdad whose staff officers had long been suspicious of Glubb's movement in the desert and disliked the impatient tone of many of his requests for support. Despite a wholehearted recommendation – 'His [Glubb's] knowledge was always at the disposal of the Royal Air Force and was, I am sure, highly valued by them' – Glubb's name did not appear amongst the RAF officers who received medals in 1930 for their part in bringing the Ikhwan raids to an end.

There is no doubt that the presence of the RAF in Iraq during the 1920s was crucial for the survival of Feisal's kingdom. 'If the writ of King Feisal runs effectively throughout his kingdom it is entirely due to British aeroplanes,' noted L.S. Amery, the Secretary of State for the Colonies, during a visit to Iraq in May 1925. 'If the aeroplanes were removed tomorrow the whole structure would inevitably fall to pieces.'[22] Without those elderly veterans of the First World War, like the DH9A and the Snipe, Iraq could not have defended its northern frontiers against the possibility of Turkish incursion while the Ikhwan raiding in the south was ended with the help of Air Control. It was also inexpensive – an important consideration at a time when colonial expenditure in the Middle East was unpopular at home – and it was efficient. As the Colonial Office was able to note with some satisfaction, during the operations against the Ikhwan the three squadrons in the desert flew over 6,000 hours worth of sorties for the loss of only one airman killed.[23]

Glubb also had good reason to feel satisfied even though he believed that there were still areas in which the use of Air Control could be refined. Throughout the campaign he had promoted the usefulness of co-operation between the air forces and forces on the ground. When it had worked, it had been an efficient instrument, but all too often bad relations between the different forces led to misunderstandings and the eruption of petty jealousies. Glubb complained incessantly that the over-punctilious interpretation of diplomatic agreements forced staff officers in Baghdad to rescind orders for the operation of air patrols close to the border. (This was a point of view he was bound to adopt, being so close to the action.) However, as he also pointed out, the system had an excellent chance of succeeding because in Iraq the armoured cars came under control of the RAF and many of the crews had experience of air operations.

Unfortunately, as frequently happened in other parts of the empire, there was an unwillingness to pay serious attention to the kind of irregular troops which Glubb raised in his Camel Corps. As they were local volunteers and, in this case, did not even possess regular uniforms they were regarded as scallywags who could not be wholly trusted during field operations. The difficulty was exacerbated in Iraq by the rivalry which existed between the regular army and the Levies, a gendarmerie raised mainly from the Assyrian Christians of the north who enjoyed a particularly close connection with the Royal Air Force and were much admired for their martial qualities. Not surprisingly perhaps, this preference was resented by nationalist officers in the Iraqi Army who regarded the Levies as mercenaries in British pay. In return, some officers in the RAF and the Levies were contemptuous of the Iraqi Army and its abilities. Because Glubb's little force was also manned by Iraqis, and even worse in the eyes of some traditionalists by Bedouin, similar criticisms were made about it. Although the British pretend that they do not take seriously military preparedness or warfare, they do take a good deal of interest in the pedigree of the forces under their command. Glubb's Camel Corps was no exception.

Nonetheless, Glubb's appreciation of the tactics required in a limited frontier war did evoke the right reactions from those who served with him. He respected the support of bomber aircraft and armoured cars, and he also realised that the only long-term method for the desert tribes to protect themselves against Ikhwan attack was for them to organise their own defence. Those tactics were to be used again when Glubb took up his new post in Transjordan.

6

Desert Patrol

When Jack Glubb arrived in Amman in November 1930 he was still a young man, aged only thirty-three, but already he had fashioned for himself a considerable reputation in the enclosed world of British Middle East politics. The Colonial Office files and correspondence dealing with Ikhwan raiding on the Iraq–Nejd frontier make clear the reliance which civil servants and politicians placed on his opinions,[1] and in Baghdad he had won plaudits from such serious believers in imperial progress as Henry Dobbs and Francis Humphreys. During his time in Iraq he had emerged, too, as a recognisable product of the British colonial system, an official who was part administrator, part soldier, yet wholly devoted to the people and the country he served. Although he had severed his links with the British Army, he was still very much a military-minded man as had been demonstrated by his sure grasp of tactics in the limited war on the frontier. He knew the value of small irregular forces and, more importantly, he knew how to use them.

The success had not been gained without some loss to himself, however. Ever since joining the army in 1915 he had been something of a nomad without a secure base from which to operate. During the war his leaves had been hurried, intense periods, overshadowed by the constant fear of death or injury at the front, while his one lengthy term of convalescence in 1918 had been marred by his mother's illness, his father's absence on active service and his own impatience to

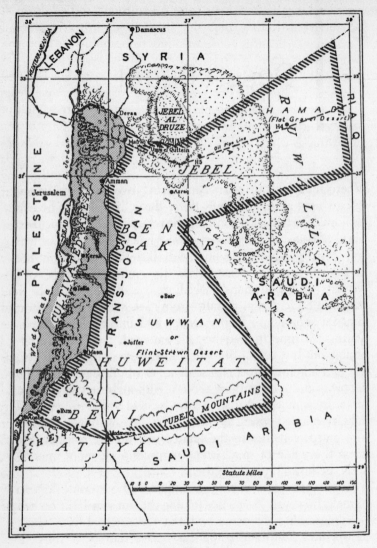

TRANSJORDAN

get back to the front. His parents had finally settled down at Pembury in Kent – their first fixed abode in thirty years of marriage – but the house was only to be home for their son during his short periods of leave which were few and far between in the early years of his service. Having left England in 1920, Glubb did not return home for another five years and during that time his parents had aged, a fact they did not always trouble to hide in their correspondence. One of the first things which Glubb noticed on his first leave was that his father had given up hunting – thus breaking one of the bonds between them – and that he had turned to golf and shooting for his recreation. For their part, his parents worried about him and his choice of career: they would have preferred him to live in England, to stay in the army and, above all, they wished that he would marry and settle down.

This thought had begun to cross Glubb's mind too. Shortly after arriving in Transjordan he confided to one of his Bedouin companions that all the worldly success he had enjoyed meant nothing to him as long as he was without a wife, a family and a place he could call his home. While he acknowledged that the kind of life he led made relationships difficult, if not impossible, he was also painfully aware of his lack of experience with women. While this was a common complaint amongst men of his class and generation – Harold Macmillan, a contemporary, wrote of his youth that it was 'an entirely masculine, almost monastic society', and that for practical purposes girls simply did not exist[2] – Glubb had been doubly cocooned. His family life as a boy had been sheltered and cosy, dominated by the love of horses he shared with his father, and his schooldays were ruled by a sturdy Christian muscularity which placed great emphasis on prayer and team games.

The war had placed another barrier on top of these. Like many other front-line soldiers Glubb realised that the closely knit camaraderie he had experienced in the intimate and all-male world at the front had driven a wedge between himself and the society he had left behind. As a result women were

167

either disregarded or placed on pedestals, thus expanding further the gap that already existed between the sexes. There was, too, the mystery of physical sexual relationships with women and, as Glubb also admitted, on that score he had been given little advice by his father. 'Don't chase after women, old boy,' he had been told. 'If you do so, you will regret it bitterly when you ultimately meet the woman you want to marry. Some men can think of nothing else, but I have not been tempted in that way and I hope you will not be.'[3]

The difficulty was 'ultimately' finding a woman whom he might want to marry. Those whom he had met so far had thoroughly unnerved him. While stationed in France he had been billeted with French families on several occasions but had always taken care to distance himself from their women-folk, especially their daughters. Shortly after being commissioned in 1915 he had found himself alone with the daughter of a tobacconist in whose house he had been billeted. His main fear at the time was that he had been compromised and that an angry father would force him to marry her.

Ten years later, while paying a visit to the British Residency in Amman, the scene returned to haunt him when he entered a room to discover 'a beautiful lady clad in diaphanous clothing lounging gracefully on a sofa'. This was Rosita Forbes, the renowned traveller and writer who was planning to cross the Empty Quarter* with St John Philby and who had already made several dangerous desert expeditions in Libya and Ethiopia. Twice married, she was a strikingly beautiful woman whose dark hair and eyes were always set off by brightly coloured and frequently revealing clothes. As one of her admirers noted, during the course of her travels her high heels and sophisticated make-up had beguiled many a man between Aden and London. Glubb, though, took the line of least resistance and, mumbling his excuses, left the room.

---

*Ruba el Khali, the great sand desert of southern Saudi Arabia.

This was the occasion when he had first ridden across the Syrian desert into Transjordan, an exploit which had drawn from Rosita Forbes the flirtatious comment that she would love to cross a desert with the young and flustered Glubb. For the rest of the decade Glubb was to use up part of his twice-yearly leaves unsuccessfully seeking a – perhaps less disconcerting – partner who would be prepared to share the kind of life he had come to lead.

There was another burden which he found he had to shoulder as his career began to take successful shape – professional jealousy. Not everyone was pleased that he had come so far so quickly and, when he was appointed to serve in Transjordan, the announcement discommoded those British officials who had been in the country since the beginning of the British mandate. Glubb's appointment had been made nominally by the Emir Abdullah but the decision had been taken on the urging of the British Resident Lieutenant-Colonel Henry Cox. The other party to the idea was Alec Kirkbride, the Assistant Resident and another of the great Arabists whose career was to run in tandem with Glubb's.

Unfortunately, the one man who should have been included in the decision was not consulted at all – this was Frederick Gerard Peake, the commander of the Arab Legion, Transjordan's gendarmerie force, which was to provide Glubb with his operational base. A veteran of the Arab Revolt and friend of Lawrence, Peake was a pre-eminent personality in the Middle East and one of the small number of British officials who had helped to establish Hashemite rule in Transjordan. As Peake noted in his diary, the decision had been made while he was on leave in England: 'On getting back, I was surprised to find that a Royal Engineers officer named John Bagot Glubb had been sent to the Arab Legion to be my second in command. He had made a very good job of raising a camel corps in Iraq and he was to raise another in Jordan.'[4]

Hardly surprisingly, Peake was upset by the decision to appoint a second-in-command without any reference to his own wishes and, initially, the relationship between the two men was strained. Matters were not helped by Cox who showed a growing contempt for Peake by leaving him out of the decision-making processes on his return to Transjordan: instead, he dealt directly with Glubb and this added to ill-feeling at the Arab Legion's headquarters. Peake was also distrustful of Glubb's promotion of the Bedouin cause, having witnessed the erratic behaviour of some of the desert tribes under Lawrence during the war. This was a common sentiment in Transjordan at a time when the country was unsettled by tribal disputes, many of which seemed to have been started by the Bedouin. To the older officials in Amman it seemed that Glubb was lavishing too much attention on the nomadic tribes and ignoring the aspirations of the new generation of Arab nationalists. 'I think it true that he remained absolutely ignorant, and indeed careless, of the mood, humour and character of the cultivated Arab,' noted one of his subordinates in the Arab Legion, R.J.C. Broadhurst.[5] Others, like Sir Philip Brocklehurst, another noted Arabist and scholar, were uneasy about Glubb's infatuation with the desert and believed that it blinded him to what was happening elsewhere. Later, these criticisms were to re-emerge when Glubb's links with the Arab world finally came to an end; and all three men, Peake especially, were to take great exception to uninformed press reports in the 1950s which spoke of 'Glubb of the Arab Legion' as the only begetter of this unique and romantic desert force.

In fact the Legion had its origins in a memorandum written on 11 September 1920 by Captain C. Dunbar Brunton, a British intelligence officer in Amman who recommended to the authorities in Jerusalem the formation of 'a Reserve Force which would be kept ready as a small striking force to re-inforce the gendarmerie when necessary'.[6] Consisting of 200 men led by seven officers and ten NCOs, it was one of several gendarmerie or irregular militia forces which operated in the occupied enemy territories of Palestine and the future Transjordan before Abdullah arrived in Amman to stake his leadership claims. One of the officials appointed by the new ruler was Peake who arrived in the country as inspector of gendarmerie; one of his first tasks was to transform and enlarge the Reserve Force into a larger militia – or 'self-contained miniature army' as Glubb described it – which became known as the Arab Legion or Jaysh al Arabi, the Arab Army. This was not accomplished without difficulty – just as Glubb's arrival had irked Peake, so too had Brunton been unhappy about the sudden transformation of his little force. Although Brunton believed that he had never been given any credit for his part in creating the Arab Legion, Peake was the right man for the task of creating a force which would combine the duties of police work with those of internal defence. Born in 1886, he was commissioned into the Duke of Wellington's Regiment but saw his wartime service with the Egyptian Army. He commanded the Egyptian Camel Corps which joined Lawrence in the attacks on the Hejaz railway and which took part in the Battle of Megiddo in September 1918. During the war he dislocated his neck but had been restored to health by bumping into a tree in a hospital garden in Dafur. On another occasion his ship was torpedoed while he was going home on leave; nothing daunted, he jumped overboard carrying a packet of sandwiches and a bottle of beer and was eventually picked up by the Royal Navy.

It was that kind of enterprise which the British colonial administrators desperately needed in the fledgling state of Transjordan in the years after the war. Originally, both Palestine and Transjordan were to be part of the same British mandate, but during the carve-up of the Middle East Churchill had decided to exclude Transjordan from the terms of the Balfour Declaration, much to the anger of the Zionists in Palestine. With a British subsidy of £5,000 a month the Emir Abdullah raised his first administration in April 1921, although from the outset it was understood that he would remain under British tutelage. In 1924 the relationship was cemented further after Abdullah had plunged his little state

171

into debt; Henry Cox of the Palestinian service was then sent to Amman as Resident with orders to force Abdullah to abdicate unless he accepted the indirect rule of the Colonial Office. A British cavalry regiment was also despatched to Amman to show that the British were serious in their intentions.

Between then and 1930 there was a period of consolidation in the country with Abdullah seemingly content to accept the fact that he was ruler in name only. A formal constitution was introduced in 1928 which gave the country a legislative council, although all its decisions were subject to British approval. That same year also saw the signature of a treaty with Britain which regularised the RAF's right of occupation – like Iraq, Transjordan depended largely on the RAF for the protection of its frontiers. By that time, too, the Transjordan Frontier Force had been created by the new High Commissioner in Palestine, Field Marshal Viscount Plumer, who wanted it to be organised on the lines of the Indian Army with native soldiers and British officers. It included infantry and cavalry formations but because it recruited mainly from the settled Arabs of the towns its efficiency as a desert force was often called into question. What was more, the force was a British imperial formation which owed its allegiance to the High Commissioner in Jerusalem and through him to the government in London.

A more sensible solution would have been to strengthen and enlarge the Arab Legion whose allegiance was to Abdullah but, without giving any reason other than he wanted to split up the military and the police functions, Plumer decided to cut it by 40 per cent and to reduce the remaining 900 men to a gendarmerie force without artillery, machine-guns or signals. Abdullah was deeply affronted by the decision but was powerless to prevent its implementation and it was not until the Second World War that the Arab Legion became an army once more. Glubb was fond of placing the blame for Plumer's decision on his first visit to Transjordan when the Arab Legion failed to come up to his expectation as a guard of honour. Although the men looked soldierly when standing to attention, he said, they collapsed into a shambles on being dismissed and Plumer was not amused. Pleasing though the anecdote may be, it seems an unlikely tale as Plumer was a pragmatic soldier who had served with irregular forces in the Sudan and South Africa and realised their limitations for ceremonial duties. It is more likely that he wanted to restrict a force which owed allegiance to Abdullah at a time when the emir was causing trouble with British officials in Transjordan. At that time, too, much faith was still vested in the policy of Air Control to keep the peace in the Middle East.

RAF bombers had shown their effectiveness in this role in 1924 when they repulsed a determined Ikhwan raid which got within fifteen miles of Amman. It was a story similar to the one that had been told in Iraq along the frontier with the Nejd, of Ikhwan-inspired raids on the shepherd tribes, of counter-raid to retrieve loot, all complicated by the rivalry that existed between the house of Saud and the Hashemite family.

On this border, too, Ibn Saud had been loath to check his unruly subjects with the result that there was more or less a state of open warfare between them and the Howeitat, the main Transjordanian Bedouin tribe. During the civil war with the Ikhwan the Howeitat had used the opportunity to raid deep into the Nejd to recover their property with the result that, by 1930, Ibn Saud was determined to punish them. In March a large force commanded by one of his cousins attacked and raided the Howeitat, stripping them of their flocks and leaving them destitute. Because the Transjordan Frontier Force rarely patrolled the Nejd border area, they had been powerless to intervene but when they did, it was to stop the Howeitat from recovering their flocks from across the border. To the Transjordanian Bedouin leaders it seemed as if their people had been doubly wronged: first by the Ikhwan who stole their property and second by the British who prevented them from recovering it. It was this impasse – and the solution of a similar problem in Iraq – that had prompted

Cox to invite Glubb to join him in the Transjordanian administration.

As well as Glubb's appointment as second-in-command of the Arab Legion, he was also given the grandiloquent title of Officer Commanding Desert. No sooner had he arrived in Transjordan, though, than he discovered that there was no settled organisation and that he had to begin from scratch. He later wrote:

> My situation was at first somewhat anomalous. I had no authority over anyone, and, being dressed as a civilian with no particular status, the troops naturally were inclined to regard me as something of an outsider. The tribes were unwilling to have anything to do with anyone who came to them from the Government.[7]

Since Peake was on leave Glubb was able to act without referring the problem to him and, as he was a new man in a new job, there was an early honeymoon period during which his needs were granted. He prepared a budget to cover the cost of raising ninety men and purchasing suitable vehicles – the force would be similar to his Camel Corps – and passed the papers to Cox for agreement. Then, as he had done so often before, he took himself off into the desert to talk to the tribes and to listen to their point of view. Once again he met Bedouin people living the same kind of nomadic existence that had so bewitched him in his first years in the Middle East. 'Only those who have experienced them can understand the joys of evening in the desert, seated in a circle round the campfire in the clean soft sand, beneath the sparkling Arab stars or in the still white light of the full moon,' he noted. 'In the glowing embers stand the brass coffee-pots, from which are poured again and again the little cups of bitter coffee. Every now and then a new bush is thrown on the fire, which flares up suddenly to a bright flame, illuminating the lean figures seated around and filling the air with a sharp aromatic fragrance.'[8]

174

Idyllic though the mood may have appeared in retrospect as he recalled it for his books about the Arab world, Glubb's purpose was to gather intelligence for the promotion of British interests in the area. Although he was accompanied by a Bedouin guide and although as an officer of the Arab Legion he was in Transjordanian service, he was well aware that his real masters were the politicians and officials of the Colonial Office in London. Glubb performed wonders in pacifying the frontier tribes and settling their grievances, it is true, but he was also circumventing the authority of Abdullah. Through Glubb, Britain was able to control the negotiations with the Bedouin tribes and to make decisions about them that would accord with their own interests. There was also a strategic necessity to put a stop to the raiding as Britain was anxious to develop its interests in the oil fields that were being discovered and exploited in Iraq and in Ibn Saud's kingdom. Throughout this period, Glubb's voluminous reports from the desert were passed by Cox to Jerusalem and from there to London where they were read by Sidney Webb, now Lord Passfield, the new Secretary of State for the Colonies. Time and time again, the officials underlined the point that any loss of prestige would weaken Britain's position in the Middle East and cause dissension amongst the Transjordanian tribes.

It was not an easy task to encourage the Bedouin tribes to break the habits of generations and to allow themselves to be knocked into a semblance of order. Transjordan was a rough and inhospitable country, four-fifths of which was desert; only the strip along the western frontier was fertile ground. A mixture of peoples made up its 350,000 inhabitants and by far the most volatile of these were the Bedouin who had not been subjected to any form of government for centuries. The Howeitat in the south and the Beni Sakhr were regarded as the most powerful, but also of significance were the Ruwalla, the Beni Atiya and the Ahl el Jebel, the hill folk of the mountainous places on the north-eastern border. Within these tribal confederations there were numerous sub-groupings, all of which lived together in varying degrees of harmony. Just as had been the case in Iraq, though, the loyalties of the tribes were contested by the rival rulers; because Ibn Saud harboured no love for the Hashemites he coveted the Transjordanian tribes and longed to bring them under his rule as a prelude to taking over the country itself. This, too, was the fear of the British administrators in Amman, for the annexation of Transjordan by Ibn Saud would undoubtedly upset the balance of power that had been so haphazardly created after the war.

There was one other reason for bringing the tribes under control. A land-reform scheme had been established in the country, and in the settled areas taxes were being collected from cultivators who in former years had paid protection money to their local tribal chief. Although many British worshipped the ideals of Bedouin culture and society, as Glubb did, they recognised that those kind of medieval excesses had no place in the twentieth century. Now that Transjordan was easing itself into the modern world, albeit under British tutelage, they wanted the tribes to settle their grievances through the law and to start paying taxes to the state. The sheikhs could still keep their romantic trappings, the black tents and the huge herds of goats and camels, but instead of behaving like brigands they would be transformed into another stereotype the British knew well, the squire with his tenants, all country manners and good breeding. In that guise, too, they would be a useful bulwark against the increasingly noisy town-based nationalists who were slowly winning ground in Cairo, Baghdad and Damascus.

The methods employed by Glubb were those which had stood him in good stead in Iraq. In the rolling hills and dry water courses of the desert between the railway and the Wadi Sirhan depression, he held lengthy meetings with the tribesmen and from them he heard a sorry story. The deprivations of the Ikhwan raids had left them poverty-stricken and the firm control of the Frontier Force had prevented them from retaliating. Moreover, they believed that the government, and therefore Britain too, were in league with Ibn Saud. Fear of further raids only served to make them feel more helpless.

For two months Glubb moved amongst the tribes and on 11 December 1930 he filed a comprehensive thirty-five-page report to Cox in Amman. Marked 'secret' it was forwarded to John Chancellor, the High Commissioner in Jerusalem together with Kirkbride's comments and those of Peake and Air Commodore C.R. Freeman, the Air Officer Commanding (AOC) Transjordan and Palestine. Taken together, the documents revealed a parlous state of affairs in the eastern desert. Glubb wrote:

> I must confess that, as an Englishman, I was utterly ashamed to discover the complete absence of prestige of Great Britain on both sides of the frontier. This lamentable situation is due to the impression that, in fining and imprisoning their tribes and returning the loot to Ibn Saud, while the latter's Governor in Jauf is openly urging the Nejd tribes to raid Trans-Jordan, His Majesty's Government is willing to descend to any depths of servility to placate Ibn Saud. I am aware that this is strong language but it is almost verbatim the language used to me by the Bedouin.[9]

The main thrust of Glubb's argument was that the Howeitat were in an acute state of distress due to the raids, that they believed Ibn Saud to be responsible by allowing the Governor of Jauf to give permission for raiding and that they did not trust the Transjordanian government or the British administrators. The report also disclosed a state of muddle in the previous intelligence-gathering which had been undertaken by RAF Special Service Officers. Their reports had been sent straight to the Air Ministry in London without Cox or Peake having sight of them for analysis, and this resulted in the mistaken belief that the Howeitat were always the guilty party in raiding activities. In these circumstances, warned Glubb, the tribes to whom he had spoken would have no option but to throw themselves on the mercy of Ibn Saud, thereby precipitating the imbalance in loyalties which Cox feared. Glubb expressed his concern in high-flown language which was underlined before being sent to London:

If the Howeitat were to transfer their allegiance to Ibn Saoud [sic], they would winter in Jauf and the Wadi Sirhan. The Sheikhs, receiving pay from Ibn Saoud and afraid of the political resentment of the Trans-Jordan Government, would probably remain all the year in Jauf. But the bulk of the tribe would continue to summer West of the Railway line from Ma'an to Kerak and down to the edge of the Jordan Valley. But they would come wearing Akhwan [sic] turbans, abusing the infidels and loudly praising Ibn Saoud. That magnetic smile, which has melted so many hearts from Mr Philby downwards (perhaps I should say from Mr Philby upwards) would have been turned upon them. They would have received money and supplies with the same noble gesture and would have been regaled by the same sweet tongue with pious expositions of the Koran and the traditions, the superiority of a Moslem over an infidel ruler. They would seem to have discovered the ideal ruler at last after the fines, impositions and imprisonments of the Trans-Jordan Government (carried out to placate Ibn Saoud), and they would proclaim the fact from the house-tops in Trans-Jordan. This is not a far-fetched prophecy.[10]

Glubb's recommended solution to the problem was one born of his experience in the desert and his knowledge of the tribes who lived there: he called it 'the goat and the tiger'.

In some countries, I believe, it is the custom for such as wish to shoot tigers to take up a position in a convenient tree and to tie up a goat in a clearing nearby. While the tiger is stalking the goat the man in the tree obtains a chance of an easy shot.[11]

In this instance the goat would be played by the Howeitat while the Ikhwan would take on the role of the tiger. Because the Frontier Force had failed to stalk and shoot the tiger and appeared to take pot shots at the goats, the best long-term solution would be to arm the goats against further attacks. This would be done with the backing of the force which Glubb hoped to raise, but the plan would stand or fall by the ability of the tribes to adhere to the kind of disciplined tactics which had been so successful at Abtiyya. In other words, defence of the desert would only be completely successful if it became the responsibility of the people who lived there.

In the short term Glubb recommended that diplomatic pressure be put on Ibn Saud to return the loot captured during the summer raids and that he should prevent the governor of Jauf from sanctioning future raids. Failing that, the government should grant the Howeitat £6,000 – the cost of a crashed bomber, argued Glubb – and that immediate steps should be taken to remove the RAF and the Transjordan Frontier Force from the desert. His last recommendation was the most radical of all – that he should place himself on the frontier with a Nejdi official in order to become the final arbiters in tribal disputes.

At first the response in Amman was one of relief. Cox had long argued that the Howeitat were more sinned against than sinning and this was reinforced by Peake who, for all his differences with Glubb, described the report as 'a most masterly exposition of the true facts and I agree with every word of it'.[12] Although Peake was frequently irritated by his subordinate's close involvement and identification with the Bedouin tribes he always insisted that the Howeitat should be given Transjordanian protection to prevent them crossing over to Ibn Saud and he could see that Glubb's plan would prevent such an outcome. The only dissenting voice came from the AOC, Freeman, who was somewhat disgruntled, not unnaturally, by the recommendation for the removal from the frontier area of the RAF bombers and armoured cars. Later, he allowed himself to be won over by the logic of Glubb's claims that a single officer in a forward position could act more decisively than the imperial forces' commanders whose movements were directed by headquarters staff in Amman or Jerusalem.

Glubb's recommendations were adopted with minor diplomatic qualifications and the Foreign Office asked the British Ambassador in Jeddah to put pressure on Ibn Saud for the return of the camels belonging to the Howeitat tribe. The first reactions from the Nejdi ruler were not promising. Not only did Ibn Saud refuse to countenance the British request, he answered unequivocally that he did not believe Glubb and accused him of being a troublemaker. This claim brought an immediate rebuke from the British Minister, Sir Andrew Ryan, who was instructed by the Foreign Office to convey 'the strong resentment of His Majesty's Government at their accusations against Captain Glubb and their allegations as to his attitude both at the present time and in Iraq'. The telegram also told him to underline the fact that Glubb had been specially selected for the job and that London had every confidence in his abilities.

The negotiations continued throughout February and at the month's end the Nejdi authorities agreed to appoint an official who would be Glubb's opposite number. His name was Ibn Zeid and he was instructed to meet Glubb in the Wadi Sirhan to discuss the raiding problem and the return of loot to the Howeitat.

Unknown to Glubb at the time, the diplomatic exchanges had not just revealed Ibn Saud's hostility, they had also brought into the open the whole question of Glubb's own personal safety. Intelligence reports reaching the Colonial Office were worrying enough for an anxious telegram to be sent to Chancellor on 18 February: 'Ibn Saud has a great respect for Glubb's influence among the tribes, and might be tempted to get rid of an opponent whose activities in Transjordan he may regard as inimical to his own policy.'[13] This brought the response from Chancellor that Glubb and Peake

– also mentioned in the signal – were capable men well aware of the risks they were running:

> It is quite true that both Glubb and Peake carry their lives in their hands all the time. Twice within the last two years Peake has been held up by hostile Arabs who threatened to kill him and he saved his life only through his coolness and his knowledge to [sic] tribal manners and customs. Over a year ago I gave instructions that he must always be accompanied by an armed escort, and I believe that he does so.
>
> Glubb is in the same position and I have told Cox to see that he is always provided with an armed escort.[14]

Chancellor ended by saying that the creation of Glubb's desert force would provide him with the protection that was needed, especially when he was on station in isolated parts of the desert, far removed from the protection of imperial forces. That both men needed bodyguards was made evident by an incident at the end of February when a sheikh was assassinated by rivals after attending a conference at Glubb's desert camp.

The first men to join Glubb's desert force were two mercenaries from Iraq who had served with him in the camel corps. Their arrival and the stories they brought with them encouraged others to join and by the beginning of March he had twenty men under his command. More importantly, Cox had received funds for equipping the force with six-seater Buick trucks armed with Lewis and Vickers guns. Thus was born the Desert Patrol of the Arab Legion.

From the very outset Glubb insisted that his new force should not only be properly equipped and armed but it should also be provided with an identifiable uniform. Rather than transform them into British imperial troops with khaki uniforms and headwear of the native design, as was the custom in the Indian Army or the Transjordan Frontier Force, he decided that they should wear a form of Arab dress that was entirely their own. The main item was a long khaki gown drawn together by a broad red belt and festooned with bandoliers. Each man carried a revolver and a silver dagger and the head-dress was 'a red and white checkered headcloth which has since then become a kind of Arab nationalist symbol'.[15] Under these clothes they wore white cotton trousers and a long white gown known as a *thob*. With their plaited hair and flowing gowns the men were an impressive sight but the British soldiers stationed in Transjordan were not slow to nickname them 'Glubb's Girls'.

In time the Desert Patrol was to become one of the most romantic of all the British irregular forces raised during the last days of empire. With their camels and horses and their dashing armed vehicles they certainly looked the part and Glubb's photographs of his men camping in the desert places of Transjordan or emerging line ahead from toy soldier forts were, like the Foreign Legion, the stuff of legend. (After 1933 Glubb instituted the attractive habit of prefacing a photograph to each of his monthly reports to the British Resident.)

The men who joined his force were idiosyncratic too. Although the Beni Sakhr provided the majority of the recruits, most of the Transjordanian tribes were represented and Glubb made a point of combining their talents to produce a unified force. In private he might have believed that the different tribes should maintain their own individual identities but as far as the Desert Patrol was concerned, he insisted that 'it is impossible to enlist and train any force in which tribal sentiment is permitted, such as, for example, a company of Howeitat, a company of Shammar and a company of Beni Shakr'.[16] Here Glubb was flying somewhat in the face of the traditions of Britain's imperial forces. In the infantry regiments of the Indian Army, for instance, it was common practice to have companies consisting of representatives of the various religious groupings – Sikhs, Rajputs, Jats and so on – although the battalions would still work together as a single unit. Presumably Glubb felt that his Desert Patrol was too small and its military duties too irregular to allow tribal divisions within its ranks.

Whatever Glubb's reasons, the Transjordanian Arabs took a great deal of interest in the Desert Patrol and within a short period it had acquired a reputation as a corps d'élite. To interested British outsiders like John Hackett* of the Transjordan Frontier Force, the standing of the Desert Patrol was entirely due to Glubb's understanding of the Arab mind:

> He was a person who carried out his business in the patri-archal way that Arabs, particularly desert Arabs – above all desert Arabs – greatly respect. And he was a man of the most enormous prestige.
>
> Arab princelings in the desert used to send their sons to serve in Glubb's Bedouin desert patrol of the Arab Legion, as potentates might have sent their sons in the European Middle Ages to do a stint as a page to the neighbouring potentate because it would be part of their education. And there were some very well-known young men serving as private soldiers in Glubb's desert patrol.[17]

Other British officers in Transjordan at the time also noted the sense of separateness, almost aloofness, that surrounded the Desert Patrol. It was not just their self-consciously dramatic uniforms that set them apart, it was also an inner belief that being a member of the Desert Patrol was also a vocation, almost like the Jesuits in its sacerdotalism. Glubb encouraged that concept because he believed that it was good for the morale of his little force and, as he told Brigadier E.H. Tinker, also for the Transjordan Frontier Force, he was well aware of the implications for himself:

> On one occasion he [Glubb] said to me, 'I am a *Regel Malaki*, I am a Royal person, and all these people are my

---

*Later General Sir John Hackett, GCB, CBE, DSO, MC, D.Litt, MA, LID sons and daughters, as it were. I am their father.' And in a way that's what Glubb was to his, originally his, desert patrol which he commanded, and later the whole of the Arab Legion when he took it over. They were, definitely he regarded them, as his children. And this kind of very paternal relationship was one that fits in very readily into the Arab scene.[18]

Although Glubb was in time to pay dearly for espousing the notion that he was an 'uncrowned king of the Arabs', in the early days of the 1930s it was a useful recruiting device for attracting the haughty desert Bedouin tribesmen into what amounted to his private army.

Glubb also believed that he could motivate his men by instilling in them the traditions of Christian knighthood whereby they would dedicate themselves to the defence of right and the protection of the poor and the weak. So strong was this feeling that he caused to be hung on the walls of every orderly room a notice bearing the injunction: 'Example is stronger than precept, so guide the people by your noble deeds.' It was a curious coming-together of Christianity and Islam, but this was a fact which rarely troubled Glubb who believed until the end of his life that the way to salvation was the life of God in the soul and that the way to it was possible for all creeds.

These pious beliefs did not prevent Glubb occasionally behaving like other imperial officials for whom the striking of natives was commonplace. While raising the Desert Patrol he lost his temper with a picket from the Khushman tribe who had left his post without permission: 'walking up to the man, I struck his sneering face with my fist. I then went back to my car and drove away.' When the aggrieved man sought redress with the assistance of his tribe, Glubb responded by rounding up their camel herds and handing them over to a Transjordan Frontier Force patrol. The camels were only returned after the Khushman had promised 'not to be naughty again'.[19]

While arrangements for the formation of the Desert Patrol

were being finalised, Glubb also had to meet Ibn Zeid in the Wadi Sirhan, an agreement which both sides discovered was fraught with difficulties. Ibn Saud refused to give his emissary plenipotentiary powers and continued to voice his suspicions about Glubb's appointment – in one letter to Chancellor in Jerusalem he accused Glubb of being a spy because no great rank was attached to his name. In response to these charges it was decided to give Glubb a new title, that of Commandant Desert Area; and at the same time Cox passed on Glubb's secret radio call sign, ZC1TP on 800 metres, to the authorities in Jeddah.

It took time and patience to fix the meeting with Ibn Zeid because both sides wanted to ensure that the agenda was suitable for their needs. The Nejdi official had been told not to make any concessions to the British and, instead, to use the return of the camels as a bargaining counter. Glubb understood the logic of that argument. Although Ibn Saud's tribesmen were guilty of raiding the Howeitat and stealing their flocks they would not admit to the crime as that would weaken their own position. Later, when Glubb asked Ibn Saud why he had attacked him so vehemently, the king replied that there was nothing personal in his attitude; he was merely fighting against any trend of events which he considered to be working to his disadvantage. Glubb summarised his understanding of that position in a thoughtful memorandum to the Colonial Office:

The abstract European worship of peace is absolutely unknown to them [Arab rulers]. They believe it to be the natural state of all rulers, princes and governments to be continually toiling to gain some advantage over their neighbouring rulers. A prince content to sit down and merely enjoy his natural dominion is regarded by them as hopelessly poor-spirited and effeminate. Moreover, it is not only the prince who conquers his enemies whom they admire. In high politics, successful lying, deceit and subtlety evoke exclamations of admiration.[20]

To Glubb's way of thinking, Ibn Saud exemplified the self-seeking ruler whose sole interest was the promotion of his own policies and who was never unwilling to ignore moral principles. Throughout Glubb's dealings with the king there is a hard-edged awareness that both men well understood the other's point of view.

For their part, the Colonial Office officials in Amman were not always so understanding about Glubb's position. As had happened in the past when the authorities in Baghdad felt that Glubb had 'gone native', so too did people like Sir Arthur Wauchope, the new High Commissioner in Jerusalem, doubt the impartiality of Glubb's monthly reports. 'I hope that this will prove to be one of Glubb's exaggerations,' he noted testily in the margin of a memorandum claiming the deaths of 'many thousands of sheep' following a desert drought; and even Peake could be irritated by the outbursts of hyperbole in Glubb's prose. As he did not share his second-in-command's passionate attachment to the desert Bedouin tribes he was moved more than once to note that 'Captain Glubb's zeal as usual slightly outruns his discretion'.

Cox, it is true, always supported Glubb but his greatest ally – and the man with whom he was to work ever more closely – was Alec Seath Kirkbride, the Assistant Resident in Amman. Like Glubb a former sapper officer, Kirkbride had served with Lawrence in the Arab Army during the war and was one of the first men into Damascus, a feat which won him the Military Cross. In 1920 he was one of a handful of young men who found themselves administering the occupied territories and for a time he was 'President of the National Government of Moab in Transjordan'. Well over six feet tall, Kirkbride could be taciturn, even standoffish, towards his fellow countrymen but he always relaxed in Arab company, an attribute he shared with Glubb. In the 1930s he became Abdullah's principal associate and mentor, acting in the same tradition as the political agents of the Indian Political Service. One story illustrates their relationship perfectly. So well did the two men understand each other's point of view that words were not always necessary. 'Why don't you like that idea?' asked Abdullah after presenting a plan to Kirkbride. 'Who said I didn't like it, Sidi?' 'Nobody, but I know that when you flick you head away like that, it means you disapprove!'[21]

For all that there continued to be misgivings about Glubb there was no doubt about his success in bringing peace to Transjordan's frontier with Ibn Saud's kingdom. After his initial discussions with Ibn Zeid, Glubb met him again at a point on the frontier sixteen miles west of Kaf. 'We met at the rendezvous at 8 a.m. on August 15, each of us bringing two tents, ten men and two cars, by previous arrangement,' Glubb told Kirkbride. 'We held conversations of about one and a half hours each in the morning and afternoon, and on the morning of August 16; I lunched with Ibn Zeid while he dined with me. The two parties separated at 9.00 hours a.m. on August 16.'[22] This was the breakthrough for which Glubb had long worked. The question of retribution was agreed and a method of compensation computed. ('If the killed person was the aggressor the compensation should be seven young camels; if the person killed was not the aggressor the compensation should be twenty-eight young camels.') More importantly, they also agreed that future complaints about raiding would be handled by Glubb and his Desert Patrol who would deal with the matter on the spot, according to the local laws of the land.

For Glubb it was a considerable diplomatic success which he was determined to consolidate by further investment in his desert force. Here he was greatly helped by the support of Kirkbride and Shareef Shakir Ibn Zeid, the President of the Bedouin Control Board and a Hashemite relative of Abdullah. Through Kirkbride's prompting the three men became close colleagues and firm friends – 'it was essential that Shaaker [sic] and Glubb, both of them excellent fellows, should pull together if the new venture was to be a success,' noted Kirkbride[23] – and the Assistant Resident made it his business to bring them together at an early stage.

187

The first opportunity was an expedition to 'show the flag' in March 1931 which allowed the two Amman-based officials to see for themselves how Glubb's tactics for the Desert Patrol would work in practice. At first all the signs for a successful operation were propitious enough. Glubb had prevented an Ikhwan raid on the Howeitat by ordering the tribe to stand its ground in armed camps to face the enemy, just as he had done with the Iraqi tribes at Abtiyya years before. However, no sooner had that danger passed than news reached him of a Howeitat counter-raid to the south through the mountainous region of Tubaiq.

This was too much for Glubb who decided that the errant raiders should be taught a lesson for disobeying his orders. Instead of pursuing them he drove to their camp, surrounded it and confiscated their camels, an action for which there was no legal justification. Once again Glubb seemed to be allowing his temper to override commonsense, for, by right, he should have arrested the miscreants and sent them to Amman to stand trial. It was at that moment that Shakir arrived with Kirkbride but, quickly summing up the situation, the President of the Bedouin Control Board commended Glubb and promised him his support. He could probably have done little else. Kirkbride was a dominating character whom he was anxious to please; how better than to fall in with an albeit hot-headed decision taken by a rising star in the British administration?

What happened next, though, came straight out of the realms of melodrama. Anxious to begin the expedition Kirkbride urged Glubb to lead them south into the wilder regions of Tubaiq where the raiding problem was still thought to be acute. The party would consist of the three officials, twenty armed men all carried in a Buick six-seater and two Dodge one-ton tucks armed with machine-guns. 'The men had only had a few weeks training,' remembered Kirkbride, 'but made up for lack of experience with an enthusiasm which was schoolboyish in its warmth.'[24]

As they made their way through an increasingly lunar

landscape, scattered with fantastic outcrops of sandstone, the expedition took on the aspect of an adventure. Soon, to Glubb's delight, tracks were found which appeared to indicate that they had come across evidence of a Howeitat raiding party returning from the Nejd. It did not take long for the two groups to make contact and when they did the three vehicles of the Desert Patrol set off in hot pursuit to try to prevent the raiders from reaching the safety of the nearby mountains.

Before leaving Amman Glubb had instructed his Bedouin soldiers to follow a system of three simple flag signals which ordered load, fire and cease fire. But in the excitement of the chase these were soon forgotten. When Glubb gave the second signal both gunners opened up at once without first getting out of the line of fire. In the leading vehicles Kirkbride was disconcerted to find the rear Lewis gunner firing over the top of his vehicle as the trucks bumped over the desert, the Buick bringing up the rear. 'As I looked back I could see the puffs of earth thrown up by the bullets striking the ground between the two cars as the muzzle of the guns jerked downwards,' he recalled. 'The gunner, wild with excitement, had thrown away his headgear so that his plaited hair blew out behind him and he was singing at the top of his voice.'[25]

Fortunately for the party's safety, the ground quickly became too rocky to continue the pursuit and the Desert Patrol was forced to unship weapons and deploy by a ravine in an attempt to cut off the raiders' line of escape. Although they failed to do this one camel was captured and in its saddle-bag was the damning evidence of a merchant's note which provided Glubb with the identities of the raiders. For him – and for his men too – it was a supreme moment:

Everybody was in high spirits after this exhilarating little hunt. The troops had worked well, and were full of enthusiasm, and the Lewis gun had fired. We watered at a little rain pool, and after posting look-out men in case any other raiders were about, we sat down to make tea. The troops were bubbling with glee at the thought of what the raiders

189

would say when they reached their homes, and found that all their camels had been seized by the Government in their absence.[26]

Looking back at this incident from the distance of over half a century it is difficult not to be amused by it. Despite the wild firing of the Lewis gunners, no lives had been lost and the identities of the raiders had been established, yet it still smacks more of a schoolboy prank than a serious military operation. As Kirkbride noted, that was part of its charm, but he was also astute enough to realise that Glubb's tactics could work and would continue to work in the future. Instead of deploying the Transjordan Frontier Force in the area and thereby fuelling local suspicions, the problem of raiding could be controlled by these poachers-turned-gamekeepers. As Glubb had forecast, the transformation of these semi-nomadic tribesman into desert policemen was not just a matter of giving them arms and uniforms – essential though these were – it was also a question of handing over to them the responsibility for their own security. Kirkbride also understood that by guiding negotiations on all frontier matters, Britain, through Glubb, was maintaining its decisive role in deciding the future of Transjordan and its frequently stormy relationship with the Nejd. What neither Glubb nor Kirkbride seem to have realised, though, was the longer-term effect of their policies on the people of the desert. Whereas the raids and counter-raids of former years had virtually turned the Bedouin into enemies of civilised society, they would now become members of it.

Hardly surprisingly, the incident in the Tubaiq and its successful outcome gave Glubb much-needed support in Amman. Kirkbride was a loyal ally and friend and Shareef Shakir remained one until his untimely death in 1935. Through both men, too, Glubb enjoyed direct contact with the Emir Abdullah who harboured ambitions to transform the Desert Patrol of the Arab Legion into a regular national army. Money and equipment became available to it and by

March 1933 Glubb reported that its strength was 200 – one-fifth the complement of the entire Arab Legion. By then, too, a chain of forts had been constructed in the desert at Bair, Azraq and Rum and the Bedouin soldiers of the Desert Patrol had been trained in the use of wireless telegraphy. This provided Glubb with the lines of communication he required for his force and the presence of the square toy-soldier forts provided the tribes with firm evidence of the administration's intention to make the desert a safer place.

The seal on the new-found peace was provided by the conclusion of a British–Transjordanian treaty with the new kingdom of Saudi Arabia. This was signed in Jeddah in June 1933, and just as he had represented Iraqi desert interests in the HMS *Lupin* negotiations three years earlier, so now was Glubb asked to perform a similar role for Transjordan.

'Thank heavens, that's over!' Glubb wrote in his diary, noting, too, that Ibn Saud had introduced a new air of formality to the proceedings and was no longer interested in making himself available for private discussions with the opposite side. For Glubb this represented an end to the old desert way of doing business and the ushering in of a new life whose pace would quicken with the discovery and exploitation of the country's oil resources. Glubb deplored the changes and came to believe that the introduction of an oil-based economy would be the ruination of Ibn Saud's kingdom. 'It is rumoured that an oilfield has been discovered in the Hejaz and that several of the great oil combinations of Europe and America have thought it worthwhile to approach Ibn Saud for concessions,' Glubb had reported to Amman in March 1933. 'If this be really true, it may indeed mean a transformation in the future history of Arabia.'[27] Glubb, in fact, was never to entirely lose his suspicion of the oil companies' activities, especially in the desert areas.

Although Glubb was pleased to see the growth of the Desert Patrol and took a delight in his men's loyalty, Peake was less enchanted. He still held that the Arab Legion should remain a gendarmerie force responsible for internal security

191

and that the obligation for the country's defence should be vested in the Transjordan Frontier Force. Paradoxically though, the creation of the Desert Patrol under Glubb's command had laid the foundations for turning the Arab Legion back into a military force. Glubb's tactical doctrine gave his men operational experience in desert warfare, including the use of modern weapons, transport and communications as well as co-operation with other formations including the Air Force. In other words, Glubb created the Desert Patrol as an élite strike force capable of operating over long distances against superior numbers. As the Legion's historian P.J. Vatikiotis has pointed out:

> [Glubb's] success in recruiting beduins [sic] and pacifying them over the next five to ten years was the result of a combination of expert diplomacy and efficient military action. To this extent Glubb was instrumental in raising and training what soon came to constitute the *striking force* of the Jordan Arab Army.[28]

The success enjoyed by Glubb in the desert and the élan with which he led his men could hardly have recommended themselves to Peake. Officially he supported Glubb and there is nothing in his reports or correspondence to suggest that he was anything but a loyal commanding officer. However, he did not always see eye to eye with Kirkbride and Cox, his civilian superiors in Amman, and this prickliness led to private tensions in his relationship with Glubb. In particular, he seems to have fallen foul of Cox whom he accused in his diary of 'doing all he could to reduce my prestige in the Arab Legion and thus force me to resign'.[29] Cox was still bypassing Peake on operational matters but, astutely, Glubb had started showing the papers to his commanding officer in an attempt to lessen the friction caused by the slight.

Nonetheless, the tension between Peake and Glubb was noticed and inevitably London became aware of it. When, in 1935, a British journalist, Kenneth Williams, asked the Colonial Office to assist him with a book about Transjordan which would contain a chapter on the Desert Patrol, officials were not enthusiastic. Glubb himself wrote to London asking that the book be read so that any reference to himself and his force might be excised because he did not want to upset Peake. 'Glubb's position vis-à-vis Peake is a little difficult,' noted an official before passing the request to the Colonial Secretary. Fortunately, Williams decided not to proceed with the book and a relieved Colonial Office noted that this result 'would not add to Major Glubb's difficulties with Colonel Peake'.[30]

Peake's own personality did not help matters. An officer of the Victorian school he seemed to believe it was a military virtue to appear to be angry at all times and to make his subordinates terrified of him. Not for nothing was his wireless code-name 'thundercloud' and it was flashed from fort to fort with much trepidation before he arrived on a surprise visit. His rages were legendary throughout the Middle East. In fairness to him, though, he was very much a man of his age and upbringing, a bachelor soldier – he married late in life – who masked his own feelings and bent his energies towards maintaining high standards of duty and service. He was also a fine soldier and something of a closet romantic who learned to fly at the age of fifty so that he could use an aeroplane to visit Glubb's outposts in the desert.

The awkwardness of Glubb's relationship with Peake, and his natural disinclination to shine in the smart colonial society of Amman, meant that Glubb himself was happiest when he was with his men in the desert. The 1933 agreement with Saudi Arabia provided for an inspector from each side to co-operate in dealing with frontier problems and, naturally enough, Glubb was appointed to deal with Transjordanian interests. His delight was doubled when he discovered that his opposite numbers, in succession, were princes of the Saudi royal household, for Glubb always believed that when he was with them he was in the company of true aristocrats. Certainly, he reserved some of his most colourful prose to describe their desert meetings which were always governed by the precepts of Bedouin hospitality.

At sunset the Saudi party would arrive at Glubb's reception tent to find a magnificent meal prepared for them. Both parties would be wearing their most colourful uniforms and costumes and, having washed and prayed, they would sit down together to eat:

> Dinner was in the old Arab style, and consisted of a heaped mountain of rice, surmounted by five sheep roasted whole. Each sheep was filled with savoury stuffing and hard-boiled eggs, while the whole contents of the dish was sprinkled with almonds, raisins and other sundries. It took ten stout men to carry the great dish from the kitchen tent, amid much staggering and shuffling of feet, and pauses for rests. The central *pièce de résistance* was placed on the floor in the centre of the dining-tent. Around it were grouped a hundred small plates containing many different varieties of meat, vegetables, sauces, chicken, buttermilk and other delicacies.[31]

The most important moment would come later in the evening when the leading Saudi and Glubb would withdraw for *ta'lila*, the evening conversation, when they could speak man to man. Coffee would be served – 'Yes, by Allah, coffee!' the two men would declare – and the discussion would range over the ways of the world, its people and religions, before returning to the matter of a lost camel. 'Eventually we rose and strolled, smiling, from our tent – the peace of the world was saved – at least until our next meeting.' Not only was Glubb at his happiest during those sessions, he always liked to think they represented a coming together of true minds.

Not everyone was so impressed. An RAF officer called Denis Newman remembered landing beside Glubb's camp in the desert and being closely followed by a swarm of locusts. Asked to join in a meal which the Bedouin said had been sent from heaven, he quickly refused. 'I didn't fancy it,' he recalled. 'As these things flopped down they'd just pull the wings off and throw them in the frying pan. You know, they were all squirming and all legs and things. And they'd say "Oh, lovely" and crunch, you know. They probably did taste nice but I couldn't fancy it, watching them all squirming in the fat in the pan. I couldn't do that. No, not for me the Desert Patrol!'[32]

During this period of rapid change Glubb became uncomfortably aware of the fact that, although he was committed to the service of Transjordan, he did not have a proper contract. In the Arab Legion he had the local rank of major, or bey; when he took over command from Peake he became a lieutenant-colonel; during the Second World War he was first colonel and then brigadier; and eventually he achieved the rank of lieutenant-general when he became the Chief of Staff of a vastly expanded Legion in the post-war years, but these were not British Army ranks, only local equivalents. (Throughout the war and until the end of his service, official papers generally referred to him as 'Glubb Pasha'.) Sonorous those military titles might have appeared, but they masked the reality of a job which was poorly paid and relatively lowly within the Palestine civil service.

In 1933 Glubb had applied to the Colonial Office for an appointment which would carry both a contract of service and a pension – he was by then thirty-six – and after much official prevarication he was appointed Assistant District Commissioner, Grade G, in the service of the Palestine government. The post carried a salary of £300 rising by £25 increments to £800, plus an annual cost-of-living allowance of £30. It was the only pensionable job he ever had in his life. At the time, though, it was a good salary, good enough to make him regret that he was still a single man. 'Looking back now on those frustrations and heartaches,' he wrote in later life, 'I can only conclude that any failures were due to my inability to perform any physical endearments. This was probably due to my innocence and my lack of experience. But

195

not entirely so – I also felt that physical familiarities before marriage was [sic] sinful.'[33]

The years of such frustration came to an end during his leave in England in 1936 when a quiet girl, Rosemary Forbes, walked into his life. She had been engaged as a German conversationalist for his mother and the two liked each other at first sight. 'He was shy and reserved but he also had a twinkle in his eye,' she remembers. 'We went out for drives in his car and our friendship developed and deepened. When he went back to Transjordan, we had a definite understanding.'[34]

They were married two years later, during the summer of 1938, in a Tunbridge Wells registry office. It was not the wedding expected of a prominent general's son but Glubb's father had died earlier in the month, on 2 August, a fortnight before his eighty-first birthday, and the circumstances dictated hasty arrangements. His widow decided to sell the house in Pembury in order to live with her son in Transjordan, a decision which startled Glubb who had been given leave to fly home for his father's funeral. During that period of intense activity he decided to marry Rosemary Forbes immediately. On 20 August 1938 they went through the civil form of marriage and the following day Glubb and his mother left for Transjordan, taking the overland route to Marseilles and then on to Beirut by sea.

Three months later Rosemary followed them out to the Middle East, accompanied by her own mother and the marriage was solemnised in the Church of All Saints in Beirut. The honeymoon was a two-day holiday spent in a local hotel – 'chaperoned by both our mothers' according to Glubb – before moving back to Amman which was to be their home for the next eighteen years. Their first son, Godfrey, was born in October 1939. He was also known as 'Faris', meaning 'knight' because Abdullah believed that he should have an Arabic name and in time Godfrey adopted it as his own. For his part, Glubb received another nickname: 'Abu Faris', or 'father of Faris'.

Fifteen years younger than Jack Glubb, Rosemary gave the impression of being a reserved, even diffident wife, but she possessed an iron will and a kindly heart. Shortly after arriving in Amman she noticed the plight of the local Bedouin orphans and quickly set about planning improvements for their lot. She rented a small building near their own house – a modest, though handsome, stone-built residence – and it became an elementary school. Later it increased in size when Palestinian refugees flocked into Jordan after the war with Israel and from her own pocket Rosemary provided the necessary pencils and paper as well as paying the stipend of a retired local teacher who took the lessons.

Generosity ran in the family, for her mother, Mrs Graham Forbes, received a medal from the Red Cross for her work in organising a milk centre for Palestinian refugees in 1948. In October 1939 she returned to Amman to help Rosemary after the birth of her first son and, due to the difficulties of wartime transport, she stayed on in the Middle East to manage the Lady MacMichael Convalescent Home for Officers in Jerusalem. It was a happy, closely knit family, for Lady Glubb also remained in Jerusalem and would not be moved until her son finally left Jordan in 1956. Only Gwenda remained in England, at Brooklands, where she and her husband set up a workshop to manufacture specialised components for military aircraft. At the end of the war she decided to follow the rest of the family eastwards to the Mediterranean and Aegean seas where she led a roving life in her yacht *Elpis*.

Wartime colleagues of Glubb liked to think of him as a quiet man who had little to say for himself – although they admired his courage and powers of leadership – but they knew few details about his personal life for, like many other successful and self-contained men, Glubb chose to keep it strictly private.

7

Arab Soldier

When Glubb had returned from home leave in 1936 he found increasingly obvious signs that the character of Transjordan and its position in the Middle East were on the point of change. One such harbinger had been the construction of the Iraq Petroleum Company's pipeline from Mosul province in Iraq to the port of Haifa in Palestine: the presence of western technicians and Arab labourers from neighbouring states had disrupted the bucolic quality of desert life and made Glubb fear for the integrity of the Bedouin tribes. The most obvious signs of change, though, were the rise of Zionist power politics and the awakening of Arab nationalism in the neighbouring state of Palestine. In the long term Palestine and all its problems were going to have the greatest influence on Transjordan as it slowly evolved into a modern state with a political role to play in the Middle East.

Although Transjordan was to remain a backwater as far as the discovery and exploitation of oil were concerned, it was not untouched by it. Oil had been found in massive quantities in Iraq in 1927 at a wadi called Baba Gurgur near Kirkus and it had to be piped through Transjordan to the Mediterranean coast. The pipeline was built by the Iraq Petroleum Company – which was owned jointly by Royal Dutch-Shell, Anglo-Persian, and a French and an American consortium – and from the very beginning it created a number of local difficulties. The oilmen who built the pipeline were tough operators, used to driving their men hard and hiring and firing them at will. Amongst the workers they employed were tribesmen of the Ahl el Jebel who were renowned for their lawless behaviour and their appearance on the IPC pipeline was the cause of a good deal of friction.

Glubb's Desert Patrol was responsible for the security of the 200 miles of pipeline which stretched between the Hejaz railway and the Iraqi border and from the very outset the relationship between the Patrol and the oilmen was difficult. Under Transjordanian law any transgressors in the desert had to be handed on to Glubb's men for arrest and subsequent trial in Amman. All too often, though, the European foremen tended to mete out their own punishments or turned a blind eye when their men fought with local tribesmen. To Kirkbride, Glubb confided in his monthly reports that this new responsibility was 'an anything but congenial task':

> The company pays a sum of money to the Transjordan government to cover the expenses incurred in the additional police needed to guard the company's camps and undertakings. This fact has caused the company's officials to assume proprietary airs over the police and even to taunt them openly with being merely servants of the company.[1]

Glubb did not hide the fact that he detested most of the oilmen whom he met in the desert. They demanded round-the-clock protection but treated the men of the Desert Patrol with an arrogance which was unforgivable to a man like Glubb. Most were foul-mouthed and aggressive and all were united in their belief that they should not conform to the legal requirements of the country in which they were working.

Their intransigence was partly due to an ignorance of the role of the Desert Patrol and a deep-seated belief in their own superiority over these quaintly dressed camelmen. Partly, too, they were driven by financial considerations to complete

the construction of the pipeline so that the company's investment could be turned into profit. By way of mitigation, it is
also true that they were suspicious of Arab law and feared
that their men would face terrible punishments if handed
over to the authorities. Many were veterans of the fields in
eastern Saudi Arabia where oil had been found at Dhahran
and they had witnessed the public beheadings, stonings to
death and severing of hands that were common forms of
punishment in Ibn Saud's kingdom.

Whatever their reasons, they failed to take Glubb's force
seriously and his monthly reports throughout the 1930s are
punctuated by his irritation with the oil company's off-hand
attitude towards himself and his men. For a man as sensitive
as Glubb those examples of modern industrialised life were
potent reminders that not all Europeans shared his sentimental attachment to the nomadic Arab way of life, with its
courtesies, hospitality, conservatism and love of the desert.

The biggest problem facing Transjordan during this period,
though, was Palestine. From the very beginning of their
postwar relationship the two countries had been linked by the
British mandate – but the connection was already centuries
old. Geography alone dictated a close affinity and the border
between the two states – created by the British – was there in
name only. No passports were required and the trading links
were long established and respected by both sides; since 1927
the two countries had shared the Palestinian pound as their
currency and while Transjordan was regarded as a ready
supply of unskilled labour, Palestine provided trained men for
the administration.

However, as Transjordan had been excluded from the
terms of the Balfour Declaration – which had established
Palestine as the Jewish homeland – and as the rate of immigration began to increase dramatically, so too had the settlers
started looking covetously across the River Jordan. After all,
counselled their elders, these were the lands of the Old Testament where the tribes of Reuben, Gad and Manasseh had
first pitched their tents and tended their flocks. One of the

aims of the Zionist movement was the unification of the two countries and, according to one of their leaders, Chaim Weizmann, one means of achieving it was the purchase of land: 'The road to the Allenby Bridge along which we cross over to Transjordan will not be paved by soldiers but by Jewish labour and the Jewish plough.'[2] Weizmann also believed that the Zionist cause would be helped in Transjordan if the local landowners were provided with evidence of the financial rewards to be gained from their dealings with the Jews. If they were seen to be making money from their investments, then surely others would follow suit. In the longer term the Zionists regarded Transjordan both as an area for future Jewish expansion and as a place where the dispossessed Arabs of western Palestine could be permitted to settle.

Under the terms of the League of Nations' Palestine Mandate Commission, Britain had a duty to 'provide special facilities for the immigration of Jews' in Transjordan but this had rarely been permitted. In 1927 the Jewish-controlled Palestine Electric Company had purchased 6000 dunams of land at Jisr Al-Majami and two years later the Palestine Potash Company had purchased the concession to extract potash from the Dead Sea. Both companies planned to use any excess land for housing development in order to attract settlers, both Jews and Arabs, into the area.[3] The move was not welcomed by Wauchope, the High Commissioner in Jerusalem, who cautioned that although the settlement of Jews in Transjordan could not be ruled out, the time for such a development was not propitious.[4] Glubb, too, was similarly minded, for the simple reason that any immigration would further disrupt the charms of Bedouin life:

I do not wish to state that the importation of foreign capital into Transjordan might not be for the benefit of the capitalists. It would probably increase the total revenue of Transjordan. It might be for the general benefit of the human race. But let us be quite clear and honest – it would not be for the benefit of the tribesmen. Perhaps the tribesmen are few and unimportant and should be sacrificed in the interests of bigger stakes – but let us not pretend it would be for the good of the tribesmen.[5]

Glubb went on to warn that although the introduction of 'foreign capital' (that is, Jewish capital) would increase Transjordan's prosperity, it would surely change its character. 'Human beings in the last resort cannot be won by money,' he claimed, adding the thought that wealth could only lead to envy and hatred and might well stir up further trouble between Jew and Arab. What he was really implying, of course, was his distrust of Jewish motives: the essay concludes with a forecast that the sale of land and the introduction of a market economy would create a society of 'haves' and 'have-nots', the Jews being the former, the desert Arabs the latter. 'It may be necessary to do such things to gain higher and greater objects, but it is an error to suppose that it would be helpful to the Arabs of Transjordan.'

In 1930 a British White Paper prepared by Lord Passfield, recommended the tighter control of land sales within the mandated territories and urged that Jewish immigration into Palestine should be governed by the capacity of the economy to absorb it. Although the recommendations never became law, the suggestions heightened the Zionists' awareness of Palestine's lack of spare land. Fortunately, in spite of all the difficulties imposed by the British administration, they were able to find a number of Transjordanian landowners who were prepared to rent land to them through the Jewish Agency. Amongst these was the emir, Abdullah, who was not averse to negotiating with his Palestinian neighbours, be they Arab, Christian or Jew. Britain had just granted him three further tracts of land in Transjordan – a useful means of increasing his income at small cost to the exchequer – but one of these, Ghawr Al-Kibd in the northern Jordan Valley, had a zero-ratable value and was therefore of little practical use to the emir. When the Jewish Agency approached Abdullah about the possibility of renting it to them he was tempted and entered into secret negotiations which were concluded in 1932. However, it was impossible to keep silent about the deal and although Abdullah issued a denial that any land agreement had been made with the Jewish Agency, few in the Arab world believed him.[6]

Throughout his life Abdullah's motives in attempting to reach agreements with the Jewish settlers in Palestine were the subject of a good deal of suspicion and distrust in Damascus, Baghdad, Jeddah and Cairo. Abdullah's ambitions to create a united Arab kingdom were also much resented, as were his claims to the kingdom of Syria. Ibn Saud regarded him with derision – Abdullah was, after all, a Hashemite, one of his traditional enemies – and even his relatives in Iraq treated him in an off-hand manner. With King Faud of Egypt he had no relationship whatsoever. The British were also wary of his motives and the Colonial Office did not always take him seriously. It would be tempting, therefore, to see Abdullah as a figure of fun, a leader ruling over a tin-pot country who owed everything to the support of the British. To do so would be scant justice as Abdullah was one of the few rulers in the Middle East who wanted to find a solution to the Arab–Jew question in Palestine throughout the 1930s and beyond.

The reason for this misrepresentation lay partly with Abdullah himself. He was an impulsive man, capable of great generosity, but his intrigues, such as the land negotiations, led to friction with the British administrators, particularly with the staff of the High Commission in Jerusalem. From the letters that passed between them and London, one could be forgiven for believing that the British regarded Abdullah more as a naughty child than a head of state. With Kirkbride, of course, he enjoyed a close and warm friendship and the two men not only understood each other well, but perhaps too well – a favourite joke of Abdullah's was to make insulting remarks in Turkish or Arabic to ill-favoured guests and then to watch Kirkbride's spluttering attempts to translate them. Glubb, too, became a member of that tight little circle and in time he was to become Abdullah's closest European associate and mentor.

Nonetheless, for all Abdullah's faults, most of which were harmless, he understood the strength of international Zionism and its importance for the future development of Palestine. Knowing that it would be impossible to encourage any degree of co-operation amongst his fellow Arab leaders, he liked to think that he could play a leading diplomatic role in reaching agreement with the Jewish settlers in Palestine. The death of his brother Feisal in 1933 provided him with an opportunity to take his place at the centre of pan-Arab politics but his earlier land dealings with the Jewish Agency still cast a long shadow over his personal standing. It was not until 1936, when civil unrest broke out between Jews and Arabs in Palestine, that British officials began to think that he and his country might be useful allies in their attempts to reach some sort accord between the two communities.

The trouble began on 15 April 1936 when the Arabs in Palestine began a general strike which quickly escalated into a series of vicious attacks on Jewish property. Two Jews were killed in Nablus, their murders setting off a chain reaction of further murders followed by retaliation, and by the end of the month there had been serious outbreaks of violence in all the main areas of population. The Haifa–Lyddah railway line was attacked; there were widespread demonstrations against the British authorities while, in the country areas, the attacks on Jewish property led to reprisals by the Irgun Zvai Leumi, the Zionist defence organisation. Initially, the British responded by using minimum force to put down the Arab revolt and defend their own interests. Not until the end of August, by which time their forces were at divisional strength, were they able to threaten the imposition of martial law as a solution to the problem.

The main reason for the Arab unrest was the increased scale of Jewish immigration into Palestine. In 1931 it had been 4,075 but by 1935 the figure had shot up to 61,854, largely as a result of Hitler's anti-Semitic regime in Germany

– in November of that year he had passed the Nuremberg Laws which deprived the Jews of German citizenship. The increased numbers of Jewish immigrants greatly alarmed the Arab nationalists in Palestine. 'The Arabs looked on with dismay,' noted the writer Christopher Sykes, at that time a frequent visitor to the country. 'Seen through Arab eyes, this great work of rescue and redemption had nothing beautiful about it and seemed on the contrary to be a stark act of oppression against themselves.'[7] This despair was heightened by the evidence of increased Jewish financial investment in the country and by the knowledge that many incoming European Jews were putting their technical and administrative skills at the service of their own community. Suddenly it seemed all too likely that a Jewish state could be created in Palestine and that the Arabs would end up as the underclass.

Perversely, some Arab leaders took comfort and confidence from Germany's actions. To them it was encouraging to see another country dealing with its Jewish population by taking away their citizenship and encouraging emigration. Moreover, all the evidence seemed to suggest that Britain either condoned Germany's action or was powerless to prevent it, for in March 1936 Hitler had been able to use his military forces to take unopposed repossession of the Rhineland. There was other evidence indicating that British power was on the wane. In the previous year neither she nor France had been able to prevent Mussolini's invasion of Abyssinia, for all that the action had been roundly condemned by an increasingly feeble League of Nations. If other countries could stand up to Britain, argued the Palestinian Arab leaders, then could not they do so too? It has to be remembered that there was widespread resentment against western – and, therefore, Christian – rule throughout the Muslim world and that the unrest in Palestine had been preceded in January and February by strikes against the French authorities in Syria and the British in Egypt. For those reasons the first violence of the Arab Revolt in Palestine in 1936 was directed just as much towards the British as it was to the growing number of Zionist settlers.

Inevitably, the disturbance spilled over the border into Transjordan and throughout that summer there was considerable public disorder in Amman, with attacks on government offices and Arabs taking to the streets to demonstrate their solidarity with the strikers in Palestine. Palestinian terrorists successfully attacked the Iraq Petroleum Company's pipeline and badly damaged a pumping station.

For all that the Desert Patrol had established itself in Transjordan and was highly regarded by most of the Arab population, Glubb had not been left immune from the nationalists' dislike of the British. In October 1933, while walking through Amman to attend a meeting of the Bedouin Control Board, he was confronted by a sizeable anti-British demonstration. At first he paid little heed to the crowd who were waving sticks, banners and clubs, but the situation quickly became nasty when the speaker gesticulated in his direction. Suddenly stones were thrown and despite the presence of a soldier from the Desert Patrol the crowd began to close in on Glubb. 'We faced round again and confronted our persecutors,' wrote Glubb later, but help was already on the way:

> ... suddenly there was a sound of galloping horses, and through the crowd burst the Amir Shakir himself on horseback, followed by three or four mounted slaves. They wheeled their horses, waved their canes in the air and ordered the crowd back. The crowd bust into cheers and clapping. The Prince was popular and was also a beautiful horseman, and to see him handling his grey pony was a pleasure in itself. A slave galloped off to fetch a car, while His Highness skirmished between me and the crowd. Soon the car arrived, and the Amir Shakir, dismounting, drove off with me to the board meeting.[8]

Although unsettled by the incident, which he believed was

uncharacteristic of the Palestinian population in Transjordan, Glubb had a clear enough understanding of the problems they faced. He believed that the Jews could make few claims on the Old Testament lands of Palestine, either by reason of historical association or by the terms of the more recent Balfour Declaration. If race alone were the deciding factor, he asked, would it make sense for the Americans, for example, 'to hand back their national home to the Redskins?'[9] Furthermore, 2,000 years of tribal migrations and consequent colonisations had left few people with realistic claims to particular pieces of territory.

As for the Balfour Declaration, Glubb, like many other Anglo-Arabs, considered that this solution had been imposed on the majority Arab population of Palestine and could only be upheld by British arms:

> Military coercion of a civilian population has always been extremely distasteful to the people of Britain. It was one of the many ironies of the Palestine muddle that the Jews, who seemed in Europe to be an oppressed minority, arrived in Palestine in the guise of European colonisers. Many of the parties which in Europe and America have been loudest to denounce European 'Imperialism' yet support the forcible colonisation of Palestine by military force. A movement [Zionism] which to Europeans stands for liberal idealism is thus transformed in Palestine into military imperialism.[10]

With the influx of European Jewish settlers into Palestine, the native Arabs had good reason to feel aggrieved, he counselled. And just as the Jews had begun to feel more of a nation than a race, so too had Arab nationalists begun to fear that they stood in danger of becoming the minority racial grouping in Palestine. Glubb believed that the solution to the problem could not be found in using Palestine as the haven for the many thousands of Jews who wanted to escape from the repressions of Nazi Germany. Instead they should be accepted far more readily into British and American society and Nazi Germany should be prevented from forcibly deporting its Jewish citizens to Palestine. (Under the terms of an agreement known as 'Ha'avara', the Nazi regime encouraged the emigration of wealthy Jews and their financial properties from Germany to Palestine between 1933 and 1938.)

As Glubb saw the position in the 1930s, the immediate solution to the difficulties in Palestine was to restrict immigration and abandon, albeit temporarily, the idea of the movement towards the creation of a Jewish national home. Britain's other aim should be to encourage Abdullah to keep Transjordan out of the unrest that was sweeping through Palestine. Fortunately, the Transjordanian emir had already stamped on potential unrest in Amman. He had also appealed to the Arab Higher Committee, the Arab leadership in Palestine, to use its influence to end the strikes and the violence. This was a sound move for Abdullah because it demonstrated to British officials in Jerusalem that he could still be a political force in the Arab world. Of course there was, too, an ulterior motive: Abdullah had high hopes that his intervention would strengthen his own position and allow him to seize the initiative. However, the Arab Higher Committee was not minded to heed Abdullah's advice in 1936 as its members still distrusted his motives and believed that he wanted to annex the West Bank and Jerusalem.

During this period Glubb, Kirkbride and Cox believed it was their duty to give all possible support to the emir in his efforts to keep Transjordan quiet and strike-free. Glubb counselled that the evidence of a settled Transjordan could increase Abdullah's standing in the Middle East and that the people 'by their obedience and good conduct [could] prove that a state governed by Arabs for Arabs had a higher standard of conscience and public devotion than a country still groaning under the brutalities of "colonial" rule'.[11] Although all three men were greatly heartened by Abdullah's determination to maintain public order in Transjordan, they were still shocked by the upheaval that was taking place before their eyes.

> To Englishmen who have worked with Arabs [wrote Glubb in May 1936] the situation is tragic in the extreme. Many of us have collaborated with Arabs for periods of from fifteen to twenty years. Throughout all this period, with many ups and downs, we have maintained and enjoyed innumerable friendships, and throughout all this time and in spite of local differences, the great majority of Arabs have maintained their faith that Britain was the greatest, the most generous and the most friendly of the great powers. It is nothing less than tragic to see this faith and friendship turning, before our eyes, into disillusionment and hatred. God alone knows how it will all end.[12]

Of particular concern to Glubb, in his capacity as commander of the Desert Patrol, was the movement of arms and men across the border into Palestine, particularly in the north from Syria. He was also worried that it might become a two-way traffic and that propaganda emanating from Palestine might suborn his men. In June 1936 he reported that the Howeitat had been greatly excited by calls to rise against the British and that only a firm demonstration by his armed cars had convinced the tribesmen of the superiority of the government forces.

Above all Glubb wanted to see Transjordan remaining a tribal and, therefore, Bedouin country; in other words, an Arab nation-state which would remain under British tutelage as a bulwark against the noisier claims of pan-Arab nationalism. With some distaste he noted that whatever happened to Palestine in the future, it had lost all hope of remaining a truly Arab state. 'In Palestine the influx of Jews and foreigners, and seventeen years of direct British administration, have made the country Levantine or Mediterranean,'[13] he wrote to Kirkbride in July 1937. Transjordan, on the other hand, had managed to contain the political extremists in Amman. Only in the desert were hot-heads to be found but they were merely lawless and excitable and unlikely to be persuaded to take action for political reasons.

The contrast between the two neighbouring countries' position was all too clear and Glubb and his coevals were determined that it should stay that way. In August Glubb told Kirkbride that the most frequent topic of conversation heard in Amman was that Arab governments should henceforth co-operate to resist foreign interference and present a united front against oppression. While such sentiments chimed in with Abdullah's own thinking – and were unlikely to come to fruition – Glubb disliked hearing them being expressed. In his private notes, and occasionally in his monthly reports, he showed a fair degree of contempt for the new class of Arab bourgeoisie in Amman whom he felt might foment the Palestine situation for their own political ends.

These he divided into two different classes: Syrian immigrants, mainly merchants whom he called 'Damascenes', and Palestinian-born administrators – 'Nablusis' to Glubb – who, he believed, 'have neglected no opportunity to propagandise and spread false reports'.[14] The former were unlikely to cause any real trouble because, although they might pay lip-service to the idea of Palestinian nationalism, they realised that civil unrest was bad for business and they had, therefore, a vested interest in supporting the status quo. On the other hand, many of the 'Nablusis' had been educated in Europe and had acquired nationalist attitudes which they (or so Glubb believed), adapted to serve the Arab cause. Glubb was never to lose his distrust of the town-based Arab politicians.

Although he disliked their political style, Glubb was willing to concede that many of the Transjordanian officials had good reason to feel unhappy about the number of British men occupying administrative posts within their country. This was a prevalent feeling at the time – Abdullah had already told Cox that he expected Peake to be replaced on retirement by an Arab officer – and it was used by the members of the Arab Higher Committee to sow the seeds of discord in Amman. In particular, the Mufti of Jerusalem, Haj Amin al-Husseini, the holder of the most influential Arab office in the country, and a thorn in the flesh of British interests, used agents to control the Arab Revolt from Damascus. Using extensive religious funds they bought weapons for guerrillas and showered Palestine, and later Transjordan, with propaganda leaflets denouncing British rule. A well-publicised part of their campaign was a 'hit-list' of British officials and during the first summer of the revolt a number of administrators and policemen were gunned down in Palestine.

After the revolt died down in the autumn of 1936 those same agents turned their attention to Transjordan, giving Glubb cause to suspect that 'some careful system for picketing and propaganding' was being operated from Damascus. Confirmation came from two of his NCOs who visited the Optical Hospital of St John of Jerusalem in February 1937. After the consultation both men were followed back to their hotel by the Mufti's agents who chided them for not supporting their co-religionists in Palestine. Although both men shrugged off the incident and reported it to their commanding officer, Glubb could see that additional efforts would have to be made in Transjordan if the tribesmen were to remain loyal to the emir and to his British backers. While he could understand that there might be natural sympathy for the Palestinian cause, Glubb was concerned lest this should boil over into actual support. Even if that did not happen, by undermining the authority of British rule, the Palestinian rebels were giving considerable comfort to disaffected minorities in other parts of the Middle East. In his monthly report for December 1937, he wrote:

Palestine has affected Transjordan in two ways:
1. By direct sympathy for the inhabitants of that country.
2. Perhaps more indirectly, by revealing the apparent inability of the government to put an end to the Palestine disturbances. This, quite irrespective of the rights and wrongs of the case, has caused every malcontent to

211

open his eyes. If discontented Palestinians can defy their government why should not the discontented elsewhere, they ask? Thus Palestine has, to some extent, undermined the prestige of settled governments everywhere.[15]

Throughout 1936 and 1937 Glubb's monthly reports had returned again and again to the Palestine disturbances to evoke the spectre of Transjordan being drawn inexorably into them with disastrous consequences. Although his reports brought the occasional rebuke from the Colonial Office – 'It is a great pity that Major Glubb does not exercise some restraint,' was a far from untypical marginal note – his recommendations for additional safeguards were heeded when he presented them in July 1937. Two changes were needed if the Arabs' natural sympathy for their neighbours in Palestine was not to erupt into violence. First, the Arab Legion should be strengthened – this was a goal shared by Abdullah – and, second, the east bank of the Jordan should be picketed to prevent Palestinian rebels entering Transjordan. Both moves would obviate the need for stationing additional British troops in the country. Indeed, at Glubb's urging, Cox quickly countered a suggestion from Wauchope that a British infantry brigade should be stationed in Amman. 'The continued disorders in Palestine have inevitably brought Trans-Jordan nearer the boiling point,' admitted Cox, 'but the Amir's authority is still sufficiently great and his determination sufficiently strong to maintain order.'[16] All the more reason, he added, to bolster Abdullah's standing and, if necessary, to increase the size and prestige of the forces at his disposal. For the next three years, with Cox's and Kirkbride's encouragement, Glubb was to spend much time and effort slowly turning the Arab Legion into a professional military force.

In 1936, for all that it carried out paramilitary duties in the desert, the Arab Legion was still little more than a police force or gendarmerie whose role extended to traffic control in

Amman and the provision of men for the country's prison service. It had an establishment of 1,200, of whom only two-thirds could be described as fully operational servicemen. Peake was happy enough with the situation as he believed that policemen should never carry out soldier's duties. Increasingly, too, he had become bogged down in administrative work in Amman and left much of the day-to-day operations of the Legion to Glubb. He was increasingly hampered also by illness and after an attack of hepatitis in 1936 he had been advised by the British medical officer that continued exposure to the heat of Transjordan during the summer would carry considerable risks for his future health. By then Peake was fifty; most of his life had been spent in the Middle East and it was probably at this time that he began to think seriously about taking early retirement.

Glubb, on the other hand, spent most of his days with the men of the Arab Legion, preferably in the desert area where, as Glubb saw it, 'one can breathe amongst friends a sigh of peace and relaxation. The terrorism and bloodshed of Palestine, the menaces of Hitler and Mussolini seem suddenly far away. To a great part of the world the desert means fear, exhaustion or at best discomfort. For ten years, it replaced for me the relaxation, the happiness and the affection of home.'[17] That was how Glubb remembered his feelings ten years later when he wrote the first volume of his memoirs *The Story of the Arab Legion* (1948), but it was a faithful enough recollection. In a 1938 interview with Tom Driberg of the *Daily Express* Glubb provided a good picture of how he and his little force fitted into the scheme of things in Transjordan:

Glubb spends few days in the year at his house in Amman; goes there only to have an occasional bath and do a bit of office work. He is never seen at social functions in Amman or Jerusalem ... This is not Lawrence coyness. It's simply that Glubb has to be constantly in touch with all the corners of his territory. He goes by car (reading a good deal of history on the way). He does not affect Arab dress;

213

when I met him he was in khaki uniform. 'The trouble all over the east,' he told me in a clear, imperial rather school-masterish voice, 'is that with improved communications and so on, British people lead an increasingly Western life. They go to each others' parties. They never mix with the people of the country. They might as well not be here.'[18]

This was very much a personal view, for the Colonial Office still regarded the Arab Legion as second in importance to the imperial troops of the Transjordan Frontier Force. Because Abdullah was still viewed with some suspicion in London, one reason for limiting the size of the Arab Legion was the possibility that it might one day evolve into a private Hashemite army whose guns could be turned against the British. Even as late as September 1940 Sir Harold MacMichael, the High Commissioner in Jerusalem, had to object to the continuation of that point of view at a time when the wartime needs of national defence required a rapid expansion of the Arab Legion Reserve.

Glubb always countered the opposition to the Arab Legion with evidence of the Desert Patrol's operational activities – during the first stages of the Arab Revolt in 1936 his men had successfully repelled Syrian guerrillas trying to enter Palestine through the Ajlun district in northern Transjordan. The experience led to the formation of a small permanent reserve of 200 men to bolster the regular cavalry and mobile infantry and the men of the Desert Patrol. A supernumerary force, consisting of ninety men, had already been raised in 1934: paid for by the Iraq Petroleum Company, its sole responsibility was for the security of the desert pipeline. It was commanded by Glubb's assistant, Norman Lash, formerly of the Palestine Police. Like many other Englishmen attracted to the deserts of the Middle East, Lash was something of an oddity; quiet, donnish and respectable, he was a fluent Arab speaker and a great admirer of the Bedouin tribesmen. Although he left the Arab Legion in 1938 to return to Palestine as a Special Service Officer with the Royal Air Force in Nablus, he later took over Glubb's responsibilities as Officer Commanding the Desert. (After Peake's retirement, which took place in 1938, Glubb was, for a time, the only British officer in the Arab Legion. The rest were all middle-aged Arabs with little modern military experience, some of whom had served in the Ottoman Army during the First World War.) At this time too (1936), Glubb received enhanced secret service funds of £1,050 a year. Most of this was distributed to the desert sheikhs in return for information or simply as 'pensions' or 'bribes' to keep the tribes loyal to Abdullah. The Colonial Office disapproved of this practice but, on Glubb's urging, it had to be continued.

The most far-reaching change to the Arab Legion and the one that allowed it to become a military force during the Second World War came in 1937 with the establishment of a mechanised regiment known as the 'Desert Mechanised Force'. It was 350 strong and its men came mainly from the ranks of the Desert Patrol who had experience of the kind of operational duties the new formation was expected to perform. To begin with, it was equipped with heavily plated Ford trucks armed with Lewis guns but, within a year, the Legion had designed and built its own 'home-made' armoured cars and once war broke it was equipped with Marmon Herrington armoured cars carrying Bren and Lewis guns as well as the Boys anti-tank rifle.

The arrival of the new mechanised formation and the presence of a permanent reserve – comprised of two squadrons of cavalry – gave Glubb's forces greater mobility in the desert area where they were deployed along a defensive chain of forts and district headquarters. As was only to be expected, the innovations did not entirely please Peake who worried lest the new, mainly Bedouin force become too powerful in the country – 'such domination can only lead to poverty and misery,' he noted.[19] His attempts to block or water down Glubb's proposals for military expansion met with little reward – the reports were passed from him to Cox in Amman and thence to Jerusalem. Later, they were read by the Colonial Office whose officials were well aware of 'the long-standing friction' (note, March 1937) that existed between Peake and the other British officials in Amman. It is notice-able, reading Glubb's monthly reports and the subsequent comments made on them in Amman, Jerusalem and London, that however much they might have been criticised for the occasional exaggeration, if there were a difference of opinion between Peake and Glubb, the latter's point of view would be invariably accepted. In that way, through a series of magister-ially argued reports, Glubb was able to push, successfully, for the expansion of the Arab Legion at a time when its commander wanted to retain it as a gendarmerie.

Later, Glubb was to be accused, both in Britain and Jordan, of giving preference to the Bedouin and the charge has more than a grain of truth. Just as there are British Army officers, even today, who swear by the fighting qualities of their Highlanders or take great pride in their 'little Gurkhas', so too did Glubb prefer the company of his Bedouin soldiers to the town-based middle-class Arabs or the *fellahin*, the peasant village farmers. 'How often did I not sigh with relief as the car wound up the hair-pin bends out of the Amman valley after one of my four- or five-day visits to the capital,' he wrote. Ahead lay the kind of experience which encour-aged him to bend his energies towards the creation of a desert-based Arab army, manned by the kind of soldiers whom he could easily understand:

'Most blessed hour which brings these guests!' cry the soldiers as they run to bring coffee and order dinner.

Outside the walls of the fort the immense desert stretches in darkness and a silence so intense that with the utmost attention it is impossible to hear any sound. Overhead the sky is covered with the sharp brightness of Arabian stars. In the courtyard of the fort by contrast are bustle and gay voices. Flames shoot high from a fire in the open court, throwing dancing shadows on the high stone walls and lighting up the scarlet sashes and cloaks of the soldiers.[20]

Instinct and experience helped to create Glubb's romantic evocation of the desert way of life, but he was nothing if not a pragmatist. The care and attention he brought to arming and equipping the Arab Legion were born both of a personal ambition to turn it into a model army and also a soldier's natural desire to be associated with the best. John Hackett noticed this trait too: to him, and to others, Glubb seemed to be becoming more Arab than the Arabs.

> Glubb was a very fine Arabist and he could have, I think, passed as an Arab from somewhere other than he happened to be. I mean, if he was in the Wadi Sirhan let's say, or in the country of the Howeitat, he wouldn't be mistaken by one of them for one of themselves. But if he said he was a Christian Arab from Ramallah or something of that sort, by the Bedu they might believe him [sic]. Or if he said he was Lebanese and they hadn't very much experience of how the Lebanese whine when they speak Arabic, but merely knew that they spoke it rather differently, he might take people in. He was very good.[21]

There was another noteworthy aspect of Glubb's intense interest in the Bedouin way of life. As well as bringing them indirectly under the influence of British colonial rule, he also provided the Transjordan desert tribes with a new role to play within the country. When Glubb arrived in Amman in 1930 the fortunes of tribes like the Howeitat and Beni Sakhr were at a low ebb. Harassed by the neighbouring Ikhwan and further debilitated by several long-lasting periods of drought, they faced an uncertain future as Transjordan slowly evolved into a modern town-based state. Like the Scottish Highlanders who lost everything after the failure of the Jacobite rebellions in the eighteenth century, the Bedouin found that they too were an anachronism, a throw-back to a period of history that had no place in the modern world. By giving them employment in the Arab Legion, as noted before, Glubb turned them from poachers into gamekeepers and provided them with the possibility of full integration into the nation-state. In time, the men of the Arab Legion were to become proud servants of Transjordan, excellent soldiers with a good understanding of fieldcraft and amenable to military discipline and, more importantly, they also became instruments of Hashemite policy, a kind of praetorian guard to the country's ruling family.

First and foremost, though, the Arab Legion had to prove itself as a military force capable of carrying out duties normally entrusted to the Transjordan Frontier Force. (Glubb's reports in 1938 and 1939 make frequent mention of the rivalry – of which he approved – between the two forces.) Moreover, any opportunity to shine in action would lend substance to Glubb's ambitions and prove the efficiency of the Legion as a national defence force.

The opportunity to demonstrate their skills came in the spring of 1939 when Palestine and Syrian guerrillas plotted a rebellion in Transjordan: had it been successful large numbers of British troops would have been needed to suppress it. As Glubb noted at the time, if it had taken two infantry divisions to contain the disturbances in Palestine, it would have required even more men to carry out a similar task in Transjordan whose terrain was considerably larger and wilder. By then, the revolt in Palestine had petered out, mainly because the population had been exhausted by the ferocity of the fighting which in 1938 alone had claimed 1,600 Arab lives, but also because a succession of British political initiatives, backed up by military firmness, had brought a period of relative calm to the country.

The first initiative had been the Peel Commission whose task had been to investigate the root of the problem in Palestine by taking evidence from the different factions. It had produced its findings in July 1937: the main recommendation was the partition of Palestine into an Arab area and a Jewish area which would consist of a coastal strip from Haifa to Jaffa together with the traditional lands of Galilee. The present mandate would be ended and a new treaty would be concluded between the Arabs of Palestine and Transjordan. Jerusalem would be subject to a new mandate. 'Partition seems to offer at least a chance of ultimate peace,' claimed the report. 'We can see none in any other plan.'[22]

Naturally enough, Abdullah was pleased with the commission's findings as the new Arab state would be incorporated into Transjordan, thereby enhancing both his holdings and his prestige in the Arab world. However, the Palestinian Arabs rejected the recommendations and vilified Abdullah for accepting them so quickly. Iraq, Syria and Saudi Arabia followed suit with the result that the partition plan was scuppered by all the parties opposed to it. Amongst the detractors were the British Foreign Office whose officials intrigued to destroy it, largely because they had little faith in Abdullah who would gain the greatest advantage:

> The proposal that the new Arab state should be incorporated in Transjordan, while no doubt sound in principle, is open to the somewhat accidental objection that this will presumably mean that it will come under the rule of the Amir Abdullah, who is regarded by most of the Arab world as very doubtfully loyal to the Arab cause ... though possessing many virtues, [Abdullah] is politically short-sighted and a good deal given to petty intrigue.[23]

Following a period of further unrest which had to be put down in draconian fashion by the British security forces, discussions were re-opened in London in early 1939, bringing together Arab leaders from Egypt, Saudi Arabia, Iraq, Yemen and Transjordan, as well as representatives of the Arab and Zionist factions of Palestine. By that time Britain had abandoned its position on partition and had also declared that the Jewish National Home had been established according to the terms of the Balfour Declaration. By that time, too, with war in Europe seeming inevitable, Britain was acutely aware of the strategic importance of the Arab and Islamic world with its oil supplies and lines of communication to India and the

Far East. Any decision would have to take the whole Middle East into account and the ensuing White Paper both reflected that new standpoint and was governed by a need to placate Arab opinion.

The White Paper's recommendations, in brief, were no partition, the creation of an independent Palestine within ten years, the introduction of severe quotas for Jewish immigration and limits placed on land sales to Zionists, all balanced by the provision of 'safeguards' for the Jewish community. However, the terms suited neither Jews nor Arabs and Britain went to war with Germany in September 1939 with both factions in Palestine committed to the long-term aim of ending British rule in their country. This signalled the end of Britain's impractical task: the creation of a Jewish National Home and the protection of the rights of Palestine's Arab population.

Because the Arab revolt had been put down with a severity which had alienated the bulk of the population, it was not surprising that its leaders in Damascus had decided to change tactics and looked eastwards for a new arena in which to take the battle back to Britain. The Mufti was also anxious to have Abdullah deposed and still held to the dream that a greater Arab Palestine could be carved out of the territory on both sides of the River Jordan. From a military and a political point of view it made sense, therefore, for his guerrilla forces to turn their attention to the previously quiescent state of Transjordan.

Previously the main problem caused by the Arab revolt had come from the frequent incursions of Syrian 'volunteers' who had made their way into Palestine to carry out guerrilla raids before escaping once more back over the border. Now, it seemed to Glubb, they would turn their attention to Transjordan, using the remote northern area of the country as their main route. In the early stages of the Arab Revolt they had followed the old smuggling routes to the north and west of the Sea of Galilee, using pack-mules to carry their equipment and explosives and travelling by night to avoid detection.

The construction of a huge wire fence along the Palestine frontier which marched with Syria prevented further penetration in 1937 but, nothing daunted, the rebels pushed further south to enter Palestine through the border with Transjordan. This was the area of the Yermouk valley and, as Glubb reported in March 1939, it was ideally suited to clandestine operations:

> Immediately opposite the Palestine frontier south of the Sea of Galilee, lies a system of very deep rocky canyons, running into the Jordan from the east, formed by the ravine of the Yermouk river and its tributaries. The ravine is on average about 1,500 feet deep with precipitous sides, in places almost vertical, and in other covered with undergrowth and strewn with boulders. The bed of this system of ravines has long contained a main depot for the despatch of men and stores to Palestine. Lying in Syria, the right bank of the Yermouk and its tributaries to Wadi Masoud and the Wadi Khalid, are yet within a few hours walk of Palestine.
>
> The virtual closing of the north Palestine frontier by the wire fence has rendered the Yermouk valley the principal base depot, firstly for stores, munitions and reinforcements for Palestine and secondly for creating disorders in Transjordan. So open are the preparations carried on at the rebel base on the Yermouk that most of the men, stores, ammunition and rations arrive by train from Damascus, and are unloaded at Wadi Khalid station in the Yermouk valley.[24]

Given its hard going, the river valley was adopted by the Syrian volunteers as a main training base where they received tactical instruction for their missions into the British-mandated territories. Although the valley was picketed on the Syrian side by French troops, no effort had been made to sweep the rebels from their positions and the Yermouk had rapidly become a 'no-go' area. Glubb's main fear was that it would now be used as a base for raids into Transjordan and that his men would be hard-pushed to prevent a determined assault.

The first sign that trouble was afoot came in the last week of February 1939 when a British forestry officer was abducted from the village of Dogara near the Syrian frontier and only managed to escape in the confusion of a fire-fight between the guerrillas and a Transjordan Frontier Force patrol which happened to be operating nearby. The first serious attack on the security forces, though, came a few days later, on 9 March, when a heavily armed gang of sixty Syrian guerrillas entered Transjordan by way of the Yermouk valley and occupied the village of Deir as Sana with the intention of heading for the Ajlun foothills. Later in the day their presence was discovered by two cavalry troopers of the Arab Legion who were able to call up reinforcements, in spite of coming under fierce rifle fire.

For reasons known only to themselves the Syrians hesitated before leaving the village and while crossing open ground in the early morning of 11 March they were engaged by a ten-man cavalry patrol of the Arab Legion, led by a sergeant. A fire-fight followed and, shortly before noon, the battle was joined by thirty more men of the Arab Legion who arrived in cars. Next to come on the scene were the men of the Desert Mechanised Force who were led by Lieutenant F.T. Macadam, a young British officer who was earmarked to succeed Glubb as Officer Commanding the Desert. The problem facing Macadam was that the guerrillas had used their early numerical superiority to deploy themselves amongst what cover there was – mainly rocks and wooded copses – and that both forces were only about a hundred yards apart. Given his force's growing strength and confidence, Macadam could probably have winkled out the enemy, but during the afternoon the RAF sent a flight of Hawker Hart aircraft to lend assistance to the ground forces. With the arrival of large numbers of infantry in Palestine the policy of Air Control was in abeyance and the three RAF squadrons in the country had hardly been used during the revolt. Here was a chance for them to engage the enemy, even though the close proximity of the front lines caused obvious sighting problems for the pilots. Alert to the danger that the Harts might attack his own men, Macadam jumped to his feet and waved his arms to signal to the low-flying aircraft. It was a tragic error: the Syrians saw from his uniform that he was an officer and immediately shot him dead. In spite of this loss the Arab Legion pressed home their attack until the end of the day when, in Glubb's words, 'the gang had ceased to exist'. In addition to the death of Macadam, the Legion had lost one sergeant killed and three men injured. Within the next few days they were in action again at Rashadiya and Gharandal: the attempted uprising had begun in earnest.

Macadam's death left Glubb as the only fully operational British officer in the Legion and he was obliged to spend the summer of 1939 leading the fighting patrols in the Ajlun area. As he saw the problem at the time, it was absolutely essential to keep a public-security presence in the area, both to take on and defeat the guerrillas and to show the local population that the government of Transjordan was in control of the situation:

The great majority of the people of Trans-Jordan appear to be opposed to the occurrence of disturbances. The Arabic press in Syria and Baghdad has been publishing articles giving accounts of the 'rebellion' in progress in Trans-Jordan. This rebellion is purely artificial. It is true that armed gangs are now at large in Trans-Jordan, and that conflicts have taken place between them and the armed forces of the government. But these gangs consist almost entirely of foreigners, Syrians or Palestinians, and seem to be meeting with little welcome from the local villagers. The latter, however, are fully aware of the terrorism which has long reigned in Palestine, and are deeply apprehensive of the gangs. Thus the issue is largely one of prestige. If the

223

government can keep the upper hand of these foreign gangs, the people may have the courage to refuse them assistance and thus to freeze them out. But if the gangs go long unpunished, the villagers will probably be terrorised into assisting them. And if the gangs appear to be gaining the upper hand, there is a large class of ex-bandits in Trans-Jordan who would be ready to join, not from any political grievance, but out of love for a [life] of banditry.[25]

This was to be a difficult and frequently intractable problem for Glubb. As happens in every guerrilla war, the insurgents needed the support of the local community for food and shelter and for gaining intelligence about government troop movements. In that way they could strike at the security forces and then melt back into the countryside; the guarantee of shelter and provisions would also allow them to make several small-scale attacks over a relatively wide area, causing constant tension amongst their opponents and forcing the commanders to spread their forces more thinly.

To prevent the Syrian guerrillas from adopting that strategy, and thereby gaining the upper hand, Glubb had to do two things. First, he had to make sure that his own men were visible to the local population; second, he had to persuade the villagers to report to him the movements of the insurgents. To achieve both ends meant leading from the front, talking to policemen, religious and community leaders and generally keeping a sharp eye on the villages of the Ajlun, a task which demanded energy, stamina and subtlety.

Far from discouraging the Syrian gangs, the encounter with the Arab Legion in March only spurred them on to greater efforts to destabilise the local population and to entice them into armed revolt against the government of Trans-jordan. As before, the focus for their activities was the Ajlun area south of the Sea of Galilee and north of Amman, which Glubb reported in April 1939:

The gangs have made their headquarters in the very rough

wooded mountains along the norther half of the Jebel Ajlun. Their base is on the Syrian side of the Yermouk valley, and their line of communications down the Jordan valley to the vicinity of Jisr Sheikh Husain, whence they turn up into the mountains. They favour this line of approach because the Jordan banks are in several places covered with thick reeds and high bushes, which enable the gangs to rest and lie concealed at intervals of their journeys. While lying up on the banks of the Jordan, moreover, they are able to obtain food from sympathisers on the Palestine bank of the river. In addition to the main line of entry of the gangs, the direct route from Ajlun mountains to Deraa is used for messengers and casual personnel. This route crosses an open plain near Remtha, which makes it unsuitable for use by gangsters in daylight.[26]

To the west lay the Jordan valley with the hills of Palestine rising blue in the distance, and both sides of the ridge were surrounded by fields of high corn rippling in the wind. 'War or no war,' wrote Glubb about one patrol through these idyllic surroundings, 'it was impossible not to be glad on such a morning, and the men in the trucks behind my car had already broken out into a camel trotting song.'[27] Somewhat to Glubb's regret, though, not all of his men were so enamoured of the scene, especially his Bedouin troopers whose mode of warfare was almost entirely waged on horse- and camelback in the open spaces of the desert.

Tranquil the scene might have appeared to a romantic like Glubb, but throughout March and April his men were in constant action, frequently taking part in close-quarter actions with the Syrian guerrillas in the wooded hillsides and sudden ravines of the Ajlun region. All too often, the enemy broke off when the Arab Legion out-manouevred them and were able to retire into the Yermouk valley where the lack of passable tracks prevented Glubb's mechanised columns from giving pursuit. (In his report for March 1939 Glubb lamented that the absence of decent roads nullified the mobility of his newly mechanised forces.) From this base the gangs were still able to mount a number of daring raids, cutting the telephone wires between Ajlun and Irbid and, on at least one occasion, cutting the IPC pipeline and setting fire to the escaping oil. As well as causing damage to the country's economy, these incidents also proved to the local communities that the rebels could act with impunity.

Glubb felt that the only way to put a stop to the outrages was to increase the size of the forces on the ground and thereby limit the gangs' freedom of movement. At the beginning of April he was joined by a squadron of the Transjordan Frontier Force; at the same time he reorganised his own forces to enable his cavalry and mechanised infantry to act in concert as mobile columns. In this way he was able to keep the gangs on the move – from local intelligence sources loyal to him he was fed a constant supply of accurate information concerning the whereabouts of his opponents. This combination of superior intelligence and improved mobility gave Glubb a decided edge in engaging the guerrillas, and whenever there was any fighting the Arab Legion always gave pursuit, thereby preventing the gangs from escaping and regrouping. Glubb later said of this period in his life that he decided to play the gangs at their own game and that the only way to defeat guerrillas was not through regular warfare but through the employment of guerrilla tactics. In those conditions he had to have the loyalty of his own men and the support of the local communities, for in the last analysis he was leading Arabs in battle against Arabs:

The whole of this unhappy affair was a sad misunderstanding. For every man in Trans-Jordan and in the Arab Legion sympathised with the cause of the Arabs in Palestine. But their leaders made a profound miscalculation when they attempted to produce a rebellion in Trans-Jordan against an Arab Government, and that by force and without the prior consent of the people. There was indeed no little difference of opinion among the rebels themselves as to the advisability of invading Trans-Jordan. In the end, as some of the Arabic newspapers in Damascus pointed out, the Arabs found themselves fighting one another, while the British and the Jews in Palestine looked on unmolested.[28]

The crunch came on 24 April when news reached Glubb that a Syrian gang, some 200 strong, had taken over the village of Beit Idis, south-west of Irbid, and had used the cover of darkness to dig trenches and mine the main road. The activity had been observed by scouts of the Desert Patrol who had quickly radioed for reinforcements. At first light an Arab Legion cavalry squadron approached the village from the south and the guerrillas abandoned their positions to take cover in the nearby woods. A second cavalry squadron then arrived and the two formations lined up to attack the defensive positions in open order. As the skirmish got under way a mechanised patrol came down the road and, attracted by the sound of shooting, the men abandoned their vehicles and advanced on foot through the woods to attack the enemy from the flank. 'A sharp running fight ensued, in precipitous mountains covered with thick scrub, the gang flitting ahead from tree-trunk to tree-trunk, the troops crashing along behind at the best pace they could,' remembered Glubb. 'Towards evening, when contact was nearly lost, a detachment of the Frontier Force arriving from the north bumped into the flank of the retreating enemy, and the action flared up again for a short time. In the day's fighting, this gang of about 200 men were reported to have suffered eleven killed and more than twenty wounded. The Frontier Force had one man slightly wounded; the Arab Legion suffered no casualties at all.'[29]

The action broke the gang's back and in small parties they drifted over the border to Syria, never to return. Although the attempted revolt in Transjordan never came to fruition, guerrillas continued to use the country as a route into Palestine and much of the Arab Legion's efforts were aimed at arresting troublemakers and preventing them from committing acts of terrorism against the country and its population. During the summer there were some notable successes. The infamous Palestinian guerrilla leader Yusu abu Durra was arrested in the Jordan valley following an Arab Legion ambush, and by the end of the summer Glubb's men had improved the roads leading into the Yermouk valley, thus putting an end to this haven for banditry.

By preventing an uprising in Transjordan Glubb had achieved two ends: the country remained an oasis of tranquillity alongside its unruly neighbour, and this he had achieved without calling on the help of British troops whose presence would have exacerbated the situation. That the operation had been accomplished by Arab troops was a bonus. Just as he had proved in Iraq, Glubb had shown that the long-term solution to Transjordan's defensive needs had to be found in her own servicemen. Hardly surprisingly, he took advantage of his strong position to press for the further enlargement and modernisation of the Arab Legion, to turn it finally into a proper army. His case was helped by the rising tension in Europe, but the real evidence had already been provided by his own men who had proved themselves in a short and sharp low-intensity anti-guerrilla war.

During the period of guerrilla incursion into Transjordan changes had been taking place in the command structure of the Arab Legion and the Desert Patrol. Glubb had taken over command of the Arab Legion, a promotion that, although inevitable, had not been achieved without some difficulty. As early as August 1938, MacMichael had written to Malcolm Macdonald, the Secretary of State for the Colonies, to remind him that Peake was due to retire and that Glubb was the only man to succeed him:

I need not elaborate my reason for this recommendation as you are fully acquainted with the capacity and qualifi-cations, of Major Glubb, as well as the distinction and success with which he has performed his duties throughout his eight years' service as second-in-command of the Arab Legion and Officer Commanding the Desert Area.[30]

MacMichael also recommended that Glubb should be promoted to Grade E of the Palestine Service and that his pay should be increased to £1,300 – Peake received £1,322 a year but he also had a free house, a legacy from the early days of the administration. There was, too, the question of a replacement for Glubb who had occupied two posts since joining the Legion – second-in-command, and Officer Commanding the Desert. On this score MacMichael was to run into trouble:

> Colonel Peake's British assistants are all too junior and inexperienced for promotion to the post of second-in-command, and, in addition, there is a number of senior Arab officers in the Legion who are senior to them in rank. Nor is there any officer at present serving in Palestine who could be recommended for appointment.[31]

As the British could not countenance the appointment of an Arab officer, MacMichael's solution had been to divide the job. He recommended that the post of second-in-command should be offered to Major H. J. Hare, 2nd King Edward's Own Gurkha Rifles, who was a 'first-class Army interpreter in Arabic' and who had impressed him with his 'officer stamp' when he visited Jerusalem to discuss the possibility of employment with the Legion. The second point was that the post of Officer Commanding the Desert should be given to Lieutenant F.T. Macadam, who had extensive knowledge of the Bedouin tribes. The new appointments would entail an additional expenditure of £700, the salary demanded by Hare.

It was on this point that the recommendations ran into problems and an increasingly acrimonious row started between the Colonial Office and Treasury officials who were opposed both to the new appointments and to the need to raise Glubb's salary. The arguments continued into the new year and were only settled on 26 January 1939 after Mac-Michael threatened to make the appointments unilaterally and to find the necessary funds from other sources within the Transjordanian budget.

Quite apart from the obvious need to get the men into their new appointments as quickly as possible due to the unsettled position in northern Transjordan, MacMichael was also anxious to forestall Peake who had offered to stay on until a solution could be found. 'I shall *not* feel bound to say that the retention of Peake for so long is necessary,' he warned the Colonial Office on 23 September 1938. 'The appointments of Glubb, Hare and Macadam, on the other hand, are of real importance. Peake, as a matter of fact, is becoming somewhat of a nuisance both to the General and myself, not to mention others in Trans-Jordan, by his inter-ference in matters which are not really his business, and I am particularly anxious to avoid rifts in the local lute at a juncture when it is essential that we should all pull together.'[32]

There is also evidence that Peake sought Abdullah's support by warning him that Glubb wanted to make the Arab Legion an all-Bedouin force. If that happened, he advised, then Glubb would destroy the Legion's integrity by sacking all the Palestinian and Circassian officers.[33] Although Glubb had no such intention, Peake's intrigues with Abdullah were greatly frowned upon by MacMichael and provided him with a further incentive to replace him sooner rather than later. In the event, Abdullah's only comment on Glubb's appoint-ment was that he approved of it, but wished that the command had gone to an Arab officer. Peake himself retired officially on 21 March 1939.

Unfortunately, by the time the appointments were announced, only Glubb was in a position to take up his new responsibilities. In April 1939 Hare had suddenly announced that he did not want to take up the offer and had settled in Egypt, and a few days earlier Macadam had been killed at Deir as Sana. In some despair, the Colonial Office turned to another Indian Army officer, a Major Faraday, but he could not accept due to his wife's illness and it was not until 29 August that a suitable replacement was found in Major R.J.C. Broadhurst. Command of the desert was then given to Glubb's old colleague Norman Lash who had left the Arab Legion following a disagreement with Peake and had returned to Palestine to serve with the Royal Air Force.

With the world slipping slowly towards war, the administration in Amman was anxious to have a settled team in office so that Britain's long-term interests could be protected. Cox had retired and been succeeded by Kirkbride who supported Glubb's appointment. Not only did he want a strong personality at the head of the defence forces, he also realised that there were still those in the Colonial Office who feared that the Arab Legion's expansion would provide Abdullah with a private army. The note attached to the letter confirming Glubb's appointment is revealing: 'There is no doubt that the post of OC Arab Legion is definitely a politico-administrative one.'[34]

Glubb, too, realised that he was in a delicate position. On the one hand he was a British colonial servant whose ultimate masters were in London; on the other, his oath of allegiance as an Arab soldier was to Abdullah. Shortly after he had been appointed he set off to the small three-roomed cottage in the palace grounds where the emir did most of his work. The memory of Abdullah's words of advice to him were to leave a lasting impression:

'You are English,' said the Amir, motioning me to sit down, 'and this is an Arab country, and an Arab army. Before you take over command, I want you to pledge me your word, that, as long as you remain in this appointment, you will act always as if you had been born a Trans-Jordanian.

'I know you would not wish to fight your own countrymen. If it should ever come to fighting between us and the English, I will hold you excused. You may leave us then and stand aside. But if, by God's will, this does not happen, I want you to be one of the people of Trans-Jordan.'

'Sir,' I answered, 'I give you my word of honour. From now onwards I am a Trans-Jordanian, except under the conditions you mentioned, and which I pray God may never come.'[35]

8

Battle Honours: Iraq 1941

War, the great bringer of change, allowed Glubb to complete the revolution which turned the Arab Legion from a modest gendarmerie force into a regular national army. At the outbreak of war in 1939 it was still a fledgling formation, well suited to internal-security duties yet neither equipped nor trained to cope with military-style field operations. Its total complement was only 1,290 officers and men, of whom 1,043 could be counted as regular establishment (43 officers, 246 NCOs and 754 men).[1] Even its equipment was spartan and somewhat old-fashioned. Its half-dozen armoured cars had been made in Jaffa by a German coach-builder and were based on the elderly South African-designed Marmon Herringtons, and the score or so of Ford trucks and station wagons were reaching the end of their useful lives. Equipment was fairly basic, too. The cavalry and infantry formations of the regular force were armed with the ordinary Lee-Enfield rifle while the mechanised forces had been given the newer short Lee-Enfield Mark V, both well-tried British infantry weapons which dated from the First World War. The men of the Desert Patrol, now the mechanised force, were permitted to carry revolvers and daggers.

Six years later, by the summer of 1945, the Arab Legion had changed out of all recognition and had become a seasoned and disciplined military institution, many of whose members had combat experience. It had the appearance of an army as well. The mechanised force had grown into a brigade with three regiments, there was a basic engineering cadre which would soon grow into a fully equipped technical services branch and there were also separate medical and communications services. Perhaps the greatest growth had been in manpower – altogether 9,000 officers and men made up the regular forces and they had been equipped by the British with modern automatic weapons, mortars and improved military transport. The long years of the war had given the Arab Legion the means and the impetus to expand, but the seeds for the rapid growth had been sown by Glubb in December 1939 when he argued for the immediate formation of a strategic reserve of two cavalry and two mechanised squadrons. Such an addition, properly equipped, would enable the Legion to carry out its police duties over a wider area – at this stage Glubb was careful not to place any emphasis on the paramilitary aspects of the expansion; that would come later. The proposal was welcomed by Mac-Michael who immediately recommended its implementation to the Colonial Office in a memorandum of 20 January 1940:

> In summary, Major Glubb's case is that [the] Arab Legion is essentially a police force whose function it is to maintain law and order. In view of the nature of the country in which it operates and the characteristics of the inhabitants, it must maintain an adequate reserve in the form of a mobile striking force. Such a reserve exists at present and the force is well-equipped to continue to carry out its role as it has done very efficiently and effectively in the past few years. But the reserve must be maintained, irrespective of the availability of military forces to aid the civil power in quelling disorder.[2]

As a result of the consolidation of his reserves, Glubb was permitted to purchase eight fast cars for wireless work and to make arrangements for the supply of additional trucks. Due to the problems of wartime supplies getting through to the Middle East from Britain Glubb was given special dispensation to order the new vehicles directly from Ford in Detroit and the first batch arrived in Haifa in the spring of 1941. The wireless cars, though, had to be bought second-hand from sources in Amman and Jerusalem. Arming the men was a different matter and, as Glubb remembered, he had to beg or borrow equipment as soon as it became available: 'We had a few machine-guns already and eventually, as British units in the Middle East were re-equipped with Bren guns for example, we were allowed to have Lewis guns which were First World War weapons and even Hotchkiss guns which were even older.'[3]

By October 1940 the size of the Desert Patrol had been doubled, the reserve forces had been equipped and permission had been granted to form an additional company for the mechanised force. The Arab Legion was growing and as the direction of the war indicated that Syria might soon become troublesome – a German armistice commission had arrived in the country following the fall of France – it seemed increasingly likely that Glubb's force would have a role to play in the defence of Transjordan. For that reason it became imperative that its duties should be regularised and recognised both by the Allies and by the enemy. Glubb was especially concerned lest his men be considered irregular forces by any invader and punished accordingly. He made his views clear to Mac-Michael in a report written in September 1940 and the matter was passed to London for the necessary approval to give the Legion military status.

> The reason for this recommendation is that should it become necessary to use the Arab Legion to assist in repelling invasion by a foreign army it is desirable that the Legion should possess military status in order to secure, as far as may be possible, that its members should not be treated by an invading army as francs tireurs.[4]

Approval, in the form of temporary Colonial Office agreement, was granted the following month and the Legion enjoyed military standing throughout the war, although legislation was not passed until 15 December 1946.

Another key factor in the growth of the Legion had been the good impression it made on General Archibald Wavell, Commander-in-Chief, Middle East, and Anthony Eden, Secretary of State for War, when they visited Amman in June 1940. As a result an Arab Legion infantry company was sent to Palestine for airfield guard duties.

In the period immediately following Britain's declaration of war, life in Transjordan, and indeed in most of the Middle East, continued very much as in peacetime. This was the time of inaction on the home front in Britain which journalists called 'the phoney war' or 'the great bore war'. With the expectation of bombing raids and huge civilian casualties, a well-prepared civil defence programme had been put into operation, but after the first scares life drifted back to a semblance of normality. Rationing and travel restrictions caused a good deal of annoyance, as did shortages of food and essential materials, but as the war dragged on the people of Britain looked back on the irritations of the phoney war with much affection for, by then, they knew what real war entailed. Of course, throughout this period British forces were in action, notably at sea and in the air, and the country was on a war footing; nonetheless, in the autumn and winter of 1939, most people found it very difficult to take the war seriously.

The same held true in Transjordan. As tension increased in Europe during the summer, Glubb had recommended that air-raid precautions should be introduced in Amman, but his report, written in June 1939, met with an unenthusiastic reception. Although he conceded that there was little immediate likelihood of Transjordan being subjected to immediate aerial attack, he urged that some precautions be taken and based his argument on two main points. First, the presence of the RAF at Amman could provoke an enemy attack – at that time there was a fear that Germany might use air bases in Turkey to launch raids on British possessions in the Middle East. Second, the country's political and military relationship with Britain could make it a target. 'If the Arab countries are involved in war,' Glubb cautioned, 'they will inevitably think that this had taken place owing to their association with Great Britain.'[5]

Having experienced bombing from the air during his service in Iraq, Glubb was well aware that enemy air raids on Transjordan could cause much damage and panic and that in extreme circumstances it could destabilise the population. Eventually, a local air-raid precaution committee was set up and, although most people told Glubb that the enemy would not take the trouble to bomb Amman, he was able to arrange for five of his NCOs to be given ARP training by the RAF as a first step to introducing a civil-defence policy for the country. With Kirkbride's help, too, he ordered a first batch of respirators which were delivered shortly after war broke out.

This was a sensible initiative for, although all the evidence pointed to Transjordan remaining loyal to the British cause for the time being at least, Glubb knew that any setbacks or shortages or even a recrudescence of the revolt in Palestine could tax that allegiance. Evidence of rising prices and profiteering was already to hand: the price of tea, sugar and paraffin had 'advanced by leaps and bounds' and, with serious implications for the Arab Legion, there was a sudden shortage of fodder for the cavalry's horses, a panic measure which Glubb attributed to hoarding and wartime profiteering. Rumours also abounded, which seemed to Glubb to change daily, but in spite of the local difficulties, he was still able to pen a reasonably optimistic report for the first month of the war:

To the rural population of Trans-Jordan, Germany is too distant to provoke much interest or sympathy. Were the progress of the war to mean a marked deterioration in economic conditions in Trans-Jordan, the tribes and villages might become disaffected, but such a development does not seem to be immediately likely. On the contrary, a

237

rise in the price of agricultural produce may mean a temporary increase in prosperity.

Thus Trans-Jordan is internally contented but is susceptible to some extent to news of Arab movements outside. If the Palestine question became revivified, they would undoubtedly be affected. If Ibn Saud were really to turn hostile, they would be thrown into confusion. If a coup d'état in Baghdad were to bring a pro-German party into power, Trans-Jordan might be somewhat disturbed, but the effect would be less than that caused by disturbances from Palestine or Saudi Arabia.[6]

Although subsequent events in Iraq were to prove Glubb wrong – Transjordan was more than 'somewhat disturbed' by a later pro-German coup in its neighbour – his fears about Ibn Saud were not entirely groundless. From his intelligence agents Glubb had received evidence that the Saudi ruler was flirting with the idea of ending his country's neutrality and siding with Nazi Germany: were that to happen, argued Glubb, Abdullah might then be temped to take a similar course, for all that he continued to support the British cause in public.

Throughout 1938 and 1939 Glubb had kept a close eye on the activities of German agents in the Middle East and watched as they attempted to spread Nazi influence in Palestine, Iraq and Saudi Arabia. It was obviously fertile territory because the Arab revolt in Palestine was directed towards the ending of British rule and many of the Arabs were fighting the Jews, the Nazis' ideological enemy. However, the Middle East had never been properly exploited by the Nazis, partly because Hitler had little real interest in the area – his lingering admiration for the British Empire contributed much to a belief that the Middle East should not be destabilised – and partly because, before the war, he had been more interested in continuing the policy of enforced emigration of Jews from Germany to Palestine. Also, most of the countries of the Middle East were already aligned: Palestine and Transjordan

Jack Glubb's mother, Frances Letitia Bagot, a spirited lady full of Anglo-Irish wit and charm.

Jack Glubb's father, Major-General Frederic Manley Glubb, Royal Engineers. He was Chief Engineer of the Second British Army during the First World War.

A lifelong devotion to soldiering: Jack Glubb with sword and 'charger' – the family dog.

Dressed for the part with trooper's helmet and sword.

'I feel quite ashamed of going about dressed in European clothes.' Glubb wearing Bedouin dress shortly after his arrival in Iraq.

Glubb's Arab household. Ali al Yunis and Yusuf Effendi in Nasiriya, 1922.

Above: Desert warriors. Armed trucks of the Southern Desert Camel Corps, Iraq, 1927.

Centre: 'Life in the desert is continuous guerilla warfare.' Men of the Desert Camel police, Iraq, 1929.

Below: The sinews of war: securing an oasis, southern Iraq desert, 1929.

Men of the Arab Legion prepare for war against Iraq, 1941.

Camel patrol of the Arab Legion, 1941.

Ships of the desert. Arab Legion camel patrol at speed, Transjordan desert.

Guarding the Royal Air Force lines of communication in Iraq: a vital task for the Arab Legion's infantry companies.

A close friendship of true minds: Glubb playing chess with King Abdullah in Amman.

Arab Legion armoured cars, 1948.

'The King still maintained his usual high spirits.' King Abdullah enjoying a joke with Glubb, 1948.

King Hussein ibn Tallal of Jordan at the time of Glubb's dismissal, 1956.

Compensation for a lifetime's service to the British cause in the Middle East. Glubb outside Buckingham Palace after being knighted by Queen Elizabeth, 1956.

to Britain through the mandate, Egypt and Iraq to Britain through treaty, Syria to France and Yemen to Italy through sphere of influence.

That left Saudi Arabia as the only country lacking a commitment to the West and it was there that Germany concentrated her efforts in the months prior to the outbreak of war. In January 1939 diplomatic relations were established when a German mission was opened in Jeddah with the aim of obtaining Ibn Saud's support or at least the promise of neutrality in return for the provision of arms. Ibn Saud was much taken with the initiative and hoped that Germany would provide him with the small arms he needed for his internal security forces – in 1937 he had made a similar request but had been rebuffed by the German foreign office. His willingness to negotiate left the German representatives, Dr Fritz Grobba, with the impression that the Saudis were antagonistic towards the British and that there were diplomatic opportunities for the Germans to gain the king as a possible ally. Although the German foreign office was suspicious of Grobba's findings, he was permitted to continue negotiations and in July it was agreed to make a gift of 4,000 modern rifles. By then Hitler had turned Czechoslovakia into a protectorate and taken over the country's industries, thus breaking the terms of the Munich agreement. Chamberlain's futile attempts to protest only served to convince the German leader that Britain was not to be taken seriously in Europe and that there was no further need to placate her. It was the evidence of the German diplomatic initiative that led Glubb to report his fears to Kirkbride and to urge that London pay attention to his findings:

Ever since the visit of Ibn Saud's emissary to Herr Hitler some months ago, reports have been generally current in the northern Arab countries that Ibn Saud had abandoned his traditional friendship for Great Britain and had concluded an alliance with Germany and Italy. Politicians embroidered on this outline by stating that the condition of the Saudi-Nazi Alliance were that Ibn Saud should declare for Germany at the outbreak of war, and that, in the event of a German victory, he should be recognised as sole ruler of the Arabian peninsula from Anatolia to the Indian Ocean. So rash a political adventure was indeed entirely out of keeping with King Abdul Aziz's past political career, for many years characterised by patient caution, but these reports were nevertheless almost universally believed in north-western Arabia.[7]

While admitting that much of his intelligence came from bazaar rumours, and that he had received a confidential memo from a Saudi official confirming that his government was 'on the best of terms with His Majesty's Government', Glubb continued to be alarmed by the uncertainty of Ibn Saud's position. Later in the same report he repeated his fears and suggested that Ibn Saud was on the point of declaring for Hitler. Here he reinforced his argument by pointing to the fact that the Saudi king, alone in the Indian and Arabian world, had remained silent when Britain went to war. If he were truly on Britain's side, argued Glubb, then he should have made his position clear. Although a Saudi declaration in support of Germany would be of little practical use to Hitler's war effort, the threat of Ibn Saud's intervention in the Middle East would tie down much-needed British imperial forces in Palestine, Transjordan and Egypt. On the other hand, if Ibn Saud threw in his lot with Britain, his support would help to convince those Arabs who had not yet decided where their sympathies would lie during the war. 'Everything that can be done, even now, to incline Ibn Saud to make public statements in favour of Great Britain will have a beneficial effect on the morale of the other Arab countries.'[8] Under those circumstances, counselled Glubb, as much diplomatic pressure as possible should be aimed at Ibn Saud in order to get from him a statement of support for the British war effort.

Far from taking an active interest in Glubb's warnings, the

Colonial Office was much displeased by these sections of Glubb's monthly reports. A tetchy handwritten note on his September report pointed out that Ibn Saud was not even bound by treaty to Britain and that his position was entirely different from the other rulers mentioned by Glubb. Both Iraq and Egypt were in treaty with Britain; Abdullah was under Britain's mandate; and the Gulf state rulers and Indian princes were feudatories of the British Crown, whereas Ibn Saud was an independent sovereign and his country was not even a signatory to the League of Nations.

The main opponent of Glubb's point of view – and the writer of the note – was John Evelyn Shuckburgh* who had begun his career in the India Office. When he was appointed to head the Middle East Department in 1921 he had been recommended to Churchill as 'really first-rate – level headed, always cool, very accurate and unsparing of himself: his only fault perhaps a tendency to excessive caution'.[9] It was that leaning towards prudence that led him to attack Glubb's proposals and to ensure that they were never acted upon. A riposte was sent to both Kirkbride and MacMichael warning that there should be no political pressure on Ibn Saud to make him side with the Allies. Even if promises of support were extracted from him they would be worthless in Arab eyes as it would soon emerge that they had been gained by coercion.

Shuckburgh had a clear understanding of the dilemma facing Ibn Saud. While the Saudi king had flirted with Germany he did not want to offend Britain: so finely balanced was his position that neutrality was his best option, even though, as Shuckburgh observed, in view of the British troops based on the Arab world, it was a special kind of neutrality. So worried was Shuckburgh by Glubb's alarmist reports that he restricted their circulation lest the information

---

*His son Evelyn Shuckburgh was head of the Foreign Office's Middle East Department from 1954 to 1956.

reached the wrong hands. The whole file was then closed for fifty years and not opened until 1990.

The incident was not the end of Glubb's fears that German intelligence would attempt to subvert those Arab leaders who had remained loyal to Britain. Because Transjordan was still mandated to Britain Abdullah had automatically been included in Britain's declaration of war. Nonetheless, the emir, according to Glubb, still sent a message of loyal support to King George VI and promised to place his forces at the disposal of the British government. Given the level of support he received from Britain – and a natural liking for the British – such a move was to be expected, but, like Ibn Saud, Abdullah was not above hedging his bets and considering an alliance with Germany as an insurance policy should the Allies be defeated.

According to Kirkbride, who passed on the information to the Israeli scholar Uriel Dann, Abdullah sent an emissary to the German Embassy in Ankara during the summer of 1940 to enquire about the possibility of German support in the event of Britain falling. Nothing came of the initiative because the Germans considered that Abdullah was only a British stooge. However, Kirkbride reasoned that the Germans would target Abdullah's son Talal if they followed up their victory in France with an invasion of England – this was considered a distinct possibility in the summer of 1940.

There is no written evidence to support Kirkbride's story – which he related privately to Dann shortly before his death in 1978[10] – but it was known that Abdullah's loyalty to Britain did waver in the early stages of the war. A 'most secret' report, written by Kirkbride in July 1942, reveals that on four occasions Abdullah's constancy had been called into question – at the outbreak of war, after the fall of France in 1940, and twice in 1941, on the entry of Japan into the war in December and when the Free French occupied Syria, which took place a few months earlier. Because Abdullah had retained hopes of becoming king of a Greater Syria – which would include Transjordan and Arab Palestine – this last blow was particularly hard, as Kirkbride reported to the Colonial Office:

> The Amir resented not being told of the British plans beforehand but his vexation on this point was negligible when compared with his feeling on seeing Syria occupied and handed over to the Free French. This dashing of his hopes gave birth to the first serious doubts as to the intention of His Majesty's Government to assist him to attain his ambitions; these doubts were increased further, firstly, by the successive failures of his attempts to intrigue in Syria, failures which he attributed largely to British action although, in point of fact, his own unpopularity was mainly responsible and secondly, by the rebuffs which he received to more official attempts to dabble in the affairs of Syria and Palestine or to extract some undertaking about the future of Trans-Jordan.[11]

Although Abdullah's confidence was restored by Hitler's decision to attack the Soviet Union in June 1941 and by the entry of the USA into the war in December of that year, he continued to believe that the upheavals in the Middle East would weaken British authority and that he himself might be abandoned. 'The difference between yourselves and ourselves is that you are fighting and we are not,' he told MacMichael in 1942, 'that you know everything and we do not.'[12] Even if the emir did not contact the Axis powers, warned Mac-Michael, such was his mood that he could 'come to the conclusion that a policy of obstructiveness would pay better than continuation of helpfulness and be more easily justified in retrospect'.[13] The report caused some alarm in Colonial Office circles, not because anyone thought that Abdullah would be taken seriously by the Germans, but because his pessimism came at a time when Britain was looking for unreserved support in the Middle East and elsewhere. Shuckburgh was minded to play down the warnings given by Kirkbride and MacMichael, but it was decided to allay

Abdullah's fears by offering more arms and equipment to the Arab Legion and to increase Glubb's own authority.

This fitted in with Glubb's thinking as he had come to believe that Britain should radically reorganise its system of imperial defence for the war against Germany and Japan and that the Arab Legion, along with other smaller forces, should be asked to play a more prominent role in the fighting. Now that he had become commanding officer of the force, his monthly reports had turned to the possibility of giving greater employment to native troops in the Middle East, thus freeing the regular army for service in other theatres:

> We are told, and doubtless correctly, that one of the most formidable handicaps imposed on the British Army is the necessity to train simultaneously for a first-class war in Europe, and also for possible guerrilla operations in Palestine or on the North-West Frontier. Moreover, as war becomes more technical and specialised the difference between guerrilla and European warfare will become more marked, and make this problem increasingly difficult. The scientific progress of war in Europe, moreover, necessitates a quantity of technical equipment, which is not only useless but positively in the way when the task imposed is the pursuit of barefooted bandits under an Eastern sun. All these complications would be avoided were it possible to maintain a colonial army for the colonies, without using the British Army for that purpose.[14]

There was no reason, Glubb argued, why the Transjordan Frontier Force or the Arab Legion should not be based on the Suez Canal or at Mersa Matruh, the main British defensive position in the Western Desert. Similarly, the regiments of the Sudan Army could be garrisoned in Palestine for the good reason that 'martial law loses half its effect if the soldiers themselves, like the police, are locally recruited'. Glubb also recommended that thought should be given to developing a new type of military formation in addition to her regular, territorial and colonial forces. This would be small, self-contained, highly motivated and trained in irregular warfare for low-intensity operations against guerrillas and terrorists. Although he did not have time to pursue the idea, the forces he had in mind were similar to the wartime Long Range Desert Group and to the later Special Air Service Regiment (SAS).

All these different reasons – the force of Glubb's own ambitions, the need to defend Transjordan's borders and the pace of war itself – played their part in determining the expansion of the Arab Legion, but the deciding factor was wartime necessity. To achieve what Glubb wanted, the Legion had to prove itself operationally alongside the British Army.

The opportunity to do so came in Iraq in May 1941.

At the beginning of the war, Glubb, like others in the Middle East, had believed that Iraq would remain loyal. Attempts had been made by the Nazis to gain influence in the country but, when war was declared, diplomatic relations with Germany were severed and Britain was allowed to retain the two large air bases, at Shaibah near Basra, and at Habaniya on the Euphrates. Both were vital staging posts on the air route to India and both housed RAF flying schools for aircrew training. Britain's treaty with Iraq also allowed her forces the right of access through the country and Iraq's railways, ports and airfields could be put at her disposal should they be required. Despite the arrival in Baghdad of the Grand Mufti, a long-time opponent, the British government still had reason to believe that they had nothing to fear. Both the prime minister, Nuri es-Said, and the regent, the Emir Abdul Illah, were solidly pro-British and had control of the four-year-old king, Feisal II.

However, in March 1940 Rashid Ali el-Gailani was elected prime minister and, supported by the Mufti and sections of the army, he took a pro-Axis line. When Italy entered the war three months later he refused to expel the Italian Legation from Baghdad and the capital soon became a centre of Axis intrigue aimed at promoting anti-British agitation throughout the Middle East. At the same time this cause was given a boost when Syria fell into Vichy French hands and German agents moved into the area. It was a difficult period for Britain, by then standing alone with her Dominion allies, and little diplomatic effort was made to retrieve the situation in Baghdad where Rashid Ali was becoming increasingly troublesome to British interests. Pre-echoing the demands made by a later Iraqi leader, Saddam Hussein,* he said that the price of his country's co-operation would be a just solution to the problems faced by the Arab population in Palestine. The threat was not taken seriously and it was only at the beginning of 1941 that steps were taken, including the appointment of the experienced Sir Kinahan Cornwallis as ambassador in Baghdad. He immediately set about bolstering the confidence of the regent and Nuri es-Said but it was an uphill task because the British government was unwilling to reinforce the garrison in Iraq. The military operations against Italian forces in British Somaliland, Greece and Libya in the winter of 1940–41 had also helped to place Iraq further down the list of British priorities. Another factor was the failure of the eastern department of the Foreign Office to act on information from MI6 that the crisis in Iraq was worsening.

On 3 April 1941 the storm broke when a military coup d'état brought to power four senior army and air force officers known as the 'Golden Square'. Rashid Ali quickly did a deal with them by which he became titular head of state. The regent, Prince Ghazi, and Nuri were forced to flee to Basra where they took refuge on board the elderly British gunboat HMS *Cockchafer*; they were later taken to safety in Palestine. Suddenly, Britain's strategic interests in Iraq had been put at

---

*After invading Kuwait in August 1990 Saddam Hussein insisted, amongst other conditions, that his forces would withdraw if the United Nations recognised the 'linkage' between his action and Israel's occupation of the Palestinian territories.

risk by a new administration which was openly hostile to them. This time, though, Britain decided to act. Although over-stretched militarily by the operations in the Mediterranean theatre, the Chiefs of Staff recommended immediate intervention and it was agreed to despatch a joint British and Indian Army infantry brigade group to Basra and to reinforce the Shaibah airfield with Wellington bombers from Egypt. At the same time the Royal Navy strengthened its presence in the Gulf with the cruiser HMS *Emerald* and the aircraft carrier HMS *Hermes*. Within a fortnight of the seizure of power, the first British troops of the 1st King's Own Royal Regiment began arriving in Shaibah. They were flown in from Karachi in aging biplane Valentia transports operated by 31 Squadron RAF which had been operating previously on the North-West Frontier.

Glubb was drawn into the planning of the Iraq operations from the very outset. With his experience of the southern Iraqi desert and his knowledge of the tribes who lived there, it had been decided that he should be responsible for organising and establishing an underground resistance movement which would threaten Rashid Ali's government from within Iraq:

> Previous to the occurrence of this open breach, a scheme had been considered in Trans-Jordan, under which a base should be established at H4 [a desert pumping station on the Iraq Petroleum Pipeline], from which subversive activities directed against the Baghdad authorities could be carried out along the whole length of the Euphrates.

> When the open breach occurred between His Majesty's Government and Rashid Ali's administration, it was decided to set these activities in motion, and Major Glubb proceeded to H4 to organise the movement. It was believed at the time that no troops would be available, and that it would be impossible to invade Iraq from Trans-Jordan. Activities were, therefore, to be limited to the despatch of agents and agitators in cars from H4 with a view to their being dropped all along the line of the Euphrates, from the Syrian frontier

to Basra. These agents were to be provided with money and letters, and were to endeavour to raise the tribes in support of His Highness and against the usurping Baghdad administration.[15]

The operations would be conducted by Glubb from the H4 pumping station on the IPC oil pipeline and would be carried out by a small number of Bedouin tribesmen drawn from the Arab Legion. Their task was similar to those carried out later in the war by the Special Operations Executive (SOE) – to make contact with groups still loyal to the Hashemite Royal Family and to organise them into an armed resistance. As the situation worsened, though, General Wavell, Commander-in-Chief Middle East, realised that he would also need all the troops that he could get, including the Arab troops of the Transjordan Frontier Force and the Arab Legion. Glubb was immediately recalled to Jerusalem to discuss the situation with the new GOC, General Sir Henry Maitland Wilson ('Jumbo').

'Will the Arab Legion fight?' asked Jumbo, to which Glubb replied, 'The Arab Legion will fight anybody.'[16] This was a bold statement since Glubb was by no means certain that his men would take up arms against their brother Arabs and co-religionists in Iraq. The situation was also complicated by the fact that Glubb was ordered to retain his status as 'political officer' and would, therefore, not come under British military command. As Glubb himself explained later to Somerset de Chair, a Life Guards officer serving in Palestine, a compromise was reached when it was agreed that the Arab Legion should accompany him as a bodyguard:

I was originally to go alone, but I asked permission to take some men of the Arab Legion as a personal escort. This task had originally no connection with the military operations; and I very nearly set off for Iraq alone. When, however, it was proposed to send a military column across the desert, it was decided that we might as well go

248

together, just for company, but I still had no connection with the column. As soon as we reached Habbaniyah I was to start on my job.[17]

Wilson was well aware of the significance of Glubb's role for British political intelligence and he wanted to avoid a clash between him and the senior British officers. Although Glubb enjoyed the local rank of lieutenant-colonel, as El Feriq, or commander of the Arab Legion, in British eyes he was still a civilian, or, at best, a retired captain of the Royal Engineers.

By the time those discussions had taken place in Jerusalem, hostilities had already broken out on 2 May at Habbaniyah where the RAF base had been surrounded by a brigade-sized force of the Iraqi Army. Although the RAF only had a motley collection of obsolete or obsolescent aircraft,* they had taken the initiative and started bombing the Iraqi positions. The British Chiefs of Staff then decided that the prime objective was to continue attacking the Iraqis in an attempt to discredit Rashid Ali and his regime before the Axis powers could intervene from air bases in Syria. Because Wavell did not want to risk the recently arrived Indian Army forces until a bridgehead at Basra and lines of communication had been established, it was decided to relieve and reinforce Habbaniyah by sending a mechanised column across the desert from Transjordan. Part of this force would be the Desert Mechanised Regiment of the Arab Legion which had already assembled at H4. It consisted of four armoured cars, four Chevrolet lorries, twelve pickups armed with Hotchkiss guns, while the men were equipped with rifles and First World War vintage Lewis and Vickers guns. Yet, as Glubb shrewdly guessed, it was ideally suited to a scouting role in the desert.

---

*Thirty-two Audaxes, eight Gordons, twenty-nine Oxfords, three Gladiators, one Blenheim and five Harts: seventy-eight aircraft in all. These were reinforced on 19 April by six Gladiators and one Wellington.

The formation sent to Habbaniyah was known as Habforce, and it was raised as a mechanised brigade of the 1st British Cavalry Division under the command of Major-General J. G. W. Clark. Although it contained three cavalry regiments (one regular, two yeomanry), a mechanised infantry battalion, a field-artillery battery and three squadrons of the Transjordan Frontier Force, it was woefully short of anti-tank and anti-aircraft weapons. Wavell thought it would be too little and too late to be of use, but the news of the successful RAF bombing campaign encouraged the Chiefs of Staff to begin the land battle against the Iraqi positions.

The need to reach Habbaniyah quickly was desperately important if the British position were to be consolidated and to do this a flying column of 2,000 men and 500 vehicles was formed under the command of Brigadier J.J.Kingstone, of the Queen's Bays. Drawn from Habforce and known as 'Kingcol', its composition was:

Household Cavalry Regiment (Life Guards and Royal Horse Guards).
237th Field Battery and one anti-tank troop, Royal Artillery.
2nd Field Squadron, Royal Engineers.
2 rifle companies, 1st Essex Regiment.
166th Field Ambulance, Royal Army Medical Corps (detachment).
552nd Motor Transport Company, Royal Army Service Corps.
No.2 Armoured Car Company, Royal Air Force.
Desert Mechanised Regiment, Arab Legion.

Because of the difficulties involved in assembling the force in Palestine it would not be ready to move into Iraq until 12 May, a week after Glubb's Arab Legion detachment had proceeded to the H3 pumping station. There it dumped its heavy equipment and proceeded ninety miles into Iraqi territory to reconnoitre the strategically important desert fort at Rutbah. This was the point where the pipeline road stopped being of any use to Kingcol – it swung eastwards – and the fort also protected a landing strip and the last wells before the desert crossing to Habbaniyah. Its capture was vital and the task was given to the Arab Legion and to 'A' Squadron of the Transjordan Frontier Force. The plan was to surround the fort while four Blenheim bombers of 203 Squadron RAF attacked it from the air – the fort at Rutbah was garrisoned by around a hundred men of the Desert Police, the same force which Glubb had raised from the Iraqi tribes in the 1920s and it was believed that they would not be able to withstand the effects of modern aerial bombardment.

It was at this early stage in the campaign that things started to go awry. On 8 May the men of the Transjordan Frontier Force mutinied and refused to cross the border into Iraq to fight against fellow Arabs: they were quickly withdrawn and sent back to H4 to be replaced by the RAF's armoured cars under the command of Squadron Leader Cassano, always 'the imperturbable Cassano' to Glubb. Early next morning the Blenheims arrived to bomb the fort and, to begin with, it seemed the attack would prove successful:

> ... after an hour and a half, one of the aircraft dropped a message to the effect that the fort was showing a white flag. The Arab Legion detachment approached, but as no sign of a white flag could be seen, the column halted. The fort then opened up with a Vickers gun, and one man of the Arab Legion was slightly wounded. On two subsequent occasions, the Arab Legion engaged the fort with machine-gun fire, the latter replying briskly.
>
> The bombing was less successful than had been hoped, although carried out from so low an altitude that several machines were hit by rifle and machine-gun fire from the fort.[18]

As the siege entered its second day, Glubb sent a message to the garrison telling them that they had done their duty and that they could surrender without losing honour or dignity.

This was not accepted by the Iraqi commander who knew that a relief force, equipped with armed trucks, was on its way and would reach Rutbah that night. Realising that his force would be outnumbered and out-gunned, Glubb slipped back to H3 to call up the RAF armoured car company. Happily, they were able to intercept the Iraqi column which withdrew after a short sharp engagement, leaving the garrison at Rutbah to its fate. A further period of bombing completed the task and the garrison surrendered to Glubb on the morning of 11 May. The following day the main Kingcol force arrived at Rutbah and final preparations were made to begin the thrust over the desert to Habbaniyah.

During the bombing raids on the fort one of the Blenheims was shot down as it made its way back to Shaibah and in the confusion the Iraqis believed that Glubb had been killed. The news was even reported on Baghdad radio and picked up by Berlin. As a result, on 20 May, the BBC announced that 'Major' Glubb had been killed on the Iraqi desert and several papers published brief obituaries. A recurring theme in all of these was the idea that Glubb had followed in Lawrence's footsteps and that he was similarly engaged on top-secret work with the Bedouin tribes. One notice, published in the *Scotsman*, was equally wide of the mark: it referred to Glubb as 'Aby el Hanek' meaning 'he of the strong jaw' (sic) and claimed that he was the founder of the Transjordan Frontier Force. The following day, 21 May, it was announced that Glubb was, after all, still alive. Fortunately, by the time the reports reached Rosemary Glubb in Amman she knew them to be untrue.

Although Glubb understood that his orders were to accompany Kingcol into Iraq where its role was 'to be independent of the army and was to consist in raising revolt in tribal areas against the Rashi Ali administration', this had not been made clear to Brigadier Kingstone. Like most regular army officers he was deeply suspicious of anything that smacked of private armies or guerrilla warfare, and in this case he was also put on the defensive by the comparisons which had been made between Glubb and Lawrence of Arabia.

Kingstone, an officer of the old school, had served with the 9th (Queen's Royal) Lancers during the First World War and had then gone on to peacetime soldiering with the yeomanry. Prior to serving in the Middle East with the 1st Cavalry Division, he had been commandant of the Army School of Equitation at Weedon in the last years of horsed cavalry and, as a result, had missed out on the opportunity to study mechanised warfare. Tall, red-faced and angular, he could be both terrifying and charming, depending on his mood: Kingstone was a good soldier but, in the desert commanding a mechanised column, he was forced to improvise. Under his command he had Household Cavalry officers who had only recently exchanged their horses for vehicles and they seemed to speak the same language. Unfortunately, he was not so certain about Glubb, and his inability to trust him and his Arab soldiers almost put the entire expedition in jeopardy.

When the two men met at Rutbah and sized each other up, Kingstone's intelligence officer, Somerset de Chair, said that they were 'like a couple of prima donnas billed to perform in the same opera, who met behind the scenes for the first time, and were eyeing each other with some misgivings'.[19] Because Glubb was wearing the insignia and uniform of the Arab Legion, Kingstone was under the mistaken impression that he was senior in rank and was also irked by the fact that Glubb had smiled and said very little. 'This fellow thinks he is the king of Saudi Arabia,' he told de Chair. 'I am going to get him out of the way as soon as we leave here.' To do this, Kingstone suggested that the Arab Legion should be employed in reconnaissance duties away from the column: had he ordered them to scout ahead it would have saved a good deal of time and trouble.

In the summer months, the Iraqi desert is a hot and shimmering place with temperatures reaching 120° Fahrenheit. On the first day out of Rutbah, 13 May, the force had made little progress, and a by now short-tempered Kingstone told the Arab Legion that they would be best employed to the north, an order which Glubb recognised was meant to keep them out of the way while Kingcol enjoyed the honour of relieving Habbaniyah. It was a bad move. Without the assistance of Glubb's men, the column's transport, especially its three-ton lorries, got stuck in the sand and had to be dug out repeatedly – no easy task given the high temperatures. One of the problems facing the British troops was their reliance on compass bearings: instead of taking the best available routes, avoiding sand-hills and soft sand, they had pushed on regardless, with the result that their heavy lorries had become stuck in sand drifts. With his water supplies running low, Kingstone feared that he would have to return to Rutbah, a prediction which Glubb thought ridiculous – his men were, after all, used to operating in desert conditions. At the evening conference he spoke up and offered the services of his Arab Legion soldiers as guides to the column.

This time Kingstone saw sense and the following day the Arab Legion reconnoitered and found a new route which would involve a detour over hard, gravelly sand suitable for the heavy lorries. Kingcol was then divided into sections, each led by Arab Legion guides and by 18 May the entire column had entered Habbaniyah. The operation was not accomplished without loss, however. Before setting off, the rear guard, composed mainly of Household Cavalry, was attacked by three Messerschmitt 110s. More knowledgeable about modern warfare, the British troopers jumped into slit trenches, but two Arab soldiers – Mutr Fuqaan and Mibrad Mohamad – refused to leave their Lewis gun. Although hopelessly out-gunned, they continued firing at the low-flying enemy aircraft until they were themselves hit. Mutr Fuqaan was killed and his number two gunner was badly injured in the face but, as Glubb noted in his report, 'this gallant performance did much to remove the painful impression of the TJFF mutiny'.[20] No doubt, too, the men's bravery raised the prestige of the Arab Legion in the eyes of the accompanying British soldiers. When de Chair came to describe the incident in his account of the campaign, he belittled the attempts of the Arab Legion machine-gunners to bring down the German planes and suggested that they were ignorant of modern warfare. That observation, and his suggestion that the Bedouin soldiers stank, brought a sharp rebuke from Glubb which de Chair was pleased to publish in the book's second edition:

> In brief, during the six weeks before the fall of Baghdad, every Arab was convinced that we were done for. Every Arab force previously organised by us mutinied and refused to fight for us, or faded away in desertions. These men of the Arab Legion alone not only stood by us, but played a most active, energetic and valuable part in our little campaign.[21]

Glubb had good reason to be proud of his men because they also played a useful role as scouts for the next phase of the operation – the advance on Baghdad to oust Rashid Ali's regime. With the the arrival of General Clark at Habbaniyah on 18 May, Glubb was also drawn more closely into the planning of the operation – Kingstone, too, had been much impressed by the performance of the Arab Legion during the advance into Habbaniyah and as de Chair noted, the two men had become 'firm friends'.

Before Habforce could begin the advance to Baghdad, an obvious preliminary move was the capture of the bridge over the Euphrates at Fallujah. While the force's artillery and infantry formations surrounded the town to prevent Iraqi troops from counter-attacking, the RAF bombed it on 19 May and by late afternoon the Iraqis had begun surrendering. Over 300 prisoners were taken and the road from the west to Baghdad lay open. Clarke then decided that his force should be split up: the bulk of the mechanised infantry and artillery under Kingstone's command would advance along the main road into Baghdad while a smaller column, composed of the Life Guards and the Arab Legion, would swing to the north and attack

Baghdad along the main railway line from Mosul. This force was commanded by Lieutenant-Colonel A.H. Fergusson, Household Cavalry.

In the week preceding the advance, Glubb was able to plan and put into action the clandestine operations which were the main reason for his presence in Iraq. His first objective was to make contact with the tribal leaders known to be loyal to the Iraqi royal family and, having secured their allegiance, to supply them with money, arms and plans for a general uprising. Glubb favoured the classic guerrilla tactics of keeping the leaders in separate 'cells', both to maintain security and to keep the different tribes apart. From past experience he knew the strength of inter-tribal jealousies and he realised the importance of ensuring that each leader thought this particular tribe had been allotted the most important task.

Two areas of operation suggested themselves to Glubb – the Middle and Lower Euphrates between Habbaniyah and Basra which ke knew well, and the area known as the Jezira between the Euphrates and the Tigris from Fallujah to Mosul. After discussing the alternatives with Clark, it was decided that the Arab Legion should concentrate its activities on the latter region, the Jezirah, because it carried the routes north to Mosul where the Germans were rapidly establishing an air base. Glubb was also ordered to cut the main Baghdad–Mosul railway line and to 'establish moral ascendancy in the area' by attacking Iraqi troop positions and other strategic targets, thereby impressing on the local population the offensive spirit of the invading army.

On 23 May Glubb's forces, accompanied by a detachment of Royal Engineers and two RAF armoured cars, were ferried over the Euphrates at Habbaniyah to begin a series of raids in the desert area between the two great rivers. In the following three days they successfully cut the Mosul railway line at Istabulet and then again north of Samarra: during this second raid they also routed an Iraqi army patrol and took several prisoners who provided the first evidence that the army was not completely loyal to Rashid Ali. Captured personnel usually provide intelligence about the opposition's morale, and this was no exception:

> All were exceedingly polite and amicable, and not one of them exhibited any signs of resentment or hostility. The majority alleged that they had been sent into battle against their will, without any knowledge of the situation. While, of course, allowance must be made for the fact that these men were prisoners, possibly hoping to obtain lenient treatment if they curried favour with us, it is still remarkable that not one of them exhibited any feeling whatever, particularly as the whole coup d'état was believed to be a military revolt. The majority of the prisoners asked to be allowed to re-enlist to serve His Highness, the Regent.[22]

This information gave much-needed encouragement to the British forces, but Clark was worried that the advance on Baghdad might still be held up by the resistance of the Iraqi Army which was thought to be three divisions strong, and by the difficulty of crossing the canals and waterways which criss-crossed the alluvial plain between the Euphrates and the Tigris. He was also concerned about the growing strength of the German air attacks which were being made by Messerschmitt 110 and Focke-Wulf ground-attack aircraft. This was Wavell's fear too: before the column left Transjordan he had warned that its lack of anti-aircraft guns could leave it exposed to German air attack.

However, the speed and determination of the British advance from the west and north sowed considerable confusion in Iraqi ranks and by 30 May both columns were in striking distance of Baghdad. The northern column had reached the holy city of Kadhimain, four miles from the capital, where they had been forced to halt because it contained shrines sacred to the Shi'ites, thus making artillery bombardment impossible. During this phase of the operations Glubb's Arab Legion forces had distinguished themselves by capturing the fortified railway station at Meshahida and successfully disrupting Iraqi attempts to bring reinforcements by rail from the north.

Meanwhile, Kingstone's forces had arrived at the Washash Canal to the west of Baghdad but, as Glubb noted, 'both columns were now at a standstill, surprise had been forfeited and the first momentum lost'.[23] It was indeed a precarious position. The British forces were faced by a numerically superior garrison which was expected to put up stout resistance in the suburbs of Baghdad. There was no question of bombing the Iraqi capital, as the raid on Fallujah had already caused disquiet due to the civilian casualties and, in any case, the RAF had withdrawn its Wellingtons to Egypt, for they were needed to bomb Benghazi. Moreover, Clark's force was now over-stretched and depended on supply and re-supply over a long line of communications which were vulnerable to attack from the air.

At this point Glubb's guerrilla operations to the north began to bear fruit: the raids on the railway lines had convinced the Iraqi leadership that a powerful British force was arrayed against them in the north. This was made clear when Glubb took prisoner Jellal Beg Khalid, the Mutassarif, or governor, of Baghdad: he confirmed that while the attack from Fallujah had been expected, the northern advance had come as a complete surprise. With the arrival of the 10th Indian Army Division at Basra, Rashid Ali and his cohorts had suddenly realised they stood in danger of encirclement. The only way of escape was the road eastwards into Persia and during the night of 28/29 May they had decided to take it. On the evening of 30 May a much-relieved Cornwallis was able to call up Kingstone on the embassy radio and arrange for a truce. The campaign was over. The new RAF commander, Air Vice-Marshal J.H. D'Albiac, immediately christened it the 'Thirty Days War' and was relieved to note that it had cost the British and their Arab allies few casualties – thirty-four killed and sixty-four wounded. All that remained was to enter Baghdad – where the British expatriate population had taken shelter in the embassy grounds – and to conclude a ceasefire with the Iraqi armed forces. As Glubb wrote:

> The writer accompanied Air Vice-Marshal D'Albiac and Major-General Clark, who left Habbaniyah at mid-night for the southern Column. At 4 a.m. of May 31st, the party passed through the British front line in the grey dawn, and at a point in No Man's Land, met a car containing two Iraqi officers, bearing a bath towel on a pole. A car was meanwhile sent in to fetch Sir Kinahan Cornwallis from Baghdad.
>
> The Iraqis had cut all the canal banks in the vicinity and water was lapping the road in the grey dawn. With water birds flapping overhead, the scene was more suggestive of the Norfolk broads than the city of the Caliphs.
>
> The armistice terms were drafted on the back of a telegram form, sitting in the General's car, and were carried back to Baghdad by the British Ambassador. The A.O.C. and the G.O.C. returned to Cavalry Brigade Headquarters for breakfast, and the campaign was at an end.[24]

With the return of the Regent and the re-establishment of a pro-British government, the British were not inclined to impose punitive terms. The ceasefire required British prisoners-of-war to be returned, Italian and German servicemen to be interned and Ramadi was to be vacated by its military garrison. Although the Chiefs of Staff in London felt that an additional clause should be inserted to allow for the establishment of garrisons at strategic points, Cornwallis, backed up by Glubb, counselled otherwise. Far better, they argued, to return to the status quo ante bellum, and vigorously uphold the terms of the 1930 treaty. Prince Abdul Illah had already made it clear that Iraq would have no objection to Britain maintaining a sizeable force in Mosul for the remainder of the war.

In the context of the global war that was being waged in

May 1941, the Iraq campaign was little more than a footnote. Indeed, it seemed to belong to another age: with his hastily improvised flying column and assorted British and native troops, Kingstone could have been Roberts on his way to relieve Kandahar almost a century earlier. Other Victorian images intruded – the garrison at Habbaniyah included women and children, as did the British Embassy compound in Baghdad, the odds against success were stacked against the relieving force and Rashid Ali's administration played the 'wicked rebels' who had risen to put the British in danger. There was also something amateurish – and therefore satisfyingly British – about the Household Cavalry and yeomanry troopers – only recently mounted on chargers – who rode into battle on lorries of questionable vintage armed with rifles and machine-guns from another age. Even 'Glubb's Girls', with their plaited hair and flowing robes, added a picturesque touch to a scene which already belonged to the history books.

And yet, to see the campaign merely in that light would do it a disservice. For the British, May 1941 was one of the worst months of a hard war, one in which everything seemed to go wrong at the same time, on land, at sea and in the air. In North Africa Rommel was preparing to advance eastwards towards Egypt and the Suez Canal, Malta was under continuous air attack, Crete was to be evacuated at the end of the month, and in the Atlantic German U-boats were sinking Allied shipping at will. 'I feel we are fighting for life, and survive from day to day and hour to hour,' said Winston Churchill in the House of Commons on 7 May. 'But believe me, Herr Hitler has his problems too.'

One of these was undoubtedly the failure of the Axis-supported revolt in Iraq. Had the Germans managed to win Iraq over to their side, Britain would have lost vital oil supplies and its whole position in the Middle East could have been threatened. Transjordan and Palestine would have been open to invasion, as would Persia, and with Rommel gaining ground in North Africa, the British forces would have had to fight on several fronts to protect the Suez Canal.

There were several reasons for the British success – which provided a much-needed fillip to morale when things were going so wrong elsewhere. First and foremost, the Chiefs of Staff insisted on a resolute response to the Iraqi uprising and overruled the wishes of Wavell who opposed military intervention. Here, they were helped greatly by the interception of a telegram from the Japanese Ambassador in Baghdad on 12 May which suggested that the Iraqi forces could not hold out without German support. This was followed a day later by fresh decrypts which revealed that German aircraft with Iraqi markings had entered Syria to support Rashid Ali's forces.

The intelligence encouraged Churchill to insist that the ground forces should advance immediately on Baghdad once Habbaniyah had been relieved. Without the promised air cover from Syria the Iraqi Army quickly lost heart when faced by British aerial and artillery bombardment and failed to put up any sustained resistance. Although German and Italian aircraft were able to fly a number of sorties, the absence of integrated tactics weakened their contribution. Despite a lack of anti-aircraft guns, too, the British forces still managed to account for nineteen German and three Italian aircraft during the court of the campaign.

In the following month the victory in Iraq was put into perspective when Hitler began his attack on the Soviet Union. Not only had the Germans been prevented from establishing a vital stronghold in the Middle East but Iraq became an important supply route for the Allies into the southern Soviet Union. 'We had no idea then that a few weeks later Germany would attack Russia,' admitted Glubb, 'and that streams of munitions and supplies would pour along the Haifa–Baghdad road and up the Persian Gulf to Basra to our hard-pressed ally.'[25] The next step was to remove the Germans from Vichy-controlled Syria where they had a more determined presence and were backed up by pro-German French forces.

Glubb remained exceptionally fond of Iraq. It was there

that he had won his spurs as a desert soldier and he felt a good deal of warmth towards the people who, he believed, had been duped by Rashid Ali and his gang. This was not just a middle-aged soldier waxing sentimental about his youthful exploits. Glubb genuinely believed that Britain had been wrong to impose a western constitution which had been all too easily hijacked by self-seeking politicians. This idea formed the basis of a lengthy report which he wrote for the Colonial Office after the campaigns in Iraq and Syria:

> Thus, a small group of politicians were able to monopolise office for the better part of fifteen years. Every cabinet contained the same old crowd who just changed round their chairs at each change of government. In this process they all became very rich, and most of them became owners of great landed estates, at the expense of the fella-heen and the small farmer, who from being small independent landholders, became agricultural labourers of the big politicians. The latter had, meanwhile, borrowed the jargon of democracy from England and America, and they also controlled the press and the radio. Thus, to the uninitiated observer, Iraq gave the impression of a model little democracy in action. In reality, a gang of political hacks were grinding out the same old tunes on the democratic barrel organ, while the men in the street, indifferent if not rather aggravated, by the discordant uproar, were occupied solely in making their livelihoods.[26]

The constitution had allowed Rashid Ali to seize power under the guise of a national democracy rightly struggling to be free and to present the British as imperialist interventionists. Publicity and propaganda, 'with a complete vocabulary borrowed from British democracy', had done the rest. In Glubb's view it would be better to introduce a constitution which reduced the power of the main cities and strengthened it in the country areas where 'the ordinary cultivators and tribesmen live on terms of social equality with their sheikhs and leaders'. Although he was unable, or unwilling, to develop this idea further, Glubb seems to have been in favour of a devolved federal system of government which would remain tied to the royal family, British-supported, of course.

While these were hardly original ideas and were based on Glubb's stated preference for the countrymen and the villagers, the paper did contain a number of astute observations about the Iraqi people and their relationship to the military ethos. Far from being loyal supporters of Rashid Ali, most people to whom Glubb spoke voiced their opposition to military adventures and cared little about the possibility of German support. Their greatest concern was to maintain the standard of living which they had enjoyed before the war and they were opposed to conscription which had been introduced a few years earlier. The dissenting voices came from the people of Fallujah who had suffered from the British bombing raids and from the Shi'ite people of Kadhimain who resented the appearance of infidel soldiers near their holy places. Glubb's old friends the Dulaim were also disenchanted, but that was because they hated the Assyrian Levies who had served with the British forces at Habbaniyah.

Another interesting discovery was that the Iraqi regular army, although superior in numbers, did not fight well; while the all-volunteer para-military police force put up more determined opposition. During the 1930s conscription had been a major political issue with Iraqi leaders demanding the creation of a large conscript army to keep the country strong. This had always been vetoed by the British military advisers in Baghdad who preferred the establishment of small volunteer professional forces. Having judged the performance of the police during the campaign, Glubb, writing a year later in 1943, feared that a small regular army, divorced from civilian life, could be used by the politicians for their own ends:

Thus Iraq will never be safe and stable, while she has an army, until a real public opinion develops sufficiently strong to convince unscrupulous politicians that any of them who use the army to seize power will be politically outlawed. Such a public opinion, should it ever develop, will certainly take many generations to form.[27]

Those words have an uncomfortable ring fifty years later. In 1979 a Ba'ath Party activist, Saddam Hussein, seized power in Iraq and used the army to consolidate an increasingly authoritarian rule. For eight years, between 1980 and 1988, Iraq pursued an increasingly fruitless war against Iran which ended in stalemate and huge casualties on both sides. During this period Iraq received considerable financial and military support from the West because most governments, particularly the United States, thought that Saddam Hussein was more likely to provide sympathetic stability than the clerics of the Shi'ite-controlled and fundamentalist Islamic state of Iran. This led the Iraqi leader to believe that the West would condone an invasion and occupation of Kuwait – a long-held Iraqi ambition – and on 2 August 1990 his army rolled into the oil-rich state. Shortly afterwards, it was declared the Nineteenth Province of Iraq, a redrawing of the boundaries which Percy Cox had fixed in 1922.

The world community reacted swiftly to the events but despite the imposition of United Nations sanctions and the steady build-up in Saudi Arabia of coalition forces led by the United States, Saddam Hussain refused to back down and withdraw from Kuwait. Inevitably, hostilities broke out and in a short and sharp land and air battle in January and February 1991 his forces were overstretched and defeated. During the fighting several Iraqi towns and cities were attacked by coalition aircraft and missiles and, as happened in 1941, there were civilian casualties at Fallujah.

Although the Gulf War was fought on a larger scale and with more modern military weapons, there are comparisons with the British Iraqi campaign of 1941. In both conflicts a ruthless dictator had taken his country into an unwanted war in which there were substantial Iraqi casualties; the Iraqi armed forces consisted mainly of untried conscripts who could not offer much resistance and superior air power in both wars proved to be decisive. And just as Glubb's Arab Legion forces were engaged in clandestine warfare north of the main British thrust, so too did American and British special forces play a significant role in the Gulf War by operating deep inside Iraqi territory.

After the war, too, a punitive peace was avoided. All that was required of Iraq in the temporary ceasefire were the return of coalition prisoners-of-war, the removal of Iraqi forces from Kuwait and southern Iraq and a restriction on flying military aircraft. Later, a permanent ceasefire was agreed by the Security Council of the United Nations and this placed further restrictions on Iraq's armed forces and prevented the further development of nuclear, chemical and biological weapons.

The big difference between 1941 and 1991 was that, whereas Rashid Ali fled the country, Saddam Hussein retained power, despite the determined attempts of the Kurds in the north and the Shi'ite opposition in the south to unseat him. As Glubb so rightly said at the time, the development of Iraqi political opinion strong enough to resist authoritarian rule would still take several generations to develop.

9

'Our Joint Enterprise in the Levant'

It was almost inevitable that Syria should be the next Middle Eastern country to be drawn into the war. Ever since France had fallen in May 1940 and Syria had subsequently come under the control of the Vichy government, it had posed a strategic threat to British interests; a year later, on 13 May 1941, a clash became unavoidable when the local administration in Syria and Lebanon permitted German aircraft to land at their bases en route for Iraq. Although the British Chiefs of Staff insisted that action should be taken against the French, Wavell argued that the use of his inadequate forces was unsound. Not only were they overstretched in North Africa and in Crete, but he had also been forced to find troops for the invasion of Iraq. Permission was granted, however, for the RAF to bomb German aircraft in Syria, even if that meant attacking French airfields.

The Free French representative in the Middle East, General Georges Catroux, also pressed for firm action to be taken and his insistence was the cause of a good deal of tension at the Middle East headquarters in Cairo. Eventually on 25 May Wavell filed a modest plan to invade Syria using a mixture of British, Indian, Australian and Free French forces. It was known as 'Operation Exporter' and, after it had been put into effect on 8 June, it was agreed that Habforce and the Arab Legion should provide a desert flanking attack from Iraq.

Syria had become a French mandate after the First World

War and, to make it easier to govern, the French colonial administration had partitioned the country into three autonomous districts: the first in the predominantly Shi'ite Alawite Mountains, the second in the Jebel Druze to the south and the third, greater Syria, centred on Damascus. All three districts were responsible to the French High Commissioner in Beirut. There in Le Grand Liban, or the Lebanon, traditionally a French sphere of influence, with a mixed community of Shi'ite and Sunni Muslims, Jews and Christians, both Catholic and Greek Orthodox, the French favoured the Francophile Maronite Christians as their power base. Although the terms of the mandate promised a constitution for both countries, France was not keen to withdraw from either country and regarded independence, especially in troublesome Syria, as no more than a distant goal. In 1936 France entered into treaty negotiations with both countries, the terms of which were similar to Britain's treaty with Iraq, but by the time the war broke out nothing had been put into effect.

Throughout the inter-war years, the French remained greatly suspicious of their British neighbours in the Middle East; their main fear was that Britain was trying to outmanoeuvre them by giving concessions to the Arabs and by encouraging Arabic and Islamic nationalism. France also possessed a weaker domestic economy than Britain, its armed forces were less effective and it could never be certain of keeping its Middle Eastern mandated territories within its sphere of influence. There was the added fear that Britain might once again attempt to redraw the boundaries as it had done in the early 1920s and pull Syria into a greater Arab nation embracing Transjordan and parts of non-Jewish Palestine. When the Druze tribes of the mountainous and lava-strewn Jebel Druze rebelled in 1925 the French maintained – not without reason – that the insurgents had been given moral and material support by Abdullah and the British in Transjordan. By the same token the British had been greatly displeased by the use of Syria and its capital Damascus as a

267

base for Palestinian guerrillas during the Arab revolt from 1936 onwards.

There was also a difference of style. France favoured exporting her own culture and traditions to the Arab world, to promote the use of the French language as the principal means of communication and to base the currencies of both countries on the French franc. The press was censored, nationalist disturbances were suppressed whenever they broke out and the colonial government was backed up by military power. Britain's role was less high-minded, more pragmatic, and more concerned with the strategic importance of oil, the Suez Canal and its large military bases throughout the Middle East. Besides, in men like Glubb and Kirkbride and others, the British possessed imperial servants who genuinely liked the Arabs and were happy to work in their best interests. Glubb was never particularly well liked by his French opposite numbers in Syria who constantly accused him of intriguing with the desert tribes to turn them against French rule. There was some truth in this allegation, for Glubb had recruited men from nomadic tribes whom the French considered to be under their control, and there had been several frosty confrontations on the frontier. In the face of considerable provocation Glubb, a fluent French speaker, never lost his temper with his opposite numbers but he was scornful of their concept of colonial control: his memorandum of a meeting in 1941 with the French General Collet, a veteran of twenty-three years of service in Syria, neatly underlines the difference between the two powers:

> Wherever the British have penetrated we meet British officers who believe the Bedouins, the Kurds, the Ghurkhas, the Sikhs or the Sudanese (whichever they happen to command) to be the most splendid fellows on earth. The French do not share this passionate interest in other races – they only praise individuals or communities insofar as they have become Gallicized.[1]

Glubb was also aware that the global war in which both countries were engaged was bringing about great changes to imperial attitudes. The defeat of France and the British struggle to wage war against Germany had given notice that neither country was any longer an invincible world power. A year after his meeting with Collet, in 1942, following the heavy defeats inflicted on Britain and America by Japan, Glubb put his feelings on the subject more strongly in one of his periodic reports to the Colonial Office:

> Whatever may be the results of this war in other directions, one thing is certain – 'coloured' races are no longer going to accept with resignation a racist status inferior to that of the white races. Japan and China are fighting on equal terms with Britain and Germany and no Ayrian [sic] or Nordic snobbishness can get away from the fact. Indian troops in the Western Desert have fought on equal terms with British and Germans and with considerably more distinction than the Italians.[2]

By pursuing an imperialist policy in Syria and Lebanon, argued Glubb, the French were storing up problems for the future. A later memorandum of 1943, on 'Peace Terms in the Middle East', suggested that France would probably have to be ejected from Syria and that the problem would be solved either by asking the United States to intervene or by turning Palestine and Syria into an Arab federation.[3]

The Free French, of course, had ample reasons for wanting to create a power base in Syria and Lebanon. Although Chad, French Equatorial Africa and Cameroon had opted for them in 1940, the larger French holdings in North Africa, the Levant and West Africa had decided to remain under the Vichy government of Marshal Pétain. It was one of the objectives of General de Gaulle, the Free French leader, to win them over to his side, not the least of his reasons being their large and well-equipped garrisons of French and French Foreign Legion soldiers. Well aware of the dangers they faced from their fellow countrymen, the French colonial administrators in Beirut and Damascus had followed the lead of the Vichy government by surrendering and then declaring their neutrality. As a precautionary warning, though, Britain had then announced that it would take whatever action was necessary to safeguard its holdings in the Middle East, and this statement was to remain the touchstone of British policy in the months to come:

> His Majesty's Government declare that they could not allow Syria or the Lebanon to be occupied by any hostile power, or to be used as a base for attacks upon those countries in the Middle East which they are pledged to defend, or to become the scene of such disorder as to constitute a danger to those countries. They therefore hold themselves free to take whatever measures they may in such circumstances consider necessary in their own interest.[4]

This was plain speaking but, in truth, in 1940 the British government was not anxious to upset the Vichy French administration and, due to the exigencies of war in other theatres, was keen to prevent any outbreak of hostilities in the Middle East. As long as Pétain was able to maintain his policy of neutrality, it was considered prudent to adopt a policy of live-and-let-live in Syria. For that reason the British government felt it would be unwise to offer too much overt support to Catroux in his desire to win back the two countries for the Free French.

That policy was to be overturned, however, in February 1941 when Glubb and Kirkbride were given funds to encourage the Druze tribes to begin a revolt against the French administration in Syria. Some £200,000 was made available by the Colonial Office[5] which agreed that, while Kirkbride would make contact with the Druze, Glubb would deal with the desert tribes of southern Syria. In both cases their task would be similar: 'to place [themselves] in touch with the people of Syria, with a view to possible resistance to the Germano-Italo-Vichy government'.[6]

Money was a possible reason for the Syrian tribes to assist Britain and her allies against the Vichy French administration. Another and perhaps more persuasive argument was the promise of eventual independence. Both Glubb and Kirkbride were happy to play this card as they believed that Britain had a duty to provide care and protection to the Arab peoples as they made their way towards self-determination. Partly this arose from the feelings of shame which Glubb – and many others – felt about the muddled Anglo-French double-dealing at the end of the First World War, but the belief was given added strength by the admiration and respect they bore towards the Arabs themselves. It was a paternalistic relationship, of course, and Glubb was never too proud to describe it thus in the memoranda which he produced throughout the war from his headquarters in Amman. Here he is writing in 1941 about Transjordan, but he also believed that the same policy could be applied to Syria at the end of the war:

Trans-Jordan has, from the British point of view, been the most successful of the Arab states created after the First World War. She is the only Arab country which has never rebelled or suffered from internal political crises, and the Government and people are still strongly pro-British.

This success has been achieved largely because the British, instead of attempting to interfere too much, have if anything gone to the other extreme, and urged the local Government to run the country. The benefits of this policy were particularly evident in the 1936–39 disturbances, when the British attitude to the Arabs was 'This is your country! You can have a rebellion if you like. We shall not mind!' This was not strictly true, but it was highly effective. The Trans-Jordan Government was obliged to exert itself to maintain order.[7]

Such a point of view was never entertained by the French

and Glubb had always been slightly scornful about their niggardly attitude towards the possibility of self-rule for the people of Syria and Lebanon. Now, in the early part of 1941, there was a chance to go amongst the Syrians and to tell them that the reward for their assistance would be the same kind of independence which Britain had granted to Iraq before the war. A goodly part of the initiative would therefore be propaganda aimed at making the Vichy French appear as the enemy of all nationalistically inclined Syrians. After the war, Glubb made that clear in his first volume of memoirs:

> In the preparatory work undertaken before the invasion of Syria, it had been assumed by one and all that French control of Syria was at an end. The official Government of France was assisting the enemy. The French rulers of Syria had refuelled German aircraft and sent trains of munitions to the usurping Government of Baghdad. Both British and Arabs assumed that Syria would be controlled by Great Britain until the end of the war, and would then become independent in the same manner as Iraq.[8]

Here Glubb was being somewhat disingenuous by providing a gloss some half-dozen years after the event. Certainly, in February 1941 when he and Kirkbride started talking to the Syrian tribes about rebellion, both men believed that Britain would control Syria until the end of the war when it would be granted full independence. They could hardly achieve that aim if the Syrians ever realised that victory would only bring a further period of colonial rule by the British or by the Free French under the tutelage of Britain. Yet that possibility was already known in the spring of 1941 and it has to be said that Glubb's and Kirkbride's initiative was a sorry distortion of British policy.

This had been made clear on 15 May when Churchill ordered the General Staff in Cairo to support the Free French intentions and to start planning for the invasion of Syria. At the same time Churchill sent a telegram to de Gaulle advising him 'not to withdraw Catroux' and to travel to Cairo himself. (De Gaulle arrived on 25 May.) This was the go-ahead for action which the Free French had been long awaiting, and to return the compliment, de Gaulle's reply was written in English for the first and only time in the war: '1. Thank you. 2. Catroux remains in Palestine. 3. I shall go to Cairo soon. 4. You will win the war.' Shortly before the attack began, Churchill again underlined the importance of Anglo-French co-operation when he sent a further telegram to de Gaulle expressing his best wishes for 'our joint enterprise in the Levant'.

The problem was that de Gaulle did not altogether trust the new initiative which he realised was a volte-face from previous policy. He also realised that the new alliance was based on shaky historical foundations. Like all Frenchmen he distrusted British intentions in the Middle East and feared that his ally was attempting to gain a foothold in the Levant from which it would be extremely difficult to dislodge them after the war. Glubb's propaganda campaign amongst the Syrian tribesmen, aimed at discrediting the French, only served to confirm those fears.

By early June, when the Chiefs of Staff ordered the attack to begin, Kirkbride would have known that the Free French planned to replace Vichy authority in Syria. He had met Catroux several times at Middle East headquarters – Glubb, too, was a frequent visitor to Cairo at this time – and he must have been aware of French intentions which by then had also been taken on board by Middle East Command. One of the main fears at Wavell's headquarters was a suspicion that any nationalist uprising in the Levant not controlled by the British could destabilise the position in Palestine by encouraging the Arabs to begin their own rebellion. That was another reason why the British government changed its mind and looked favourably on the idea of supporting the Free French in Syria, even if that meant contradicting the instructions which had been given to Glubb and Kirkbride three months earlier.

Glubb complained later that the British government should have made its intentions clear before the operation began as this would have prevented him from misleading the Syrian tribesmen. Of course, he was only carrying out his orders – which were in any case agreeable to his point of view – but the incident left a bitter after-taste. The most likely reason for the muddle was the general uncertainty which hung over British political policy in the Middle East theatre of operations. There was, too, a clash of ideology in London where the Colonial Office was responsible for Palestine and Transjordan, the Foreign Office for Egypt and Iraq and the War Office for the direction of the war. As the Official History makes clear, May 1941 was a month when orders and political and military intentions were subject to rapid and regular change:

> The Free French movement and the stability of Syria were matters of deep concern to the British Government and telegrams flew to and fro between the Commanders-in-Chief and Chiefs of Staff, the British Ambassador in Egypt and the Foreign Office, the High Commissioner in Palestine and the Colonial Office, and between General de Gaulle (now in French Equatorial Africa) and General Catroux and Major-General E.L. Spears, the head of the British Liaison Mission with General de Gaulle.[9]

During the month of May, while Wavell was having to cope with operations in North Africa, Crete and Iraq, most of the running for an invasion of Syria was made by Catroux. In the third week he told Wavell that the Vichy French were about to pull back into Lebanon, leaving Syria to the Germans, who would still be too weak to put up much resistance. A quick and determined attack by the Allies would win an easy victory, counselled Catroux who was given additional support by de Gaulle.

The Chiefs of Staff were also in favour of an early attack but Wavell refused to be rushed and his caution was rewarded on 21 May when British intelligence revealed that, far from pulling out of Syria, the Vichy French were digging in and preparing to fight. Four days later, having finalised his plans, Wavell told Churchill that Operation Exporter was ready and that he could afford to send forces consisting of 7th Australian Division (less one brigade), part of the 1st Cavalry Division and the Free French forces. Although this was too small – Wavell suggested that at least two infantry divisions and an armoured brigade would be needed to complete the successful invasion and occupation of Syria – it could be effective if the Turks agreed to move into northern Syria to seize the strategically important airfields, including the base at Aleppo. At that stage Turkish intervention was a possibility as they had been alarmed sufficiently by the German presence to move up large numbers of troops on to their border with Syria: it was not until 2 June that the Turkish government decided against taking military action.

Throughout this period Wavell was under tremendous pressure on all fronts. Between 28 May and 1 June some 16,000 Allied soldiers were evacuated from Crete after fierce fighting with German airborne troops but the operation was only completed at great cost to the Royal Navy. In North Africa Rommel had recaptured the Halfaya Pass on the Egyptian-Libyan border and his army had been reinforced by 15th Panzer Division. As the Axis powers seemed to be taking an inexorable grip on the eastern Mediterranean, Wavell was forced to conserve his armoured and air forces for Operation Battleaxe, the long-awaited attack to relieve Tobruk which had been surrounded by the Germans since the first week of April. Churchill was particularly keen that this attack should succeed, but he also understood the importance of 'shutting the back door' on the possibility of a German presence to the east of Egypt and Libya. 'Personally, I think we shall win, in spite of the physical difficulties of reinforcing by tanks and air,' he told President Roosevelt in a message pressing America to declare war on Germany. 'But I adjure you, Mr President, not to underrate the gravity of the consequences which may follow from a Middle East collapse. In this war every post is a winning post, and how many more are we going to lose?'[10]

As part of his policy to prevent that collapse of British power, Churchill then insisted that Wavell's forces for the proposed invasion of Syria should be increased to provide it with adequate air cover and naval support. Initially, the RAF was only able to grant the use of a Blenheim bomber squadron, a squadron of Hurricane fighters and an army co-operation squadron. Later, these were reinforced by additional fighter and bomber aircraft operating from bases in Palestine and by a Royal Australian Air Force squadron flying American-built Curtiss Tomahawk fighters. Naval fire support was provided by three cruisers and eight destroyers whose task was to bombard the Syrian coastline; overall command was given to Maitland Wilson, and his final ground forces consisted of:

7th Australian Division (less one brigade)
5th Indian Infantry Brigade Group
Two cavalry regiments – Cheshire Yeomanry (horsed) and mixed Staffordshire Yeomanry/Royal Scots Greys (mechanised)
Free French forces – six battalions, one artillery battery
One squadron armoured cars
Three regiments Royal Artillery – field, light, heavy anti-aircraft
A Commando, C battalion, Special Service Brigade

Wilson's main objective was Beirut, the seat of government and the headquarters of General Henri Dentz, the Vichy French High Commissioner in the Levant; at the same time he hoped to take Rayal and Damascus and thereafter to advance on Homs, Palmyra and Tripoli. In the first stages of the advance – the operation began on 8 June 1941 – the rapid advance made by the Indian brigade encouraged Wilson's commanders to think that the Vichy forces would offer only token resistance and that there would be no heavy fighting. This was wishful thinking. Although Dentz's forces often fought less than zealously against British and Dominion troops, they reserved their real hostility for the Free French. One Gaullist officer, Captain Paul Repiton-Preneuf, previously the French representative in Palestine and a man whom Glubb admired, later remembered that his fellow countrymen considered the Free French forces to be 'the Devil incarnate, the scapegoats for all the anger, resentment and weakness which had been lurking in the dark places of their consciences for a year'.[11] There were also Foreign Legion regiments on both sides and in one bloody engagement the Free French 13th Legion Demi-Brigade encountered the Vichy 6th Legion Infantry Regiment: neither side gave way. Five weeks later, after some bitter and unpleasant close-quarter combat, the short and sharp war was over – the Allies had suffered 3,500 casualties, the Free French 1,300 and the Vichy forces 6,000.

From the outset of the campaign Wilson's forces were hampered by a lack of suitable transport and armour and this shortcoming prevented him from making a rapid advance on a broad front – although the experienced 5th Indian Brigade made good progress on its way to Deraa and Damascus. It was on the left flank, where the steep hills and valleys made the coastal road easy to defend, that the Australians encountered determined attempts to block the route to Beirut. A third advance, mainly Free French, was made from the Palestine border towards Merjayun where the road then wound westwards to the coast at Sidon.

The topography of the Levant dictated that the advance should be three-pronged to take account of the narrow coastal plain, the valley of the River Litani which was surrounded by a parallel range of mountains rising to 9,000 feet, and the low hills and open desert to the east. As the Official History also recognises, the campaign usefully fell into three parts. The first, between 8 and 13 June, saw the initial advance and the first Vichy resistance. The second, between 14 and 22 June, was 'a period of sharp cut and thrust' during which the Vichy forces offered spirited resistance at Ezraa and Kuneitra; during this period, too, Wilson was reinforced by two brigades of 6th (British) Division. In the third phase of the operation, 26 June to 12 July, the initiative passed to the British and success was ensured by the deployment of Habforce and the 10th Indian Division on the desert flank. Once again, the Arab Legion played an important part, acting as scouts for Habforce and fighting alongside them at the battle for the important oasis at Palmyra.

At the end of the campaign in Iraq Glubb had taken his men back to Transjordan while the cavalry, yeomanry and infantry regiments of Habforce had remained at Habbaniyah. When news came through of the advance into Syria Glubb feared that the Arab Legion might not be deployed and that its only role would be to check the tribal raiding which always broke out in time of war – in one action early in June a sergeant and four men of the Arab Legion gave chase to a raiding party and followed it deep into Syrian territory to retrieve two large flocks of camels. After the heady days of the invasion of Iraq, it seemed once more that the Arab Legion would be confined to paramilitary duties within Transjordan.

That all changed during the second period of the Syrian campaign when General J.D. Lavarack, an Australian, took overall battlefield command and it was decided that encirclement would be the best tactic to defeat the enemy; to do this successfully an attack would have to be made on the right flank from Iraq and the task was given to Habforce. Glubb had been fretting for this moment and, when the orders came, he recalled that for his Arab Legion soldiers the campaign suddenly took on the aspect of a mission:

In the Iraq campaign, agitators had endeavoured to convince the troops that they were to be employed to fight their fellow Arabs in the interests of Great Britain. No such political motives could be attributed to the invasion of Syria. The Arabs for twenty-five years past had resented the presence of the French in Syria, but the alliance between France and Britain had made it impossible to oust them. Now by a fortunate coincidence, as it appeared to the Arabs, the British and French were on opposite sides. The hour for the redemption of Syria had struck.[12]

Before leaving Transjordan the Desert Mechanised Regiment assembled at Mafraq to be inspected by Abdullah who told them that it was an historic moment, that the time had come for Arabs to join forces in the cause of liberty and independence. His gesture, though well meant, had political undertones: throughout this period of uncertainty the emir continued to promote the long-held idea that he should become the ruler of a greater Syria embracing Transjordan and parts of Palestine. Abdullah was nothing if not consistent in his ambitions and his barely concealed scheming also provided grounds for the French suspicions about British intentions in the Middle East.

The Arab Legion's first goal was the base at the pumping station H3 where the greater part of Habforce was waiting for them. As they moved across the gravelly desert they had their first taste of the difficulties that would face them from the absence of air cover when their column was attacked by Vichy French Morane-Saulnier 406 fighters. Habforce, too, had been attacked by Vichy bombers – apart from a battery of light anti-aircraft guns and mounted Bren guns captured from the Iraqi Army, the absence of suitable anti-aircraft weapons was to be a severe handicap to the force throughout their short campaign. This time Brigadier Kingstone provided a warm welcome for Glubb, for he realised that the Arab Legion soldiers would be invaluable, both as flanking guards for his column and as guides across the 150 miles of desert which lay between them and their first objective, Palmyra. There was a five-day delay at the pumping station to allow

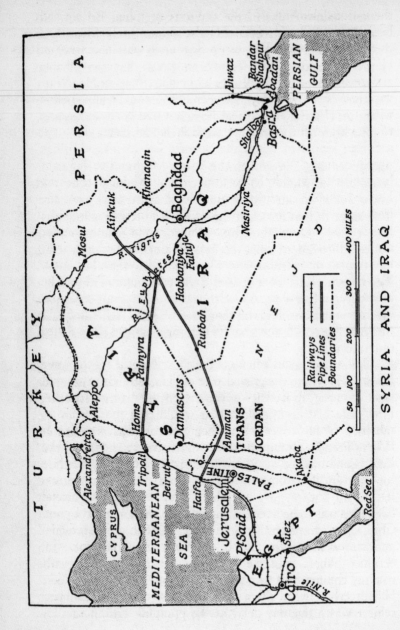

the various elements of Habforce to reassemble, as they had been given different tasks after the successful conclusion of the Iraq campaign. The Essex Regiment was in reserve at Habbaniyah while the cavalry regiments were on active service in the desert – the two yeomanry regiments (Warwickshire and Wiltshire) were guarding the Haifa pipeline while the Household Cavalry Regiment had been attempting to track down the Palestinian guerrilla leader Fawzi al Kaukji, a Syrian who had taken the opportunity to attack British supply columns. When the cavalrymen returned to H3 they bequeathed their elderly Hotchkiss machine-guns to the Arab Legion, having captured a number of Bren guns from the Iraqi army. It took some time for Glubb's men to master the French-built Hotchkiss: though reliable it was greatly inferior to the British Bren which had been supplied to the Iraqi Army but not to the British forces serving in the Middle East. Major-General Clark was again in overall command and he insisted on waiting for the arrival of an Australian anti-tank battery equipped with two-pounder guns as he had heard that the French might be able to call on light tanks for the defence of Palmyra.

Clark's plan was alarmingly simple. Habforce would leave H3 on 20 June, cross the desert and capture Palmyra that same evening. The way would then be open to capture the French base at Homs before attacking Hama and Aleppo in northern Syria. It had been estimated that the entire operation would take forty-eight hours and that casualties would be kept to a minimum – but Glubb thought differently. His spies had advised him the French Fort Weygand at Palmyra was larger than the fort at Rutbah, that it was garrisoned by some 500 men of the Foreign Legion and the French Desert Companies and that they were equipped with armoured cars and artillery. However Glubb was not in a position to make any comment on Clark's plan and he contented himself with passing the information to Somerset de Chair. After all, Habforce had its own RAF armoured cars and had also been reinforced by a battery of twenty-five-pounder field guns.

When the force left H3 early in the morning of 20 June it had been divided into three columns – an advance party of the Wiltshire Yeomanry and Arab Legion guides under Lash's command whose task was to take up position to the west of Palmyra; the Household Cavalry and Warwickshire Yeomanry, led by Kingstone who would capture the hills to the north; and the main investment force of the Essex Regiment, artillery, engineers and five troops of the Arab Legion together with Clark's headquarters. This latter column would also be responsible for maintaining the lines of communication between H3 and Juffa, to the south of Palmyra.

At first, everything seemed to go according to plan. An Arab Legion patrol captured a French picket at Juffa and first indications suggested that they had prevented it from reporting the British presence to the main garrison at Fort Weygand. By evening, too, all three columns were approaching their pre-arranged positions and hopes were high that Clark would be able to force the French to surrender but it was then that the plan started falling apart. Kingstone found his way blocked by an unexpected French command bunker at the T3 pumping station and stopped to lay siege to it instead of proceeding to his position in the hills above Palmyra. While addressing this fruitless task – the artillery shells merely bounced off the well-made French pillboxes – his column was attacked from the air by Potez 63 bombers and was forced to dig in.

Meanwhile Lash and the Wiltshire Yeomanry had discovered for themselves that Palmyra did indeed present a difficult obstacle. The French fortifications were solidly built and stood to the east of the town itself – an astounding cluster of pillars and ruins dating from Roman times. Standing at the crossroads of the main trade routes between India and the Mediterranean, Palmyra had been a wealthy and important town, the home of Queen Zenobia, the Arab 'Queen of the East' who had been defeated in battle by the Emperor Aurelian in AD 272 and led in triumph through the streets of Rome. Although some Arabs and Turks still lived amongst the ruins, the French had built new quarters nearby but, as Glubb noted, this was 'an ugly new village with straight shadeless streets and cheap houses'. Initially, Glubb thought that his men could perform a useful task fighting amongst the ruined buildings, but before the operation began Clark made it clear that the Arab Legion would only be used in a reconnaissance role and were unlikely to see combat. Ironically, it was this order which enabled the Arab Legion to play the key part in the campaign.

By the evening of 22 June Habforce was scattered over a large area of the desert in front of Palmyra but Clark and his senior officers seemed bereft of ideas for bringing the siege to a successful conclusion. The delay allowed the French to reinforce the small garrison of Foreign Legion and Desert Companies with additional men and a handful of light tanks of the 6th Chasseurs d'Afrique. It also enabled them to call up aircraft and Habforce's days were made miserable by the frequent intrusion of Potez bombers and modern Dewoitine D520 fighters which bore an uncanny resemblance to the RAF's Hurricane. Casualties began to mount, and in one air raid Somerset de Chair was injured in the foot and shoulder by cannon fire; he was eventually evacuated to Jerusalem and later wrote *The Golden Carpet*, his personal account of the two campaigns.

Unfortunately the battle was also soured by a regrettable incident at the T3 position when a troop of the Warwick-shires was ambushed and shot up by Arab tribesmen whose vehicles were carrying white flags of surrender. This led to rumours that the Vichy French were involved – their vehicles carried white aircraft-recognition panels which often confused the Allied soldiers. However, the attack at T3 was not the only time during the campaign when the French were accused of opening fire under the white flag and stories abounded of the practice being used throughout the campaign. Most of the rumours were born of frustration, for suddenly the bright hopes of a quick and cheap victory seemed to be vanishing into Syria's desert sands, as Glubb described:

The spirits of Habforce were dampened by their lack of success in capturing Palmyra by a *coup de main*, as had been intended. The unceasing enemy air attacks and the complete absence of British aircraft from the sky was even more depressing. In Britain, in Africa, in Greece, in Crete – everywhere the British Army and Air Force were struggling against five or ten times their numbers of enemy. Was this invasion of Syria to be another fiasco like the recent expedition to Greece? Could we carry on indefinitely with no aircraft, while enemy machines seemed to fill the sky?[13]

Attack from the air was the main problem facing Habforce. On 25 June French bombers and fighters staged what Glubb called a 'full dress' attack on their positions and the British Bofors guns were unable to offer much protection. Not until three days later was some revenge gained when a squadron of Australian Tomahawks shot down six French Martin Maryland bombers in full view of the cheering troops. By then, too, Clark had been greatly encouraged by news of another success after Glubb had made the first move to break the deadlock. On 25 June he had announced to Clark: 'It has just occurred to me that it might be a good idea to take Sab Biyar.' The following day this strategically important French communications base to the south of Palmyra surrendered to Glubb without a struggle. Not only did this give a much-needed fillip to morale, but it allowed Habforce to move its supply base to H4 in Transjordan, thereby shortening the lines of communication by at least 100 miles and saving supplies from air attack. A few days later, the Arab Legion added Sukhna to the battle honours when they took part in one of the most colourful and unorthodox battles of the war.

While the Arab Legion was carrying out a sweep in the northern plain on 1 July, Glubb heard that a powerful French motorised column guarded by armoured cars was loose in the desert. Early that same morning on a gravelly ridge near the village of Sukhna, some forty miles north-east of Palmyra, his small force – one troop each of infantry and armoured cars, backed up by a squadron of Household Cavalry – encountered the French column coming up the road from Deir-ez-Zor. Eighteen vehicles strong, and heavily armed, this was the 2nd Desert Company and the speed and élan of their advance suggested an immediate attack on Glubb's badly defended position. On seeing the Arab Legion troops, the French unloaded their own infantrymen and machine-guns and took position to fight a pitched battle against what they took to be inferior opposition – they did not know that the Household Cavalry squadron was breakfasting half a mile to the rear.

The sight of the French soldiers taking up combat positions was too much for some of Glubb's men, some of whom had fought with Lawrence at Deraa during the march on Damascus. 'These old worthies were indifferent to tactical combinations,' remembered Glubb. 'Military discipline sat on them but lightly. All they knew was that this was a battle. If the enemy would not come to them, they would go to him.' Without further ado, the Bedouin soldiers charged the French lines and with many blood-curdling yells scattered the French position with the violence of their first charge.

This was too much for the drivers who turned their vehicles and quickly retreated back down the road to Deir-ez-Zor with the Arab Legion's trucks and armoured cars in hot pursuit. A fierce running battle developed, which the Household Cavalry also joined, but the day really belonged to 'Glubb's Girls'. Later a Household Cavalry NCO admitted that, although he had been doing 60 mph in his truck, he had been unable 'to live with the hounds'. At the conclusion of a short and sharp engagement eleven French soldiers had been killed and eighty officers and men captured along with their transport and armoured cars. More importantly perhaps, the news of the success boosted Habforce's morale and dented that of the defenders in Palmyra. Realising that resistance was no longer possible, the garrison surrendered to Clark on 3 July. A week later, following the collapse of the Vichy forces in the west and in Lebanon, General Dentz contacted the Allies by radio and requested a general armistice. The Syrian campaign was at an end and the Arab Legion had played a significant role in bringing it to a successful conclusion.

It had been an odd campaign, short and ultimately victorious, yet it also had an other-worldly quality. Those who took part in it, and who later saw service in the Far East or in Europe, admitted afterwards that the fighting, as in Iraq, seemed to belong to another age. One reason was that it was fought on a smaller scale and, apart from the Vichy French use of modern military aircraft, the weapons were less formidable than those used in other theatres.

There was also a matter of style. While the fighting was often bitter and protracted between the opposing French forces, some of the British formations, particularly those in Habforce, adopted a lighter approach and tended to regard it as an extended period of games. On one occasion Glubb had been highly amused by the sight of General Clark refusing to take cover during an air attack: as the bullets from a Dewoitine fighter ripped through the sand, he merely took out his sandwiches and said, 'How extremely unpleasant!' At the end of the campaign, the novelist John Masters, serving with a Gurkha regiment in 10th Indian Division, watched in disbelief as a yeomanry colonel forgot the name of one of his own officers. 'Memory like a sieve,' he exclaimed. 'I'll be forgetting the names of me hounds next.' The mood was caught by Gawain Bell of the Sudan Political Service who found himself serving in the Jebel Druze with a clutch of yeomanry officers of 5th Cavalry Brigade:

Most of them were countrymen and before the war they had hunted. Some had brought their own horses with them and as batmen they had brought their peacetime grooms. Conversation was mainly of well remembered fox-hunting runs. Each morning we rose early and rode. The more thrusting spirits would set off on what was known as a 'Tantivy', a cross-country scurry to include as many jumps as possible. A point-to-point was held. This was exactly how Wellington's young officers spent their spells of winter inactivity in the Peninsula.[14]

The following year Bell transferred to the Arab Legion with the rank of qaimaqam, or colonel, and became one of Glubb's growing circle of British commanders.

For all that the Syrian campaign occupies little more than a passing reference in most histories of the Second World War, and for all that it seems to have been touched by amateurism it was taken seriously at the time. In a summer when the heavens seemed to be falling, Britain and her allies had achieved a victory to compensate for the loss of Greece and Crete and the failure of Wavell's June offensive in Libya. Winston Churchill put the seal on the campaign when, in the House of Commons on 15 July, he paid tribute to the men who had planned and taken part in Operation Exporter: 'If anyone had predicted that we should already, by the middle of July, have cleaned up the whole of the Levant and have re-established our authority there for the time being, such a prophet would have been most imprudent'.

To be sure, at that juncture the British prime minister had good reason to be pleased. Despite the lack of air cover the ground forces, especially the Indians and the Australians, had given a good account of themselves, fighting over difficult terrain in high summer temperatures. British stock had also risen amongst the Arabs and there was a general feeling of good will towards them amongst those Levantine nationalists who hoped that independence would be granted to Syria and Lebanon. Some doubting Thomases claimed that the invasion of Syria need never have taken place as the German threat to the Levant had disappeared with Hitler's invasion of the Soviet Union which began on 22 June. While it is true that the Germans had indeed withdrawn from Syria before the invasion was finally planned, it was still strategically important for Britain to have control of the Levant as Hitler's

287

strategy in 1941 included a possible German pincer movement against Palestine and Transjordan, aimed on one side from Libya and Egypt in the south-west and from the northwest from Bulgaria through Turkey.

Unfortunately, as often happens in the middle of warfare when minds are engaged elsewhere, Britain made a mess of the peace. On 12 July 'Jumbo' Wilson summoned Catroux and the Vichy French General de Verdilhac to Acre to discuss the peace settlement; two days later it was announced that it had been agreed to repatriate the Vichy forces without giving them the freedom of choice to join the Free French forces. In fact, the Free French were not even mentioned in the accord and Catroux was not invited to sign it; furthermore, the pre-campaign promise to recognise the Free French in the Levant was also conveniently forgotten.

Wilson was roundly castigated by Oliver Lyttelton, the War Cabinet's representative in the Middle East who believed that the Free French had been badly treated, but the British general had sound reasons for acting as he did. As a soldier he believed that magnanimous treatment of the Vichy forces would make them less likely to throw in their lot with the Nazis or to cause further trouble in Syria before their departure. There was, too, the undeniable fact that, as Britain was not at war with Vichy France, Wilson was not in a position to impose a punitive peace. Perhaps, too, he preferred the Vichy forces to those representing Free France: the former were, after all, regulars who were merely doing a soldier's duty, while de Gaulle and his followers seemed more like rebels, beyond the pale of decent military society. This was made clear a few days later when an Australian military band played the Marseillaise on the quayside as the Vichy high command embarked for France.

Not surprisingly, the news of the peace settlement enraged de Gaulle who believed that Britain had manoeuvred herself into a position of power in the Levant and that French interests had been disregarded. By allowing Dentz and his forces to be repatriated, the British had also denied de Gaulle the use of trained soldiers whose possible change of allegiance would have given him a much larger army. On 20 July he descended on Cairo and made his anger clear to Major-General Sir Edward Spears, his principal British liaison officer, who pointed out that the long-term intention was the defeat of the Nazis. 'Do you think I want Britain to win?' he retorted. 'No, the only thing that matters to me is a French victory.' When Spears suggested that that was the same thing, de Gaulle replied, 'Not from my point of view; not at all!' The following day, in acrimonious discussion with Lyttelton, de Gaulle threatened to use his forces against the British forces in Syria who had raised the Union Flag over the important forts at Jezireh and Suweida, the capital of the Druze country. This was already the cause of no little local provocation and even Spears, by then equally angry with the Free French leader, had to agree that this could provide a flashpoint for trouble. Although Lyttelton was shocked by de Gaulle's arrogance, on 25 July he offered an 'explanatory agreement' to the Acre treaty which permitted the Free French to make direct contact with the Vichy forces and, equally importantly for de Gaulle's self-esteem, he agreed that Britain's authority in Syria would be confined to military issues. In other words, tacit approval was given to de Gaulle to take up the reins of colonial authority in the Levant.

This last point enraged Glubb who had taken the Arab Legion to Deir-ez-Zor where he was busying himself with the kind of peace-keeping duties – settling local disputes, returning stolen camels and so on – which were his responsibility in Transjordan. He had also continued to tell the Syrians that, with the defeat of the French, independence would be theirs in the near future and that they could count on fair treatment from the British. Funds were still at his disposal and he continued to use them to good effect to bolster his proaganda campaign against the French. It is not difficult to imagine his chagrin, therefore, when he saw the local Vichy French administrators suddenly switching their allegiance to de Gaulle – so short of trained administrators were the Free French that they had to rely on Vichy personnel. This 'quick turn of coat' greatly angered Glubb because it bewildered the local Syrians and frustrated his own efforts. So vociferous did he become that it did not take de Gaulle long to take an interest in this 'intelligence service specialist' who was preaching sedition against the French. Not without reason, de Gaulle asked for Glubb's removal. Spears, too, was in favour of sacking Glubb 'for rousing the natives against the representatives of France', but when the order reached Wilson he was inclined to question it as Glubb had a high reputation. The matter was passed to London and Lyttelton got his way: on 28 August he contacted Wilson again telling him to remove Glubb and the Arab Legion from Syria. 'Glubb's presence in Syria would be so misinterpreted by Free French as to defeat its object. French suspicions of British policy in Syria are unfortunately of long standing.'[15]

At the end of the month the Arab Legion pulled out of Syria and returned to Transjordan, a victim, said Glubb, of 'parochial jealousies'. Later he claimed that his propaganda work was aimed solely at the Vichy French but given his hostile attitude towards French colonialism it is not difficult to believe that his shots were also aimed at the incoming Free French who had determined to rule the population, whatever their wishes. He said as much after a visit to Damascus later in the year: 'Mr Churchill was uttering a paradox when he said that Syria would be granted her aspirations but France would, at the same time, retain her pre-eminence. The chief and principal Syrian aspiration is to get rid of the French.'[16]

For Glubb the whole episode left a sour taste. Being too close to the action at the time he could not see that the Anglo-French invasion of Syria had been a compromise – one of the necessary expedients of a war which was not going Britain's way – and that misunderstandings had been built into the operation from the very start. With weightier matters taking precedence elsewhere, in North Africa and on the home front, Britain's War Cabinet was desperate for a victory to bolster her position in the Middle East. They failed to understand the strength of de Gaulle's belief that he needed to win control of the Levant to give substance to his national revival and that Syrian independence, therefore, would be a long time coming. Instead, the British regarded Syrian independence or the promise of it as a means of winning the war by preventing the kind of nationalist unrest which would jeopardise their position in the region.

The removal of the Arab Legion from Syria not only dented Glubb's self-esteem, it was also a blow to Wilson's plans for the defence of the country. British intelligence decrypts of German top-secret Enigma signals confirmed that an enemy attack on the Middle East through the Balkans was a key part of Hitler's future plans. If Russia succumbed quickly – as was thought possible at the time – the Germans would then be able to turn their attention to the Middle East, using Trans-Caucasia as a jumping-off point. Hitler also hoped that the collapse of his enemies would encourage the Arabs to rise against the British in the Levant, Palestine, Transjordan, Iraq and Egypt, thus tying down valuable Allied forces to deal with revolt and public disorder. To guard against this possibility Britain needed strong forces in northern Syria and the Arab Legion's performance in the two campaigns suggested that they would be the ideal force to guard the exposed desert flank.

However, it was impossible to ignore the role played by the Arab Legion and, as the British had promised to reward Abdullah for his support, a first step was taken by increasing Arab Legion's annual grant and by implementing plans to turn it into a national army. To replace the ageing armed trucks 400 new Ford truck chassis were ordered from Detroit; when they arrived they were given armour plating by the simple expedient of bonding two sheets of mild steel plate with heavy plywood in between – this caused bullets to splay and reduced their power to penetrate. South African-built Marmon-Herrington armoured cars were also made available. On the manpower front, the Desert Mechanised Regiment was brought up to full strength and steps were taken to raise a second and, later, a third regiment. The men received British Army battledress uniforms and webbing equipment and gradually the colourful Bedouin clothes came to be used only on ceremonial occasions. By the end of the war, too, a brigade headquarters was added and Transjordan soldiers were able to take over most of the logistical tasks from British REME and Ordnance Corps specialists.

As these modern military developments were introduced, the all-Bedouin nature of the Arab Legion also began to change. As Glubb pointed out, 'You can teach a Bedouin or anybody else to drive a truck, but maintenance requires of course a fitter ... we were obliged to take educated townspeople and curiously enough the great majority turned out to be Christians.'[17] Glubb was obliged to recruit these newcomers because he wanted the Legion to thrive, but he felt uneasy about the development. Town-based recruits were usually educated and through their families they enjoyed influential political connections, an important factor in Arab life. It had always been Glubb's objective to keep the Arab Legion out of Transjordanian politics – just as the British Army keeps itself aloof from any political involvement – but the introduction of the townsmen and the *fellaheen* villagers meant that the complexion of the Legion would inevitably change. Many of the men who joined the Arab Legion during this period became NCOs and then went on to gain commissions: by promoting from within Glubb hoped to avoid the kind of problems experienced by other Arab countries whose army officers were almost entirely political appointments. As P.J. Vatikiotis has written: 'In so small a country as Jordan, it is most important *not* to recruit officers from important or powerful families. This applies as much to the sons of tribal chiefs as to those of cabinet ministers.'[18]

As it was to turn out, though, the recruitment and promotion of many of these officers was later to lead to increasingly insistent calls from them for the replacement of Glubb and the British officer cadre by Jordanian and Palestinian officers.

A move to introduce British officers into the Arab Legion was a necessary concomitant of its expansion. Amongst them was Gawain Bell who feared that he might have to return to the Sudan Political Service after his experiences with the yeomanry in the Druze and had pleaded with Glubb to find a place for him. (He returned to Sudan after the war.) Eventually, after a period of apprenticeship and further training, he was given command of the 3rd Desert Mechanised Regiment. When he first arrived in Transjordan he lived in a small mess in Amman where he was encouraged to learn as much as possible about Bedouin life and culture. Other members in early 1942 included the Arabian traveller Wilfred Thesiger, the historian Stewart Perowne, and Lord Apsley. Kirkbride's new assistant Hugh Foot (later Lord Caradon) was also a member and in his autobiography he left a vivid account of the self-conscious Arabism which they all practised in their day-to-day lives: 'We became Arab enthusiasts. We didn't drink or smoke.* We carried the string of Arab beads which we would run through our fingers as we talked of an evening. I gave more and more of my time to Arabia.'[19] A desire to maintain Glubb's own high standards was one reason for the enthusiasm, a sense of purpose and a love of the Arabs for their own sake another, but as Bell makes clear, they all wanted to live up to Lawrence's *Twenty-Seven Articles*,† the precepts laid down as 'stalking horses for beginners in the Arab armies'. In addition to offering sound advice about wearing Arab dress in the desert, the importance of creating mutual respect and the necessity of avoiding discussions involving women or religion, Lawrence's final exhortation to those who followed him was the study of the Arab himself:

---

*Bell denies this: 'I am not sure that we were all non-smokers and entirely teetotal as Hugh suggests.'

†First published in the *Arab Bulletin* in 1917 they were kept in print as a guide for British officers in Arab countries.

Bury yourself in Arab circles, have no interests and no ideas except the work in hand, so that your brain shall be saturated with one thing only, and you realise your part deeply enough to avoid the little slips that would undo the work of weeks. Your success will be just proportional to the amount of mental effort you devote to it.[20]

Glubb was particularly keen that his new officers should live up to that example, and in Bell he had a man not only well versed in Arab culture generally but also prepared to study life in Palestine and Transjordan in particular. At Glubb's insistence, Bell's first duties were lengthy mounted patrols along the Druze frontier or in the Yarmuk valley where he and his men 'slept and fed in the villages, occupying the *Mukhtar*'s or Mayor's guest chamber at night, stretched out on blankets and rugs alongside the walls. The smell of sweaty shirts and socks as the men pulled off their boots and settled down made sleep difficult at times, and the snoring of my companions was monumental in volume. The hillsides and valleys were green and fruitful. The Yarmuk river tumbled and foamed down its steep sided gorge.'[21] This was the only life that Glubb knew and he was determined that those who served with him should experience it as well.

Cassano, too, soldiered with the Arab Legion after the Syrian campaign and with officers of their calibre Glubb felt secure because they were committed to the Arab cause, but he was also obliged to accept other British officers as instructors and technical staff for the new regiments. Amongst these was a number of experienced tank officers including Robert Melville, John Salmon and Tony Bliss who had all served in the North Africa campaign. Melville was later to play a key role in the development of the post-war Legion as liaison officer in London but as Salmon recalled, the opportunity of serving in the Arab Legion in 1944 provided them all with a colourful interlude in their wartime military careers:

It wasn't so much a technical exercise as a co-operative

and international exercise ... but we used to do a lot of sheep feasting. Any time you were on exercise the men would say, come and eat with us, and that could be a four-hour job! They weren't really professionally inclined soldiers but they were remarkably pleasant people. The Bedouin had by far the greatest charm – and really wanted to be soldiers. For the whole of their lives they had been involved in tribal raiding and they had a great respect for anyone who bore arms. To be a soldier was the height of their ambition – they were rather like overgrown school-boys. If we were due to go on a march and everybody was told to be ready to move by eight, they would all be up by seven, ready in their trucks, singing.[22]

Glubb's administrative duties in Amman meant that he could not spend large amounts of time with the brigade but he was careful to monitor the new officers' progress – Salmon was not alone in remembering the avalanche of papers which emanated from Glubb's headquarters. Although Glubb understood that the new men were first and foremost British Army officers who had been seconded to Transjordan in a technical capacity, he was keen that they should share his belief that service in the Legion was more of a calling than a job of work.

Whenever Glubb visited Cairo he was disturbed by the presence of British officers who held typically 'colonial' attitudes and who tended to treat Indian or Arab servicemen in an off-hand way and he was determined to keep such types out of the Legion. (In this he was largely successful.) Glubb had been brought up to believe that there was no need to tell officers how to behave, for if they did not understand the unwritten rules then they were hardly likely to be gentlemen and should not, therefore, hold the King's Commission. This was a common sentiment amongst professional army officers of his generation but the appearance in the Middle East of conscripted wartime officers, most from non-military backgrounds, forced him to revise his opinions. In some exasperation he issued a set of guidelines for headquarters in Cairo which were as forceful, sensible, and colourful, as those written by Lawrence twenty-five years earlier. This was followed by regular exhortations urging his own officers to apply standards to themselves which the Arab soldiers would then willingly follow. An order of the day, written as late as 30 December 1944, showed that it was not always easy to get his colleagues to appreciate his point of view:

> Few of us realise that the British are known for their rough manners amongst other nations. Educated Arabs rarely make due allowance for this national quality, nor do they understand that it is natural. They too often receive it as a deliberate insult and are accordingly resentful. Any officer who wishes to live and work with Arabs should immediately master the conventions of Arab politeness and will as a result find all his work with the educated classes easier and happier.[23]

That Glubb had grounds for feeling aggrieved by the behaviour of his fellow countrymen is made clear by a note of a security briefing which he attended at 9th Army headquarters in January 1941. Following obligatory warnings about the need to exercise high security standards, the briefing officer reminded the meeting that the British Army was stationed in a part of the world whose populations were potential enemies:

> The British Army has been in the Middle East long enough to know that constant vigilance is required to ensure military security. You chaps get on pretty well with the Wogs and Oozles as you call them, and treat them very sensibly, *but* you know that there was fighting here as recently as 1939 and there are still hostile elements among the population.[24]

That kind of attitude infuriated Glubb who always reminded

his officers that they could hardly expect to win the loyalty and respect of their men if they were always roaring around losing their temper. He had disliked that aspect of Peake's personality and he did not want to see it in his own officers. Not that he was regarded by others as a hard taskmaster. Bell remembered that Glubb had little patience with men who enjoyed the lighter social side of life – 'poodlefakers' in army parlance – and he could be cold and censorious with those who failed to match his own high standards. There was an element of aloofness in his make-up and although he was always unfailingly polite to others, his reserved, even retiring personality made him a difficult man to know intimately. His domestic life was quiet and orderly, too. As the senior officer in the Arab Legion he had to attend Abdullah's regular Friday levees, dressed in a stiff and uncomfortable ceremonial uniform when he would have preferred to pull on an old pair of trousers and read a book in his garden. Although never gregarious, Glubb enjoyed entertaining at home and was always happy to welcome Arab friends with tea or coffee and British colleagues with sherry or whisky – a heavy smoker in his younger days, he gave up cigarettes completely for reasons of health in 1939. Otherwise he regarded his private life as his own affair – a necessary qualification given the propensity of his Bedouin soldiers to make demands on him – and his leisure hours were usually spent reading or pottering in his garden.

Something of the desire to keep his private life separate from his public existence can be seen in an incident in 1947 when the Glubbs were devastated by the untimely death of a second son – during the war, in 1944, they had added to their family by adopting Naomi, a baby Bedouin girl. Following Godfrey's birth, Rosemary had undergone two serious gynaecological operations and her second pregnancy was a great source of delight to herself and Jack. However, the baby was born prematurely, only five-and-a-half months old, and although everything possible was done to save him in the Italian hospital in Amman the lack of an incubator meant that there was no hope of his surviving. The death and the realisation that Rosemary could not risk further pregnancies had a lasting effect on the Glubbs: grief stricken, Jack arranged for the tiny body to be buried at dawn in the small cemetery reserved for Arab Christians.

> There were no British mourners. Not that they would have been unsympathetic, but there were few of them then in Amman. Besides, I did not feel as if I wanted to tell anyone. Two Arab Christian priests read the burial service. My Arab orderly and my driver stood by the grave.[25]

Like many other self-contained men – soldiers often show this kind of reserve, even stoicism – he preferred not to show his feelings and believed that they should always be kept under control. His strongest feelings of affection outside his family were reserved for his Bedouin soldiers and he was fond of relating an incident which he felt proved the existence of a bond between simple soldiers:

> A few men were taken prisoner in the attack on Palmyra and were taken off to a prisoners-of-war cage with a number of British prisoners-of-war. The French sorted them out and said, 'Arabs could go over there but British prisoners would be accommodated here'. And the British prisoners-of-war refused, they wouldn't co-operate at all unless the Arab Legion troops were allowed to live with them at the same prisoner-of-war camp. And the French had to give way ... the Arab Legion were heroes to the British Army ... there was an extraordinary feeling of friendship, comradeship between the two. The Arab Legion was aware that this was owing to their prowess; the British welcomed them as comrades which had a profound moral effect.[26]

Unfortunately the Middle East high command did not always view the Arab Legion in the same light and Glubb had to work long and hard – and ultimately fruitlessly – to secure an operational role for his men. In 1942 it was thought that the 1st Desert Mechanised Regiment might join the British 8th Army in North Africa following the Battle of Alamein but the speed of the victory meant that they were not needed. Then 'Jumbo' Wilson put forward a suggestion that they could be employed to prevent the Kurdish tribes attacking convoys taking supplies from Persia into Russia. It was the kind of politico-military task at which Glubb would have excelled but the administration of Teheran objected to the operational deployment of Arab Legion soldiers because Transjordan was controlled by a British mandate and had not declared war herself on Germany. Similar reasons were put forward to prevent the Legion from serving in Greece during the Allied invasion in the winter of 1944. The only positive step was taken in 1942 when a party of Arab Legion soldiers under the command of Captain Mark Pilkington, Household Cavalry, joined the Long Range Desert Group in operations behind enemy lines. Their ability to operate in desert conditions made them ideal candidates for this special force which had been raised by Major Ralph Bagnold, Royal Signals, for covert warfare in difficult terrain, but the end of the war in North Africa in 1943 put paid to that idea. Unfortunately, Pilkington was killed during the first operation involving Arab Legion soldiers.

One reason for the British lack of confidence in the Arab Legion was the generally held belief that its soldiers were incapable of withstanding the rigours of a lengthy campaign. In attack they were known to be fierce fighters – they had underlined their prowess at Palmyra – but as the majority of the Allied fighting in the Second World War was marked more by dogged determination than by any genuine flair it was felt that the Arabs might give up if subjected to the discipline required by the British Army in field operations. There was, too, a racial element at work in this line of thinking. Whereas the Allies were prepared to use Indian troops in most theatres the relationship between the British and Indian armies was well-tried and it was easy to place mixed regiments in composite brigades. No one in Cairo thought that it would be possible to use the Arab Legion in this way as the men seemed so wild and untamed; it was too easy to dismiss them as 'Glubb's Girls'.

Glubb himself was something of a stumbling block. For all the love and admiration he lavished on his men, and for all that he never tired of praising them to others, he could appear diffident in front of British generals and their staff officers and it is not difficult to imagine that he was overawed by their rank. A different, more outgoing personality might have been prepared to curry favour with the great and the good and to push his claims at private gatherings or at official receptions. Such a course of action, though, was anathema to Glubb: as he had already told Tom Driberg, there was no point in serving in the Middle East if most of his time were spent at parties in Cairo or Jerusalem. Kirkbride was aware of this stubborn, diffident stream in Glubb and in his reports to the Colonial Office he took it upon himself to argue for a more positive role to be given to the Legion, in one 1944 report pointing out that 'at a time when there is a shortage of manpower, it seems curious that the unit cannot be permitted to make a more adequate contribution to the war effort'.[27]

Inevitably, perhaps, it was the shortage of manpower which gave the Arab Legion profitable employment – although it was not to be in an operational role. As more and more British and Dominion troops were needed for combatant duties in Europe and the Far East, there arose an acute need for men to guard the lines of communication throughout the Middle East. This task was entrusted to the Arab Legion and, from 1942 and 1945, their infantry companies served throughout the area, guarding road and railway routes from Cairo to Baghdad, policing the strategically important pipelines and airfields in Palestine and Iraq, protecting fuel and ammunition dumps and acting as garrisons to the ports of Haifa and Aqaba. It was inglorious though essential work, demanding concentration and self-discipline and, surprisingly perhaps, the Arab Legion soldiers had little difficulty adapting to it.

Glubb was especially pleased when, at the end of the war, General Paget, GOC Middle East, wrote to thank him for the services of the Arab Legion and ended the letter by praising the men for a display of discipline that was almost without parallel in the Allied armies during the Second World War. Not one criminal incident had been brought to the GOC's attention throughout the period; no one had gone absent without leave, there had been no rioting, no drunkenness, no rape and no thieving – no bad encomium for a force which but a few years earlier had consisted almost entirely of desert raiders. When asked by Cairo to supply a note on the Arab Legion for a publicity brochure, it was not without pride that Glubb described them as both the successor to Lawrence's Arab Army and a modern force with a huge potential:

The Arab Army of Lawrence and Feisal, which became so famous in the First World War, was a hasty improvisation which tried to make up in enthusiasm for what it lacked in training, equipment and discipline.

Its successor in the Second World War, the Arab Legion is a veteran force with a quarter of a century's history and traditions, an ésprit de corps of its own, and no less enthusiasm than Lawrence's first raiders. The horses and camels, the swords and cloaks which we associate with picturesque Arab warriors, have perforce given way to more prosaic and deadly weapons of modern warfare. Perhaps we do not expect to meet Arab sheikhs in battle dress and steel helmets. But when the first glamour (or disappointment) has worn off, we find them remarkably like ourselves, loyal to their comrades, full of humour, grumbling about their rations, and sometimes worried about their families (for postal arrangements are primitive in Arabia).[28]

Quite apart from rightly praising his men's virtues, Glubb had another reason for wanting to keep the Arab Legion in the public eye. With the ending of the war, the Palestine problem would re-emerge and Glubb believed that his force would have to be called upon to keep the peace between Jew and Arab. Through Kirkbride he had heard that the subsidy to the Arab Legion might be cut and he was determined to do everything in his power to keep changes to a minimum. Far from being a period of calm, the post-war years brought fresh tensions to the Middle East, unrest that would test to the limit Glubb's dual loyalties to Britain and the Arab world.

10

Abdullah's Man

When the war finally came to an end in August 1945, following the surrender of Germany in May and the dropping of atomic bombs on Hiroshima and Nagasaki, the men of the Arab Legion were still scattered throughout the Middle East. The first units to be withdrawn and brought back to Transjordan were the infantry companies which had been guarding roads and installations in Iraq and Persia, but even as late as 1947 Arab Legion soldiers still remained in Palestine where they had a substantial presence in Gaza and Haifa. In most places their presence was welcomed as the whole of the Middle East was in a state of flux and British forces were gradually being pulled out and replaced in the inevitable demobilisation and budgetary cutbacks. Glubb was able to report to the Colonial Office that the Arab Legion enjoyed a high reputation in the area, even amongst nationalist groups in Syria, Palestine and Iraq, largely because it was the only identifiably Arab army which enjoyed high standards of training and discipline and was equipped with reasonably modern weapons. In the immediate post-war period, it was Glubb's main objective to make sure that things stayed that way.

The necessary reductions in Britain's armed forces came about principally because the country could no longer afford to maintain armed forces on a large wartime scale. Fighting the Second World War had drained Britain financially, and Clement Attlee's postwar Labour government found itself having to grapple with the problems of recession, shortages and financial restrictions. In a world which saw Britain negotiating a loan of $3,750 million from the United States, followed by harsh domestic economies, massive expenditure on the armed forces was a luxury the nation could ill afford. Between 1946 and 1948 the RAF Estimates shrank from £255.5 million to £173 million. The Naval Estimates for 1949 totalled £153 million, a decrease on the previous year of £44 million, and on both services the government urged further economies in manpower and matériel. Expenditure on the army was reduced, too, to £270 million, and Second World War equipment was not replaced in any quantity until well into the 1950s, prompting Field Marshal Lord Montgomery, Chief of the Imperial General Staff between 1946 and 1948, to remark that 'the Army was in a parlous condition, and was in a complete state of unreadiness and unpreparedness for war'. In April 1945 the total strength of the British armed forces was 4,984,300; a year later it had shrunk to 2,685,000.

Not surprisingly, perhaps, the position of the Arab Legion was also under scrutiny, simply because it had expanded during the Second World War and had become a drain on the country's exchequer. In 1939, the British subvention had been £200,000; by 1945 this had increased ten-fold, although £800,000 of the total was earmarked for the retention of the garrison companies which had been used for guard duties in Palestine in the latter stages of the war. Even so, £1.2 million was a tidy sum, well above inflation – the Treasury reckoned that the true rate of growth should have provided the Arab Legion with a grant of £500,000, a figure with which Glubb was inclined to agree, provided that it was used as a baseline for further negotiation. As it seemed entirely possible, though, that cuts might still be the order of the day, Glubb set about arguing the case for the retention of a strong and well-equipped Arab Legion if British interests in the Middle East were to be safeguarded.

In a series of discussion documents for the Colonial Office

he based his arguments on military and political necessity. Before the war the Legion had been an internal security force but by 1945 it had become a national defence force whose prestige in the Arab world was closely linked to Abdullah's authority. Any hint of excessive cutbacks would be a blow to the emir and therefore to British interests at a time when Palestine was threatening once more to become unstable. While the Colonial Office accepted this point of view its officials were concerned about the advisability of continuing to fund a fully blown army and by the war's end were pressing the War Office to take over this responsibility. Glubb resisted the proposal because he believed that it would remove Transjordanian control and turn the Legion into an imperial force. In the end, Transjordan's independence in 1946 brought it under the aegis of the Foreign Office who then took over the funding responsibilities, but Glubb realised that, before any decisions could be taken about the size and strength of the Legion, he had to make sure that the Treasury understood the special circumstances surrounding the seemingly large amounts of money awarded during the war years.

In an impressive document, 'A Note on the Future of the Arab Legion', one of several composed in late 1945 and early 1946, Glubb accepted that £1.2 million was an inflated figure but he was also quick to point out that some £360,000 represented capital costs for new equipment, most of which had been bought at face value from the British Army and was therefore only a transaction on paper. This was elementary accounting but, even so, Glubb was not above pointing out that some of the items were no longer front-line equipment and that the Legion was probably doing the British Army a good turn by taking it off their hands. 'Incidentally,' Glubb noted in an aside, 'it may be worth mentioning that the Armoured Cars supplied were obsolete for European warfare and if they had not been issued to the Arab Legion would probably have been broken up as scrap, although the Arab Legion were debited with their full cost price.'[1] The argument obviously had some effect for, when the Foreign Office took over responsibility for the Arab Legion's grant, wartime capital costs had been written off and permission was given to re-equip the Legion with modern transport and armoured cars similar to those used by the British Army.[2]

During this difficult transitional period it was noticeable that Glubb began employing harder and more pragmatic arguments in the discussion papers which were sent back to the Colonial Office after perusal in Amman and Jerusalem. Now aged forty-eight, Glubb stripped his style of bucolic references to the simplicity of Bedouin life or the chivalric nature of the troops under his command and based his arguments instead on the strategic grounds that Britain needed a strong ally in Transjordan and that, if the country were to be fully supported, it needed a strong army, one based on the wartime model. Like everyone else in the Middle East, Glubb was also aware that the ending of the war would reawaken the Arab–Jew confrontation in Palestine and that in the event of further armed struggles, Transjordan would need a strong defence force to protect its own borders and to prevent the kind of infiltration that had taken place during the revolt of 1936–9.

At this stage no decisions had been made about the employment of the Arab Legion should fighting break out again, but Glubb was uncomfortably aware that if Britain withdrew from Palestine and, indeed, from Egypt – both possibilities had been mooted in 1945 – then Transjordan would be isolated and a prey to hostile neighbours. Even if Britain were to remain in Palestine for the time being, the internal control of the country would be more complicated without Arab Legion help and Glubb did not hesitate to point out that his forces were already employed under the direction of the British Army. There was also a possibility that Transjordan itself would have to be granted independence as a reward for the loyalty and steadfastness to the British cause it had shown during the war. This prospect, but not the consequences, had been seen by the Colonial Office as early as 1941 when Britain was arguing the case for Syria to be made independent of French rule:

> If we are prepared to put an end to the mandate in Syria to buy the support of Arabs who might otherwise be our enemies, are there any grounds on which we can continue to retain the mandate in Trans-Jordan, where the ruler and his people have for twenty years been our most consistent friends?[3]

The answer was obviously no; but at that stage of the war Britain was in no mood to think about granting independence to Transjordan – or indeed to any other part of the empire – while she was engaged in a global struggle for her very existence. Although the Colonial Office remained amenable to the idea of granting independence to Transjordan at some future date, it also recorded the observation that there was much to be said for preserving the status quo as Abdullah had not pressed for independence and there was no discernible nationalist movement within his country.

Although he did not admire nationalism as a credo, Glubb knew only too well that it could become a potent force in Transjordanian politics and to control it Britain would have to bolster Abdullah's authority. In one of his periodic reports, written in 1942, he agreed that while it was right to reward Transjordan because it had 'the only Arab army where men still stood in queues' to enlist, complete independence would be an abnegation of responsibility unless Abdullah were offered military and financial support:

> It is difficult, when war is over, to allot suitable rewards to friends and enemies, but it is sincerely to be hoped that HMG will find some way of showing their appreciation to His Highness and Trans-Jordan, although free gifts of 'independence' without stability may not necessarily be the best form of reward.[4]

In other words, when Transjordan became independent, as

307

Glubb and others hoped it would after the war, Britain should continue to pay the cost of the Legion as part of the price for maintaining her influence and keeping the region comparatively stable. In the years to come, this reasoning was to form the basis of Glubb's view of British policy in the Middle East. 'Whatever the future may bring in the seething cauldron of Arab politics,' he claimed in a periodic report to the Colonial Office, 'a strong and efficient Arab Legion will always be a factor for making stability, democracy and co-operation with Great Britain.'[5]

While this view was largely accepted in London, there were continuing doubts within the Colonial Office about Transjordan's readiness for independence and there were still officials in the Middle East Department who remained suspicious of Abdullah's meddling in regional politics. There was a fear, too, that the continued payment of the Arab Legion grant and the retention of the military bases – a necessary prerequisite of any agreement – would anger Transjordan's neighbours, especially Ibn Saud who retained territorial claims on Malan and Aqaba. Iraq, too, was suspicious of Transjordan's ambitions, despite the family relationship between the two rulers, while to the north, Syria, now independent, had accused Glubb of fomenting unrest amongst the Druze tribes by supplying them with weapons. Any agreement would also have to fit in with Britain's policy towards the Middle East in general. The arrival in power of a Labour government in the summer of 1945 had given rise to hopes that the new administration would be more sympathetic to nationalist aspirations but from the very outset the new Foreign Secretary, Ernest Bevin, had made it clear that he wanted to maintain Britain's dominant military position in the Middle East.

In return, Britain would support the idea of Arab independence and supply the necessary economic and military infrastructure which would lead friendly Arab states to identify their own interests with those of the protecting power. Federation was also encouraged – this was one of the features of

Britain's colonial policy – and in March 1945 the Arab League had been established with its headquarters in Cairo and a permanent staff headed by a secretary-general. Its members were Egypt, Iraq, Saudi Arabia, Transjordan, Yemen, Syria and Lebanon and its professed aim was pan-Arab unity.

Despite the fact that the granting of independence to India and Pakistan in August 1947 seemed to make a mockery of the need to retain expensive military installations in the Middle East and to guard the lines of communication, Britain still had good reasons to preserve an active policy for the area. There were substantial British investments in Egypt and Iraq and it was vital to protect the supply of oil. There were also growing fears of Soviet incursions, particularly in Syria and Iraq, and these were to continue well into the post-war period. National prestige was a further factor: there was a strongly held belief in many government circles that the Middle East and Africa were the last areas where Britain could play a decisive role in shaping future events. Not the least of these was in Palestine which the Foreign Office felt could be settled by negotiation in spite of the country's rapid and dismal post-war descent into anarchy.

It was against that background that Abdullah visited Britain in February 1946 to negotiate the treaty which would give his country independence. He was in a good position. Firstly, he had been a loyal supporter during the war – in spite of his momentary doubts in 1942 – and his Arab Legion had performed well in the field; secondly, he was known to be amenable when it came to the question of negotiating a settlement with the Zionists. His one fear was that Britain might use the Arab Legion as a bargaining counter and threaten to withdraw its subsidy, thus leaving him bereft of power in the Middle East and a prey to his larger neighbours. (Abdullah was also painfully aware that his prestige in the Middle East depended more or less entirely on the Arab Legion.)

As an insurance policy, therefore, Abdullah entered into

secret discussions with Iraq a fortnight before he was due to leave for London – by then Kirkbride, who would have opposed such a move, had left for London – and the way was clear to talk to his Hashemite cousins. An Iraqi delegation, led by the Regent Abdul Illah, arrived in Amman in January and, studiously ignoring their previous enmity towards Transjordan, offered to pay for the Arab Legion should Britain refuse to continue the annual grant. In return the Arab Legion would expand into the national army of both countries at a time when Iraq herself felt threatened by the other members of the Arab League – for despite all the pronouncements about Arab unity, the new organisation had soon divided into two loose camps, Egypt, Syria and Saudi Arabia in one and Transjordan and Iraq in the other. The Iraqi Army, too, had performed badly in dealing with a Kurdish rebellion in the Mosul province and Iraq's leaders were worried about the threat of Soviet invasion from Armenia in the north. Having reviewed the whole situation the delegates agreed that Iraq's needs and the continuing uncertainty about British aims meant that the Arab Legion might be better served by coming under Arab control.

Quite apart from providing a safety net should the treaty negotiations fail, Abdullah had another good reason for entering into talks with Iraq. Ever conscious of the weakness of his position in the Arab world, and suspicious that he was only considered a British stooge, he believed that an agreement with a fellow Arab state, in this case a Hashemite country, would provide him with the necessary stepping stone to further his territorial ambitions elsewhere. Fortunately, Glubb had been alerted to the content of the talks when the Iraqi delegation requested the Arab Legion's Order of Battle and, as he reported to London, he was able to intervene and to induce Abdullah to change his mind:

The present writer approached the Amir Abdullah privately during these negotiations, and pointed out to him the dangers involved. The acceptance of something like

£2,000,000 a year from Iraq would reduce Trans-Jordan to the status of an Iraqi colony. His Highness admitted the danger but claimed that he had no alternative, if His Majesty's Government would not pay for the Arab Legion. To disband it, he said, was quite unthinkable. He would be obliged to use his own wits and prestige to prevent Trans-Jordan from becoming an Iraqi colony. He relied on the fact that he was head of the family, the Regent of Iraq his nephew, and the King his great-nephew. Arab ideas of family solidarity obliged all members to obey the head of the family.

The writer pointed out that the throne in Iraq was very much less powerful than in Trans-Jordan, that the Iraqi Parliament would have a good deal to say on the matter, and that Trans-Jordan might find herself receiving orders from a Baghdad politician not from the Royal family.[6]

Glubb's arguments had the desired effect and Abdullah left for London minded to use the Iraqi offer only in the unlikely event of the Colonial Office refusing to continue funding the Arab Legion. The subsequent treaty gave Transjordan independence from Britain and paved the way for Abdullah to crown himself king later in the year, on 25 May 1946. On paper, it seemed to the world that Transjordan had achieved self-determination and was free to carry out its own policies, but in practice, the country remained under British tutelage, still economically and strategically dependent on Britain. The Americans and the Soviets certainly saw it in that light and refused to support Transjordan's application to join the United Nations.

Both countries remained suspicious of British imperial intentions in the postwar period: America had made it clear that it was not fighting a world war to bolster the British Empire and the Soviet Union feared the creation of a western power bloc in the Middle East which might threaten the frontiers of Soviet Central Asia. As evidence of these fears they pointed to the military annex which Britain had insisted was the price of Transjordanian independence. Basically, this held open the offer of continued support for the Arab Legion in return for the presence of British military bases and installations in Transjordan. The agreement was summarised in Article 8 of the military annex to the treaty:

> HM The King will afford financial assistance to His Highness the Amir in meeting the cost of the military units of the Amir's forces which are required to insure the purpose of Article 5 of the Treaty [mutual assistance in the event of war]. The strength of such units will be agreed upon annually by the High Contracting Parties and His Highness the Amir will enable His Majesty's representatives in Transjordan to ascertain that the funds in question are expended for the purpose for which they are issued.[7]

Later in the year, after discussions between Glubb, Kirkbride, now the British minister in Amman, the Foreign Office and the War Office, it was agreed that the British assistance to the Transjordanian government should be based upon the following provisos: 1. Arab Legion to consist of three mechanised regiments plus logistical support; 2. The garrison companies to be funded by the War Office for as long as they were needed in Palestine; 3. Funds for 1947–48 to be fixed at £500,000; 4. Kirkbride to oversee all expenditure; 5. British officers to be paid from Transjordanian funds and not by the War Office; 6. No inspection unless requested by the Transjordanian government.[8]

This was a satisfactory outcome for both parties as it allowed the Arab Legion to retain its wartime strength – Glubb's argument – and it was to provide the Foreign Office with a pawn in the coming British discussions over the future of Palestine. Any further increase in the Arab Legion grant would be governed by Glubb's recommendations and Britain would retain a military presence in the area even if its own troops were withdrawn. Moreover, there was the bonus of the responsibility of funding the garrison companies remaining with the War Office and in turn their operations would come under the local military command of the British Army in Palestine. Small wonder, then, that the two postwar super-powers not only regarded Abdullah as a British puppet but remained highly critical of Britain's continuing involvement in the affairs of Transjordan and, by association, of Palestine as well.

There were good grounds for their cynicism. Throughout this period the reports written by Glubb and Kirkbride always implied that, while Abdullah was the King of Transjordan, he was ruler in name only and that despite the constitutional changes Britain's interest would continue to be safeguarded by the military provisions of the treaty. Kirkbride went one step further and reported to Bevin, the Foreign Secretary, that following an initial burst of enthusiasm, Transjordan's political leaders had soon reverted to their old habit of discussing immediate problems with himself and Glubb:

> As regards the Transjordan Government, immediately after the ratification of the treaty, a tendency was evident on the part of the prime minister and the members of the Council of Ministers to stand on their dignity and to be on the look-out for action by His Majesty's Minister which might not be covered by the terms of the treaty but this phase soon passed and the consultation of an informal nature which used to take place between the Prime Minister and the British Resident on current affairs has resumed between the Prime Minister and His Majesty's Minister. I am now frequently asked by the Prime Minister to use my personal influence on King Abdullah on matters of purely local and internal concern.[9]

Abdullah was probably too wily a ruler not to have under-stood the nature of the relationship he shared with Kirkbride but, as Glubb noted, when the king returned to Transjordan, he seemed 'immensely relieved' by the outcome of the nego-tiations. Now he felt he could speak on equal terms to his fellow Arab rulers, especially to Ibn Saud, and to Glubb's amusement Abdullah began bombarding the Saudi ruler with well-meant advice about the necessity of entering into a long-term political relationship with a powerful country, just as he had done with Britain.

Although little changed immediately in the relationship between the king and his British political advisers, there was one subtle shift of power which affected Glubb. He remained the commanding officer of the Arab Legion but, as King Abdullah was now the constitutional head of the country's armed forces, his position in Transjordan was no longer as secure as it had been during the war. He was still in the nominal employment of the Palestine Service but he knew that Britain's days were numbered in that country and that it might make sense to make a break at this crucial juncture, while Transjordan was enjoying the first fruits of independence. Accordingly, he set down his thoughts in a rambling letter to General Sir Alan Cunningham, the new High Commissioner in Jerusalem, and suggested that the time might have come for him to transfer to another service, perhaps the Middle East section of the Foreign Office 'while I am still young enough to take up slightly different work'. Another suggestion was a proposal to put his experience of Arabic culture at the disposal of the British Council which had been established in 1934 to promote abroad a wider knowledge of Britain and its culture and languages. Glubb had two reasons for suggesting a move: first, he wanted to remain in employment in order to fund his children's education and support his family, and, second, he feared that his continuing presence in an independent Transjordan could become a focus for Arab jealousies:

> I should, however, like to add that I am not trying to work myself into a better job, or to threaten or demand. I have spent all my life in Government service, as did my father and grand-father before me. I have no higher ambition than to serve my country as they did. Should His Majesty's

Government be of the opinion that I am best employed in Trans-Jordan I will continue in my present post without complaint. But I should be grateful if it could be placed on record that I have little private means, that the vicissitudes of my career have deprived me of any pension worth mentioning, that I have a young family and that my present post may well be precarious, through no fault of my own. This being my position I trust that His Majesty's Government will protect my interests until at least my family is grown up and launched in the world.[10]

Cunningham passed the letter to the Colonial Office as the department responsible for Palestinian affairs and asked for their advice. He was in two minds about Glubb's position. Like most British officials in the Middle East at the time, he recognised the importance to British policy of Glubb's remaining as head of the Arab Legion in a settled Trans-jordan. On the other hand, Cunningham was a professional soldier who knew all about the dangers of seeking the bauble reputation. During the war he had made his name through his successful prosecution of the campaign against the Italians in Ethiopia but had then been promptly sacked whilst commanding the 8th Army after Rommel's strike into Libya in November 1941. He was not the kind of man to be swayed either by sentiment or by the relative importance of a man's position. Moreover, he was not at all sure about the military proficiency of the Arab Legion: sitting on his desk was a critical report written by Lieutenant-General Sir Evelyn Barker, GOC Palestine and Transjordan, who was sceptical about Glubb's leadership qualities and thought that the training of the Legion should become the responsibility of the British Army:

As you know, Glubb is not a soldier and I don't think understands the organisation and training or the interior economy of a unit and as he is more interested in politics no doubt leaves a good deal of soldiering to the brigade commander [Lash].

315

I have reason to believe that orders which emanate from the Headquarters of the Arab Legion are not always carried out by subordinate commanders and that Glubb accepts this. I am told, also, that the senior Arab officers are mostly ex-Turkish officers who have become fat and lazy, and I am equally doubtful as to the efficiency of the British officers.[11]

Although Barker's criticisms had been promptly rebuffed by Kirkbride, who pointed out that the Arab soldiers in Transjordan would refuse to give their loyalty to abstract bodies and preferred men like Glubb and Lash whom they had known for a long time and trusted, Cunningham was less than impressed. He agreed with Barker that the Arab Legion should be subjected to twice-yearly inspections and he also feared that the presence of Arab Legion units in Palestine might be a breach of international law. While wartime legislation passed by Abdullah permitted the Legion to serve outside Transjordan – a measure intended to protect the British officers from being regarded by the enemy as *franc tireurs* – Cunningham held that the position in peacetime was different and that the Arab Legion should be confined to Transjordan. He wrote to the Colonial Office:

In the field of international politics, the presence of what is constitutionally a foreign force will inevitably give rise to a series of embarrassing questions. Although the Arab Legion would, of course, never be used offensively against the Jews, units might be, and in fact have been, involved in incidents with the Jews. In such circumstances a situation might arise which would be calculated to arouse considerable adverse comment in both the United Kingdom and America. On the other hand it would not be advisable in a crisis to rely on the Arab Legion for offensive action against the Arabs. For both constitutional and political reasons, therefore, I must urge that the War Office be asked to consider the replacement of the units of the Arab Legion now in Palestine by other troops.[12]

Implicit in Cunningham's letter was the recommendation that Glubb should be quietly replaced when the Legion returned to its bases in Transjordan. The Colonial Office passed the files to the Foreign Office and the War Office and immediately the alarm bells were set ringing as both had a vested interest in maintaining a strong British-backed Arab Legion presence in the Middle East. The War Office responded quickly by underlining the strategic necessity of maintaining the garrison companies at full strength in Palestine as no British or imperial troops were available to take their place.[13]

The Foreign Office was more cautious as they had to deal with all the implications of Glubb's future service. While acknowledging Glubb's experience of Arab affairs, his role as a figurehead and his influence over Abdullah all of which 'must redound to Britain's credit', the minute, written by G.W. Furlonge, also expressed reservations about Glubb's prominent pro-Arab stance and about his supposed relationship with Abdullah's expansionist policies. If there were a strong case for Glubb's replacement, the minute seemed to suggest, then the Foreign Office would bow to the wishes of the Colonial Office. Eventually the matter was settled by Ernest Bevin who decided that the time was hardly ripe for any changes to key British personnel in the Middle East and Glubb was told that, while it was not possible to set an exact timescale on his appointment in Transjordan, it was hoped that he would continue in the post for the time being and that his name would be carefully considered in connection with any suitable vacancies that might occur when his time in Transjordan came to an end.[14]

There the matter was closed for the time being. Glubb was permitted to remain at the head of the Arab Legion because it suited British policy in the Middle East and because his replacement so soon after Transjordan's independence could unsettle the country, but the difficulties surrounding his appointment had been noted and it was not the last time that the question of his official position would return to trouble him. As General Barker had astutely noted, the position of the commanding officer of the Arab Legion was mainly political: even though Glubb refused to admit it at the time, or indeed later in his life, he was very much a key player in Britain's moves and counter-moves in the policy towards post-war Palestine. As John Hackett observed, pressures were starting to build up in Glubb's appointment as he was having to act simultaneously as army commander, chief of staff and minister of defence.

The attention given to Glubb's papers and reports from Transjordan confirm the view that he was an influential voice in government decision-making. Just as the Colonial Office had done, some Foreign Office officials complained at the time about their length and prolixity but they were still impressed by his pro-Arab stance which was very much in keeping with the views held by the Middle East Department. Time and time again, references to the Arab Legion are annotated with queries like 'what does Glubb think?' and it was always made clear that the future of the Arab Legion was bound up with British policies in Transjordan and Palestine.

In the later part of 1946 the linkage between the two countries was underlined when orders were given for more British military equipment to be transferred from Palestine to the Arab Legion. These items included 62 Marmon-Herrington Mark IV armoured cars equipped with two-pounder guns and coaxial Bren guns: similiar to the British Humber, these vehicles provided the Legion for the first time with modern strike and reconnaissance weapons. Also supplied were large numbers of Sten guns and two-inch mortars, as well as 12 twenty-five-pounder field guns, 24 six-pounder anti-tank guns and a further 115 trucks and jeeps.[15] At that time, too, the first tentative steps were taken to start an Arab Legion air force when a request was made for the supply of seven Auster observation and communications aircraft which would be invaluable in a sprawling country like Transjordan. The request was passed to the Air Ministry for comment, though it was not until 1950 that a fledgling air force was formed; Glubb was a firm supporter of the proposal, having enjoyed the use of a privately purchased aircraft during the war.

Equally important to him was the question of the British officers required to assist with the development of the Legion. Glubb's standards were high and in the aide-mémoire he prepared for the War Office on the selection of officers, he made it clear that he considered the Arab Legion a corps d'élite and that he was only interested in choosing from the best available candidates:

> The most important point of all however is that all such Officers should be of first-class quality. If really good Officers are not available, it is better to have none. Inferior Officers are not useless, they are actively harmful ... For combatant Officers, the first essential is the quality of leadership, high moral character and a natural affinity and affection for the Arab soldier. Any Officer who possesses these qualities will be able to make himself efficient in the simple weapon and tactical training required for a small Arab Army.[16]

Glubb also recommended that they should be well paid and that it would be a false economy to cut back on any expenditure which might lead to local allowances being cut or, just as important given his own experiences, their pensions being reduced. Eventually it was agreed that a special Transjordan allowance of £300 a year would be paid on top of salaries and that the War Office would continue to maintain pension funds with additional payments being met by the Transjordan exchequer. As it turned out, Glubb was extremely fortunate with the quality of the officers who served with him in the post-war years, men like James Lunt, Peter Young, Desmond Goldie, Sam Cooke, Rea Leakey and 'Teal' Ashton, amongst others.

Despite all the changes that were taking place around him,

Glubb continued to lead the kind of life he had enjoyed throughout his period of service in Transjordan. His office in Amman was always open to anyone who wanted to discuss a problem with him, be it a young officer requiring additional ammunition or a private soldier anxious to go on leave to visit a sick relative. John Salmon remembered the patient queues of men who were prepared to wait several days, if necessary, to hear Glubb's judgement on any subject under the sun. He was generous with his own limited funds, too – a virtue much admired by the Bedouin people – and he frequently paid for his men to go on courses or to attend clinics. James Lunt was told by one senior Jordanian officer that Glubb had saved his career when he had tuberculosis by paying for his treatment in a Beirut clinic, and in January 1945 Glubb dreamed up a scheme which would have allowed young Arab boys to attend British boarding schools. In this way they would be immersed in British ideas and might return to their countries with a better understanding of the British point of view. Despite an approach to Lord Nuffield to finance such a scheme, Glubb's proposals came to nothing although he never lost sight of the notion that if Arabs were exposed to British influence at an early age, they would remain loyal to Britain throughout their lives.

To supplement his income and to propagate his ideas Glubb had started concentrating on writing during his spare time and while he was on leave in England. As a young man he had hoped that one day he might write a great book which would lead to greater human understanding but his career had been so packed with action and adventures that he had found no time to further that ambition. His first literary efforts, essays on various aspects of Bedouin life, had been encouraged by St John Philby who passed them on to the editor of the journal of the Royal Central Asian Society and these appeared as a series before the Second World War. Glubb was a meticulously careful writer and took great trouble over the correction of his proofs which were always sent out to him in Transjordan after he had submitted the articles while on leave in England. He wrote everything in long hand and the manuscript would then be typed by his secretary Thelma Toogood at Arab Legion headquarters. The lengthy monthly reports which he produced throughout the 1930s show that he was a natural writer with an eye for detail and a pleasing ability to bring incidents to life – unlike the writing produced in similar documents by Kirkbride and others, Glubb preferred literary flourishes to dry administrative details.

Given his undoubted ability and his ambition to turn to literature, perhaps as a means of supplementing his income in his retirement, it was hardly surprising that Glubb should have given thought to writing an account of his adventures with the Arab Legion. In fact, as early as 1942, he had already contacted a publisher when he proposed such a book to Stanley Unwin who had been enthusiastic about the idea: 'We are confident that we could make an outstanding success of any book you may see your way to write when the appropriate time comes.'[17] Once more the exigencies of service life made it impossible for Glubb to write the book during the war, but in 1946 and 1947 he turned his spare time to profit by writing *The Story of the Arab Legion* which was published in 1948, not by Unwin but by John Attenborough of Hodder & Stoughton who later published several other titles. After completing the first draft Glubb submitted the manuscript to the Colonial Office and War Office but neither department offered any comment as it was felt that the official view should be that the author was 'Glubb Pasha, a servant of the King of Transjordan who was during the war thrown by circumstances into contact with British forces'.[18]

Although not a particularly wealthy man, Glubb rarely allowed lack of funds to hamper his or his family's enjoyment of life. Horses continued to be a passion – he rode whenever he could – and he encouraged his children to do the same. After the distressing experience when his second son was delivered prematurely and still-born, the Glubbs adopted two more children in addition to Naomi – Mary and John, both Palestinian refugee children, in 1948. Godfrey, the eldest son now aged eight, increasingly preferred to use his Arabic name of Faris and was often found in his father's company wearing a specially made copy of the Arab Legion's uniform, complete with *shamagh*.

During this period of his life Glubb was forced to work hard and put in long hours at headquarters but he never neglected his family and was fond of quoting Dr Johnson's dictum: 'To be happy at home is the ultimate result of all ambition, the end to which every enterprise and labour tends, and of which every desire prompts the prosecution.' Afternoon tea with the family was an important ritual and the children always looked forward to seeing his official car drive up outside the house and the bodyguard dismissed – a sure sign that work was over for another day.

Moments like that gave Glubb great pleasure, too, and he especially liked hearing the piano being played and the sound of 'fresh young voices' singing a nursery favourite – Naomi had become an accomplished pianist who played regularly at school concerts in Amman. 'Deedee!' the girls would shout to him as the drawing room doors opened and two small figures would wrap themselves round his knees. Those happy memories found their way into his book *A Soldier with the Arabs*, his account of the confrontation with Israel during the early 1950s.

> 'Oh Deedee! Do you know what has happened? We'll give you three guesses! you'll never guess! What do you think?'
>
> I gave it up. They looked at one another in triumph.
>
> 'Tibby's had her kittens in the cupboard! On top of your shirts! Two are tabby and one is yellow! Come here and see!'
>
> I was seized by both hands and dragged into our bedroom.[19]

Glubb never forgot that his family were an important part of the responsibility he felt towards Abdullah's kingdom.

For the whole family, the highlight of the week was Friday, the day of rest, when a picnic would be arranged and they could leave Amman for a well-deserved period of privacy. Sundays, too, were important days and Glubb frequently led the services in the small Anglican church at Zerqa. Hardly surprisingly, given Glubb's official position in the country, their existence in Transjordan was rather like living in a goldfish bowl. It might have lacked the glamour, élan and snobbishness of social life in British India, where it was said with some truth that the country provided a vast system of outdoor relaxation for Britain's ruling classes, and it contained nothing of the dangerous scandal-mongering of White Settler Kenya, but Transjordan was not without its share of petty social manipulations and intrigues. If Ronnie Broadhurst saw too much of the emir, for example, he was accused of social-climbing, behind his back of course, and eyebrows were raised when, in a typically effusive act of generosity, Abdullah presented Glubb with an expensive Cadillac for his private use.

Being an important man in Jordan, Glubb had to be given police protection and whenever he and his family went out they were always accompanied by a jeep carrying an armed escort. 'I was well aware at the time that my father had had threats made on his life,' remembers Naomi. 'Even when we were on leave in England we had the protection of Special Branch detectives who always followed us around in a similar kind of car to ours. They shadowed us wherever we went – except, of course, when we went to the continent, which we usually did.'

There were good reasons for providing Glubb with a high level of personal protection. Early in 1948 the Foreign Office had received warnings from the US Central Intelligence Agency (CIA) that Glubb's name had been found on a Stern Gang list of 'British criminals sentenced to death' and that the 'sentences would be executed as soon as possible'.[20] This was no idle threat as the gang, more properly the Lohamei Herut Israel, was a much-feared terrorist organisation which regarded murder and assassination as legitimate means to the political end of forcing the British to leave Palestine. They had been responsible for the murder in Cairo during the war of Lord Moyne, the British Minister of State in the Middle East, and for the summary execution of several members of the British security forces. The gang's murderous activities encouraged other terrorist groups to indulge in acts of violence and, in the spring of 1948, a little-known Syrian group attempted to murder Glubb by placing a bomb outside his house in Amman. Only Rosemary was at home at the time, as she was recuperating from a bout of influenza; although all the windows were blown in and the house suffered some structural damage, Glubb acknowledged that his wife was lucky to survive the attack. 'She was stunned by the explosion, but when she recovered her presence of mind, she found that her pillow and her hair were full of splinters of glass. If she had been lying on her other side, she would have received this hail of broken glass in her face and eyes. The door of our bedroom was on the opposite side of the room to the window under which the bomb had exploded.'[21]

By this time it had become only too clear to Glubb that the Middle East was about to erupt into violence again over the problems that had been fermenting in Palestine ever since the beginning of the British mandate. During the war there had been a slight hiatus in the armed struggle between Jew and Arab and the British colonial administration and at least 30,000 Jewish servicemen had fought alongside the Allies against Nazi Germany. Others, like Menachem Begin, continued the struggle against the British, fighting in guerrilla units like the Stern Gang or the Irgun Zvai Leumi which carried out terrorist attacks on police posts and personnel and against British Army units stationed in Palestine. The fact that Britain was engaged in a war against the Nazis restricted the size and scale of the Jewish attacks but after peace had come in the spring and summer of 1945 the Holy Land rapidly became a new armed camp.

The problem facing the British was – as many

commentators have noted – of Sisyphean proportions: no sooner had one faction delivered a possible solution or proposed a compromise, than it would be dashed by another group and the whole process would have to begin again. Before war broke out in 1939 partition of Palestine into Jewish and Arab areas had been the favoured solution and this continued to be the policy of the Colonial Office. (But not of the Foreign Office which opposed partition as it would damage Britain's relationships with the surrounding Arab countries.) However, by then, Palestine was not merely a British problem; it had become an international predicament in which the two super-powers, the United States and the Soviet Union, also wanted to have a say. In the United States international Zionism had a formidable ally as American Jews were an influential sector of the American electorate. One of President Truman's first pronouncements on the problem was to demand the admission into Palestine of 100,000 Jewish immigrants, a move that would have left Britain, the supervising power, with the difficulty of keeping the peace between the Jewish population and the Arabs who would no doubt start a fresh revolt, just as they had done in 1936. As for the Soviet Union, far from wanting to support the Zionists, they saw in Palestine the opportunity to destabilise the Middle East and to promote their own interests in the area. Glubb foresaw this possibility: in his immediate post-war reports to the Colonial Office he had warned that if Syria and Iraq were not kept within the British military sphere of influence 'the leaders will turn to Russia, a country with an autocratic regime'.[22] The problem was compounded by the differing attitudes of the Arab states and also by the continuing political presence of the Mufti as a focus for nationalist discontent in Palestine. His nephew Jemal al Husaini put the matter at its starkest when he was supposed to have remarked: 'The Arabs agreed with the Jews on one point only, and that was that British troops should withdraw and allow the Arabs and the Jews to fight it out.'

Meanwhile, there was fighting a-plenty in Palestine as the

Irgun and the Stern Gang continued their terrorist campaign. 'Not only were British soldiers and police murdered, but some were kidnapped, flogged, ill-treated and hanged,' said Glubb whose own Arab Legion forces were being used for internal security duties in Palestine. 'Mass murders were carried out, such as the blowing up of the King David Hotel, which was in use as the secretariat of the Palestine government. British, Arab and Jewish officials alike were buried in the ruins.'[23] Against that violent background an Anglo-American Commission visited Palestine and took evidence in a vain attempt to find a solution which would also mollify American public opinion, but its motives were so ambiguous that it was hardly surprising that its findings were only wishful thinking. Not only did the commission recommend continued Jewish immigration but they also favoured the creation of a state under the joint administration of the Jews and Arabs under the trusteeship of the United Nations. At the same time the Americans kept up diplomatic pressure on Britain to permit the entry of the 100,000 immigrants. There was also a good deal of anti-British feeling in the American press and, stung by criticism of his government, an enraged Ernest Bevin delivered a sharp counter-attack at the Labour Party's annual conference in June 1946. Not only would Britain have to pick up the pieces by deploying additional troops in Palestine – a move he was not prepared to recommend – but America, too, should take some of the burden herself. 'I hope I will not be misunderstood in America,' he said, 'if I saw that this was proposed with the purest motives. They do not want too many Jews in New York.'

It was a point of view with which Glubb sympathised for he had not lost sight of his belief that the Jews were more of a people bound together by a common religion than a race with any unique territorial claims to Palestine. He also failed to understand why it was not possible for the dispossessed and persecuted Jewish refugees of wartorn Europe to find homes in other parts of the world and he could not take seriously the Jewish claim that a return to Palestine was in some way a fulfilment of biblical prophecy: 'To drive a million Arabs from their homes and country cannot be justified by any consideration.' In an ideal world he would have preferred to see Arab and Jew living together in harmony – an aim of the Anglo-American Commission with which he agreed – but he knew only too well that the ferocity of the opposing factions made such a move impossible. After the members of the Commission hasd visited Transjordan in March 1946 Glubb summarised their options in a series of gloomy clerihews.

> A Jewish State of Palestine?
> If you do it
> You'll rue it.
>
> An Arab State of Palestine?
> Hardly a proposition
> When you consider the opposition.
>
> Federation?
> What situation
> Follows separation?
> A divorce of course.
>
> Partition?
> To partite and be neighbourly
> Then putting up with banditry
> And blaming the mandatory.[24]

Sadly, the political position in Palestine at that time was not dissimilar to Glubb's verse delineation of it, and with neither side willing to agree to a solution, and with an economically depressed Britain under continued international attack to retrieve the situation, the Labour government admitted defeat in February 1947 and announced that the problem would be handed over to the stewardship of the United Nations. The result was the formation of the United Nations Special Committee on Palestine (UNSCOP) which was set up on 15 May 1947 and got down to work immediately there-after. 'It did the usual tour,' said Glubb tartly; 'it has the same old evidence and it disappeared again.' Three months later, at the end of August, UNSCOP submitted its report which came down on the side of arbitration and ending the British mandate as soon as possible.

Like most international concords, the commission's find-ings contained a strong hint of compromise. They also seemed to favour the Jewish population in Palestine by not only giving them some 60 per cent of the territory but also awarding them the fertile coastal strip between Haifa and Jaffa, the plain of Esdraelon and eastern Galilee. The majority Arab population was given western and central Galilee, Samaria, the Judaean Hills and the Gaza Strip; at the same time Jerusalem was designated an international zone, safe-guarded by the United Nations. It was also hoped that there could be an economic union between the two territories and that Britain would continue to provide the necessary forces during the period of UN administration. In other words, Britain would have to continue quasi-mandatory responsibi-lities while at the same time appearing to play a role in the creation of the new Jewish state of Israel. Such a position would be untenable as it would endanger Britain's position in the Arab world at a time when it was necessary to safeguard oil supplies and other trading rights: realising that the UNSCOP proposal was inimical to all British interests and could hardly be squared against previous policy, the govern-ment decided to remain neutral and to withdraw from any further involvement in the settlement of the Palestine issue. On 17 October, while the UNSCOP plan was being debated in the General Assembly, Arthur Creech Jones, the British Colonial Secretary, told the United Nations that 'His Majesty's Government would not accept responsibility for the enforcement, either alone or in cooperation with other nations, of any settlement antagonistic to either Jews or the Arabs or both, which was likely to necessitate the use of force'. Between then and 15 May 1948 – the date fixed for the final British withdrawal – Britain would take no further responsibility for any action which implied the implementation of the policy of partition. As Glubb noted at the time, the British seemed to be saying: 'Well, if you don't like us, you can sort yourselves out as best you can.' This was not entirely true. While the international community, with or without Britain's assistance, was feeling its uncertain way towards a policy of dividing Palestine into two separate areas, the Foreign Office, abetted by the War Office, had been doing its best to rebuild bridges with Britain's Arab friends and, as Harold Beeley of the Foreign Office put it, to revise the idea that Britain was about to 'simply slide out of the problem'.

Given the tortuous nature of Britain's previous diplomatic initiatives in the Middle East, there were many reasons why frantic behind-the-scenes activities were undertaken to safeguard Britain's position. Not the least of these was the traditional pro-Arab stance of the Foreign Office's Middle East Department and the feeling of shame that Britain seemed to be surrendering her responsibility for the Arab communities in Palestine. There was, too, a belief that imperialism, as practised by the British at least, was still a beneficent power and that Britain had a duty to remain a force in world politics. To this idealistic notion was added the more pragmatic view that in order to be considered an internationally respected nation, Britain had to safeguard her oil interests and imperial lines of communication throughout the Middle East. A dislike of Zionism may also have had a role to play: 'It's partly their aggressive and superstitious assumption of European superiority which is responsible for the present friction,' wrote Glubb in an unguarded moment towards the end of 1947, shortly after the United Nations had voted by a two-thirds majority in favour of accepting the partition plan for Palestine.

By then officials in the Foreign Office had already started scouting around to redeem Britain's strategic interests and to safeguard the old relationships with the other Arab states.

The most obvious starting point was Transjordan. Not only did Britain retain formal treaty links with Abdullah, but Transjordan was entirely dependent on Britain for military and financial support. There was also the very good reason that in the Arab Legion Transjordan possessed the only modern and disciplined army in the Middle East and that it could play a vital role in peace-keeping operations in Palestine should violence follow Britain's withdrawal from the region in May 1948. Moreover, as Glubb had already made clear, the change in the local balance of power could leave Transjordan in an isolated position and liable to interference from unfriendly Arab states like Syria and Saudi Arabia. Its position would also be weakened if the creation of the new Jewish state prevented access to the eastern Mediterranean: to guard against that possibility Glubb had already suggested that Transjordan should annex the southern Arab areas of Palestine, including the Gaza-Beersheba district, in addition to the UNSCOP areas allotted to the Arabs:

> For Trans-Jordan and King Abdullah this would mean the creation of a state which would have some hope of permanent stability. For the Palestine Arabs it would mean independence under an Arab government of their own, with the capital in their midst, whether in Amman or Nablus ... the only tool for securing this solution, so ideal for Trans-Jordan and Great Britain alike, would appear to be the Arab Legion.[25]

To do this, though, Abdullah would require a strong Arab Legion, hence Glubb's pleas for his force to be further strengthened and not cut back. Coming on top of the demands he had made at the time of the treaty negotiations, Glubb's further requests could have been seen as just another piece of self-promotion, the kind of ploy normally employed by any commander anxious to do the best for his men. In this instance, though, both the Foreign Office and the War Office were anxious to retain the services of a sound Arab Legion, the former because they wanted to see Abdullah move into the Arab areas of Palestine to create what would in effect be a Greater Transjordan, the latter because the British Chiefs of Staff feared that the removal of the British garrison from Palestine would leave a power vacuum which would be harmful to Britain's global strategy. This point was made clear in the Chief of Staff's appreciation of the Arab Legion's contribution to British defence policy in December 1947:

The strategic importance of Transjordan lies, in general, in its position in relation to the Middle East area as a whole, and in particular because of its importance in regard to the supply of Middle East oil. We understand, moreover, that the Petroleum Development (Transjordan) Company has recently obtained an oil concession in Transjordan. If oil is discovered in quantities which allow for economic production, Transjordan's strategic importance will be increased. It is strategically important that the distribution of existing oil supplies should continue and that new ones should be developed.

We have stated that in any major war in the Middle East the defence of Egypt will have to be conducted mainly in the area of Northern Palestine and Southern Syria. The territory of Transjordan can scarcely fail to be embroiled. Transjordan is therefore of strategic importance to us in peace and war. In peace we require a friendly Transjordan with stable conditions; in war we require the free use of her territory and the co-operation of her armed forces within the limits of their ability.[26]

Although oil was not discovered in sufficient quantities to justify the Chiefs of Staffs' fears, it was obvious that Transjordan remained the cornerstone of British strategy in the Middle East, both to safeguard the Suez Canal and as a bulwark against hostile incursion from Arab, or indeed Soviet, enemies. Both departments were also uncomfortably aware that any move to strengthen the Arab Legion prior to the end of the mandate would have to be kept secret – otherwise Britain would be accused of attempting to interfere in a United Nations policy which she refused to support in public. After agreeing to provide the Arab Legion with supplies, ammunition and equipment from the British forces leaving Palestine, Cunningham warned the Foreign Office that 'this agreement may cause some comment if it comes to Jewish ears'.[27] At the same time arrangements were made to allow the Arab Legion to use the old Transjordan Frontier Force base at Zerqa.

As the months ticked by towards the end of the British mandate in Palestine, the Foreign Office worked hard to bolster Transjordan's strength and to encourage Abdullah to show his hand by planning the occupation not only of the Arab areas of Palestine but also those other places where there was an Arab majority. As Kirkbride noted in October 1947, Abdullah had the best claim of all to inherit the residue of Palestine and that the seizure of the Arab areas would greatly lessen the chance of a bloody conflict between Jews and Arabs once the British had pulled out.[28]

In fact, Abdullah was fully prepared to take up the running on his own account. Ever since he had entered into a treaty agreement with Britain he had been prepared to abandon, albeit temporarily, his ambitions for the creation of a greater Syria. Now with Palestine about to be partitioned, he saw opportunities for Transjordan to extend her territories by taking over responsibility for the Arab areas, a move that would not only help to keep order by offering protection to the local populations, but one that would also prevent the Mufti, a lifelong opponent, from seizing power. Realising that both outcomes would be welcomed by the Jews – with whom he was always prepared to treat – Abdullah arranged to meet a high level Jewish Agency delegation, led by Mrs Golda Meyerson (Meir), on 17 November 1947, shortly before the UN was due to deliver its verdict on the UNSCOP proposals. The meeting lasted fifty minutes and the gist of the discussion was quite simple: to prevent the possibility of fighting between Transjordan and the new Jewish state, Abdullah would order the Arab Legion into the Arab areas to prevent the Mufti from establishing an independent Arab state. For obvious reasons the discussions were kept secret and no records were kept – any hint would have destroyed Abdullah's reputation within the Arab League – but both sides left the meeting fully aware of Abdullah's intentions. His next step was to square the matter with the British and that meant taking Glubb and Kirkbride into his confidence.

Although recent Israeli historians have claimed that Abdullah kept the matter secret from his British advisers,[29] the Foreign Office papers dealing with this period reveal that both men knew about Abdullah's negotiations and understood the implications for Britain. When Glubb was in London in January and February 1948 he briefed the British Director of Military Intelligence on the subject and from the beginning of December 1947 onwards Kirkbride kept up pressure on the Foreign Office to endorse Abdullah's proposals and to incorporate them into British policy. It was a move fraught with hidden dangers for if it were ever revealed that Britain was secretly supporting the implementation of partition in Transjordan's favour, while refusing to do anything at the United Nations, her reputation would be badly sullied.

Bevin, the Foreign Secretary, was well aware of the difficulties involved in such a course of action but he also realised that, properly handled, the plan could benefit both Britain and Transjordan by bringing the designated Arab areas into the British sphere of influence through the treaty relationship with Abdullah. However, it was important to keep the matter secret as any suggestion of a British conspiracy with Transjordan would not only be seen as a violation of the UN decision but it would inevitably poison Britain's relationship with her main ally, the United States – and in 1948 Britain was well-nigh dependent on US loans for her economic survival. The problem was put in the hands of Harold Beeley, the Foreign Office's leading Middle East expert, who set the ball rolling with a series of meetings both within his depart-

333

ment and also with officials from the Colonial Office, the War Office and the Treasury. Meanwhile, the official British line was that the Arab Legion would withdraw from Palestine before 15 May and that it would do everything possible to prevent British attached officers from leading the force on active service. With these understandings the British officials began their investigations and discussions on 6 January 1948.

During the course of their deliberations it was made clear that Britain would support Abdullah's plans provided that he waited until after the British withdrawal and that he kept to the areas designated by the UNSCOP findings. Privately, it was conceded that if he moved the Arab Legion into other high-density Arab areas then Britain would not disapprove, provided that he was prepared to reach an early understanding with the Jews. Throughout the discussions it was made clear that the protection of British interests was the overriding necessity.

> It is generally agreed that the maintenance of our position in the Middle East is vital to His Majesty's Government as much from the economic as from the political standpoint. The withdrawal of our forces from Palestine weakens our direct influence in the Middle East at a time when the United Nations decision on Palestine creates a state of tension. Our aim is to maintain and indeed strengthen our links with the elements in the Middle East which are known to be favourable to us and of these King Abdullah of Transjordan is one. Further it is very much to our interest that conditions of security should be restored in Palestine as soon as possible after our withdrawal and if King Abdullah and the other Arab leaders agree on the use of the Arab Legion in that part of Palestine allotted to the Arab State by the United Nations, law and order might be restored to that part of Palestine quite rapidly.[30]

Before he could proceed further with the proposal to support Abdullah's aims, Beeley had to take soundings from the Arab states in order to gauge their attitudes to an Arab Legion occupation of parts of Palestine. The replies made interesting reading. Iraq was only in favour if the Arab Legion moved into the whole of Palestine; Syria stated that it would 'intensely dislike' any Transjordanian move, while both Egypt and Saudi Arabia said that they would regard an invasion as a 'treacherous and insupportable' piece of Hashemite territorial aggrandisement. Only Lebanon supported the idea as they believed that Britain was at the back of it anyway. Beeley understood the drift – the Arab states wanted Abdullah's professional and highly disciplined army to confront the new Jewish state and establish an independent Arab state in the whole of Palestine. Beeley minuted:

> The general conclusion which emerges from these replies is that King Abdullah can count on a large measure of support in the Arab world if his action involves defeat of the United Nations and invasion of the territory assigned by them to the Jewish state. But if he confined himself to occupying what the Arabs have already been given, his actions will be interpreted as personal aggrandisement and will isolate him from his neighbours and Arab opinion generally.[31]

As Abdullah was well aware of the dangers contained in Beeley's final sentence, he wanted Britain to pay the proper price for carrying out policies which would benefit both countries. This, too, Beeley understood:

> Abdullah wants the revision of the Trans-Jordanian treaty because, in the present state of Arab feeling, it is impossible to emerge as the Arab liberator while known to be subservient to Britain. He does not mind if there is a secret agreement which guarantees Britain all she requires in Trans-Jordan as long as there is an overt revision which puts him on a par with other Arab states.[32]

To keep himself in that happy state Abdullah needed a strong army and that same day, 6 January, steps were taken to increase the size and strength of the Arab Legion. The meeting was attended by representatives of the Foreign Office, the War Office and the Treasury and the main item on the agenda was Glubb's proposal to bring the Arab Legion up to the size of a British mechanised division and to supply it with full supporting arms. As the plans had the backing of the Chiefs of Staff, the meeting was prepared to give additional support to the Arab Legion as 'a firm indication that we are determined to keep our place in the Middle East and to take the necessary action to do so in spheres in which action is open to us'.[33] This was exactly what Glubb had requested:

It is not, of course, possible exactly to foresee when and where the Arab Legion will intervene. But nor is it possible exactly to foresee when and where the British Army will next go on active service. All we can say for the British armed forces is that their maintenance at a high level of efficiency will be a factor for peace in a disturbed world.

The same, on a much smaller scale, can be said for the Arab Legion. Whatever the future may bring in the seething cauldron of Arab politics, a strong and efficient Arab Legion will always be a factor making for stability, democracy and co-operation with Great Britain.[34]

The deal was finalised a few weeks later while Glubb was in London as military adviser to a Transjordanian delegation consisting of Taufiq Pasha abu al Huda, the prime minister, and Fawzi Pasha al Mulqi, the foreign minister. Their mission was to renegotiate the terms of the Anglo-Transjordanian treaty to give Abdullah a greater degree of sovereignty – his price for co-operating with Britain – and to finalise the military arrangements for the secret annex. After the meeting, Taufiq Pasha requested a private audience with Bevin on Saturday, 7 February, and asked Glubb to accompany him as his translator. This was done to discuss the hidden agenda for the visit: to reach an understanding on the situation in Palestine following the end of the mandate. Bevin went into the meeting well briefed by his civil servants:

> It seems likely that the Prime Minister may wish to put forward the idea of an action by Trans-Jordan in Palestine which would lead to eventual agreement with the Jews. This might take the form of occupation by the Arab Legion after May 15th of some or all of the areas alloted to the Jews. Then after a suitable lapse of time, King Abdullah would come to a *de facto* agreement with the Jews that they would not encroach on each other's territory in return perhaps for a share of Jewish autonomy.[35]

As recalled by Glubb in his memoirs of this period, this was more or less what Taufiq Pasha told Bevin. Then he went on to say that, while the Jews had an army in the Haganah, the Arabs in Palestine had no means of defending themselves once the British had left:

> Consequently, Taufiq Pasha explained, if the situation were left as it was, one of two things would happen. Either the Jews would neglect the United Nations partition plan and would seize the whole of Palestine up to the River Jordan; or else the Mufti would return and endeavour to make himself ruler of Arab Palestine. Neither of these alternatives would suit either Britain or Trans-Jordan.[36]

Because Abdullah had received requests from the Palestinian Arabs begging for protection, he intended to send the Arab Legion into the affected areas once the mandate had formally come to an end. Taufiq Pasha explained that he was giving this information to the British foreign secretary in the spirit of the treaty arrangements between the two countries. Begin replied, 'It seems the obvious thing to do.' Then, after Glubb reminded the prime minister that the invasion would only involve UN-designated areas, Bevin again concurred, 'It seems the obvious thing to do, but do not go and invade the areas alloted to the Jews.'

In Glubb's version of the meeting, written ten years later, he makes much of his recollection that Taufiq Pasha only agreed to enter the areas 'contiguous with the frontier of Trans-Jordan'. However, the official minute, written at the time, suggests that the understanding was less precise. In Glubb's version he warns Taufiq Pasha about the dangers of entering non-designated areas, but in the minute, this appears as a question: 'I asked His Excellency whether, when he spoke of the Arab Legion entering Palestine, he referred to the Arab areas as laid down in the UN decision or whether it would also enter the Jewish areas.'[37] To this, Taufiq Pasha replied non-committally that it would be the designated Arab areas only, unless the Jews attacked the Arab Legion which was extremely unlikely, given Abdullah's secret negotiations with the Jewish Agency.

The 'cordial' meeting ended with both sides agreed on the main question: at the end of the mandate and following the withdrawal of British forces from Palestine, Transjordan would occupy the Arab areas which had been agreed by the UN, thus imposing the very kind of partition which Britain had refused to support. In other words, by acting in collusion with Transjordan, her partner by treaty, Britain had put her weight behind Abdullah's plot of dividing Palestine between himself and the new Jewish state of Israel. In this way it was unlikely that a separate Mufti-controlled Arab state would come into being, an outcome which neither side desired. What Bevin wanted, and what he seemed to have achieved, was the possibility of a greater Transjordan carved out of the Arab areas of Palestine, thus allowing the new Jewish state to come safely into being. After all, this was very similar to what had happened to India and the new state of Pakistan in August 1947.

To cement further this new working relationship with Transjordan – which was something of a turning point in Britain's post-war policies in the Middle East – it was agreed that Glubb should continue to provide London with military and political information from Transjordan which might otherwise not have been received through the usual channels. During an earlier meeting with the Director of Military Intelligence, Glubb had countered a proposal to appoint a British military attaché in Amman by suggesting that he could fulfil the same kind of function: now he could make good that offer. Although he was still a Transjordanian employee who owed his loyalty to King Abdullah, Glubb obviously wanted to remain helpful to the British government and promised to supply London with confidential information about Transjordan by what he called the 'backstairs method'.[38] This would be particularly useful to the Foreign Office in view of Abdullah's conflicting relationships with the Jewish Agency and the Arab League.

By taking on this undercover task, Glubb was technically infringing the promise of loyalty he had made to Abdullah ten years earlier, but, clearly, he felt able to square the decision with his own conscience. Either he thought that his work would not compromise his allegiance or he continued to believe that, as a British subject, his ultimate duty lay with Britain. Whatever his reasons, the problem of being a servant to two masters was to cast a shadow over his career for the remainder of his service in the Middle East.

11

The First
Arab-Israeli War

(i) To the end of the mandate

During the six-month period leading to the official termination of the mandate, Britain's abdication of political and military responsibility in Palestine did nothing to lessen the dreadful round of murder and violence, followed by equally appalling acts of revenge. Over thirty members of the British security forces lost their lives during this period but shameful though these murders were, the main emphasis of the terrorist war had changed to the struggle between the Jews and the Arabs. As Glubb noted in his diary, all past friendships and co-operation had turned into hatred while Britain refused to intercede and sulked, like Achilles in his tent.

An equally impotent Cunningham bombarded London with reports that chaos was looming and that the violence was being exacerbated by the growing confidence of the Haganah, the fledgling Jewish defence force, as it moved into Arab areas to search for arms. If the Arabs retaliated – the inevitable result – a firefight would ensue, men, women and children would be killed and in some instances whole communities were wiped out. Just as the British had done during the Arab Revolt, the Jews would then blow up houses owned by Palestinian Arabs, a form of punishment that continued to be practised in the occupied territories throughout the 1980s and 1990s. To complicate matters further, deserters from the British Army threw in their lot with

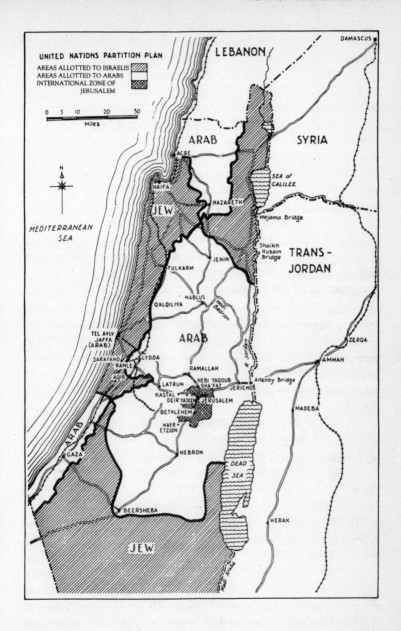

UNITED NATIONS PARTITION PLAN
AREAS ALLOTTED TO ISRAELIS
AREAS ALLOTTED TO ARABS
INTERNATIONAL ZONE OF
JERUSALEM

0 5 10   20   30
Miles

N

MEDITERRANEAN
SEA

LEBANON

DAMASCUS

ARAB

SYRIA

ACRE

HAIFA

JEW

NAZARETH

SEA of
GALILEE

Mejama Bridge

Shaikh
Husain
Bridge

TRANS-
JORDAN

JENIN

TULKARM

NABLUS

QALQILIYA

Wadi Bethran

R. Jordan

ZERQA

TEL AVIV
JAFFA
(ARAB)

ARAB

SARAFAND
RAMLE
AQIR

LYDDA

RAMALLAH

Allenby Bridge

AMMAN

LATRUN

KASTAL
DEIR YASEIN

NEBI YAQOUB
SHA'FAT

JERICHO

JERUSALEM

MADEBA

BETHLEHEM

KAFR
ETZION

ARAB

GAZA

HEBRON

DEAD
SEA

BEERSHEBA

KERAK

JEW

Wadi Araba

341

both sides, on one occasion taking their Cromwell tanks with them to provide the Haganah with its first armoured fighting vehicles. Large numbers of Arab irregular forces, supported by Egypt, Syria and Iraq, also moved into Palestine at the beginning of 1948 to protect the Arab population and, ultimately, to prevent the establishment of a Jewish state.

Sometimes the violence got out of hand and resulted in atrocities which resembled those committed on a larger scale in Europe during the dark days of the Second World War. At the village of Deir Yassin over 200 Arabs – men, women and children – were massacred by Jewish terrorists of the Irgun in April and as a result hundreds of Arab refugees were forced to flee from the area, never to return. This incident left a lasting impression on Arab minds and in time became a leitmotiv for Jewish frightfulness. Glubb himself had already been made aware of long-term Jewish intentions following discussions between one of his officers and a Jewish official. Asked if there would be impossible tensions between Jews and Arabs after 15 May, the Jewish official replied, 'Oh, no. That will be fixed. A few calculated massacres will soon get rid of them.'[1] As Glubb noted, this was not a statement made by a member of the Irgun or the Stern Gang, but by a responsible official employed by the mandatory government.

Not that the Jews were alone in perpetuating violence. The main road from Tel Aviv to Jerusalem was regularly blockaded by Arab terrorists at the Bab el Wad defile and Jewish convoys were always shot up with heavy loss of life. Arab snipers on Mount Scopus attacked and killed medical personnel from the nearby Hebrew University of Hadassah Hospital and, at the settlement of Kfar Etzion between Bethlehem and Hebron, Jewish villagers were gunned down by vengeful Arab terrorists on 13 May after the settlement had been captured by the Arab Legion. In this instance Glubb's men were not to blame – they had left the village after the action and returned the Jewish soldiers to Amman as prisoners-of-war – but the mud stuck. David Ben-Gurion, the

Jewish leader, announced that Glubb would be arraigned for war crimes once the state of Israel came into being.[2]

By that time, April and May 1948, Palestine had slipped into anarchy as Jews and Arabs entrenched themselves in their own areas and made incursions into opposing areas where they felt themselves to be the majority. By that time, too, Arab irregular forces had started arriving in Palestine in considerable numbers: as during the Arab Revolt, many came from Syria, using Transjordan as the means of access, a move which the Arab Legion was powerless to prevent as Abdullah could not withhold transit rights without antagonising the rest of the Arab world. They formed the Arab Liberation Army which was commanded by the Levantine mercenary Fawzi al Kaukji whom Glubb had last encountered in Iraq in 1941 when he had supported the pro-Rashid Ali faction. By the end of January his forces had taken up position in the area around Nablus and were ready for action. Also growing in strength in Palestine were forces loyal to the Mufti, led by his cousin Abdul Qadir Husaini, the one Arab leader with a talent for military organisation and tactics. All the forces had support of one kind or another from the members of the Arab League but as Glubb told London they were barely effective from a military point of view:

The Mufti's Force

The Mufti was daggers drawn with King Abdullah. The Mufti's Force could only be termed that of a 'gang' and as such, its leader, the Mufti, was at the moment losing considerable kudos throughout the more respectable classes in Palestine. His 'troops' were unpaid and therefore relied on scavenging and pillaging.

The Arab League Force

This is a semi-disciplined force which is in the process of being formed under Fauzi Kawukji in Palestine. Fauzi Kawukji is touting for any Arab who has received any training in any Army. Its 'troops' receive good wages which are presumably paid by the Arab League. Its Head-quarters up to the moment have been outside Damascus.[3]

In addition to the forces mentioned by Glubb in his report to the War Office, there were also guerrilla elements of the extremist Muslim Brotherhood in southern Palestine but despite its relatively large numbers the Arab military presence was weakened by a lack of overall command, tenuous lines of communications and an absence of tactical awareness. Given such a muddle on both sides it is little wonder that the early stages of the fighting in Palestine were described by Chaim Herzog, a staff officer in the Haganah, as 'a series of city riots, bloody urban encounters, hit-and-run operations that left scores of dead, maimed and wounded civilians on both sides'.[4]

As the situation deteriorated, Abdullah's position came under fire, both from the Jews who believed that by allowing the transit of guerrillas from Syria he had broken his under-standing with the Jewish Agency, and from the Arabs who believed that he was not concerned with the plight of the Palestinian Arabs but only interested in enlarging his kingdom by seizing the west bank of the River Jordan. Both sides remained highly suspicious of the Arab Legion which was acknowledged to be the only effective military instrument in the Middle East. In fact, during this period, the Arab Legion remained largely in Palestine under British command to keep open the important lines of communication along the road from Gaza to the Allenby Bridge which ran through Beersheba, Hebron and Jerusalem. There were also infantry companies in Haifa and Hebron but all were supposed to withdraw into Transjordan before the end of the mandate as part of the British withdrawal. Although in his memoirs Glubb insisted that the majority of his forces were 'back over the border by May 14th', this was not entirely true. Under pressure from Abdullah he had agreed to keep men in the West Bank area to protect the roads between Jerusalem and Hebron, and between Ramallah and Jericho. He himself had made several visits to local leaders in order to convince them that the Arab Legion would move in quickly to protect them once the British handover of power had been effected and that they should therefore not put their faith in the forces representing the Mufti.

By then, in mid-April, there was little likelihood that the Arab Legion would be able to avoid involvement in the forthcoming struggle. The Jewish forces had already seized Tiberias, Haifa and Jaffa, and when Abdul Qadir Husaini was killed in action at Kastal in April the Arabs lost their most able military leader. The growing numbers of refugees flocking into the Arab areas also put pressure on Glubb's men who were themselves becoming increasingly uneasy about the Jewish aggression which had caused the flood. By then, too, Abdullah had been forced to play a more active role and, under pressure from the Arab League, he decided to enter the fray provided that his move was supported by the other Arab countries. On 10 April the Arab League met in Cairo and decided to intervene in Palestine, both to protect the Palestinian Arabs and to prevent the creation of an independent Jewish state. At the same meeting the Transjordanian delegation made the surprise announcement that their forces would enter Palestine at the end of the mandate, thus making public what the other countries had long suspected, and five days later, Abdel Rahman Azzam, the secretary-general, issued the official invitation to Abdullah:

> The committee is of a unanimous opinion that the presence in Palestine of the Arab Legion makes it possible for the Legion to accomplish this important task with the required haste.
>
> The Political Committee adjures Your Majesty to allow please the Trans-Jordan Arab Legion to do this duty.
>
> I avail myself of the opportunity of presenting the Committee's thanks for the well-appreciated magnanimity and generous preparedness you have shown.[5]

Abdullah had been in a difficult position. With the Jewish

Agency he had reached agreement to enter the designated Arab areas – Samaria, Judaea and Hebron – and this plan had the backing of the British, but when the arrangements had been finalised there was little likelihood of all-out war. He had come under pressure from the Arab League countries to declare his hand and to counter rightly held suspicions that he was only interested in territorial gains. Now it seemed to him that as the peace initiatives were floundering, he had no option but to join the other Arab forces in the invasion of Palestine. It is likely, too, that he had been swayed by the Deir Yassin massacre and by the Jews' aggression and growing self-confidence. Certainly, on 26 April, he made his feelings clear at a press conference in Amman and, although he was well known for his colourful public pronouncements, these are hardly the words of a ruler interested in keeping out of the conflict: 'All our efforts to bring about a peaceful solution have failed. The only way left to us is war. To me has fallen the honour to save Palestine.' Besides, he needed the financial support of the Arab League: Glubb had already warned him of the dangers inherent in committing the Legion to a protracted war without sufficient funds and reserves.

The Legion's budget for 1948 allowed for an establishment of some 8,000 officers and men, 4,500 of whom were in a state of combat preparedness, but they only possessed sufficient reserves of weapons, ammunition and men for one major battle. While the British Army had been stationed in Palestine it had been responsible for providing services to the Legion – supply and equipment, medical, ordnance and workshops. There was also an understanding that the British would hold the Legion's reserve ammunition for its rifles, Bren guns, mortars and twenty-five-pounder field guns and that it could be drawn as needed – an arrangement which provided the Legion with reserve strength without incurring major financial investment. Now that the British had almost departed, these reserves would no longer be available, although under a secret agreement small-arms ammunition and a quantity of weapons, including Sten guns and mortars, had been made available from surplus stock before the final pull-out.[6]

Glubb also contacted the Commander-in-Chief Middle East, with a request for further supplies of ammunition and weapons from HQ MELF and although two attempts were made to ship them from Egypt to Aqaba, both failed, the first due to the seizure of the transporter SS *Ramses* by Egyptian customs officials and the second due to a UN resolution prohibiting the supply of warlike supplies to the Middle East. Fortunately for Glubb, though, the Arab League's plea to Transjordan carried with it the promise of funds and, following the visit of the secretary-general to Amman, Glubb received a down payment of £250,000 from the League's reported war-chest of £4 million. Abdel Rahman Azzam also proposed that Glubb should be the Arab commander-in-chief, an invitation he wisely refused, and the post was then offered to Abdullah in recognition of the Arab Legion's role.

In fact, as Glubb soon discovered, the king had been created commander-in-chief in name only, and was never to be given a general staff or any real military authority. This was made clear when the Arab chiefs of staff met in Amman to discuss their objectives: the agenda under discussion was less concerned with the creation of a viable invasion plan than with the demarcation of Palestine into areas to be attacked by the individual armies. At the end of the conference, Lieutenant-Colonel Charles Coaker, Glubb's principal staff officer for operations, drove the senior Iraqi officer back to his hotel. When Coaker asked how the conference had gone, back came the reply: 'Splendidly. We all agreed to fight separately.'[7]

As it turned out, that was exactly how the war was fought. What the plan amounted to was a general agreement about the invasion areas assigned to each of the armies. The Lebanese army (1,000) would move down the northern coast towards Nahariya; the Syrians (3,000) would move into Galilee; the Iraqis (3,000) would cross the Jordan south of the Sea of Galilee and advance to Netanya on the Mediterranean coast in order to cut the Jewish areas in half. To the Arab Legion would fall the task of seizing Nablus and Samaria with one brigade while a second brigade would take Ramallah on the approaches to Tel Aviv. Meanwhile the 10,000-strong Egyptian Army would launch a two-pronged attack from the south along the coastal plain towards Gaza and Tel Aviv and a second towards Beersheba and Hebron to engage the Jewish forces south of Jerusalem. To these regular armies were added the guerrilla and militia formations of the two Palestinian Arab irregular forces.

Throughout the fighting Glubb's lack of field intelligence led him to believe that the Jewish forces opposing him were 65,000 strong and that they were well equipped and organised but these fears were greatly exaggerated. According to Chaim Herzog, at that time a staff officer in the Haganah, the Jewish forces never numbered more than 45,000 but two-thirds of these were lightly armed men and women who were limited to local defence duties; their weapons, too, were a 'hodge-podge' mixture, including locally made Sten guns and a number of field guns of First World War vintage. In their favour, though, they possessed a superior command system based on brigades situated in identifiable military districts and their lines of communication allowed them to co-ordinate the movement of reserves and reinforcements from the rear areas to the front. 'Above all,' recalled Herzog, 'the Israelis were consciously and literally fighting for their lives and those of their women and children, and enjoyed outstanding and committed leadership.'[8]

On 14 May British rule in Palestine came to an end when General Cunningham inspected a guard of honour drawn from the Highland Light Infantry before flying to Haifa where a Royal Navy cruiser was waiting to take him away from Britain's unwanted possession in the Holy Land. No sooner had the warship left at midnight, and the Union Flag been pulled down, than the opposing factions emerged into the open to plunge the country into a state of war. The state of Israel came into being and was immediately recognised by the

United States, though not at first by Britain whose government was still wary of alienating Arab opinion.

As the region slipped ever more quickly towards chaos, Glubb recalled falling on his knees and praying, 'Oh God, I am not equal to these events. I entreat Thee to grant me Thy help. I beg Thee to direct everything to a good ending – if it be Thy will.'[9]

The first Arab-Israeli war – a 'curious imitation of a war', according to Glubb – was fought intermittently on several fronts between 15 May 1948 and 3 April 1949 but it was the fighting in and around Jerusalem involving the Arab Legion that was central to the conflict. There had already been bitter confrontations between Jews and Arabs in the Holy City as the Jewish forces attempted to gain strategic control before the final British evacuation. (It was in this struggle that the Arab Legion had captured Kfar Etzion on 13 May in order to prevent the Jewish stranglehold on the road to Hebron.) The Jews were particularly anxious to get the upper hand in the city before the Arab Legion could move in, and although a truce had been arranged by Cunningham and continued under a triumvirate of neutral consuls-general, it was obvious that Jerusalem would remain the major flashpoint in the early stages of the war. Not only was the city a holy place to Arabs, Christians and Jews, but it also controlled the main lines of communication and was therefore an important military prize. Glubb understood this, but he also realised that the battle for Jerusalem would be extremely costly:

The Jews were expert in street fighting and in house-to-house encounters. The Arab Legion would lose much of the advantage of its higher standard of tactical training and mobility. Even if two thousand men (or nearly half the Arab Legion) were put into the city, they would be greatly outnumbered by the Jews. With our slender man-power and no reserves, we could not afford a slogging match.[10]

Unfortunately for Glubb, Abdullah had set his heart on

winning Jerusalem, mainly because it held for him an emotional, even mystical significance, and he could not bear to think of it becoming a Jewish bastion. While Glubb's heart was also drawn to Jerusalem, he preferred to continue the albeit shaky truce, thus avoiding the kind of street-fighting which he dreaded, and thereby attracting the Israeli forces into the open where the superior mobility and firepower of his forces would give him a decided advantage. The problem was exacerbated by the pleas of the Arab inhabitants of the city who feared that they would be massacred unless the Arab Legion moved in, yet Glubb could hardly protect them *and* control the area bounded by Hebron, Ramallah and Nablus which was as large as the combined counties of Kent and Sussex. Glubb therefore made one final secret attempt to come to an arrangement with the opposition. His chosen instrument was Lieutenant-Colonel Desmond Goldie, a Royal Scots Fusilier officer, who commanded the 1st Brigade of the Arab Legion.*

For reasons which have never been made clear – he would not discuss the incident in later life and there is no mention of it in his books – Glubb decided to make contact with the Haganah to discuss the possibility of arranging a truce in the event of an outbreak of hostilities. He had already made informal contact with Jewish representatives of the Potash Company on the Dead Sea about the need to protect their works, and, clearly, he felt that a last-ditch attempt had to be made to keep the peace. The task of briefing Goldie was left to Lash at headquarters in Mafraq for, although the orders emanated from Glubb, he was also anxious to distance himself from the whole project. Why he did so is something of a mystery, for the initiative was instigated at his insistence, and that he was anxious to avoid fighting the Jewish forces, especially in the built-up areas of Jerusalem, is clear from other

---

*Glubb's second formation, numbered 3rd Brigade, was commanded by Lieutenant-Colonel 'Teal' Ashton, Welsh Guards.

written evidence. Presumably he wanted to avoid association with the mission should it ever become public knowledge – as Abdullah's military advisor he knew that the other Arab states already suspected Transjordan of setting up secret deals with the Jews. Whatever his reasons, they proved to be mistaken as the Haganah commanders did not take Goldie seriously and believed that Glubb was acting to protect Britain's interests behind Abdullah's back. Shlomo Shamir, the senior Jewish officer present, admitted later that he might have reacted differently if Glubb himself had appeared at the meeting.

For a last-minute peace initiative the meeting at the Jewish settlement of Naharayim on 2 May was a curious mixture of farce and high drama. First, although Goldie was an experienced British regimental officer, he spoke little Arabic or Hebrew and by his own admission knew little about politics in the Middle East. Second, the journey across the lines to the settlement was a dangerous undertaking as Goldie was forced to cross the Jordan at a place where the Arab Legion's 4th Regiment was engaged in a running battle with Jewish forces. Having convinced his colleague, Lieutenant-Colonel Habis Majali, to cease fire, he crossed the river, to find himself surrounded by angry Palestinian Arabs and only escaped through the intervention of an Arab Legion soldier who happened to be standing nearby.

Given such half-baked planning it was hardly surprising that the meeting itself failed to achieve anything. Goldie began by explaining that he spoke on behalf of Glubb who wanted to open up lines of communication with the Haganah in order to prevent an open battle developing between the two opposing forces. Shamir welcomed the initiative but retorted that there was no need for any fighting provided that the Arab Legion did not instigate offensive operations. The Jews were only interested in occupying legitimate areas, he said, and would only occupy other areas to protect their strategic interests. Furthermore, there would be no fighting in Jerusalem if the Arab Legion did not attempt to cut the main roads into the city. The meeting concluded with Goldie saying a few words about the difficulties facing Glubb: that he wanted to avoid a fight but had to be seen upholding the Arab cause. Although Shamir gave Goldie a fair hearing and passed Glubb's official letter to the Jewish high command, the initiative was doomed because the Jews did not have enough confidence in Glubb's promises. A week later, Mrs Meyerson met Abdullah again in an attempt to revitalise their earlier understanding but that, too, came to naught.

Nonetheless, back in London, Bevin was pleased to hear that Glubb had made the attempt, for he continued to place his faith in the belief that, by adding Arab Palestine to Transjordan, Abdullah would avoid the necessity of fighting the Israelis. (Like others at the Foreign Office, Bevin thought that Abdullah's increasing bellicosity was a cover designed to keep his Arab allies happy.) Bevin also realised that if war did break out he would come under pressure from the Americans to withdraw the British officers from the Arab Legion and possibly halt the subsidy. As he told the War Office and the Minister of Defence, A.V. Alexander:

> I am reluctant to do anything which might prejudice the success of these negotiations which appear to aim at avoiding actual hostilities between the Arabs and the Jews. Since their conduct, and no doubt also their implementation, seem to depend to a considerable extent on British officers serving with the Arab Legion, I feel sure that we ought not to withdraw the latter prematurely.[11]

So important was it to Bevin to uphold the agreement with Transjordan and, indirectly through Abdullah's initiative, with Israel that he was prepared to fight hard to keep Glubb and the other British officers in their key positions. By the same token, he also warned that any breach of the understanding would lead to the freezing of the Legion's funds and the withdrawal of the British officers. None of these moves was ever made public and to the rest of the world, especially to the international Zionist community, Bevin was thought to be working against the best interests of the Jews. The odour stuck and in time Bevin was castigated by Israeli historians for what seemed to be a pro-Arab and anti-Zionist stance, whereas, in fact, his moves to prevent the establishment of a Palestinian Arab state actually made it easier for the fledgling state of Israel to come into being.

Meanwhile, with tension rising in Palestine, the question of Glubb's position suddenly became a source of potential embarrassment and steps were taken to distance the British government from his presence. The first warning shot was fired by Alexander on 27 April, when he warned Bevin that there were some thirty British officers in the Arab Legion and that their presence could 'lead us into trouble in the event of fighting between the Arab Legion and the Jews'.[12] Alexander suggested that Kirkbride should indicate to the men concerned the delicate nature of their appointments and warn them not to become involved in offensive operations.

The immediate problem, though, was Glubb who, along with Lash and Broadhurst, was still employed by the Palestine civil service and came under the administration of the Colonial Office. Bevin passed the matter to Lord Listowel at the Colonial Office and back came the reply that Glubb's appointment would be terminated on 15 May when the mandate came to an end and the Palestine civil service ceased to exist. However, one difficulty remained: Glubb still had a period of leave, worth 302 days, and that would have to be taken into account in calculating his final period of service. Perhaps he could simply go on leave? asked the Colonial Office, only too anxious to pass the buck back to the Foreign Office.

Not for the first time in his life Glubb's position became the subject of forces beyond his control and his long-term prospects suffered accordingly. While the Colonial Office wanted to absolve itself of any responsibility for Glubb's position, Listowel did point out to the Foreign Office that they should take into account Glubb's importance to the British position in the Middle East.

353

I am particularly concerned about the case of Brigadier Glubb himself. As Commander of the Legion he will necessarily play a considerable part in its operations whether he remains in Amman or enters Palestine. I should have thought it would be extremely difficult for us to allow him to remain in command if the Arab Legion were fighting the Jews in Palestine. I recognise however that, on the assumption that Glubb will have severed his connexion with the Colonial Service, I shall have no departmental responsibility in this matter after termination of the Mandate.[13]

In effect, the Colonial Office washed its hands of the matter and Listowel told Bevin that Glubb would be informed that he was no longer in Colonial Service employment after 15 May. Meanwhile, further investigation by the Foreign Office revealed that there were three categories of officers serving with the Legion – those, like Glubb, employed by the Palestine civil service, private individuals in Abdullah's pay, and the British Army officers seconded to the Legion. While it was easy enough to warn the latter about avoiding incidents which would put them in 'the extremely embarrassing situation of having British officers taking part in fighting between Jews and Arabs in Palestine', the Foreign Office recognised that Glubb's case was different because 'by virtue of his position in the Arab Legion [he] must be particularly associated with all its activities even if he himself does not enter Palestine'.[14]

Despite his officials' warnings, Bevin's intuition told him to 'wait and see'; war had not yet broken out and provided the Arab Legion kept to the designated Arab areas, the dangers were still fairly remote. On the other hand, he knew that the presence of the army officers alarmed the Americans who believed that Glubb was acting as the instrument of a secret policy to aid the Arabs and that there was, therefore, a good case for demanding his removal. It was difficult to do anything about the British Army officers at that juncture –

their withdrawal would destabilise Abdullah's position – but it was possible to deal with Glubb's case. Accordingly, with time running out, Bevin offered no objections to the Colonial Office decision to release Glubb from their service and allow him to become an employee of King Abdullah – the only option left open to him. In other words, he had become a mercenary in the service of a monarch who was friendly to Britain.

When he came to write his memoirs of this period Glubb made light of the fact that his position had changed so dramatically and even claimed to laugh off a warning that he was now liable for prosecution under the terms of the Foreign Enlistment Act of 1870 which prohibits British subjects from serving foreign countries 'without His Majesty's cognisance'. At the time, though, with the Middle East about to erupt in mid-May, he took the warning rather more seriously. Kirkbride had to tell London that the information had caused a major upset in Glubb's life, and that Glubb was having considerable difficulty keeping his temper – another of those occasions when he allowed his normally calm veneer to be cracked by his true feelings:

> For your personal information, Glubb took the message very badly and wrote me a long temperamental letter closing with the statement that, unless His Majesty's Government could promise his officers immunity from a criminal charge, he would resign his post immediately. However, I have become a master in soothing temperamental people, I have had no lack of practice during the past weeks, when my day's work started frequently with the pacification of the King, the Prime Minister and Glubb (in that order).
>
> Please try and assist me by sending a soothing reply to this problem.[15]

By then, the third of week of May, the Arab Legion had become involved in the fighting in and around Jerusalem and

Glubb had no time to deal with other matters. Fortunately for all parties, Kirkbride's plea produced the not-unexpected response that the Act's provisions could be bent to meet the current British requirements in Transjordan.

> On further consideration, we have come to the conclusion that the Foreign Enlistment Act does not apply at all to persons who accepted service at a time when no hostilities were in progress. This being so, it is unnecessary to go into the question whether the officers concerned accepted service in the Arab Legion with the licence of His Majesty, seeing that the question of licence is only relevant to cases where the Act would otherwise by applicable.
>
> You may therefore assure Brigadier Glubb that neither he nor any of those in a similar position can or will be regarded as having committed an offence under the Act.[16]

Despite the reprieve – which seems to have been engineered simply to soothe Glubb's outraged feelings – there remained one further problem: Glubb was still on the Regular Army Reserve of Officers, having been placed on the list after his retirement in 1927. Although his name ought to have been removed in May 1947, his period on the reserve having come to an end, the War Office decided not to proceed with the deletion at a time when the position of the British forces in Palestine was still unclear. On 12 May this information was passed to the Foreign Office.

> While he is on the Reserve of Officers, he can, it is considered, properly be described as a 'member of the British Army'.
>
> In view of the possibility that it may be deemed advisable to ensure that there are no British Army officers serving with the Arab Legion if it undertakes operations in Palestine we would now like to take the necessary action to remove Glubb Pasha from the Regular Army Reserve of Officers. This could be done without it appearing in the London Gazette which is put on sale.[17]

With other more pressing matters on its hands, the Middle East Department fell in with the War Office proposal and agreed that Glubb's name should be removed from the War Office list and that to prevent any outcry the move should be given no publicity. On 19 May Major-General J.E.C. McCandlish reported, 'You can take it that Glubb is no longer a member of the British Army.' Glubb, of course, was not told about the recommendation at the time, for fear of upsetting him further, and by the time the relevant papers reached him informing him of the decision, there was nothing that he could do about it.

And so it came to pass that by the time Glubb took an active role in the first Arab-Israeli war, he was still in an anomalous position. Stripped of any official connection with Britain, he was a servant of King Abdullah, a mercenary in foreign pay, yet as the Foreign Office and War Office papers make clear, the British government still expected him to provide them with sensitive information by the 'backstairs method'. It was perhaps fortunate for Glubb that the greater problems of the moment prevented him from thinking too deeply about the rights and wrongs of his official position. For the time being it was enough for him to prevent his beloved Arab Legion from being sacrificed in a useless gesture.

(ii) To the First Truce

The reckoning came sooner than anyone expected. Shortly before midnight on 14 May King Abdullah committed his forces to invade Palestine when he stood on the Allenby Bridge, symbolically fired his revolver and shouted 'Forward!' as the Arab Legion moved to take up position on the Ramallah ridge and in the Judaean highlands around Jerusalem. Two brigades were involved – 1st Brigade (1st and 3rd Regiments) and 3rd Brigade (2nd and 4th Regiments). A 2nd Brigade was also included in the Legion's order of battle, but this was a shadow formation designed to make the Israelis believe that Glubb's forces were larger than they really were, and to complete the deception a dummy 4th Brigade headquarters came into being at Ramallah.

While the Arab Legion was moving into its positions around the city, Israeli forces had taken control of most of Jerusalem, right up to the Old City walls and including the Arab quarter of Shaikh Jarrah. Although the Arab defenders mounted a fierce resistance they were fighting against the odds and were soon forced to make a series of increasingly desperate appeals to King Abdullah asking him to send in the Arab Legion to protect them. From the very outset, Abdullah had set his heart on capturing and defending Jerusalem and, although he knew that Glubb did not want to intervene, he was greatly affected by the Arab pleas for help. For forty-eight hours Glubb's view prevailed – he still hoped that the United Nations would call for a ceasefire and truce – but by 17 May Abdullah had had enough and decided to send in his troops. Shortly before midday the king ordered a general advance towards Jerusalem and followed this up with a further order insisting that Glubb use infantry and artillery 'to attack the Jewish quarters in Jerusalem'. That Abdullah understood the stakes and the risk is made clear by the personal letter to Glubb which came hard on the heels of the operational orders.

My dear Glubb Pasha,
The importance of Jerusalem in the eyes of the Arabs and the Muslims and the Arab Christians is well known. Any disaster suffered by the people of the city at the hands of the Jews – whether they were killed or driven from their homes – would have the most far-reaching results for us. The situation does not yet give cause for despair. I accordingly order that everything we hold today must be preserved – the Old City and the road to Jericho. This can be done either by using the reserves which are now in the vicinity of Ramallah or by sending there a force from the

general reserves. I ask you to execute this order as quickly as possible, my dear.

Abdulla [*sic*].[18]

Glubb had little choice but to follow the king's orders. As he told the Foreign Office, he had visited the Arab Legion's units at Nablus and Ramallah 'principally in order to escape the insistence of the King and Prime Minister for immediate action' but he found his men in such a state of indignation that he feared he could not restrain them unless the order were given to attack Jerusalem.[19] One possibility for channelling their energies would have been an attack on a Jewish area outside the city – this had already been suggested by the War Office who favoured a rapid advance towards the coast at Haifa – but Glubb rejected this because he realised that a successful attack 'to save the Holy Places of Jerusalem would give Transjordan great merit in the Arab world'.

As a first step Glubb ordered an infantry company of 100 men to take up position on the walls of the Old City at first light on 18 May. Not for the last time in the campaign Glubb was struck by the significance of the places over which most of the fighting took place. As the 1st Infantry Company moved down from their positions on the Mount of Olives they passed Gethsemane and marched through the valley of Kidron, the reputed burial place of the Virgin Mary. A few days later, when the Legion's 3rd Regiment assembled for the first major attack, Glubb noted that their start line had been used centuries before by the Seleucid army which attacked Jerusalem in the days of the Maccabees.

While the arrival of the Arab Legion riflemen within the walls of the Old City boosted the confidence of the Arab defenders, Glubb clearly had to attack in some force if his little army were to make any impression on the heavily defended and tightly knit Jewish-controlled areas of the city. Normally a break-in battle requires much time and planning to prevent the costly attrition associated with this kind of manoeuvre, but time was not on Glubb's side and he had only a matter of hours in which to commit the necessary forces.

His first step was to assemble a mini-battle group consisting of an infantry company, a squadron of armoured cars and a battery of four field guns, backed up by anti-tank guns and heavy mortars – 300 men in total. Its main objective was the Shaikh Jarrah quarter which was entered at dawn on 19 May; by midday the strategically important French Hill overlooking the northern approaches had been captured and at nightfall forward units had reached the Damascus Gate and were in touch with the defending Arab forces. While the Arab Legion's field guns started to pound Jewish strongpoints from the north of the city, Glubb decided to consolidate his initial successes by calling up the only reserve he possessed, the 3rd Regiment in the Nablus area, and they began their attack on Saturday 22 May.

Their initial objective was the Musrara quarter of the Old City where a body of the Israeli forces had taken possession of the vast Nôtre Dame monastery and the Italian Hospital, both of which were well-defended obstacles. In spite of the difficulties involved in attacking the buildings, the 3rd Regiment made good ground in the initial stages of the assault, firing over the open sights of their six-pounder anti-tank guns and fearlessly pushing the armoured cars forward into the narrow streets but they suffered dreadful casualties – by the afternoon of 24 May over half their number were either dead or wounded. Against them, the Israeli defenders had made good use of Molotov cocktails and anti-tank rifles to attack the armoured cars, and in one encounter the Old City wall by the New Gate was dynamited to hold up the advancing Arab Legion vehicles. That evening, at 5 p.m., Glubb bowed to the inevitable and called off the attack in west Jerusalem simply because he was left with only a fortnight's reserves of ammunition and because he was not prepared to accept further casualties.

If it was a victory of sorts for the Jewish defenders – as most Israeli historians claim – the battle for the Old City was not yet over as far as Glubb was concerned. Fighting with forces trained for the open spaces of the desert, he had used his resources cleverly, with due regard to their safety, and he was still in a good position to attack the Jewish quarter from the south where his men had joined up with the guerrilla forces of the Muslim Brotherhood. Besides, he realised that the sight of his men on the battlements of the walls of the Old City had given a wonderful fillip to the Arab population. 'There was something strangely moving to me in seeing my own soldiers on those historic walls, their rifles thrust through mediaeval loopholes, shaped long ago to the measurement of cross-bows,' he wrote later.

However, the last shots had not yet been fired in the battle for the Old City. While the 3rd Regiment entered the city from the north, an Israeli Palmach force, drawn from the 4th Battalion of the 'Havel' brigade, had fought its way into the Jewish quarter from Mount Zion bringing with them fresh supplies of ammunition and food. Mount Zion overlooked the Jewish quarter from the south and while it remained in Jewish hands their snipers were able to make full use of the tall belfry of the Church of the Dormition which provided an open field of fire into the narrow passageways of the Old City. As Glubb noted, it was here that Peter heard the cock crow after his betrayal of Jesus, and nearby was the building in which the Last Supper had taken place. And as he remembered later, historical the scene might have been, but it was a fearful place in which to fight a battle between well-armed soldiers:

The whole of the Old City was built in mediaeval style, houses crowding on top of one another, and cellars and courtyards sinking down into the earth. The only thoroughfares were narrow streets, often paved in steps. In many places the narrow bazaars were roofed over, while the cobbled alley-ways were spanned by bridges of flying buttresses connecting houses on opposite sides of the street. Sometimes these bridges carried whole buildings, so that the narrow lanes passed through tunnels under blocks of houses. Old Jerusalem, moreover, is built on several small hills divided by little valleys, with the result that the narrow paved streets often enough climb up and down in steps, or in steep irregular slopes between overhanging houses.[20]

Before the two Arab Legion companies fought their way into this teeming warren they had put additional pressure on the defenders by fighting their way to the Zion Gate, thus preventing any tactical liaison between those inside the quarter and the forces on Mount Zion. This gave the Arab Legion a useful advantage as the Israelis were now besieged; but Glubb's forces, never more than 400 in strength, were still outnumbered and still had to deal with ferocious counter-attacks along the walls of the Old City. Besides, the narrow confines of the Jewish quarter turned the fighting into a hand-to-hand affair, with whole houses, and often single rooms, having to be taken one by one, to allow the men of the Legion to advance.

It was possible to call in artillery fire from the gun positions to the north but, as the men fought their way further into the quarter, the shelling had to be restricted – nonetheless, during the fighting fifty-eight synagogues were destroyed and much of the quarter was razed to rubble. Throughout the battle the men of the Arab Legion demonstrated a patient discipline which surprised and pleased their officers. They also showed themselves to be adaptable. Because heavy mortars could not always be used they hit on the idea of employing their PIAT short-range anti-tank weapons to break down walls and breach masonry in advance of the infantry attacks. And, as always happens in close-quarter combat, most of the fighting was ruthless and bloody, with few prisoners taken.

By 28 May it was all over and with their food and ammunition running low, over 1,000 Israelis – civilians and active servicemen – surrendered to the Arab Legion and the Old City fell into Arab hands and would remain so until the Six Day War of 1967. The Arab Legion's capture of the Old

City was a signal victory and immediately boosted Abdullah's prestige at a time when Syrian and Egyptian forces were being less than successful against the Israelis in the north and south of the country.

With the Old City of Jerusalem secure Glubb was able to turn his attention to the new Jewish city to the west where, rather than risk further costly street fighting, he decided to use the indirect approach of starving it into surrender. To do this, the Arab Legion had to hold Latrun, a fortified hill-spur which dominated the road between Jerusalem and Tel Aviv. If this could be defended successfully, the main supply route into the Jewish city would be closed down and, inevitably, its inhabitants would run short of essential supplies.

Fortunately for Glubb the Israeli forces had been slow to realise Latrun's tactical significance, thus allowing him to move in the 4th Regiment on 18 May. It was commanded by one of his most able Arab officers, Lieutenant-Colonel Habis Majali, whose family was close to the Hashemites and who later became a field marshal in the Jordanian Army. Taking advantage of the lack of Israeli interest in the position, he had had ample time to deploy his forces which were soon dug in amongst the ruins of the old Crusader castle which sat on top of the Latrun spur and which gave his men a clear field of fire down to the main road. Shortly before the Israelis decided to attack Latrun, Majali received reinforcements from the 2nd Regiment and these were deployed in the rear areas of Yaslu and Deir Ayub. Equipped with Bren guns and heavy mortars and protected by a covering artillery battery, the Arab Legion force presented a formidable obstacle to any attacking army.

Ironically, the Israeli forces given the task of attacking Latrun were commanded by Shlomo Shamir, the Haganah officer who had spurned Goldie's earlier peace mission. Under his command he had a force of brigade strength – the 7th Brigade – which consisted of an armoured battalion equipped with armoured cars and half-tracks, and two infantry battalions whose numbers had been increased by poorly trained volunteer soldiers recently arrived from

Cyprus. Shamir's plan was to attack Latrun and then strike north-east along the mountain ridge towards Ramallah; there he hoped to meet up with the 'Havel' brigade which would have fought its way up from Bab el Wad. However, everything depended on his men's ability to capture Latrun and it was there that the Israeli plans ran into immediate difficulty.

In the early morning of 23 May, shortly before first light, Shamir's experienced 'Alexandroni' battalion, a recent reinforcement, reached its start line by the Jerusalem road and advanced across open ground with the intention of capturing the village of Latrun. It was a tragic blunder. From their superior positions on the ridge the men of the 4th Regiment had sufficient time to select their targets before opening up with a devastating barrage. It was more of a turkey-shoot than a real battle and after a brief engagement the Israeli battalion was forced to withdraw. At least 600 of them had been killed in the hail of bullets. At the same time, a second Israeli battalion protecting the right flank also came under Arab Legion fire and was quickly pinned down. Majali then exploited his advantage by calling down artillery fire thereby increasing the panic amongst the rapidly retreating Israeli troops. As they fled from the battlefield they abandoned their weapons, many of them modern Sten and Bren guns, whose acquisition was a much-needed boost to the Arab Legion's reserves. Those who lay wounded on the open ground stood little chance of surviving the oppressive heat as many of them had neglected to take their water bottles with them into the battle. As Chaim Herzog was forced to admit, Latrun was 'a serious defeat for the Israeli Defence Forces at the hands of the Arab Legion'.[21]

The Arab Legion's position was further strengthened on 26 May when the men of the 1st Regiment took Radar Hill to the north of the Jerusalem road. This strategic point provided their gunners with a useful observation post to direct fire in support of the position at Latrun. Despite the setback of the first battle, the Israelis made two further attempts to break the Arab Legion's stranglehold, but both ended in disaster.

The next attack was led by Colonel David Marcus, a US infantry officer serving with the Israeli forces who used armour and infantry in a three-pronged frontal attack on 30 May. Although his men succeeded in securing the flanks, the ferocity of the Arab Legion counter-attack halted them in their tracks and, once again, they were forced to retreat in panic. Marcus himself was killed during the course of the battle. A third offensive on 9 June was equally ineffective but by then, with a UN ceasefire looming, the Iraelis had discovered a means of bypassing the obstacle at Latrun and getting their supplies into Jerusalem. This was the so-called 'Burma Road' which skirted to the south and was built hurriedly by engineers working in the high temperatures of summer.

Thus, although the Arab Legion remained 'the master of the battlefield', as Glubb had it, and although the Israelis had suffered a major setback in Latrun, the road to Jerusalem had been opened, an important consideration as at 10 a.m. on 11 June the UN-inspired ceasefire had come into effect. This was a British initiative in the Security Council proposed by Bevin in an attempt to stop the fighting in the area while the politicians talked, and, just as importantly, to heal the breach which was opening up between Britain and the United States. As soon as the Arab Legion entered the fray in Jerusalem, America had stepped up its criticism of Britain's financial assistance to Transjordan and George Marshall, the US Secretary of State, had been particularly upset by the continuing presence of the British officers in the fighting. Partly, Marshall's dismay was aroused by his distrust of British motives in the Middle East but he was also under pressure from Zionist supporters in America who kept up a barrage of protests about the British involvement in the affairs of the Arab Legion. Under pressure from the Prime Minister, Clement Attlee, the Foreign Office informed Marshall that while Britain had treaty obligations to help Abdullah, the British loan officers had been told to avoid fighting with Israeli forces in any areas designated by the UN for the new

Jewish state. While this was true – none of the fighting had taken place in Jewish areas – the secret message skated over the fact that British officers had been involved in the fighting throughout the short conflict:

> As regards the officers, for the top secret information of Mr Marshall, their instructions are to withdraw to Trans-Jordan if the Legion becomes involved in hostilities with the Jewish state, as a result of an attack on the State within the frontiers recommended by the Assembly ... the Arab Legion attack on parts of Jerusalem was the direct conse-quence of the breaking of the cease-fire by the Jews. We are confident that the attack would not have taken place if the Jews had accepted the truce for Jerusalem. Latest infor-mation suggests that the Arab Legion will henceforth be manning the defences of Jerusalem.[22]

As Bevin understood it, the danger was that America might be forced to lift its arms embargo and supply weapons to Israel, thus putting the pressure on Britain to honour her own treaty obligations with Transjordan. Britain had already abstained from voting for a US resolution on 17 May calling for sanctions on all aggressors in the Middle East and this intransigence had enraged Marshall. Obviously, an immedi-ate ceasefire would help to clear up the growing misunder-standings between the two allies, but before Bevin could support any move in that direction he had to make sure that, in theory at least, there were no British officers of the Arab Legion engaged on active operations in Palestine.

Accordingly, on 24 May, Kirkbride was instructed to with-draw all British officers for a forty-eight hour period on 28 and 29 May while the UN passed a resolution calling for a ceasefire.[23] This would allow Bevin to claim that as far as he was concerned no British officer of the Arab Legion was directing warlike operations against the Israeli Defence Forces and that all were on other duties in Transjordan. Officially, this is what happened and the officers were allowed to trickle back to their posts once the ceasefire had been agreed but some officers, like 'Teal' Ashton of the Welsh Guards, had refused to move, because such an action would have impugned their honour as British soldiers. Although the little ruse hardly affected the Arab Legion's efficiency, Glubb did suffer from the temporary withholding of the British government's subsidy which was part of Bevin's deal with the Americans. This prevented him from re-equipping and rearming the Legion during the ceasefire, while the Israelis hurriedly restocked with modern weapons, many of them Soviet-built from sources in eastern Europe.

(iii) To the Second Truce

The British decision to stick rigidly to the embargo of arms and ammunition to Transjordan was a tremendous hindrance to Glubb's military plans which were themselves based on the defensive deployment of his over-stretched forces. Moreover, it seemed to make a nonsense of the British treaty with Transjordan: the unpublished annex to that treaty agreed that Britain would be entirely responsible for the upkeep of the Arab Legion, yet at the time of its greatest need, when arms and ammunition were at a premium, the British were refusing to supply either of these necessities. Within the War Office the general and dispassionate view was that Glubb had two options open to him: the first was to hold Jerusalem as this would give a great boost to Arab morale; the second was to act boldly and drive to the coast in strength with other Arab forces, thereby cutting off the Jews in Tel Aviv and Haifa and 'possibly securing a military victory of the first order'. However, the ideas were only mooted in theory because of Britain's obligation to come to Transjordan's aid in the event of enemy attack, and it was recognised that any offensive strategy would be dependent upon British armoured and air support. In the aftermath of the fighting, whenever the Chiefs of Staff made recommendations about the size and

367

strength of the Arab Legion, the treaty obligation was always in the forefront of their thinking and Glubb's army was considered therefore to be an integral part of British defence policy in the Middle East. As such, it should be treated as a modern army and supplied with sufficient reserves of men, ammunition and equipment.

At the time of the four-week long truce, though, Glubb had little choice but to re-organise and redeploy as best he could. One improvement was the formation of the 5th and 6th Regiments with men from the six independent infantry companies; although this did not provide adequate reinforcements it did improve communications and command for the defence of Jerusalem. Glubb also had meetings with Count Folke Bernadotte, the Swedish negotiator appointed by the United Nations to produce a revised partition plan. With emotions still running high, Glubb doubted if the impartial Bernadotte could find a solution which would be acceptable to everyone – and so it proved. On 28 June Bernadotte issued his findings: their main thrust was that the Arab areas of Palestine should be united to Transjordan and that there should be an economic union between Israel and the new 'Jordania'. Territorial adjustments within the plan included the ceding of the Negev to Transjordan in return for western Galilee passing into Israeli possession; Jerusalem would become an Arab city and Haifa would become a free port, thus giving Transjordan access to the Mediterranean. Although Glubb largely approved of the recommendations, he feared that there was little likelihood of them finding universal acceptance simply because they appeared to favour Transjordan – and Egypt; Syria and Saudi Arabia would never agree to that. 'The only thing now,' Glubb told Bernadotte, 'is for the Security Council to take really strong action. They must insist on an immediate cessation of the fighting.'

Nothing happened. The Security Council was still in its infancy and incapable of intervening effectively in the Middle East and the ceasefire duly expired on 8 July without any hope of settlement which would suit everyone. Later in the year, in September, Bernadotte himself was assassinated by Jewish terrorists in Jerusalem, an incident which caused only momentary outrage. Glubb never tried to hide his scorn for the 'ineffectual and impotent' United Nations and when he came to summarise his thoughts about the fighting of 1948, he put most of the blame on the aggressive attitudes of the new Jewish state and on the inability of the United Nations to act as peacekeeper:

> We have seen that the policy of the Jordan government was to co-operate with the United Nations, which had declared Jerusalem to be an International Zone under its own jurisdiction. The government believed that the United Nations included nearly all the governments in the world, and that its power would be quite irresistible. It was to learn by bitter experience that Israel believed in force, and took no notice whatever of the United Nations.[24]

Not that Glubb ever absolved the Arabs from any blame: indeed, the Egyptian-inspired Arab League decision to renew the fighting on 9 July came as a severe blow because he knew that his forces were hopelessly over-stretched and running short of ammunition. Transjordan had hoped to have the truce prolonged but Taufiq Pasha had found himself in a minority of one and knew that any attempt to remain neutral would only have increased Arab hostility towards his country. In despair, Glubb asked the prime minister how the Arab Legion could operate without reasonable reserves of ammunition. 'Don't shoot unless the Jews shoot first,' was the unhelpful reply, and that was in fact the Israeli plan: to go on the offensive before the Arab forces could react in concert.

The tactics worked, too. On the northern front the Arab Liberation Army was defeated at Sejera, and Nazareth fell into Israeli hands; while in the south, during some of the fiercest fighting of the war, the Egyptians suffered heavy losses along their defensive line in the Negev and were never able to mount a successful counter-attack against an Israeli army which was gaining in confidence daily. By that stage of the conflict the Israelis had managed to acquire air support in the shape of Messerschmitt fighters and three Fortress bombers as well as a number of French-built Hotchkiss H-35 tanks and assorted armoured cars and Bren carriers. The key to the battle, though, remained Latrun, the central front which Glubb realised had to be guarded at all costs.

It was on this front, too, that the lack of an integrated strategy almost proved to be the Arab forces' undoing. The Arab Legion was still dug in on the well-nigh impregnable ridge at Latrun but there was a fifteen-mile gap between them and the southern flank of the Iraqi forces in Samaria. This was mainly a flat coastal plain whose key points were the villages of Lydda and Ramle; moreover, Lydda (modern Lod) contained the vital international airport and guarded an equally important railway junction. Obviously, these would be prime targets for the Israelis and Glubb was alive to the threat. However, he was never able to convince the Iraqis to extend their own front south to protect Lydda and Ramle and his own forces were too few in number to defend the two villages in any strength. If he sent men into that breach they would run the danger of being surrounded and forced to surrender: far better, he reasoned, to concentrate his defences on Latrun, because if that position was lost, the Israelis would threaten Ramallah and Jerusalem and the Transjordanian border would be left unprotected.

Accordingly, Glubb decided only to reinforce Lydda and Ramle with lightly armed volunteer forces backed up by a handful of armoured cars and the men of the 5th Independent Infantry Company, the latter under orders to withdraw in the event of an overwhelming Israeli attack. At the same time Glubb placed the bulk of his artillery with the 2nd and 4th Regiments at Latrun to stiffen the impediment which stood in the way of an Israeli thrust towards Jerusalem. While this made sound tactical sense – any heavily defended obstacle which prevents enemy movement is advantageous – he also laid plans to fight a mobile defensive battle which would allow his armoured cars and mechanised infantrymen to be deployed in several successive positions. This would enable them to channel the enemy into areas where they could be attacked and destroyed more easily and, to achieve that end, the 1st Regiment was deployed somewhat to the north of Latrun in the rear areas of Lydda and Ramle where the plain gave way to the first foothills.

The Israeli offensive, codenamed Operation Danny, began on 9 July and continued right up to the second ceasefire on 18 July. Using their superior armoured and mechanised strength, the Havel and Yiftak brigades swept through the plain in a pincer movement aimed at the two villages and after three days of bitter fighting the Arab defenders were forced to surrender. Once again, as happened during the fighting in Jerusalem, Glubb was forced to listen to increasingly frantic Arab pleas, begging him to send in his forces to protect the settlements, but this time he had no option but to stick to his plan, order his forces to withdraw and to concentrate all his efforts on Latrun. Unfortunately, during the enforced march to the nearest friendly area, many Arab women and children were overcome by heat exhaustion and the casualties were heavy. The incident left a lasting impression on Glubb:

> It is true of course that the persecuted Jews of Europe suffered far worse tortures, but these were not inflicted upon them by the Arabs of Palestine. One would have hoped that people who had suffered as much anguish as have the Jews would have sworn never to inflict on others the tortures which they themselves had endured. The Arab Legion endeavoured to fight the Israeli army but not to injure civilians. Perhaps nowadays such standards are obsolete.[25]

Hardly surprisingly perhaps, Glubb's decision to withdraw from the two villages was regarded by many Arabs as a disgraceful retreat and, indeed, the incident almost led to his downfall. Certainly, that night in Ramallah Arab Legion soldiers were spat at and stoned as the first refugees began their long trek back towards the west bank of the Jordan.

With the northern flank of the Jerusalem corridor now open to them, the Israelis turned their attention to Latrun which was suddenly vulnerable to a flanking attack. Sensing the danger, Ashton, the 3rd Brigade commander, had moved two companies of the 2nd Regiment northwards to the defensive position at Beit Sira where they joined the 5th Independent Infantry Company. During the heavy fighting which followed on 16 July the Arab Legion formations were able to inflict damaging losses on the advancing Israelis mainly because, against all the usages of armoured warfare, their armoured cars attacked the enemy in much the same style as their grandfathers had done in the desert, charging full-tilt at the enemy columns, well ahead of the supporting infantry. The following day saw the arrival of the 1st Regiment and their enfilading attack from the north stopped the Israeli advance in its tracks: the attempt to outflank Latrun had failed.

With time running out before the onset of the truce ordered by the UN Security Council, on 13 July, the Israeli forces decided to mount a final frontal attack on the position in the hope that their superior armour would give them the advantage in what would be a hard-fought break-in battle. Once more, though, the attacking forces could make no impression on the Arab Legion's defences. Although the Israelis possessed two Cromwell and three H-35 tanks, ten Bren carriers and a number of half-tracked vehicles, these were no match for the single six-pounder anti-tank gun which the 2nd Regiment had deployed on the roof of the local police station. Firing over open sights the Arab gun crews – several gunners were killed during the fighting and had to be replaced – knocked out the tanks one and by one while infantrymen moved forward to finish them off with their PIATs. Faced by this extraordinary and unexpected setback, the Israeli infantry hurriedly withdrew from the battlefield and the last battle for Latrun was over. The position remained in Arab hands until 1967.

It was a considerable victory, made more complete by the fact that the Arab Legion had been outnumbered five-to-one and had also been facing tanks and other armoured vehicles. If there was an element of luck – the Arab Legion possessed only five days worth of ammunition for all arms and for all fronts, and the supplies in Latrun were exhausted[26] – that does not detract either from Glubb's strategic awareness or from Ashton's handling of the battle. (No other commander has inflicted such a heavy defeat on the Israeli Army in the course of over forty years of fighting between Arab and Jew.) Glubb should have been praised for winning such glory for Transjordan: the Old City was in Abdullah's hands, the Israelis had been repulsed at Latrun and Ramallah had been safeguarded, albeit at the expense of Lyddah and Ramle. Instead, Glubb had to face the obloquy of the king and the rump of Transjordanian politicians, headed by Taufiq Pasha, who believed that he had been pretending to serve Abdullah while secretly obeying the instructions of the British government.

The loss of the two villages and the resultant exodus of refugees had been bad enough, but as Glubb pointed out in a terse report to the Foreign Office, the last straw had been Britain's decision to comply with the UN embargo on arms supplies:

It so happened that the Arab Legion withdrawal from Lydda and Ramleh had occurred on the day on which Sir Alexander Cadogan [the British Ambassador to the UN Security Council] had expressed Britain's intention to support the American motion in favour of sanctions. Arab politicians seized on the coincidence. Britain had reversed her policy and joined the USA and the Jews against the Arabs. The Arab Legion was commanded by a British officer and hence had retired from Lydda and Ramleh on secret orders from HMG, to ensure an Arab defeat!

This was exactly the scapegoat which the politicians of the other Arab states were looking for. Trans-Jordan, subservient as ever to British orders, had betrayed the Arab cause.[27]

Coincidentally, and with equally unfortunate timing, Bevin had also called for a ceasefire, thus reinforcing in Arab minds the idea that Glubb's decision to withdraw from Lydda and Ramle was a deliberate attempt to weaken Arab morale. Throughout this period British policy on the Middle East was at sixes and sevens because while the government was under a treaty obligation to assist Transjordan, the Foreign Office was under enormous pressure from the Americans to distance itself from Abdullah. Of course, Arab countries like Syria and Egypt were not privy to these negotiations and to them the position was clear-cut: as they had long suspected, Abdullah was a British stooge and the Arab Legion an instrument of British policy. Although Glubb consistently denied this interpretation, by an accident of British policy there was a grain of truth to the Arab accusations for, by withholding the subsidy and by refusing to supply arms and ammunition, the British government was in fact restricting the effectiveness of the Arab Legion.

Glubb's silence at the subsequent enquiry also served to put him in a bad light. Following his withdrawal from the Lydda–Ramle front, he was summoned to Amman on 13 July to face what was described as 'an unpleasant interview'. In front of Abdullah and his Council of Ministers Taufiq Pasha told Glubb that nobody believed his claims that ammunition was running low and that he stood accused of acting in accordance with Foreign Office instructions to force a truce with the Israelis. It was a bitter moment, made worse by the king's icy statement that Glubb was free to demit office if he so desired. However, instead of arguing his case, Glubb said nothing, presumably because he realised that Abdullah and his ministers were using him as a scapegoat in the event of a military collapse at Latrun.

Following this fiasco, the Transjordan government brought

the Arab Legion under the control of a ministry of defence, a move welcomed by the Foreign Office because it lessened the suspicion that Glubb was a tool of the British and that nothing took place without London's agreement. Glubb was not invited to comment on the decision.[28]

As Pirie-Gordon, the assistant minister in Amman, was forced to point out to the Foreign Office, Britain's relations with Transjordan had never been at such a low ebb, mainly because it was believed throughout the country that Glubb was a traitor to the Arab cause. But some good did come out of the affair. Abdullah was not inclined to prolong the dispute because he knew on which side his bread was buttered and, privately, Kirkbride had explained to him the seriousness of the situation facing Transjordan. Evidence of the ammunition shortage became abundantly clear when a Transjordanian delegation to Syria was given a supply of outdated and useless Belgian ammunition; then the Egyptians sullenly agreed to supply the Arab Legion with 400 rounds of twenty-five-pounder shells from the British Army supplies which they had confiscated in May. It was also made clear to the king that if the fighting continued, the Arab Legion would be cut off at Latrun and destroyed, thereby hastening the demise of Transjordan. 'The eventual happy outcome and acceptance of the ceasefire arrived none too soon,' Pirie-Gordon reported to London on 25 July:

In the event the Arab Legion defeated all Jewish attacks on July 18th, and maintained all their positions. They could not have continued to do so, however, as ammunition was almost exhausted. Up to the present, the indignation of thwarted 'patriotism' in the town, though still intense and bitter against the British, has not caused any explosion.

With the ceasefire it will be possible to strengthen the security forces in the capital which had previously been dangerously thin on the ground, and provided fighting does not break out again we can safely say that we have survived this particular crisis.[29]

With the all-out war in temporary abeyance – fighting continued intermittently along the truce lines until 15 October – Abdullah suggested to an exhausted and demoralised Glubb that he should return to Britain for a spell of leave, both to prevent him becoming a focus for Arab hostility and, more importantly, to renegotiate British support for the Arab Legion under the terms of the treaty agreement.

In August, therefore, Glubb and his family set off for London, flying via Cairo where he found that his departure had become a source of international speculation. Awaiting him at the airport was an army of reporters anxious to ask if it were true that he had been sacked by Abdullah. Similar scenes awaited him in London where journalists besieged his hotel, asking him how it felt to be a target for Jewish terrorists, following his success in holding Latrun. For a man who refused to court publicity it was a very trying moment, but it was also an indication of the interest now being taken by the world's press in Glubb's role in Middle East politics.

12

The Divided Peace

Glubb returned to Britain with a detailed report on how the current political and military situation in the Middle East affected the relationship with Transjordan. It was dated 12 August 1948, the day before he left Amman, and it presented the Foreign Office with three problems which had to be tackled if Britain were to regain her credibility in the Arab world. First, the political relationship between Britain and Transjordan had been tainted by Abdullah's doubts about British motives in the United Nations; second, the Arab Legion would cease to exist as a fighting force unless it received fresh supplies of arms and ammunition; third, the Arab Legion was on the point of bankruptcy and its subsidy would have to be renewed. Unless the British government turned its urgent attention to these problems, Transjordan would collapse, her territory would be divided amongst Syria, Iraq and Saudi Arabia, and Israel would seize the West Bank territories. 'Should this occur,' warned Glubb, 'the extremists in all Arab countries will really have a good excuse for claiming that the British and their tool – Trans-Jordan – have really let down the Arab cause.'[1]

In conclusion, Glubb reminded the Foreign Office that the British connection was a double-edged sword for Transjordan. When the Arab Legion moved into Jerusalem to capture the Old City, Abdullah was hailed as a saviour – he was able to visit Baghdad and Riyadh on the strength of his success – and fellow Arab leaders marvelled at the good sense of his treaty with Britain. However, when Glubb was forced to withdraw his forces from Ramle and Lyddah, those same rulers were loud in their condemnation of Transjordan because it seemed to them that the Arab Legion, by acting on the secret instructions of the British, had betrayed the Arab cause.

To retrieve the situation in the short term, suggested Glubb, Britain should take immediate steps to re-arm and re-equip the Arab Legion, even if that meant infringing the UN embargo; but the longer-term solution would require greater subtlety, he suggested, because it would undoubtedly affect Britain's relationship with the United States. Here Glubb recommended that Britain should publicly guarantee Transjordan's independence in accordance with the treaty agreement; furthermore, Britain should support Transjordan's right to take possession of the West Bank and warn the Israelis not to make incursions into any of Abdullah's territories. Glubb wrote:

> I venture to submit that it is essential to keep Trans-Jordan alive through the next months, because:
>
> (a) Trans-Jordan, in spite of all that has happened, has not departed from her traditional policy of friendship with Britain. Only circumstances too strong for her compelled her to fight the Jews, and to acquiesce in the futilities and follies of the Arab League.
>
> (b) Trans-Jordan is notorious in the Middle East and further afield as the staunchest friend of Britain. For her to be the first to collapse would be disastrous for British prestige.
>
> (c) If we can hang on a little longer, Trans-Jordan may receive a substantial increase of territory, which will make her a more valuable ally. If we abandon her now and she collapses, the solution of the Palestine problem itself will be rendered much more difficult.[2]

So sensitive was Glubb's visit to London that not only was he given a round-the-clock Special Branch guard, but his meeting with Bevin took place at the Foreign Secretary's private flat in Carlton House Terrace as it was thought that an official visit to the Foreign Office would attract too much attention. When the two men met on 19 August Glubb produced a rambling private letter addressed to Bevin from Abdullah in which the king spoke of the possibility of the Soviets gaining a foothold in the Middle East and the subsequent danger to British and Transjordanian interests. (At this stage Abdullah was convinced that the re-arming of Israel with Eastern Bloc weapons meant that the new state would become a Soviet puppet.)

> We do not wish [Abdullah wrote] to render Britain's position more difficult in the United Nations Organisation, but on the other hand we have to weigh the relative importance of avoiding trouble with the United Nations on the one hand, and the absolute necessity of preventing a further strengthening of Soviet propaganda in the Arab countries on the other. I feel that it is our duty to obtain the means to resist the Soviet expansion, and I am also persuaded that it is the duty of our friends to help us in this, whatever may be the consequences.
>
> This seems to me to be a reasonable measure, which it is essential to carry out, if necessary without it becoming publicly known.[3]

Neither Glubb nor Bevin was particularly convinced by the king's argument – which seemed to be more of a plea for increased British support than a veiled threat about Soviet intentions in the Middle East – and Bevin agreed to reply with a non-committal letter, thanking Abdullah for the forthright expression of his views. For the moment, the Foreign Secretary was more interested in the situation report and wanted to hear what Glubb had to say about it in private.

Glubb opened the discussion by explaining the operational problems he had faced at Latrun due to the acute shortage of ammunition: this could be solved without drawing too much attention to the fact by transferring ammunition from the Canal Zone to Amman. Two Dakota loads of twenty-five-pounder and three-inch mortar ammunition would be sufficient in the first instance and this could be held in reserve by the RAF until hostilities broke out again. The return of the subsidy would also be of immense benefit as the Arab Legion's account in the Ottoman Bank was overdrawn by £200,000.

Although he was sympathetic to Glubb's plight, Bevin explained that he would have to enlighten the United States government about the aggressive Jewish behaviour during the ceasefire as this would give him some grounds for reinforcing the Arab Legion. Glubb was asked to provide the necessary evidence. In the meantime, the Foreign Office would explore ways and means of transferring some ammunition to Amman by air as Glubb had requested.

Finally Glubb moved on to the main thrust of Abdullah's argument: if hostilities broke out again and if Transjordan were attacked by Israel, would Britain come to her aid under the terms of the treaty? Bevin replied that this was a question which ought not to be asked. Pressed further by Glubb, he replied: 'We had our treaty and we would not go back on it. We would not abandon Transjordan or give Transjordan territory. But Transjordan must not rely on the treaty or this assurance to create an incident. Glubb Pasha said there was no danger of this. The only risk arose from an Irgun attack of the Arab Legion.'[4] The meeting ended cordially with Bevin promising to pass the summary of their discussion to Abdullah through Kirkbride:

> You should inform King Abdullah very confidentially of the gist of this conversation. You should add that we are very actively examining the whole Palestine situation with the Americans with a view to clearing our minds on the prospects of a long-term settlement there. We are carefully bearing in mind Transjordan's position and will do our utmost to see that her interests are safeguarded so far as

this is possible. You should also say that as King Abdullah will see from the above, we continue to attach considerable importance to the existence and integrity of Transjordan, to the maintenance and development of our close relations with Transjordan and to the continued existence of the Arab Legion as an effective fighting force in close relations with the British Army.[5]

The last sentence in particular gave Glubb some grounds for hope: the War Office had been much impressed by the performance of the Arab Legion in battle and the Chiefs of Staff had given their support to a further recommendation from Glubb that fifteen days worth of ammunition should be flown by the RAF into Amman where it could be stored pending a resumption of hostilities. There were to be other benefits from the War Office's interest – henceforth the subsidy from the Foreign Office would be based on the Chiefs of Staff's assessment of the minimum force needed to protect Transjordan from external aggression.[6]

While Glubb was keen to see the War Office taking a greater interest in the Arab Legion and supporting it over arms and ammunition, he also had occasion to be alarmed by the bellicose stance adopted by Field Marshal Montgomery, the Chief of the Imperial General Staff. Even before the mandate had come to an end Montgomery had advocated the use of British forces to keep the peace, and when fighting had broken out in May, he had gone on record with the hope that the Jews would 'get it in the neck', an attitude which Glubb felt was out of kilter with the military reality in the Middle East.

Nonetheless, following his meeting with Bevin, Glubb went to the War Office to discuss the situation with Montgomery who insisted that not only would war stocks be provided by British forces in the Canal Zone but he would also make arrangements for the RAF to support the Arab Legion's ground operations. Glubb was much taken aback by this offer but rather than risk a confrontation he passed on

381

the information to the Foreign Office with the recommendation that they put a stop to this train of thought. A confidential minute was passed to Bevin to take the appropriate
action as any hint of a possible British confrontation with
Israel would only harm Transjordan.

> He [Glubb] feels that this would make it more difficult for
> the Jews to accept the absorption of Arab Palestine into
> Transjordan and would also be likely to make the Jews
> think that they could occupy the whole of Palestine with
> impunity, provided they did not actually threaten Trans-
> jordan.[7]

Before going on leave proper, Glubb supplied the Foreign
Office with a further paper outlining the problems being
faced by the Arab Legion in the aftermath of the conflict.
The main difficulty was the refusal of the Israelis to obey the
terms of the ceasefire while the UN was debating the problem
at Lake Success in the United States: 'The Jews are playing
power politics as crudely as the Russians, on a smaller scale.'
In addition to harassing Arab positions, the Israelis were also
moving into areas which would provide them with a tactical
advantage if fighting broke out again – and Glubb's gloomy
prognosis was that further bloodshed was inevitable. The
most serious Israeli incursions had been along the Jerusalem
to Jericho road, and if Jericho fell, he warned, the Arab
Legion and the Iraqi Army would be cut off and Transjordan
would collapse. The knock-on effects for the civilian population would be disastrous: the refugee problem would be
exacerbated and in a prophetic aside, Glubb feared that the
flight of the Palestinian Arabs would cause untold problems
in the years to come:

> There are probably nearly 400,000 Arab refugees now
> destitute or nearly so. About half of them are in Trans-
> jordan or being supported by her. A further Jewish offen-
> sive might produce another 300,000 Arab refugees. It may

take many years and millions of pounds to re-settle these wretched people. They will probably die in thousands next winter.[8]

At last, at the end of the third week in August, Glubb was allowed to relax. Exhausted by the tensions of the recent months and worn out by the protracted in-fighting in Transjordan, he only wanted to return to a lost pastoral world: 'It was pleasant to have time once again – time to write letters, to have a bath, to look out of the window at the quiet fields and trees – time to try to think what it was all about.'[9] There was also time for a trip to Switzerland – a favourite holiday haunt – where he and Rosemary met up with his mother, still a spry and determined traveller. On Glubb's modest salary, the costs of continental travel were a burden but he was always generous with his family and in the years to come Naomi always remembered that the annual leaves were a time out of life when all the family could be together. This was especially true when the children were sent to boarding school in Britain – Godfrey was sent to Wellington where he soon demonstrated a spirited, though disconcerting, unwillingness to conform to the tenets of an English public-school education.

On 17 September Glubb and his family returned to Amman, travelling to Cairo through Paris and it was there that they heard the news of Count Bernadotte's assassination by Jewish terrorists. 'Surely the United Nations would vent signal punishment on those who had so brutally assassinated their emissary,' wrote Glubb. 'As the days passed, and nothing happened, we began to slowly realise how utterly ineffectual and impotent UNO was. As far as we could discover, no retribution was inflicted – indeed, there was scarcely criticism.'[10] The main reason for the international community's unwillingness to condemn Israel was the ever-changing nature of the political situation. Within a fortnight of Bernadotte's murder, the Arab League announced the creation of an Egyptian-inspired Arab Government of All

Palestine, a clumsy attempt at national unity. At the same time Egyptian forces had started preventing Israeli convoys from crossing the Negev, thereby breaking one of the conditions of the UN truce. This intransigence led indirectly to the resumption of hostilities on 15 October. Under the terms of the revised Bernadotte peace plan, the idea for economic union between Israel and Transjordan had been dropped, the Negev was to be given to the Arabs and western Galilee and Jaffa to the Jews: this solution was also rejected by all sides. Rather than wait for the UN decision to be implemented, though, David Ben-Gurion took the law into his own hands and ordered Israeli forces to push south towards Sinai and Aqaba. Possession of the Negev would give him the right to retain the area and if the Egyptians could be heavily defeated in the process, it would be a blow to hopes of Arab unity.

The final stages of the war were fast-moving and decisive, but during this phase the Arab Legion was spared further heavy involvement in the fighting. Glubb's main concern was to move into the area south of Jerusalem to preserve Hebron and Bethlehem for the Arabs and to prevent them from falling into Israeli hands. Ostensibly this tactical move allowed him to press south towards the Negev where the Egyptian Army was involved in heavy defensive fighting with the Israelis, but there was also an ulterior motive. With a force of only 350 men Glubb could do little to offer realistic help to the Egyptians, part of whose forces had already been cut off in Hebron. He was aware, too, that the Israelis would defeat the Egyptians and that there was therefore no point in sacrificing his men in a hopeless cause. However, by making the effort, Glubb could appear as the only Arab commander willing to assist the hard-pressed Egyptians who by then, 21 October, had been pushed back into their defensive positions in the Negev. On the other hand, the sight of Arab Legion soldiers being welcomed as saviours by the local population of Hebron and Bethlehem was obviously a marvellous coup for Transjordan.

Nonetheless, it was still a dangerous mission, made worse

by the Iraqi refusal to extend their line south to Latrun in order to give the Arab Legion greater freedom of action and there was some fierce fighting at Tarqumiya. As Glubb warned Goldie, any failure would have resulted in the British officers once more playing the part of scapegoats:

> Kirkbride also sent for me today [21 October] and told me that he thought that for political and economic reasons, it was essential not to let the Jews take Bethlehem and Hebron. Politically we should have another Lydda and Ramle, especially as the King ordered me to send a regiment there [Hebron] two days ago ... It looks from the news as tho' the Jews will accept a cease-fire in another two or three days, so that they can get the maximum advantage of their victory first. It is really essential to hold Bethlehem and if possible Hebron for those three days. Please arrange accordingly even if you have to send a company from 8th Regiment or anywhere else, *or weaken your front temporarily.*[11]

Having taken Hebron, Glubb's forces were in a handy position to make contact with the besieged Egyptian garrison in the Faluja pocket, the defensive position covering the road to Gaza. Although the United Nations had called for a further ceasefire on 22 October, fighting continued throughout the period between Egyptians and Israelis who were anxious to capture Faluja as part of their strategy to gain control of the Negev. Because the besieged garrison had become something of a symbol for the Arab cause, the Arab League discussed the possibility of finding the necessary forces to raise the siege and produced the unlikely solution that a brigade-sized force should be formed from battalions representing Transjordan, Iraq and Syria. Realising the impracticality of the idea, Glubb once more asked the Iraqis to take over Latrun so that he could concentrate his forces on the relief of Faluja. When his requests proved fruitless he sent an officer, Major Geoffrey Lockett, to Faluja with a proposal that the Egyptians should pull out towards the east where the Arab Legion would be able to engage any Israeli forces which attempted to bar the way. However, Brigadier Said Taha Bey was under orders from his government not to co-operate with the Transjordanians and his garrison remained under siege until an armistice was signed between Israel and Egypt on 24 February 1949. (It has to be admitted that Glubb was also half-hearted about the operation because Abdullah did not want to see an Egyptian victory in the Negev.)

During the final stages of the fighting – confrontation between Israeli and Arab forces continued into the spring of 1949 – Glubb's main concern was to hold on to the central Palestinian ridge and the Old City of Jerusalem so that the designated Arab areas could be controlled by Transjordan:

> The Arab Legion enjoys the immense advantage in Palestine of being close to its home country. It can remain in occupation of the Ramallah district for a long time. The Iraqis must eventually withdraw, and it should then be comparatively easy for the Arab Legion to occupy Nablus also. Barring a renewal of war with the Jews or some powerful external intervention, the Arab Legion seems to be in a very strong position ultimately to annex the Ramallah and Nablus areas, and probably also Ramleh should it be returned to the Arabs by UNO.[12]

Although Kirkbride claimed that Glubb was 'very like the Arabs in his alternating waves of optimism and pessimism' and that he was 'at present on a crest', the Foreign Office agreed that Britain had little option but to support Abdullah's ambitions for the retention of the West Bank as part of a greater Transjordan. Egypt was becoming increasingly anti-British, Syria had fallen victim to a military coup, and Iraq was casting covetous eyes on Transjordan. On the other side, Israel had scored a brilliant success: what had begun as a battle for survival had ended as a war of conquest, with some four-fifths of the former mandated territories of Palestine falling into their possession – at the cost of starting a refugee problem which remains unsolved over forty years later. Between February and July 1949, the United Nations, through its mediator Ralph Bunche, signed separate armistice agreements between the Arab states and Israel but no peace treaty was ever signed and the main participants considered themselves to be morally, if not legally, still in a state of conflict with each other.

In the midst of these uncertainties, Glubb never lost an opportunity to remind the Foreign Office that Britain's best bet was continued and strengthened support for Abdullah. He was known to be 'our man', Glubb told London, and because the Arab world identified Transjordan with British policy in the Middle East, it was important that the political and military support should be strong and, above all, consistent. If anything untoward happened to Transjordan, it would not just affect Abdullah but it would also be regarded as a further setback for Britain. In this instance Glubb had a ready ally in Kirkbride who stoutly rebutted a Foreign Office suggestion that Britain was in danger of putting all its diplomatic eggs in one basket: 'What else can we do when other baskets available seem to be unwilling to accommodate our eggs?' Kirkbride went on:

So long as the other Arab states continue to protest their friendship for Great Britain and, at the same time, consistently disregard our advice and, in some cases, frustrate our policy, it seems worthwhile taking some trouble to keep Trans-Jordan alive, and on our side.[13]

As part of that support Britain had informed Abdullah on 2 November that she would come to Transjordan's aid under Article 3 of the treaty if Israel attacked across the River Jordan; however, this support would not apply to territories whose status had not yet been guaranteed by the United Nations. This was a good incentive for Transjordan to enter into an agreement with the Palestinian Arabs on the West

Bank and the official incorporation was accepted on 1 December. A fortnight later the Transjordanian parliament altered its constitution and the Hashemite Kingdom of Jordan came into being with its territories on both sides of the river. Not every Palestinian was enamoured of their new political status: some hated the Hashemites, others regarded Transjordan as a backward country but as the majority were homeless refugees they had little option but to accept Abdullah's annexation as a temporary solution to an intractable problem.

Although the Israelis had been anxious to seek an accommodation with Abdullah and had held informal peace talks with him at Shuna, the emir's winter residence in the Jordan valley, in December 1948, they were in a position to drive a hard bargain over the frontier and showed an unwillingness to come to grips with the sudden refugee crisis which had left thousands of Palestinians homeless. As Glubb was all too painfully aware, the impasse meant that there could be no security and no stability along the newly created border with Israel and that to meet the new demands the role of the Arab Legion would have to change once again. Glubb elaborated on the problem some years later:

A new phase followed during which although there were quite frequent bursts of shooting, nobody made a military advance or attack on the other side. But the Arab Legion alone was left facing Israel. During the Israeli advance, or its occupation of Jaffa, Lydda and Ramle and other various places, the Israeli army had driven out all the Arab inhabitants. Any place they came to they drove all the inhabitants out at pistol point. The result was that streams of refugees in the clothes they stood up in started pouring into Jordan. All these refugees had left all their property behind, they came on foot, running. Some were country people who'd had farms and land and crops and orchards, others were townspeople who had shops and houses and so on. When the armistice began – firing nominally ceased – a number of those fugitives tried to go back either to see what had become of their homes or to try to rescue some of their property. The Israeli army shot everybody whom they found as it was called infiltrating, that is, crossing the line between the armies. We in Jordan did the best we possibly could to prevent the refugees from going back to look after their property, but it was impossible. We had a three hundred and fifty mile long border and it's quite impossible to prevent people crossing at night. But when these refugees found that they were shot whenever they were captured, they themselves took arms with them to defend themselves and so gradually a guerrilla warfare built up.[14]

In his memoirs Glubb called the task 'guarding the frontier of hate' and there was good reason for such a sensational description. Following the agreement signed between Israel and Jordan on the island of Rhodes on 3 April 1949, a border was fixed between the two countries and a Mixed Armistice Commission came into being to deal with all cross-border disputes. Unfortunately for the Palestinian Arab communities, though, not only were the boundaries fixed in Israel's favour, but the men who agreed them had not been sensitive to the lie of the land with the result that, in some cases, Arab villagers were cut off from their traditional grazings or routes to market. It was only human nature to ignore the border and cross over, but whenever there were incidents of that kind it was Israeli policy to open fire on the transgressors, despite the fact that complaints were supposed to be lodged with the Commission in Jerusalem. Under these difficult conditions Glubb attempted to develop a *modus oper-andi* with the Israelis whereby cross-border incidents would be investigated jointly by the Arab Legion and the Israeli Defence Forces, but his proposals fell on deaf ears. 'Nothing was any good, the Israelis refused to do anything at all,' he said later. 'My own opinion – I don't state this as fact but I was in charge for six years under this situation – is that the Israelis didn't want to stabilise. They hadn't got as much territory as they wanted and so they wished to keep the thing constantly on the boil so that it would be open to recommencement of hostilities under some pretext whenever it suited them.'[15] Indeed, the Israelis adopted the policy of reprisals, shooting 'infiltrators' and taking savage revenge whenever the Arabs attacked their settlements. One of the worst incidents of this kind took place early in 1950 when the village of Gibea, two miles inside Jordanian territory, was attacked, its inhabitants shot and the buildings blown up. This was in retaliation for a Palestinian attack on a Jewish settlement where a woman and two children were killed.

The problem for Glubb was exacerbated by the sheer length of the border and by the fact that the Arab Legion only had an agreed establishment of 7,000 trained infantrymen to defend it.* Fortunately, the British War Office was well aware of his predicament and, having been impressed by the performance of the Arab Legion, defence planners were anxious to bolster its operational efficiency by increasing its manpower and providing it with better equipment. Following an inspection of the Arab Legion by General Sir John Crocker, Commander-in-Chief Middle East, the Chiefs of Staff published a favourable report, 'The Size and Shape of the Arab Legion for 1949/50', which singled out for particular praise the excellence of the brigade workshops commanded by Lieutenant-Colonel Vane. The report recommended that the Legion should be increased to 17,000 men, with a reserve of 3,000, and that it should be reorganised on the lines of a regular British division with full logistical backup. Although the paper contained no detailed financial breakdown, the Chiefs of Staff recommended that the budget for the financial year 1949–50 should be no less than £6 million with additional capital being made available to meet

---

*According to a War Office report in 1948, the Arab Legion was twice that size: '14,000 organised into a Headquarters, two Brigades and certain supporting troops.'

the costs of purchasing modern transport and replacement armoured vehicles.

At first sight, this was a revolutionary proposal, demanding the expenditure of large sums of money – the total grant for the previous financial year had only been £2.3 million. However, it was tacitly agreed that the war had cost Jordan £6 million and as the Arab League had only supplied £250,000 and Jordan £300,000, Britain had been forced to make up the deficit. As Glubb noted later, there was no other option for, if Britain had refused to foot the bill, Jordan would have been bankrupt since no other Arab country would have been prepared to help. Clearly this was an unsatisfactory arrangement and, as the threat of war between Jordan and Israel had not disappeared, it made sense for the British government to put the funding of the Arab Legion on to a realistic footing. As the report insisted, the first and foremost threat remained Israel:

> Extreme Zionism aims at the absorption of the whole of Palestine and the greater part of Transjordan into the State of Israel. There is more than a possibility that these extreme elements will come to power and pursue their claims.
>
> The greater the area of Palestine which is obtained by Transjordan the greater is the likelihood that Israel will make early demands.
>
> If the present flood of immigrants continues, or if at any future time it is restarted by pogroms in any part of the world, even the moderate elements will be forced by the pressure of events to demand more territory.[16]

Because the Israeli Defence Forces consisted of a regular element (Palmach) of 30,000 men organised in six infantry brigades backed by a part-time militia (Haganah) of 80,000 and an air force consisting of around 100 modern war-planes, the Arab Legion could never be expected to defeat them in open battle. It became a tenet of War Office policy, therefore, that the Arab Legion should be strong enough in terms of equipment, men and experienced field officers to withstand the first Israeli attack for a two-week period to allow British reinforcements to arrive from their bases in the Canal Zone. This change of policy had a serious side-effect: under the War Office plans the Arab Legion would be given an operational role, acting in concert with Britain's Middle East forces in the event of a major war. According to War Office predictions the most obvious danger was a Soviet attack from the Caucasus into Iran and Iraq with the objective of seizing the Suez Canal: this would force Britain to occupy a defensive line between Lebanon and southern Syria. With the bulk of her armoured and air forces in the Canal Zone, Britain would require the Arab Legion to meet the first assault and thereafter to play a harassing role on the enemy's flanks.[17]

This was very much a notional plan, based on a purely military interpretation of the situation but it did underline the seriousness of the War Office's thinking – far from being a minor client organisation, the Arab Legion should be organised and equipped to divisional strength so that it could be integrated into Britain's plans for the defence of the Middle East. It also gave the Chiefs of Staff, concerned about continuing defence cuts, the opportunity to maintain the strategic forces required for the region and during the coming years the War Office was to stress again and again the need to keep the Arab Legion up to full fighting strength. For example, a year later, in January 1950, a similar report claimed that the government's failure to follow War Office recommendations was placing Jordan in considerable danger:

> We have, during the past year, stressed that the Arab Legion, as at present organised, could not put up an effective opposition to an Israeli attack. Furthermore, the paucity of British troops in the Middle East would not allow us to honour effectively, at the start of operations, our existing obligations to Jordan in the event of the Anglo-Jordan treaty being invoked.[18]

It was a classic problem. The Foreign Office wanted to maintain its commitment to Jordan, the War Office provided the evidence of military need to meet those obligations while the Treasury did its best to restrict budgets to a bare minimum. As already noted, Britain was in the grip of a serious recession and the economy was bedevilled by an almost perennial balance-of-payments crisis. Rationing was still in force – butter, bacon and fresh meat did not come off until 1954 – and following the bitterly cold winter of 1947 scarcity and austerity were the norm for most people living in Britain and were to remain so until at least the mid-1950s.

Despite the financial difficulties, though, Britain could not completely disregard its international obligations for which it required substantial armed forces. While there had been reductions after the war, from which the Middle East was not exempt, there were still large garrisons in the eastern Mediterranean area, most of them manned by conscript National Servicemen. The army alone still supplied the following formations in 1949:

Egypt/Canal Zone: three infantry battalions, two armoured regiments
Libya: three infantry battalions, two armoured regiments
Cyprus: one infantry brigade
Somaliland: two infantry battalions
Sudan: one infantry battalion*

Although the granting of independence to India and Pakistan in 1947 had helped to cut back the army's overseas commitments, British troops were still needed to guard oil interests and the route to the Far East through the Suez Canal. It was something of a charade, though. Lack of trained manpower

---

*The other major British presence was in the Far East (thirteen infantry battalions), Jamaica (one infantry battalion) and West Germany (eighteen battalions, eight armoured regiments).

and an acute shortage of weapons and supplies in the Middle East meant that Britain was ill-equipped to offer a convincing strategy in the region, hence the War Office's desire to see the emergence of a powerful ally in the shape of the Arab Legion.

Glubb welcomed these proposals, even though he realised that the War Office's more optimistic recommendations would be blocked by the Treasury. However Field Marshal Slim, the outstanding Chief of the Imperial General Staff of the immediate post-war period, proved an enthusiastic supporter – as a former Indian Army officer Slim understood the Legion's needs better than his predecessor, Montgomery. Shortly after his appointment Slim pointed out to the Foreign Office that Glubb's army was 'a most effective formation both from the point of view of internal security and from the wide point of view of the Middle East in a global war'.[19] Following his first meeting with Glubb on 22 May 1950 he was instrumental in getting the Arab Legion subsidy increased to £4.9 million for the current financial year. Although Glubb was greatly cheered by his support, he also recognised that there should be no slackening of effort on his part and, not for the first time in his life, he bent his energies to writing extensive discussion papers on Jordan's future defence needs.

Most of the papers are little more than routine requests for additional funds, based on the familiar argument that Jordan was Britain's only friend in the Middle East and that any slackening in the relationship would not only ruin Abdullah but Britain too. However, one document written in 1950 is particularly arresting because it makes sensible proposals for the long-term future of the Legion's manpower which Glubb believed should be predominantly Arab in composition – he argued that the mid-1960s was the earliest date for full 'arabisation'. While it was vital to receive funds for new equipment, argued Glubb, an investment had to be made in the future by sending potential officers to Sandhurst and experienced officers to staff college. In other words Glubb was looking forward to the day, however distant, when the Arab

Legion would be led by Jordanian officers and he wanted to prepare for it well in advance:

> To build up a force of this [technical] nature in a backward country requires certain conditions.
>
> (a) Long-term planning making it possible to engage potential officers and technicians for long periods and to spend money on training them to the necessary standards. In some cases, secondary school boys have to be selected and their technical training completed at government expense, in order to enable them to reach the necessary standards.
>
> (b) The offer of a career sufficiently attractive to tempt the best type of young man to make service in the Arab Legion his profession on leaving school. The annual output of professional soldiers and technicians from the schools in Jordan is very small compared with the demand in the Arab Legion. It is therefore absolutely essential to offer reasonably secure terms if the right type of young man is to be obtained.[20]

Until that happened, Glubb realised that a condition of the continuing support for the Arab Legion would be the provision of experienced British Army officers to supply the necessary technical expertise for the growing logistical arms, as well as operational experience for the three brigades. To make sure he only got the best, Glubb still found time to write to the War Office emphasising the need to prepare detailed background notes for candidates so that they could understand Jordan's defence needs before they applied for secondment. He also insisted that they should be properly paid, with decent local allowances, and that there should be financial incentives for learning Arabic. Above all he wanted them to be committed to the Jordanian cause and, on his further insistence, it was agreed that every seconded officer should also receive a commission from King Abdullah.

While Glubb regretted the passing of the old days when he

and Lash alone had been responsible for running the Arab Legion, he realised the importance of cultivating the interests of the British officers seconded to him during the 1950s. His motto for them had always been 'very few but very good' and as he told General Sir Brian Robertson, the new Commander-in-Chief Middle East, in 1951, in order to avoid difficulties with Arab nationalists, the seconded officers should commit themselves wholeheartedly to the Arab Legion:

> The gradual disappearance of the old Arabist tradition and the introduction of purely British staff and technical officers necessary for the modern mechanised force into which the Legion is being organised, gives a chance to Arab nationalists, anti-Hashemite and Communist agitators to exploit anti-British prejudice.[21]

By the same token, Glubb confirmed that he would not promote Arab officers to positions of responsibility simply because they were Arabs, as such a move would inevitably lower the Legion's standards. Later, Glubb was to be accused by some Jordanians of doing too little to advance the cause of Arab officers and in some cases of actually preventing their advancement. While he never grew to like the Palestinian and town-based officers, and retained an exaggerated affection for the Bedouin soldiers, his papers from this period reveal a complete honesty in preparing the Legion for eventual long-term 'arabisation'. During the Korean War, for example, he pressed for a party of Arab officers to be seconded to the Commonwealth Division so that they could gain battlefield combat experience. Unfortunately, this was rejected by the Foreign Office on the grounds that 'we must be careful to avoid the allegation that we want the Korean War to continue because of its training value'.[22] At the beginning of the war in September 1950 the Americans had also requested the services of an Arab Legion battalion to join the UN forces in Korea but this had been vetoed by the Foreign Office on financial grounds.

In this approach to the administration of the Arab Legion Glubb was a stickler for appearances. Once his discussion papers and reports had been drafted and revised they would be carefully typed and then sent to the Legion's Liaison Office in London where Colonel Bob Melville acted as an intermediary, looking after Arab Legion officers attending courses in Britain and ensuring that all the papers got through to the Foreign Office and War Office. Melville was also responsible for maintaining the lines of communication with Jordan and for arranging the provision of supplies and equipment through the Crown Agents and other organisations – one of the disadvantages of Britain's withdrawal from Palestine was the sudden absence of readily available supplies and technical back-up for the Arab Legion. Now Glubb had to fashion his own ancillary, technical and supply services from scratch and, through Melville, had to make sure that his men were properly equipped and fed. This task also supplied him with further ammunition about the need to provide a higher subsidy: as he told London in the spring of 1950, the Arab Legion's soldiers had received no pay increases since 1945, rations were issued on a scale which were two-thirds of the minimum laid down for British troops, clothing was second-hand and vehicles were expected to do ten years' service before replacement. Even then, much of the kit supplied by the British to the Arab Legion was surplus stock from the desert campaigns of the Second World War.

Whenever he was on leave Glubb took the opportunity to press the case for the Arab Legion and to arrange meetings which were not always welcomed by Foreign Office officials. 'I fear we shall have a long and possibly acrimonious discussion on the Arab Legion's subsidy,' was a typical minuted remark on a signal announcing Glubb's impending presence in London.[23] Melville remembered that Glubb always took meticulous care over the presentation of his arguments and marshalled his main points before any meeting took place. 'He always seemed very calm – that's probably why the Arabs liked him. But he could be very obstinate in argument, deter-

397

mined to get his own way, not for himself, but for the Arab Legion.'

Inevitably perhaps, the task of building up the Arab Legion in the early 1950s and the strain of being responsible for the defence of the Israeli-Jordanian border took its toll on Glubb. Not only was he responsible for the reorganisation of the Legion into three brigades, consisting of ten infantry battalions, three artillery regiments, one armoured-car regiment and an engineer regiment, but he also had to negotiate the subsidy with the Foreign Office and Treasury and deal with the day-to-day administration of all aspects of the Legion's work. In other words, noted friends like John Hackett, he was being forced to act as chief of staff, commander-in-chief and minister for war:

In trying to discharge all these functions at once he was trying to do too much. He was over-burdened. Particularly, you see, as his style of being chief of general staff was to be available to everybody who came and sat at his door asking for an audience. And in Amman Glubb's door was always surrounded by people, each coming with a little grievance to be redressed. And he heard them all and did what he could for each one. He was a father figure who fitted so well into his Arab environment that I know of nobody in that respect to touch him.[24]

Complimentary though Hackett's final accolade undoubtedly is, it does mask the fact that Glubb was increasingly regarded as a one-man band. Never a clubbable man, Glubb tended to keep himself to himself and preferred the company of his family to mixing with his fellow officers. As the officer commanding the Arab Legion he had to keep himself reasonably aloof from his subordinates but some of the younger British officers mistook his demeanour for coldness and felt that they could never get to know him intimately. (Not that Glubb ever had much time to himself: his day began at 5.30 a.m. and rarely finished before 8 p.m.) The routine was a hard one and although Glubb appeared tireless, there was a suspicion in the Foreign Office that he took too much responsibility on his own shoulders and disliked delegating work to his senior commanders.

There was also the question of Glubb's successor. In 1952 he announced that he wanted to retire within seven or eight years and that steps should be taken to find a suitable replacement. The first choice would be Major-General 'Sam' Cooke, Lincolnshire Regiment, who had been appointed to command the 1st Division in 1951 but his secondment was due to end in 1956 and he would only be the successor if anything untoward happened to Glubb during that period. Gawain Bell was suggested, but he was unwilling to leave the Sudan service to which he had returned at the end of the war; eventually it was agreed that the matter should be passed to General Robertson and that he should find a suitable British officer 'who could be discreetly groomed for stardom during the next few years'.[25]

As a result of the Arab Legion's fine performance during the 1948 war Glubb had become a reasonably well-known international personality whose views on the Middle East were eagerly sought by journalists and political commentators. Glubb would not have been human had he not been flattered by their attentions but he soon realised that publicity for himself and the Legion could be a double-edged sword. This was brought home to him in May 1949 when, against his better judgement, he agreed to give an after-dinner speech to the Anglo-Arab Association while he was at home on leave in London. During the course of the talk he made some mildly critical remarks about the government's policy in the Middle East, particularly the decision not to supply Jordan with arms and ammunition during the periods of ceasefire. Far better for Britain, he said, arguing a well-worn theme, to increase its support for Abdullah and to show the rest of the world that he was a valued ally. Unfortunately for Glubb, although the dinner was a private occasion, a Labour Colonial Office minister, Lord (Glenvil) Hall, was present and he took Glubb's remarks to be an attack on government policy. There was an angry altercation after the meeting during which Hall threatened to expose Glubb in the press and to report the matter to the Foreign Office. Not to be outdone, Glubb wrote a spirited response to the Foreign Office declaring that he was entirely innocent of any intent to criticise the government:

> I am, of course, no longer a British officer, and can say what I like. But my intention is quite otherwise. I still wish to work as if I were a servant of HMG and my object was to improve, not to injure, the understanding between Britain and Trans-Jordan (not the other Arab states). I was therefore somewhat distressed by this unfortunate incident.[26]

On this occasion the Foreign Office was prepared to pour cold water on the incident and a formal complaint was not made by Hall; but worse was to follow two months later when the *Palestine Post* published an alleged interview with Glubb who was supposed to have told their reporter Lawrence Grisewold:

> So far as my information is concerned [said Glubb], the Palestinian Arabs are doomed to another winter and spring of privation and cold. It seems odd, doesn't it, that 800,000 peaceful Arab farmers, whose ancestors worked their lands through centuries, should die dispossessed and thrown out upon the desert to die?[27]

Grisewold had only met Glubb once – during a visit to Amman to meet Abdullah – and he had never been granted a formal interview: in spite of that drawback he fabricated a complete article which concluded with the warning that Glubb 'breathed no good will but war'. The *Palestine Post* was well known for its pro-Zionist stance and Grisewold was an American Jew and Glubb felt that it was his duty to issue a statement denying that any interview had ever taken place. He was on the point of doing this when messages of support started flowing into his headquarters at Amman, mainly from Palestinian leaders anxious to congratulate him for taking such a firm stance. There the matter might have died but when the Foreign Office heard about the incident from Kirkbride they demanded an explanation. Attempts were then made to retrieve the situation by claiming the right of reply but by then, 25 August, the story was dead and the subject had to be closed with the Foreign Office telling Kirkbride that he should reprimand Glubb for his lack of judgement. Until then Glubb had always been open and forthcoming with journalists and had enjoyed particularly the company of Tom Driberg and Robin Maugham, both of whom had published flattering interviews in the British press, but Grisewold's article was a new and unpleasant departure. Like others who have been misrepresented in the press, Glubb tended thereafter to be more cautious when in the company of journalists.

Glubb's high profile also increased his personal security problems, both in Amman and when he was at home on leave in London. The most serious threat had come from Israeli terrorists, former members of the Stern Gang which had been outlawed after the assassination of Count Bernadotte, but after 1949 he also became the target of disgruntled Palestinian nationalists. In May 1950, British intelligence picked up information about a plot to assassinate him at Damascus airport while he was en route to London for a spell of leave. Because there was no direct international link from Amman Glubb either had to travel to Damascus to join a flight to Cyprus or to Cairo which enjoyed direct links to London through Rome or Paris. Glubb was badly shaken by the threat to murder him and immediately suggested to the Foreign Office that they should put pressure on BOAC to open a route between Amman and Cyprus; such a service would also provide secure transportation for the growing number of British officers seconded to the Arab Legion.

Fortunately on this occasion, Glubb had been forewarned

about the plot and was able to change his plans but he was not at all pleased to discover later in the month that the plan to take his life had been hatched by one of his former officers, Abdullah el-Tel. Described by many former officers of the Legion as one of the most promising Jordanian soldiers of his generation, el-Tel had distinguished himself as a battalion commander during the fighting in Jerusalem and had become a particular favourite of the king's. However, he had quickly fallen victim to ambition and, while acting as governor of the Old City, he became involved in Jordanian politics. A request to Glubb to promote him to the rank of brigadier had been turned down and in despair he had taken up residence in Cairo where he became an outspoken critic of Abdullah's role during the fighting with Israel. Glubb, too, was a target of his attacks and, although these were at first little more than rabid articles in the Egyptian press, it came as a shock to discover him conspiring against his former commander and working with the complicity of the Syrian government.

Tragically for Jordan, el-Tel was also involved in the terrorist plot to assassinate Abdullah, the first inkling of which had been picked up by British intelligence in Beirut and Damascus at the same time as the plot to kill Glubb. Nothing untoward had happened then but similar warnings were passed on by the CIA a year later, in July 1951, after the assassination of the Lebanese prime minister Riad as-Sulh. Abdullah paid no heed to the warning and insisted that he would follow his usual practice of attending Friday prayers in the Great Mosque of Jerusalem. 'Until my time comes, no one can harm me,' he told Kirkbride. 'And when my time comes, no one can guard me.' On 21 July 1951 Adbullah was gunned down by a Palestinian terrorist as he arrived outside the Great Mosque – ironically one of his last acts was to order the men of his bodyguard, drawn from the 10th (Hashemite) Regiment, to make more room for him as he wanted to acknowledge the large crowd. The assassin, Mustafa Ashu, was shot dead and four other plotters were arrested and hanged; el-Tel was tried and sentenced to death in his absence, but a few years later he was pardoned by King Hussein.

Glubb was in Amman at the time of Adbullah's murder and in the tension-filled atmosphere he called out Arab Legion units there and in Jerusalem to prevent any outbreaks of rioting or looting. At the forefront of his mind was the fear that there would be trouble from the West Bank where many of the Palestinians regarded Abdullah as the author of all their misfortunes. Three years earlier, during one of the lulls in the fighting against the Israelis, Glubb had warned the Foreign Office that Abdullah stood in danger of failing to consolidate his military victories and that as a result the Palestinians were more anxious to establish their own government than fall under Hashemite rule: 'They would probably even prefer union with Egypt to partition but as the former is hardly practical politics the only remaining choice is a Palestinian Arab government under the influence of the Mufti and his party.'[28] The news that Abdullah had now fallen victim to a Palestinian plot only confirmed his fears that the acquisition of Arab Palestine had been a far heavier blow to Jordan than anyone had realised. Kirkbride said as much in the preface to his last annual report from Amman:

The transformation of the tribal patriarchy of Trans-jordan into the pseudo-democracy of Jordan, complete with the nationalistic ideologies of the modern Arab state which began with the union of Transjordan with Arab Palestine in April 1950, was continued in 1951. The assassination of King Abdullah in July was the most outstanding event in this process.[29]

Shattered by the king's death, Kirkbride applied for a transfer to Libya, thus breaking completely the trinity of talents which had looked after Abdullah's kingdom for twenty-one years. Inevitably the change affected Glubb, too. He had admired and respected Abdullah and regarded him as his principal ally in his attempts to build up the Arab Legion as a national defence force in which the people of Jordan could take pride. At times Abdullah had irritated him with his ideas for annexing parts of Syria, plans which Glubb was always at pains to block; the king's verbosity and his inability to keep state affairs secret were also annoying, but there is little doubting the strong bonds of friendship which were created between these two very different men. As Glubb admitted at the time of the king's death, life in Jordan would never be the same: it was the end of an era.

Abdullah was succeeded by his son Tallal, a bright, courteous young man who was unfortunately bedevilled by increasingly unpleasant attacks of hyper-mania which left him unable to rule. As a young man he had fallen out with his father and, indeed, with Britain's connivance, Abdullah had taken steps to remove Tallal from the line of succession during the Second World War. This had only been corrected as late as October 1948 when Kirkbride was able to report that Tallal had become more amenable to supporting British interests in Jordan:

> As I have already said, he is, however, intelligent and, after his succession to the throne, if he will follow the advice of his Prime Minister, and that of the British Minister, he should be able to find his feet and keep Trans-Jordan func-tioning reasonably well.[30]

Tallal ruled for a mere year before it became obvious that his ever-increasing bouts of insanity could threaten the internal security of his kingdom and in August 1952 he was forced to abdicate in favour of his eldest son, the seventeen-year-old Hussein.

In the last years of his life Abdullah had continued his attempts to find an accommodation with Israel and latterly he had held out hopes of concluding an agreement for an open land border with his Jewish neighbours. At the time of his murder much was made of the suspicion – in the Arab world at least – that he had paid the ultimate penalty for talking to the Israelis and that his death should be a warning to others who wanted to follow the same path. Understandable though this interpretation was, it fell somewhat short of the truth. Abdullah died as the result of a Palestinian plot hatched by the Mufti who had been the real loser in the war with Israel. Denied access to the Old City of Jerusalem, robbed of his political base in Palestine and badly let down by his Egyptian allies, the Mufti had every reason to want to avenge himself on his arch-enemy. The fact that Abdullah's death was seen as a punishment for breaking the Arab consensus, though, certainly deterred others. Gamel Abdul Nasser, shortly to become ruler of Egypt, told acquaintances that he 'did not want what happened to Abdullah to happen to him', and that the king's fate coloured his own attitudes towards bargaining with the Israelis.[31]

One of Abdullah's prime concerns in his negotiations with the Israelis in 1950 was the need to demilitarise the border between the two countries. One way of doing this was the creation of a joint militia force which would be responsible for patrolling set areas under the direction of the Arab Legion and the Israeli Defence Forces but Abdullah's suggestions had been rejected by Moshe Dayan, the Israeli military advisor who believed that Israel should be responsible for her own defences. Abdullah had also promoted Glubb's plans for cross-border co-operation to deal with reported incidents but when the Israelis refused to deal with the Arab Legion, Glubb was led to believe that the Israelis were only interested in sub-jugating the Palestinian Arabs by force:

It would seem probable that the Israeli Army (or indeed perhaps the public) experience a psychological urge to shoot, burn, blow up and destroy by violence, and to work their free and uncontrolled will on persons of some other race, as a psychological compensation for the years during which they endured such treatment at the hands of others ... It is surely remarkable, after all the Jews have suffered from militarists from Titus to Hitler, to hear them appealing to military strength as the true arbiter between nations.[32]

Glubb faced a seemingly intractable problem on the frontier. The Israeli forces were not content merely to police the border areas but they often went on the offensive when cross-border incidents were investigated. A typical operation would involve a platoon of infantry who would enter a village suspected of housing smugglers or terrorists; half-a-dozen villagers would be shot as an example to the others and their houses would be dynamited, often with families still inside them. To the Israeli officer in charge, this would be regarded as a reprisal for an Arab attack on a Jewish settlement, but to the Arabs in the border areas, it was outright terrorism.

Not that it was one-sided. Arab hit-and-run attacks on Israeli settlements increased from 137 in 1951 to 238 in 1955, but the main difference lay in the way the security forces dealt with the outrages. Glubb had given strict orders to his men not to cross the border and to avoid contact with the Israeli Defence Forces unless fired upon first, whereas it was always Israeli policy to retaliate in an attempt to stop governments like Syria and Egypt supporting the Palestinian *fedayeen* terrorists. Being the source of all the trouble, it was generally Palestinian villages in Jordanian territory which suffered most.

Obviously the Arab Legion could not police the entire border as it was still in the process of building up to divisional strength and had other internal security and operational duties to perform. Something more flexible was needed: Glubb fell back on his experience of defending the borders in Iraq and his early days with the Desert Patrol in Transjordan, and decided that the defences should be locally based with each village taking on the responsibility for its own security. The result was the National Guard which Glubb believed to be his most significant contribution to the Legion during the early 1950s. Based loosely on the concept of Britain's Territorial Army, but more like the modern Home Defence Force, the National Guard was a part-time militia whose main role was the self-defence of the villages and settlements in the border areas. It would be separate from the Arab Legion but its men, all locally raised, would be trained by regular NCOs who would also oversee the provision of local armouries and establish the lines of communication with headquarters staff. In the event of an Israeli attack it would be the responsibility of the local National Guardsmen to provide the first resistance until regular units of the Arab Legion arrived on the scene: in this way the Israelis would be denied the 'search and destroy' tactics which they had used previously against Arab settlements along the Jordanian side of the border.

Glubb sent his first proposal to the War Office in London in September 1949 and it received a warm though cautious welcome. The first drawback, according to the War Office analyst Lieutenant-Colonel H.B. Calvert, was that retention levels would be low and that it would only be a passive defence force, incapable of withstanding attack from professional soldiers:

> However, certain other factors outweigh these objections. One is the morale value of maintaining such a force and another its political effect, particularly in Israel. Further, once the force is equipped and trained, it may well be able to take over certain duties at present carried out by the Legion. This in turn would render it unnecessary for the Legion to be strung so thinly over all the front. The more the various formations within the Legion can concentrate, the easier it will be to reorganise and re-equip them. Training will also be much more effective, at present little can be done. Any concentration would also reduce the burden on their at present much over-worked transport.[33]

Acting on Glubb's proposals, the War Office agreed to the scheme and promised to provide up to 15,000 rifles which would start arriving in Jordan early in 1950. Given the British Treasury's general unwillingness to pour money into the

Arab Legion, this was a welcome encouragement, although it was made clear that in future years the National Guard's expenditure would have to be included in the annual grant for the Arab Legion. However, in Jordan itself, Glubb found a less enthusiastic welcome for his scheme. For the nationalist politicians on the West Bank, any involvement in an Amman-inspired organisation would imply an acceptance, in the Arab world at least, that they had given up any hope of establishing an independent Arab Palestine and had reconciled themselves to Jordanian rule. On the other hand, Jordanian politicians in Amman were nervous about arming the Palestinians for fear that they might one day turn their weapons against the government. (This was no idle fear: British weapons passed to the Malayan resistance during the war were being used against the British Army by the same men, now 'communist terrorists', or 'freedom fighters'.) When the National Guard was finally established – by 1956 it numbered 30,000 men – further attempts were made to bring it under pan-Arab control but these were resisted by the Jordanian government which realised its importance as a front-line home defence force. By then, too, it was properly armed and equipped and even possessed some heavy weapons. As early as 1951 Glubb had arranged for the British Army to supply them with 240 Bren guns, 312 Sten guns and 45 two-inch mortars complete with ammunition.

Steps were also taken at this time to consolidate the Arab Legion's air support wing and turn it into a proper air force. The first machines – four Percival Proctor observation and communications aircraft and two Tiger Moth trainers under the command of Wing Commander John Deverill, RAF – had been delivered in July 1948 and an elderly De Havilland Dragon Rapide had been supplied for VIP duties. In May these had been disposed of and four modern De Havilland DH-104 Doves were bought for VIP and communications duties, the bulk of the money coming from a special tax imposed by Abdullah. Welcome though these aircraft were – they were supplemented by new Auster observation aircraft –

the Jordanian government had also pressed for three Spitfires to help with the air defences of the country, at that time undertaken by the RAF at Amman. In fact senior Jordanian officers of the Arab Legion would have preferred the creation of an air wing which came under their tactical control but the Air Ministry's view was that such a move would upset the balance of air power in the region. It was not until 1951 that they agreed to the secondment of an RAF Wing Commander to be responsible for operational and training matters in preparation for the later supply of Vampire jet fighters. Britain had good reason for supporting, albeit tardily, Jordanian ambitions in this respect, for after Abdullah's death the Iraqis made a determined attempt to annex Jordan by offering, amongst other blandishments, the bribe of increased funding for the country's armed forces, just as they had done in 1939.

Although Glubb supported the moves towards the creation of an air force – he was after all an early convert to air power – he was less happy about the appointment of a fairly senior RAF officer to oversee its development. Under the original Air Ministry proposal the officer concerned would have reported back to them while keeping open links with the Jordanian defence ministry. In Glubb's eyes the new chain of command would have subverted his own authority for it seemed that the RAF officer would enjoy equal prestige and status in London and Amman and he complained bitterly to the Foreign Office. It was an awkward situation. Britain wanted to provide Jordan with the beginnings of an air force – in return the Jordanians promised to build a new runway at Amman – but they could not afford to proceed without Glubb's wholehearted support. He was, after all, still Britain's main military representative in Jordan. Eventually, a compromise was reached whereby the RAF officer would report to Glubb on all local operational matters and to the Air Ministry in London on technical questions.

Although it was a minor upset and one which was relatively easily handled, the Foreign Office's minutes on the file reveal a sense of irritation that the matter had been raised at all.[34] The incident also renewed suspicions that Glubb was exercising too much control over the Arab Legion and running it almost as a private army, just as he had done with the Desert Patrol back in the old days when border raiding was more of an extended outdoors game than a matter of life and death.

There was some truth in the department's doubts for, just as the political conditions in the Middle East had become more complicated, so too had the Arab Legion developed from a small tribal force, with its origins in the Arab Revolt, into a modern professional army. As far as the military innovations were concerned, most of the improvements had been for the better, as befitted a British officer-led national defence force. In spite of Glubb's annual complaints about 'always nagging for money', the grant increased annually (£6.5 million in 1951, £7.7 million a year later), a training centre and cadet school were established, an engineer regiment came into being in 1952, the artillery wing expanded to three regiments and plans were laid to establish an armoured regiment equipped with tanks. The command structure embraced a mechanised division created on British lines, as well as the police and the National Guard. In other words, the Arab Legion had become a completely different army from its romantic beginnings as a desert police force which Glubb had commanded with such élan against native opposition.

In this brave new world Glubb was pulled by two conflicting needs: he had to provide the leadership for a modern technically minded army while continuing to represent British political interests. Long ago he had decided that he could live with this split in his loyalties but, as the Arab Legion grew, he had to face up to the fact that his own position was changing. As Chief of Staff, with two Jordanian deputies, he was responsible for the overall command and direction of the Legion as well as providing the point of connection between the army and the Jordanian government. (Command of the division was in the hands of Sam Cooke.)

In this role Glubb's staff work was impeccable, as his papers to London show, and he was a meticulous planner who paid a great deal of attention to detail – Bob Melville constantly marvelled at the complexity of Glubb's arguments when pushing for additional sums of money for the Legion. At the same time, though, Glubb had to deal with political problems and as a result of this burden he tended to keep many of his worries to himself.

The view, in the eyes of some of his colleagues and associates, that Glubb was becoming increasingly overworked and taking too much responsibility for details, began to gather strength. 'If these two papers are the strongest case General Glubb can put up to support an increase in the Legion, they must confirm our judgement that no increase is justified this year.' This was the Foreign Office response to Glubb's application for increased funds in 1954.[35] Most of his evidence was based on the build-up of military strength in Syria and Iraq and the increased size of the Israeli Defence Forces and the picture he painted of life in Jordan was of a country racked by famine – there had been a plague of locusts in the summer of 1953 – and surrounded by hostile neighbours. The Foreign Office view was that Glubb was going over the top and refusing to discuss matters with his subordinates – a tendency noted by General Robertson after his official visit to Amman in September 1952.[36] Glubb was always happy to co-operate with British forces in the Middle East – a successful joint exercise had been held in 1952 – but he also wanted to keep them at arm's length and it was noticeable that he often preferred keeping important matters to himself and could be taciturn in the company of his colleagues – a characteristic he shared with Field Marshal Lord Kitchener, an earlier sapper officer who served much of his career in the Middle East.

Kitchener was often accused of being 'oriental' in his way of thinking and it is interesting to note that, as Glubb's career in Jordan drew to a close, similar conclusions were drawn about the Pasha's tendency to think like an Arab. Friends and colleagues noticed that Glubb seemed more at ease in

411

Bedouin company and enjoyed speaking to trusted Arab officers while generally keeping his distance from his British colleagues. Another (anonymous) British Arab Legion officer went further. 'You never knew what was going on with Glubb,' he told the American journalists Larry Collins and Dominique Lapierre. 'His mind had begun to work like an Arab's. He was all subtleties. He had the kind of mind that could understand the illogic of the Arabs and anticipate it. He knew they would act from their emotions, and he knew what those emotions were. He dealt as an Arab with the King's palace, as a Bedouin with the tribes, as a British officer with London. No one except Glubb knew everything that was going on.'[37]

However, there was no doubting that Glubb possessed several of the virtues found in all good commanders, the first of these being courage. 'He was absolutely fearless,' remembered Bob Melville. 'As soon as anyone began firing a gun, he'd put his head up over the top to see where the noise was coming from. Once I'd read his First World War diaries, I recognised where that courage came from.'[38] By all accounts, he also possessed self-confidence, as well as physical and mental energy – other vital attributes for the successful leader of soldiers. Tactical and strategic support was not lacking from his British-trained staff officers and battalion commanders, and he was a great believer in the value of planning. Where he fell down was his lack of experience in handling a large force and orchestrating its various parts, especially the air and armoured components, while maintaining its lines of communication and logistical support. This was a failing of many infantry officers who served in the trenches during the First World War and who then achieved tactical command in the early stages of the Second World War: certainly, according to officers like Lunt and Melville, Glubb himself was acutely aware that he lacked the operational expertise which staff college training would have given him.

In no other area were the problems facing him more clearly delineated than in the defence of Jordan's borders which faced both the possibility of all-out attack from Israel and the day-to-day reality of cross-border incidents. As Glubb saw it, the major difficulty was Israel's numerical superiority and her commanders' ability to call up aircraft, both in support of the ground operations and for reconnaissance. Apart from the communications aircraft of the fledgling air force, Jordan as yet had no fighters or fighter-bombers and had to rely on RAF support which would only be given in the event of all-out war and then only after the Anglo-Jordanian treaty had been invoked. As in most wars, the main problem remained the unequal levels of manpower. In 1953 the Arab Legion numbered 17,000 officers and men, 12,000 of whom were combat-trained. Against them, the Israelis could field 30,000 regular troops and 65,000 reservists, many of whom had experienced the fighting in 1948. Israel had also introduced universal conscription in 1951 and Glubb reckoned that this would provide their armed forces with 150,000 trained men by 1955.

According to Glubb's intelligence sources, never of the best admittedly because he relied heavily on word-of-mouth information, much of it based on rumour, large-scale immigration meant that Israel would have to expand its territory by the same year, 1955. The most obvious target would be the West Bank because this was the wasp's waist which joined together Galilee in the north with the Beersheba–Aqaba area in the south. Religious fervour could also supply the spur for any Israeli attack because many Jewish leaders believed that Israel was nothing if it did not possess all of Jerusalem including the Old City with the Temple of Solomon and the Wailing Wall. To achieve those aims, Glubb believed that the Israelis would mount a cleverly orchestrated attack with the object of defeating Jordan before Britain could come to her aid:

The Jews possess considerable political skill and an enormous power over world publicity – particularly in the USA. Israel, imitating the methods of Hitler and Stalin,

413

would start with a publicity campaign that the Arabs were attacking her. Her 'publicity superiority' is so over-whelming that she could work up a world-wide press campaign with no foundation of fact at all (we have seen it done). She would then launch 'police action' to 'restore order', and would be able almost simultaneously to produce 'quisling' Arabs in Palestine prepared to tell pressmen that they would sooner be ruled by Israel than by King Abdullah.[39]

The immediate answer to this threat was to push ahead with the planned increases in the Arab Legion and to reconsider the level of British support. By 1953 it was obvious that the expensive British base in the Suez Canal Zone would have to be abandoned, thus putting in doubt Britain's ability to rein-force Jordan in the event of Israeli attack. One solution was the positioning of a British armoured brigade in Jordan and this option was first considered by the British Defence Co-ordination Committee Middle East in September 1953 in response to Jordanian fears that the Israelis were planning a strike on the West Bank. Other proposals included streng-thening the National Guard, placing non-perishable stores in Jordan and planning for a naval blockade of Israel. The committee's views were reinforced by the Foreign Office who told Geoffrey Furlonge, the ambassador in Amman: 'It remains our view that on strategic grounds alone it is highly desirable that an armoured brigade should be stationed in Jordan in peace time, on a permanent basis, in advance of any imminent menace of hostilities.'[40]

However, it was also recognised that such a move could threaten Jordan's relations with her neighbours and it would take several months of negotiation before the first British armoured elements were pre-positioned in the country. (Seemingly unknown to the Foreign Office at the time, the Arab League had expressed surprise that, given Britain's friendship with Jordan, British troops had not already been stationed in the country to prevent any pre-emptive strike by Israel.)

Before these longer-term plans could be put into practice, the first priority was to lay operational plans to meet a hostile attack and, as he had done so often in the past, Glubb put his faith in the tactics of mobile defence. His main consideration was to deploy his forces according to the ground they were defending and the type of opposition they would encounter. The main defensive line in the West Bank was a salient which ran north to a narrow neck in the Jordan valley with a road leading from Beisan to Jericho. Glubb realised that this was the most likely area for an initial Israeli thrust while a flanking attack would be made towards Jerusalem from the west. To counter this threat he had to establish a large mobile force in the Jordan Valley whose task in the event of war would be to move from one defensive position to another to resist any rapid enemy thrust.

At the same time Glubb had to consider the continuing defence of the large border area in the West Bank. Here it was impossible to concentrate his forces in any strength along the frontier as they were simply too few in number. Instead of spreading them thinly he decided to place companies at the principal road junctions where they could reach any village or settlement threatened by attack. In other words, they would be a rapid-reaction force whose primary task was to respond quickly to any war-like situation which might arise; but in the event of all-out war they would act as a delaying guard force and would gradually pull back to stronger defensive positions in the foothills to the rear of their area.

Sensible though the plans were, given the size of the Arab Legion, they did produce problems. First, it was Israeli policy to booby-trap with mines the roads leading to any village they were about to attack, thereby slowing up the Arab Legion's response; second, although Glubb's tactics looked sound on paper, they were not designed to inspire confidence in the actual border area. All too often, political leaders in the settlements would claim that the Arab Legion was acting treacherously by laying plans to withdraw to better positions, or, worse still, that the British-led units were acting

415

in collusion with the Israelis. Far better, they argued, to stretch the soldiers along the frontier where they could die where they stood rather than withdraw, so it seemed, to save their own skins. Naturally, these critics neither understood the military necessities which guided Glubb's plans, nor did they have any knowledge of battlefield tactics but the criticism stuck and took root. More importantly perhaps, their fears reached the ears of King Hussein who had returned to Jordan in the spring of 1953 after a period of tutelage at the Royal Military Academy, Sandhurst. Unfortunately for Glubb, the young king took heed of the criticism and, anxious to assert his independence, he gave some credence to the belief that the Arab Legion was failing to carry out its responsibilities. Unfortunately, too, an Israeli force crossed the border that October, attacked the village of Qibya and massacred its inhabitants. Suddenly Glubb's plans seemed to be in tatters and the Arab Legion found itself vilified for its inability to defend the Palestinians who lived on the border with Israel.

It has to be said that those Palestinians had some grounds for their criticism, for the Qibya incident carries all the hallmarks of a major error of judgement on the part of Brigadier 'Teal' Ashton who had responsibility for the area. The day before the outrage, on 13 October, the Israeli settlement at Tirat Yehuda had been attacked by Palestinians and the Arab Legion had co-operated with the Israeli Defence Force in an attempt to track down the terrorists. Although the scent was lost, Ashton must have realised that the Israelis would retaliate and should have been prepared for what happened next. In fact, the first Israeli attack did not start until 9.30 p.m. on 14 October when Arab watchmen at Qibya were overpowered by Israeli troops who opened up on the village with rifle and mortar fire. The National Guard was called out and a fierce firefight developed. During the course of this stage of the fighting an urgent message was sent to brigade headquarters at 10.30 p.m. but, according to Glubb's evidence, Ashton was in no immediate hurry to respond because so many similar messages had turned out to be false alarms.

Instead, he sent a message to the 10th Regiment at Budrus and asked them to investigate; then he went to bed and ordered his staff to wake him if any further signals came in.

Meanwhile, back at Qibya, the National Guardsmen had run out of ammunition and could not reach the reserves which were held by the head man. The way was now open for the Israelis to enter the village where they shot up everything in sight before dynamiting the houses, most of which still contained families sheltering from the battle. All told, the Israelis blew up forty-two houses and killed sixty-six civilians: it was one of the worst massacres ever perpetrated on the frontier and it was matched in horror only by the Deir Yassan incident of 1948.

In the aftermath Glubb had no option but to sack Ashton and retire the battalion commander of the 10th Regiment. At the time, many of the other British officers felt that Ashton had been made a scapegoat and that he was being sacrificed for political reasons; some even felt that Glubb should have done more to defend him. Glubb obviously felt unhappy about having to sack Ashton and there is little doubt that he was only carrying out the orders of the Jordanian government, but it is difficult to see what else he could have done. Qibya was a dreadful incident and its emotional significance for the people of the West Bank was great. Had Glubb not acted decisively and sacked Ashton the trouble would have festered and no one would have emerged with any credit. In any case, it is often the commander's unhappy duty to sack subordinates and to carry out policies which are not always universally popular.

For Ashton, though, the decision was a personal tragedy. Even amongst those Arab Legion offices who knew and understood the Middle East and who loved the Arab way of life, he stood apart. After being commissioned in the Welsh Guards he served with the Iraq Levies and quickly became a fluent speaker of Arabic with a lively interest in the archaeology of the Holy Land. A bachelor, he liked Arab company and eventually adopted a Bedouin boy as his son, and hoped to settle in Jordan after his retirement. Instead, he returned to his family home in Wales and became something of a recluse, a life that probably suited him – Melville remembered that at one point in Ashton's career he had made his home in a cave-like hole in the ground. As Glubb said, of all the officers in the Arab Legion, 'Teal' Ashton was the one most emotionally attached to the country.

But if Ashton had good reason to rue Qibya, so too did Glubb: in his diary James Lunt wrote prophetically, 'I do not see how the Pasha can long survive this.'[41]

13

Farewell to Arms

At the time of the Qibya incident Glubb had been in the Middle East for over half of his life – he was then fifty-six – and it was almost thirty years to the day when he had first stepped foot inside the lands to the east of the River Jordan. In that time there had been many changes to the region: the Second World War had helped to bring the state of Israel into being and the war with the Arabs which followed on its heels had changed the boundaries and ushered in the seemingly intractable problem of the Palestinian refugees. The Middle East had also become a unique strategic centre with the discovery of the world's greatest concentrations of oil giving it an undisputed place in the world's economy. By 1949 the area produced 12 per cent of the world's oil supplies and, within a decade, this had been doubled as the Gulf states joined Iran, Iraq and Saudi Arabia as the main exporters of oil.

With the new wealth came changes in the infrastructure, as modern roads and airports slowly but surely replaced the traditional camel routes and rickety biplanes which Glubb had known in his youth. Political nationalism was much in vogue, too, as a replacement for the romantic pan-Arabism preached during the First World War. Urban intellectuals began to question British support for the conservative factors in Islam and the problem of the Palestinians added a new focus for anti-imperialist feelings. For all their love of the Bedouin and support for the Hashemites in Iraq and Jordan,

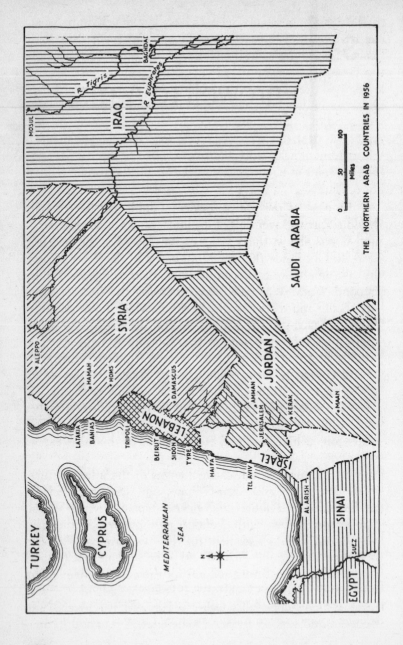

THE NORTHERN ARAB COUNTRIES IN 1956

the British administrators seem to have lost the old imperialist touch by the 1950s. Freya Stark said as much when she told Evelyn Shuckburgh, head of the Middle East Department of the Foreign Office from 1954 to 1956, that his officials no longer had the patience or the will to deal with the Arabs and no longer understood them. 'Instead of sending men out who will spend their lives there and get to love and be loved by the Arabs we deal them institutions, pacts, etc,' she told him. 'Short-term officials who change every two or three years and have no spirit in it, are a poor substitute for Cornwallis, Kirkbride, Glubb.'

In the midst of these uncertainties Glubb was regarded as one of the pillars on which British policy in the Middle East would stand or fall. Governments might change, rulers could come and go but Glubb would go on if not forever then at least until his retirement – and there were optimists within the Foreign Office who hoped that he would see it out until his sixty-fifth birthday in 1962. There was some desultory talk about finding a replacement, papers were written and letters exchanged, but nothing positive was done and the Middle East Department hoped that just as Glubb had managed to control Abdullah, he would do the same with the youthful Hussein.

Sadly it was not to be. The drift had started but Glubb and his Foreign Office mentors seemed to be unaware of the direction it was taking and between 1953 and 1956 there was a growing absence of reality in British policies towards Jordan and the Middle East. Not only was the country growing impatient with the British connection but the new king was becoming increasingly unhappy with Glubb's conservative approach to military matters. It would take another two years before the storm broke; many different factors would be involved, such as the Egyptian influence, maladroit British handling of the political situation, Jordan's own aspirations, but, in many people's minds, the rot began at Qibya because it was there that the widely discussed shortcomings in Glubb's defence policy seemed to have been laid bare.

In fact, the Qibya incident forced Glubb to readjust his tactics to take into account, at least for the time being, the indignation it had created throughout Jordan and the Arab world; and, as a result, he deployed two infantry brigade groups along the frontier to counter the possibility of further attacks. Local commanders were also ordered to go on the offensive and by turning to a policy of active patrolling, the Legion was able to reduce the number of shooting incidents along the border. Although the Israelis continued to take reprisals, these were gradually pressed home with less enthusiasm and the last major incident involving Israeli Defence Forces and the Arab Legion took place at Beit Liquya in September 1954. Skilful use of reinforcements allowed the Legion to take the offensive against the attacking Israeli battalion which was forced to retreat, having sustained heavy casualties and lost much of its equipment.

Although Beit Liquya was an important punctuation mark in the border fighting and the area became relatively quiet thereafter, the gain was quickly balanced by renewed political tensions along the frontiers with Syria and Egypt, both of which had put pressure on the Jordanian government over its continuing political relationship with Britain. The first inkling had come in 1953 when the Arab League attempted to take over the military leadership of the National Guard and had also decided to pay a £500,000 subsidy to the Arab Legion in recognition of its peacekeeping role in the West Bank. Although the money was small compared to the British subsidy, Glubb feared that the payments would threaten Jordan's independence by bringing the country into closer contact with Egypt, the main instigators of the payment. Glubb was particularly concerned about the influence of the Ikhwan al Musilman, or Muslim Brotherhood, a strict Islamic political and religious organisation which had been founded in 1928 and which believed that Britain's presence in the Middle East had introduced alien values, public immorality and imperialist domination:

Political activity in the Middle East is nearly always destructive. They [Arab nationalists] always set themselves to destroy the regime they dislike, long before they consider how to replace it. Thus contact between Egyptian officers and the Arab Legion would mean agitation to get rid of British influence. The agitators would not think what would happen after Britain had left until she actually did leave. Disaster would then follow, but it would be too late.

It may be said that the subsidy is from the Arab League not from Egypt alone, and this is true. But the fact that some of the contributors are well intentioned would not prevent the Egyptians from using the Arab League to establish their own influence in Jordan. Moreover Egyptian activity in other spheres – the Muslim Congress in Jerusalem, the Ikhwan Muslimin, the invitation to King Husain to visit Egypt, the unending attacks on British officers of the Arab Legion in the Egyptian press – all these factors show Egypt's increasing desire to dominate Jordan.[1]

In Egypt the Muslim Brotherhood had originally enjoyed close links with the Free Officers' movement which had seized power in 1952 and, although these had been weakened after an unsuccessful attempt on Nasser's life in 1954, they still held considerable religious and political power in the country and throughout the Middle East. The Jordanian government, for example, tended to favour them as being a fairly moderate Muslim society because they formed a counter-weight to the Ba'ath and Communist parties.

The main bugbear to the West, though, was Gamel Abdel Nasser who had come to power in Egypt through the Free Officers' revolution (see below, p. 425) and had succeeded General Neguib as president in the spring of 1954. One of his first acts had been to reject British demands to keep 7,000 servicemen in the Suez Canal Zone and in July that year it was agreed that they should move out by April 1956 at the latest. At the time Nasser spoke hopefully of a 'new era of friendly relations' but his optimism was not shared by the ruling Conservative government which had come to power in Britain in October 1951. Anthony Eden, the Foreign Secretary, entertained ill-concealed personal animosity towards Egypt in general and Nasser in particular and his attitudes were to exert a baleful influence on British policies in the Middle East after he became Prime Minister in April 1955.

Nasser's inexorable rise to a position of authority in the Arab world introduced a new feeling of pan-Arab nationalism amongst many ordinary people in the Middle East. Although he himself was suspicious of the concept of Arab unity – he never came to trust fully the Arab League and regarded it as an imperialist showpiece – he did believe in putting an end to western domination in the Middle East and wanted Egypt to be the focus of that intention. It was hardly surprising, then, that as his popularity flourished, so did he come to be feared and detested by those Western leaders who felt that he was upsetting the balance of power in the region.

Glubb in particular had ample reason to feel affronted by Nasser's presence, as much of the Egyptian leader's political rhetoric about foreign domination seemed to be directed at him. In some sections of the Egyptian press, Glubb was always referred to as 'Kalb' ('dog') Pasha and when he went home on leave in July 1954 the same papers immediately announced that he had been sacked by the Jordanian government. Glubb was well used to being the target of political venom and did his best to brush off the attacks as being little more than crude propaganda. However, as he told Charles Duke, the new British Ambassador in Amman, he now feared that the Egyptians were concentrating their efforts on him in order to vilify British policies in Jordan. Equally worrying to him was the feeling that the Foreign Office was no longer taking his warnings seriously. Duke commented:

> I do not know if you know Glubb but for all his quiet and unruffled manner he is a sensitive little man, as Furlonge warned me. He seems to feel that although he can in the War Office reach a level at which he can discuss his

problems with responsible people, he is liable to be 'brushed off' in the Foreign Office.[2]

Glubb had some grounds for his fears. In response to a well-argued document outlining the extent of the Egyptian attempts to infiltrate the Arab Legion and to sow discord amongst the Jordanian officers and men, the Foreign Office merely noted: 'We have had this before. Glubb's intelligence is usually quite good, if his treatment is at times melodramatic.'[3] In fact Glubb's main contention was that Nasser wanted to destabilise the regime in Jordan, get rid of the British officers and create a new united front against Israel with the intention of handing Palestine back to the Arabs. Propaganda was one weapon – Cairo had a powerful radio transmitter and the regime published several widely read broadsheets – and the promotion of cross-border incidents another, but Glubb's main concern was that Egypt would subvert the Arab Legion through the establishment inside it of a Free Officers' movement.

This was particularly worrying as a similar political grouping had brought Nasser to power in Egypt. Originally a clandestine movement which had been founded in the 1930s by a handful of progressive Egyptian Army officers, it adopted a higher profile in 1949 after the disastrous war with Israel and three years later, in 1952, it was responsible for toppling King Farouk's regime. According to the evidence of Lieutenant-Colonel (later Brigadier) Peter Young, who commanded the 9th Regiment, a Free Officers' movement came to prominence in the Arab Legion in 1954 but was probably active even earlier. Indeed, James Lunt puts the date at 1950. Certainly, Glubb seems to have been aware of its presence and was able to supply British military intelligence with the names of those officers who had used the Free Officers' movement to forge links with the Egyptians.

The list makes interesting reading because it reveals the high level of personal information which Glubb had gleaned about those officers under his command whom he suspected

425

of various degrees of disloyalty. Amongst them was a once-trusted gunner officer, Shakir Yusuf, who had links with the Ba'ath Party – 'why he commanded an Independent Brigade I don't know!' was Glubb's tart comment. Others included Abdul Majid Debbas, 'a nasty fellow given to intrigue and alleged to be immoral in other directions'; Adeeb Abu Nuwar who 'played soccer for Sandhurst and never recovered from the ill-effects on his vanity. A very nasty type. Extremely conceited, lazy and disliked by the other officers'; and Qasim al Nasir whose principal failing was to have conspired with Colonel Mahmud Salah ed Din Mustafa, the Egyptian Military Attaché, and to have accepted bribes from him.[4]

Appointed to Amman in June 1955, on Nasser's personal recommendation, Mustafa was an artillery officer who had been through staff college and was well versed in the arts of subversive warfare. One of his first initiatives was to invite members of the Egyptian Army Staff College to Amman ostensibly to discuss joint defence problems but in reality to turn the Arab Legion's Free Officers' group into a pro-Nasser cell. Later that year he spent considerable time on Jordan's borders talking to peasants about their attitude towards Israel and, as Glubb feared, in some cases inciting them to acts of violence. Glubb passed on this information to the Foreign Office who agreed that 'the appointment seems a notably unfortunate one'.[5]

Not everyone agreed with that assessment. Mustafa was liked by a number of British officers who considered him to be a real professional, but he was also responsible for the dissemination of Free Officers' propaganda pamphlets which were printed in Cairo and distributed freely throughout the Arab Legion, often using the ordinary postal system. The message was always clear and direct: Jordan had to rid itself of the British influence and the Arab Legion had to come under Jordanian control.[6] If this did not happen soon, continued the message, then Jordan would be ruined because in the event of war with Israel the British officers would refuse to go into action. (This was more or less true: the Foreign Office had made it clear that British officers were forbidden to take part in offensive operations against Israel unless the treaty obligations with Britain had been brought into effect.) Although the pamphlets were little more than an irritant – the Foreign Office's attitude was one of superficial disdain – they did add considerably to Glubb's sense of unease when considering Egyptian influence in Jordan. 'The one ambition of the Egyptians is to dominate the Middle East,' he warned in November 1955, 'and to this purpose it is essential for them to get rid of British and American influence.'[7]

That message was by no means untypical of the flood of signals which Glubb sent back to London throughout 1954 and 1955 and while the Foreign Office did not always pay the greatest attention to them the government was sufficiently alarmed by the growth of Nasser's influence in the Middle East to ask the Chiefs of Staff to comment on the new strategic position. Their discussion acquired a new urgency in September 1955 when Nasser entered into a deal with Czechoslovakia for the supply of modern Soviet-built tanks and aircraft in return for rice and cotton. Not only did this break the policy of neutrality which the Western powers had introduced to curb arms sales in the Middle East, but it alarmed the new Prime Minister, Anthony Eden, who believed that British interests in Jordan were under a new threat. (Eden's biographer, Robert Rhodes James, believes that the arms sale 'provided the spark that lit the fuse' for the Suez crisis a year later.) Nasser's action also stirred up antagonism in Washington because of America's friendship with Israel and in Paris where the French felt that Egyptian influence was being used to ferment trouble in Algeria.

Nasser's purchase of arms also paved the way for a renewal of Soviet influence in the Middle East and Glubb feared that the next clients for Eastern Bloc weaponry would be Syria and Saudi Arabia. Not only would such a move destabilise the region, he warned, but once again it would demonstrate to the other Arab countries that an alliance with Britain brought few tangible benefits. Above all, Glubb wanted to avoid a loss of British face.

427

If Egypt, Syria and Saudi Arabia receive large consignments of Iron Curtain weapons Egyptian propaganda will not hesitate for a moment to point out that the friends of Russia are going from strength to strength while Britain's satellites are kept on a minimum starvation diet.

The Egyptians would undoubtedly brief their subversive organisations in Jordan on the same lines and would try and organise press campaigns, street demonstrations, secret circulation of pamphlets in Jordan, demanding that the Jordan government abandon the British alliance and seize the opportunity of Russian generosity to arm themselves to fight the Jews. The Russians might slip in with a simultaneous offer to give Jordan a subsidy of £15 millions a year to support the Arab Legion.[8]

To avoid that possibility, counselled Glubb, the British government should give urgent consideration to expanding the Arab Legion *pari passu* with the neighbouring forces so that it could resist both an Israeli attack and ward off the possibility of an Egyptian attempt at annexation. Such a move would also convince those Jordanians who believed that it was hardly worthwhile accepting British military support if it were so meagre. The immediate requirement was the provision of an armoured regiment to replace one of the armoured-car regiments and to raise two further infantry regiments so that a fourth infantry brigade group could be established. The new formation would also require a new brigade headquarters.

In response to Glubb's request for the provision of sufficient forces to form a fourth infantry brigade group it was agreed that General Sir Charles Keightley, the new GOC Middle East, and Field Marshal Sir Gerald Templer, the Chief of the Imperial General Staff-designate, should visit Amman at the end of May to assess the situation. By then the headquarters of Britain's Middle East Land Forces had been moved from the Canal Zone to Cyprus and the two men were anxious to inspect the condition of Britain's military contributions to Libya, Iraq and Jordan. They arrived in Amman on 31 May and dined that night with King Hussein who did not make a good impression on Templer by keeping the British party waiting. The following day Templer visited several Arab Legion frontier posts, travelling by Land Rover with Glubb who used the opportunity to press for additional funds and equipment for the Legion. Templer was suitably impressed and promised to speed up the deployment of a full British armoured regiment – a squadron of Royal Scots Greys had already been deployed in Ma'an in southern Jordan.

In return, Templer offered Glubb some well-meant personal advice. With his experience of 'winning hearts and minds' of the local population during the recent terrorist campaign in Malaya, he told Glubb that it was vital 'to keep one jump ahead of nationalist demands to promote Arab officers'. Wherever possible, senior Arab officers should be given command of the brigade groups with a British full colonel as their second-in-command. In that way, said Templer, Arab pride would be satisfied and Glubb could continue to retain control through the British officer. This was a sensitive point with Glubb, for he was already under pressure from Hussein and others for his refusal to give rapid promotion to Arab officers. While he was prepared to face the fact that Arab officers would eventually take over responsibility for the Legion, he still held to the point of view he had outlined to General Sir Brian Robertson in 1952:

In conclusion, let me explain that I am not opposed to the advancement of officers because they are Arab; far from it. What I do say is that if the Jordan government insists on the promotion of officers because they are Arab and not because they are efficient, it will wreck the Arab Legion and run a grave risk of losing the subsidy which supports it.[9]

Faced by Glubb's obduracy on this point, Templer did not press the matter; instead he told Charles Duke, the British

Ambassador, that he was 'impressed by the position held by Glubb throughout the country'. His one worry was that Glubb seemed to have lost touch with the embassy and felt that his views were not being taken seriously in London. This failing should be corrected, warned Templer, for Glubb still had a vital role to play as the figurehead for British interests in Jordan:

> It was agreed between the Generals and the Ambassador that it was important for our interests that Glubb should continue to command the Legion for as long as possible and that in any difficulties he might have with the Jordan palace or government he should receive unqualified support from Her Majesty's Government.[10]

Templer flew back to Cyprus on 2 June and a week later was back in London where he warned the Foreign Office that, in order to bolster British influence in Jordan, the Legion should be strengthened and, on the diplomatic front, Israel should be warned once more that Britain would come to King Hussein's assistance in the event of an attack on the West Bank.

Meanwhile, another related difficulty had emerged to trouble Britain's relationship with Jordan: the question of the annual payment to the Arab Legion. Under the terms of the Anglo-Jordanian treaty the Foreign Office paid the money direct to the Arab Legion through the Ottoman Bank in London. The main reason for adopting this policy was to prevent the funds being misappropriated and used for other purposes by the Jordanian government; this was matched by the British belief that he who pays the piper calls the tune. Glubb, too, had made a contribution to the formulation of that policy by advising that, if the Jordanian parliament were given access to the funds, the politicians would be able to interfere in the Legion's affairs and thereby reduce its operational effectiveness. When the British Treasury offered the opinion that the subsidy could be paid direct to Jordan provided that there were adequate safeguards, Glubb's response was incredulous. It arrived by telegram on 5 January 1955:

> If subsidy paid to Jordan government parliament would debate Arab Legion budget in detail and government would be placed in most awkward situation. Consider most important remember this point. Request may be repeated in future years. Agreement as to how money would be spent valueless. As soon as money paid to Jordan government parliament could compel government to change budget or could refuse to pass budget unless British officers reduced or impose other conditions. Jordan Cabinet would then be unable to carry out any promises made to the HMG.[11]

Glubb also believed that the unsettled political situation in Jordan made such a move dangerous – the prime minister, Samir Rifai, was elderly and unwell and Hussein's relations with Glubb were still stiff and formal. However, the Jordanian parliament did not see matters in that light. They believed that, as a matter of principle and national self-respect, the military subsidy should be paid directly to them. Under pressure from the Arab League they had accepted funds for the National Guard and it was only with some difficulty that they had prevented a move to provide it with an Arab commander from outside Jordan. By way of retaliation the Arab League had implied that Hussein was a tool of imperialism and that the British officers would refuse to carry out their duties in the event of war with Israel.

In March 1955 the Jordanian Ambassador in London made a formal request for the subsidy to be paid directly to Amman but, acting largely on the advice given by Glubb, the Foreign Office blocked the proposal. While there were good reasons for following that policy during a period of tension in the Middle East, it was clumsily handled and Glubb seemed to be out of sympathy with the changing times. Direct payment smacked of old-style imperialism, of a time when administrations in far-off London held sway over possessions whose inhabitants simply did as they were told. By the mid-1950s, the old empire was crumbling, the Union Jacks were being pulled down and imperial red was slowly disappearing from the maps of Africa and the Far East. Even in Jordan, where people generally welcomed the British connection, there were rumblings that Glubb was out of touch and failed to recognise the drift away from British paternalism. Given that failing it was hardly surprising that Egyptian propaganda enjoyed a wide currency in Jordan. Templer was right when he said that Glubb was still the top man in Jordan – but he was only seeing the surface: beneath the veneer there were unmistakeable signs that his position was becoming increasingly precarious.[12]

In an attempt to bring some order to the strategic position in the Middle East the so-called 'Baghdad Pact', formed on similar lines to the North Atlantic Treaty Organisation (NATO), came into being in 1955. Basically, this was a series of defensive treaties between Iraq, Britain, Turkey, Iran and later Pakistan, which bound them together as a 'northern tier' defensive grouping to prevent possible Soviet incursions into the Middle East and to curb Egyptian and Syrian ambitions for territorial expansion. Although the pact had its origins in American policy, the United States only had observer status as it quickly became obvious to them that the Arab states were more interested in countering the Israeli threat.

For Britain, though, the alliance provided an ideal opportunity to retain her own position in the area and the government cemented its relationship with Iraq, the principal partner, by supplying modern Centurion tanks in return for over-flying rights and the right to use the former RAF bases in the event of war. The British Foreign Secretary, Harold Macmillan, described the Baghdad Pact as one of the more pleasant things to have happened to British policy in the Middle East but although it was a sensible enough proposition as a defensive alliance, in the long term it caused more problems than it solved.

For a start, it was not strong enough to offer a positive counterweight to the Soviet Union which, emboldened by the arms sale to Egypt, wanted to create similar deals with Syria and Saudi Arabia. The pact also upset Arab opinion throughout the Middle East and it was vehemently denounced by Nasser who regarded any western-dominated alliance as a continuation of imperialist policy. Here he had the support of many Arabs and although he failed to sway Nuri as-Said, the Iraqi prime minister, he did win a substantial diplomatic victory by preventing Jordan from throwing in its lot with the Pact when Britain pressed Hussein to do so at the tail end of 1955.

Jordan, of course, already had a defensive treaty with Britain but this did not preclude her joining the pact, a fact which the Foreign Office realised could be tied in with the strengthening of the Arab Legion. However, the government was still dithering about the proposals put forward by Glubb earlier in 1955 and endorsed by the Chiefs of Staff – these called for the creation of an additional brigade group – and matters had been made worse by a Foreign Office decision to withhold £250,000 of the year's subsidy. If this were not paid, warned Glubb, he would be forced to reduce the Legion's strength by one infantry battalion, a move which would disrupt his already precarious border defences. Worse, when he went to Britain to argue his case in September, the Foreign Office's refusal to pay the money only served to aggravate his relationship with Hussein. In some desperation Glubb asked Melville to take up the matter in London and the sum was eventually paid after the War Office intervened on the Legion's behalf:

King subsequently told number of people that my mission had been a failure. King Husain has again been difficult and temperamental since I came back from England. Good effect of his official visit to England in June seems to be wearing off.[13]

According to Shuckburgh the Egyptian Ambassador had used the opportunity of Hussein's visit to demand arms from Britain because he believed that the Arabs could only deal with Israel from a position of strength. Later that year, Nasser claimed that Britain's refusal to supply him paved the way for Egypt's arms deal with the Czechs.[14]

One way of giving the Arab Legion what it wanted would be to hold out the lure of additional arms provided that Jordan joined the Baghdad Pact – a course of action which had already been suggested to Hussein by President Bayar of Turkey. The first definite steps, though, were taken at a meeting of the Baghdad Pact members in Baghdad at the very end of November 1955 when Duke flew from Amman to brief the British team on events in Jordan. According to Shuckburgh, the British Ambassador spoke about 'the parlous state of that country, torn between joining the Baghdad Pact and linking up with Egypt. Needless to say the remedy is said to lie in our doubling the subsidy of £10 million by giving them an extra division if they will join the Pact.'[15] Although Shuckburgh was not duly impressed by the arguments – he always felt that Glubb was alarmist and that his pessimism rubbed off on Duke – he felt that a suitable package of arms and finance could be offered instead, a suggestion which Macmillan was happy to accept. 'After all, we were paying large subsidies,' he said later. 'Why should we continue our support if they would do nothing in return?'[16]

The package in question contained both military and political elements. For the Arab Legion the subsidy would be increased in 1956 and immediate steps would be taken to provide it with the means and equipment to establish a new brigade headquarters. Two regiments would be provided with seventeen-pounder anti-tank guns, the armoured regiment would receive Comet tanks and an artillery regiment would be equipped with 5.5-inch medium breech-loading guns. As an added incentive Jordan would be presented with a squadron of ten Vampire jet interceptors, thus bringing to a successful conclusion the long-running discussions about the future of the Arab Legion's air force. At the same time it was decided to replace the 1948 treaty with a new agreement which would allow Jordan to join the Baghdad Pact. In return for the increased aid Jordan would provide the RAF with staging facilities and over-flying rights and Britain would continue her treaty agreement to come to Jordan's assistance in the event of attack by a third party.

The man chosen to carry out the negotiations was Field Marshal Sir Gerald Templer, who travelled to Amman on 27 November with Michael Rose, the head of the Foreign Office's Levant Department. On their arrival they were pleasantly encouraged to discover that Hussein was minded to accept the British offer. However, during the discussions which followed in the first week of December, it became obvious that the new prime minister, Said el-Mufti, was unhappy about the possibility of offending public opinion by signing a new agreement which many people thought was a prelude to a treaty with Israel. The Palestinian ministers in his Cabinet were particularly concerned as, thanks to the success of Nasser's propaganda initiative, the Baghdad Pact had become an extremely unpopular political concept amongst the inhabitants of the West Bank. Within the Arab Legion, too, there were some doubts about the wisdom of rushing pell-mell into new treaty obligations which involved the establishment of co-operative defence systems, and the Free Officers' movement increased its propaganda campaign from Cairo. One leaflet published in November by a so-called 'Group of Jordanian Free Officers Engaged in the National Struggle' was sufficiently alarming for its contents to be passed back to London for comment. It read:

We can now perceive the threads of a new conspiracy which is being hatched in the dark against our interests, namely, forcing Jordan to join the Turco-Iraqi pact. We are opposed to the trend. Glubb Pasha's attempts are only to mislead Jordanian public opinion and keep it far from facts through this feeble logic.[17]

By way of action the Foreign Office asked the British Ambassador in Cairo, Sir Humphrey Trevelyan, to take up the matter with Nasser and to impress upon him the government's displeasure at the continuing attacks on Glubb. It would not be the last time that Trevelyan would make fruitless attempts to halt the Egyptian propaganda machine as throughout December and continuing into January and February press and radio attacks on Britain and Glubb in particular became daily occurrences. Another difficulty was suddenly posed by Saudi Arabia which had revived the rivalry between the House of Saud and the Hashemites and whose agents were also providing the opposition press with funds for their attacks on Glubb.

Against that uncertain background the Jordanian government had every reason to feel threatened and, on 13 December, four West Bank ministers resigned rather than proceed with a policy that had been condemned by their own people and also by Nasser in far-off Cairo. A few hours later the prime minister, Said el-Mufti, also resigned, a victim of bad health and loss of political nerve. Although Hussein offered to sign the agreement himself he was dissuaded by Templer who made immediate arrangements to return home. The next day Hussein appointed Hazza Majali prime minister, but no sooner had he accepted office than rioting broke out in Amman and quickly spread elsewhere. Majali resigned a few days later and the king dissolved parliament on 19 December as the country plunged deeper into chaos. As a result, remaining attempts to bring Jordan into the pact were dropped on the instructions of Eden who believed that it would be a mistake to put pressure on Hussein at a time when his throne was in danger. When Samir Rifai was reappointed prime minister in January, he told London that he would be pursuing a policy of strict neutrality with both Egypt and Iraq and had no interest in entering the Baghdad Pact.[18]

Templer had a reputation for being an over-forceful negotiator, impatient of detail and anxious to press home his argument, but, being the kind of man he was he blamed himself, amongst others, for the failure of the mission. Even by his own strict standards this was doing himself an injustice for the attempt was doomed to failure even before the negotiating team left for Amman. Little thought had been given to Hussein's requests for additional arms – the 'package' was a hastily concocted compromise – and time should have been spent on preparing the ground before pushing ahead with the attempt to force a new agreement on Jordan. Meanwhile, Egyptian propaganda fuelled the rioting, which quickly got out of hand, and Nasser was left with a positive advantage in his dealings with the Palestinian population of Jordan. So alarmed was Glubb by the sudden turn of events that he discussed with Templer the possibility that the Arab Legion might be forced to take control of the country. In a subsequent letter which he described as 'thinking aloud' about the political situation, Glubb confirmed that the subject was already a matter for discussion amongst some of the younger officers:

> Since the army has taken control [of the rioting] a number of Arab officers have come to me and expressed indignation that corrupt politicians can make a lot of money and reduce the country to chaos, and then merely tell the army to restore order. Whereupon another corrupt cabinet takes office and the process is repeated. As one officer said to me only last night, 'The only body of Government servants which does not take bribes is the officers of the Army.' Of course, being British, one has always regarded with horror any idea of the army going into politics, but I now see how it happens. The army is the only decent, honest, practically minded body in the country, and it resents pulling chestnuts out of the fire for politicians.[19]

If the Arab Legion were ever to take control of the country the British officers would have to be replaced or take up new positions as 'military advisers'. Logically, Glubb would have to go, too, but as he told Templer, he would hold on as long as possible, simply because he believed that he could exert a calming influence on the younger officers. His letter was passed on to the Foreign Office and its contents were considered important enough for the Middle East Department to conduct a brief theoretical exercise on its political implications.

The most cogent response came from Charles Duke in Amman. As he saw it, although there was little immediate threat of a military coup in Jordan, a situation could arise whereby the Arab Legion could be the decisive political influence. There would be no question of the Legion making a first move; rather, the senior officers might become involved in a 'king's cabinet' of mixed civilian and military leaders, should parliament ever be dissolved. Duke also confided that this possibility had already been mooted by Hazza Majali who had been anxious to build a close relationship with the Legion's senior Arab commanders. The proposal had an attractive ring for, although this would cause difficulties for the British officers, Duke believed that under certain circumstances – a national emergency involving the breakdown of government, for example – the military could safeguard the monarchy and 'could provide, at least for a period, good, sincere and honest government which might give the promise of some stability'. It has to be remembered that Duke was writing at a time of rioting in Jordan, but, in the short term, he was anxious that any talk of a military coup should be stifled, lest it reach the wrong ears. What Jordan needed was a period of settled government under British tutelage:

On balance, however, in spite of the vacillating general unsatisfactory character of most of the governments which Jordan has had, I would regard the assumption of government by officers of the Legion as an unwelcome development, unless the situation had deteriorated a great deal further than it has now; and I do not give up hope that it may yet be corrected without recourse to such a drastic measure. I do not therefore think that we should encourage the King or anyone else to think that we should favour the establishment of anything like a military government in this country. It would almost certainly get a generally bad world press, no less in America and even in some sections of the British press than in the Arab world. It would be regarded as a British creation and as conclusive evidence that Jordan was really no more than a British colony.[20]

And that really was a problem which refused to disappear: to the rest of the Arab world, and to the Americans and the Soviets, Jordan was little better than a British possession which only possessed some artificial trappings of independence. It was certainly the main thrust of Egypt's propaganda which was picked up daily by the inhabitants of Jordan – several British residents also admitted that it was difficult to avoid the all-pervasive Egyptian presence. Even those who did not speak or read Arabic well enough to understand Cairo radio or the many broadsheets recall seeing more Egyptians than usual in the souk and remember the number of occasions when Nasser's name entered casual conversations in the officers' club.

In most of the Egyptian attacks Glubb was described as 'an imperialist scorpion' and, although he hardly deserved such a vulgar epithet, he had not helped his position by some of his actions during the rioting which followed Templer's visit. In the same letter which spoke of his fears that there might be a military coup, Glubb admitted that the Arab Legion had used the operation to quell the riots as 'our ideal opportunity to close down political parties and known subversive organisations and have a firm Government on the lines of the present administration in Iraq'. While the tensions of the time might have excused his actions, Glubb's admission sits uncomfortably beside Duke's reasoned interpretation of British political aims in Jordan. This was a far cry from his credo of earlier years when he held firmly to the belief that nobody could control Arab affairs better than the Arabs themselves and that Britain should stop meddling and allow the Arabs to stand on their own two feet.

Of course these views were not common knowledge at the time, and it is true that Glubb was under considerable strain, but the Legion's actions in putting down the riots were used by the Egyptians for their own propaganda purposes. In a typical Voice of the Arabs broadcast, Glubb was castigated as an arch-imperialist and the author of all the ills facing the people of Jordan:

> The Arabs refuse to take filthy hands, hands stained with our blood, hands which killed and continue to kill our sons, hands which worked and continue to work to immortalise colonialism ... Glubb is the one who imposes fines on you. Arabs, Glubb must go ... It is a question of your freedom and your unity ... the matter is left to you entirely, the Arabs of Jordan, the officers and soldiers of Jordan, and the authorities of Jordan.[21]

This attack was very much par for the course as far as Glubb's name was concerned and, although the broadcast was full of stock phrases, the cumulative effect of the Voice of the Arabs must have influenced broad public opinion in Jordan. After all, in military terms, propaganda is a means of forcing the opposition to do something which they otherwise might not have wanted to do. It is probable that Egyptian propaganda added to the general mood that held that the British influence was a bad thing. Cleverly the propagandists, especially Nasser's ghost-writer, Hassanein Heykal, argued that while Glubb was all-powerful, Hussein was merely a pawn in hands; the king could never be in control of his destiny while Glubb remained head of the Arab Legion. Glubb certainly believed in the dangers posed by the Egyptian propagandists and recommended several times that it should be countered by a powerful transmitter based in Jordan, and, as he later told members of the Conservative Parliamentary Foreign Affairs Committee he thought that the BBC foreign services should do more to present the British point of view:

Egypt's chief weapon was subversion, and in this we have badly underestimated the effect of unceasing propaganda by radio and in the Press. Cairo newspapers were flown into Amman daily, including illustrated newspapers which particularly appealed to Arabs who read only with difficulty. There was no paper in which the Jordan government could give its own view, still less the British view. All were 'bought', and this could be done for as little as £20,000. But HMG took a sanctimonious view that they could not stoop to bribes. We could combat this campaign, but we had not started to try. The BBC was far too academic and olympian.[22]

It is unlikely that Hussein paid much heed to the propaganda but he was a young and impressionable man who had come to the throne at an early age and was surrounded by a coterie of older aides, some of whom were susceptible to Nasser's message. Moreover Hussein had been brought up in a mixture of backgrounds, having attended school in Alexandria before going to Harrow where he had managed to combine the life of a conventional English public schoolboy with that of a young man about town. (Against the rules he kept a car for forays further afield.) Later, he finished his education at Sandhurst which introduced him to weekend night-life in London and Paris. 'There was no lack of male companions,' wrote his biographer James Lunt, 'and London is after all full of attractive young women only too happy to be taken out to dinner and dance with a handsome and well-mannered young king.'[23] He was only eighteen, a boy king; two years later he married his first wife Sharifa Dina Abdel Hamid. It was as if his boyhood had passed all too quickly and while still a youth he had been asked to assume the manners and lifestyle of a much older and wiser man. Glubb had noticed the sense of separateness during the king's discussions with Templer and later wrote about his strong feelings of paternalism towards Hussein:

441

I felt a deep affection for the young King, so courageous, so entirely deprived of disinterested advisers and plunged in such a vortex of intrigue, falsehood and power politics. It occurred to me that, if he could survive until he reached forty-five years old, he might well become another King Abdulla. For King Husain's grandfather had also been headstrong and impetuous in his youth; it was only when his hot-headedness became cooled with age that he became a great ruler.[24]

That was perhaps the truth. To Hussein Glubb might have appeared as one of the ancients, a venerable counsellor, a confidant of his grandfather and a man so versed in Jordan's ways that he seemed to know everyone in the country and to have a hand in everything that was happening. It would not have been unreasonable for Hussein to question Glubb's seemingly all-powerful authority. Also, it was hardly surprising that he should want to surround himself with people nearer his own age who shared his interests and his sense of fun.

Amongst them was Ali Abu Nowar, a rising star in the Arab Legion who had attended Sandhurst and the Staff College at Camberley; debonair and high-spirited, he had first come to Hussein's notice while serving as military attaché in Paris, a posting engineered by Glubb who suspected that he had a hand in the Free Officers' movement. Given his attractive personal qualities, though, Hussein was entitled to demand his recall in September 1955 when he needed a new ADC to replace Colonel Mohammed Sa'adi who was being posted to London. Court rumour had it that Glubb was violently opposed to Ali's transfer and had greatly angered Hussein by refusing to permit it. Although this would have been neither an unlikely nor an unworthy course of action, given Ali's political tendencies, the truth is that Glubb welcomed the transfer because he believed that Ali's presence at court would reveal the man's shortcomings. Moreover, he hoped that the concession would improve his own relationship with the king. Here he was to be much mistaken, for Ali had not changed his politics since Glubb had first discovered that he was making them public in Amman. Just as Charles Duke warned, Ali was a sinister political influence:

> The Ambassador, however, expressed his doubts about the wisdom of this course to Glubb: whether in the first place the King will realise Nuwar's failings and secondly, even if he does realise what the man is, whether he will be firm enough to dismiss him. His appointment would also be 'one in the eye' for Glubb, who is known to have opposed it in the past.[25]

Another flamboyant figure in the king's entourage was Jock Dalgleish, an RAF wing commander who was the principal flying instructor in the Arab Legion's air force (by then known as the Royal Jordanian Air Force). He had a particularly warm place in the king's affections because he had looked after Hussein in the immediate aftermath of Abdullah's assassination and had later taught him how to fly. The story of Dalgleish's close friendship with the king through their shared love of flying is well enough known but there was another, more personal side to their friendship. Both were high-spirited young men and both shared a liking for high jinks which did not always go down well with Glubb. One incident in particular speaks for itself and Dalgleish admits that he still breaks out in a sweat when he thinks about it.

While he was being taught the art of night-flying Hussein casually suggested that the two men should fly over to Cyprus for dinner and asked Dalgleish to make the necessary arrangements. Astonishingly – the absence of the king from Jordan for however short a time created constitutional problems – the trip went ahead and although it was free of any untoward incident there were repercussions for both men. Hussein was reminded of his responsibilities by the prime minister and Dalgleish received a dressing-down from Glubb who reminded him of his duty to the country and 'in that high-pitched voice of his launched off into a tirade ... how Glubb got all the information so quickly about our truancy I never found out, neither did he leave an opening for me to put forward any defence of what was an indefensible action ... a curt nod of his head indicated the interview was concluded.' Before dismissing Dalgleish Glubb had reminded him of the fate that had befallen Abdullah, and that he did not want it to be repeated with his grandson: 'In future you must let me know when anything untoward is planned,' he told Dalgleish. 'You must have confidence that I am not going to clamp down on any particular activity of the King's. I just want to know what's happening so that I can be prepared.'[26]

While Glubb was sincere in his belief that he did not want to hamper the king's private life it was made obvious to Dalgleish that he did not approve of that kind of behaviour. It is also likely that Glubb did not like the idea of a close friendship being established between Hussein and a serving British officer – Dalgleish's house had become for the king something of a second home where he could escape from the responsibilities of court life – but he was prepared to accept it as long as it benefitted the special relationship with Britain. This was Duke's attitude, too, but inevitably perhaps, the friendship gave rise to charges of royal favouritism. More damaging in the long term was a rumour that Dalgleish did not see eye-to-eye with Glubb who was therefore anxious to have him replaced. As luck would have it, Dalgleish's tour of duty was due to come to an end as 1955 drew to a close, thus giving Glubb a further opportunity to win the king's approval by recommending the reappointment of this popular officer – just as he had hoped to do with Ali Abu Nowar. However, on this occasion Glubb did not press the Air Ministry to extend Dalgleish's posting, even though he must have known that the decision would upset Hussein. Earlier, in August 1954, Glubb had also blocked a proposal to make Dalgleish one of

Hussein's ADCs because he felt that he did not exercise enough control over the king's flying.[27] Inevitably, the king took the news badly and his Defence Minister Farhan Shbeilat made the complaint known to Duke who passed on the information to London:

> The Defence Minister said that he had told much of this to Glubb himself and had suggested that when the King comes back he and Glubb should have it all out with him. He did not think that the King really had any intention of trying to get rid of Glubb now or that the situation could not be satisfactorily arranged. The cause of the King's ill humour towards Glubb, he thought, was probably our insistence on replacing Dalgleish, which he said had annoyed the King, and he indicated that in his view Dalgleish himself did not make matters any easier for Glubb.[28]

The Foreign Office response was to agree that Dalgleish was an unsettling influence and that it would not make sense to move on his behalf. Initially, Shuckburgh believed that Dalgleish should have done more to use his influence with the king to improve matters with Glubb, but he had been told by his officials that Dalgleish was 'a "King's Man" and ... it would really be useless to ask or expect him to influence the King in the way we want, unless that happened to coincide with the King's whim'.[29] It was therefore decided to let Dalgleish return to Britain and Shuckburgh explained the British position to Hussein on 21 October while he was visiting Britain.

Did Hussein use that opportunity to tell Shuckburgh he was anxious to drop Glubb and to make changes in the leadership of the Arab Legion? Although Shuckburgh's diary makes no reference of any such conversation, the author himself believes that the topic was not raised, despite the fact that it was the main item on the agenda. On 5 November Shuckburgh wrote to Duke to urge him that it was of 'the greatest importance that our position in Jordan, which depends quite considerably on General Glubb's prestige, should not be weakened. We must, therefore, take all possible measures to ensure that this does not happen.' Furthermore:

> An opportunity of tackling the King about his relations with Glubb occurred when I saw His Majesty at the Dorchester on October 24, during his visit here. I said bluntly that I had heard rumours that the King was not pleased with the General and was there anything we could do to help. The King said he had always admired and liked Glubb who, as he put it, was 'one of us'. He still had the greatest affection for him and confidence in his loyalty. There was no doubt, however, that Glubb had formed the Arab Legion a long time ago and there were those who thought his methods were becoming a little out of date.[30]

The meeting ended with Shuckburgh winning a promise from Hussein that he would inform the Foreign Office if he ever lost confidence in Glubb and wished to sack him – an eventuality that seemed entirely possible as, shortly before leaving for London, the king had told Glubb that the 'Arab Legion was a rabble and lacked any proper organisation'. In the same letter, of 6 October, Duke had told Shuckburgh that Hussein was 'behaving in a manner most calculated to undermine the organisation and discipline of the Legion'.[31] Therefore, even before Templer embarked on his ill-starred mission to persuade Jordan to join the Baghdad Pact, Glubb was in serious difficulties and the British position in the country was far from secure.

However much the rows over Dalgleish and Ali Abu Nowar had been magnified out of proportion, they were further blows to Glubb's rapidly deteriorating relationship with Hussein. On one level it was a matter of age and outlook – both men were very different and had diverging views on the satisfactions and pleasures of life. It is difficult, for example, to imagine Glubb enjoying an evening of dancing and music in the Dalgleish household as Hussein did. But the real rift between the two men lay in the Arab Legion which the king obviously believed was being badly mismanaged by Glubb. There were two main criticisms. First, Hussein thought that Arab officers were being refused promotion, that good men were being held back while incompetent British officers took their place. Second, he thought that the Legion lacked strategic supplies and that the defence plans for Jordan's borders were seriously flawed as they did not take into account the feeling that no part of the country should ever be surrendered without a fight. The king also felt that Glubb occupied too powerful a position and naturally enough, he was not amused by British newspaper reports which spoke of Glubb as 'the uncrowned king of Jordan'. With voices at court reinforcing these suspicions and with the Voice of the Arabs spreading similar stories to the people of Jordan, Glubb's position could not have been worse at the beginning of 1956.

In the end it all boiled down to the army. As Shuckburgh feared, Hussein was extremely worried that the Arab Legion was being overtaken in size and strength by his neighbours' armies and that his closest advisors had warned him that the British connection was to blame for this state of affairs. Matters had come to a head at the beginning of 1955 when Glubb gave a presentation of his defence strategy at the palace in Amman in front of Hussein, the prime minister, Taufiq Pasha, and a party of the king's advisers. This followed several weeks of prompting by Glubb who felt that he should be given the opportunity of explaining in full his policy of mobile defence in depth – a few days earlier, Hussein had visited the West Bank frontier defences to see for himself the Arab Legion's deployment. After a lengthy briefing Glubb sat down and awaited the king's comments. He could hardly have expected what followed next:

'I do not agree with any of the plans we have heard,' he

447

began. 'I will never surrender one hand's breadth of my country. The army will defend the demarcation line. Then we shall attack. I will sanction no withdrawal.' He proceeded to denounce many other 'mistakes' in the command of the army. He claimed that officers' promotions were not properly handled, that we were wrong in planning to build new headquarters, and other points of detail. 'Finally,' he said, 'we are grateful to the Chief of the General Staff for all the work he has done, but I think now it is time for him to enjoy a rest.'[32]

Hussein's remarks were met with applause from his party and shocked outrage by Glubb. For the first time in his career he had been criticised openly by his Jordanian masters and it was a humbling experience which signalled a serious rift in the British relationship. However, following Taufiq Pasha's intervention and the king's subsequent visit to London in June, the matter seemed to have been papered over and Hussein refused to refer to it again: he even spent a period in the field to observe an Arab Legion exercise and seemed thereafter to be convinced by the sense of Glubb's plans.

Later still, Hussein seemed to change his mind again when he used his lack of confidence in Glubb as one of the main reasons for sacking him. This was doubtless true, but Hussein's frustrations over the Legion ran deeper than disagreement over a defence plan which he wanted to be based on the mystical belief that no Jordanian soldier should ever surrender any piece of his homeland without a fight. Far more serious was his oft-voiced criticism that Arab officers had a low standing in the Legion and that Glubb was unwilling to promote them. There is much truth here. Although Glubb was not opposed in principle to the promotion of Jordanian or Palestinian officers, he did have a paternalistic view of his young – and not-so-young – charges. He also believed that 'arabisation' of the Legion should be conducted at a slow and steady pace and that the rapid acceleration of educated officers, some of whom were politically inclined, would lead the Legion into a more political role, as had happened to the armies of Egypt and Syria. Shortly afterwards Glubb reiterated his belief to a visiting party of senior Canadian officers who were impressed by the sincerity of his views but appalled to hear him admit that it would take time for Arabs to reach positions of authority:

> Glubb explained, for example, that the Arab Legion had a ten-year plan (subsequently reduced to three years) for the replacement of British officers by Arab officers but, Glubb had gone on, 'you could not possibly make an Arab officer into a Brigadier when he was only forty-one years old and had only fifteen years of service'. As many of his hearers had themselves been Brigadiers at thirty-one in far more difficult circumstances and dealing with much more complicated equipment, and then after perhaps only two or three years of military service, this statement had not gone down well. In comparing notes afterwards, the students had decided that Glubb should be written off as being completely out of date.[33]

The Canadian officers were remembering the experience of the Second World War when outstanding junior infantry officers were frequently promoted on the battlefield, only to return to their former ranks in peacetime, but the criticisms of Glubb stuck. His attitude also led to accusations that he favoured the martial demeanour and fierce loyalty of his Bedouin officers, in much the same way that British Indian Army officers had preferred Gurkhas, Sikhs and Punjab Muslims to the educated Bengali Hindus. In his heart of hearts, Glubb still longed for the simpler days when he could visit distant encampments or settlements and after dinner and coffee gossip with the elders far into the night beneath a starlit sky.

In some frustration with Glubb's conservative and possessive attitudes, Hussein began to interfere in the Legion's affairs and throughout September 1955 he began bombarding the Arab Legion's headquarters with ideas and suggestions for promotion and transfers. Through ADCs like Ali Abu Nowar he talked directly to Arab Legion officers, a situation which no self-respecting commander could possibly allow. It was during this period, shortly before Templer's visit, that Glubb confronted Duke with his *cri de coeur* that the king had lost confidence in him. 'General Glubb came to see me the other day, soon after his return from leave and told me with some distress that he had found that his position with King Hussein had gone right back to where it was before the King's visit to England in June,' Duke told Shuckburgh on 6 October. This led Shuckburgh to bring the problem into the open by speaking to Hussein at the Dorchester Hotel and asking him about the unsettled relationship with Glubb. It is hard to avoid the impression that if Hussein had seized the nettle that October, Glubb's early retirement could have been arranged and the unpleasantness of the following year avoided. Instead, the Foreign Office kept to its policy that Glubb was far too important a personality to be cut adrift and that everything possible should be done to keep him in Jordan during a difficult period in the country's internal affairs. Britain was also determined to maintain her authority in the Middle East in the face of possible Soviet incursions and, at the beginning of 1956, was making an effort to appease Nasser by supporting the Anglo-American initiative to fund the Aswan High Dam, a prestigious engineering project, designed to provide increased water storage and prevent flooding of the River Nile.

Not everyone in London was so certain that it was a good idea to keep Glubb in Jordan. His former colleague, Ronnie Broadhurst, had returned home to Northern Ireland and throughout that winter warned a number of politicians that Glubb was out of touch and therefore actually harming British interests. His local MP for County Down, G.B.H. Curie, took the trouble to present this viewpoint to the new Foreign Secretary, Selwyn Lloyd:

I am told that Glubb Pasha may now, in spite of his good work in the past, prove to be an embarrassment to our interests. It seems that he cannot, or does not, mix socially with those Jordanians with whom one would expect him to be persona grata.[34]

Lloyd replied that he had 'complete confidence' in Glubb – the Foreign Office view – a statement that stung Broadhurst into a new and more bitter attack in a letter addressed to Peake Pasha who was also critical of Glubb's position in the period before Hussein decided to act. In particular, Broadhurst thought that this supposed absence of any goodwill 'made the educated Arabs prepared, indeed eager, to pile on his every misfortune':

It used to amaze me that he [Glubb] never entered an Arab's house (save in the open parties, at village receptions or on feast day formal visits) and so far as I know, never had a genuine conversation (i.e., not 'shop') with any Arab. It is a strange thing to say that although he lived in the M.E. for 35-odd years, I think it is true that he remained absolutely ignorant and indeed careless of the mood, humour and indeed character of the cultivated Arab.[35]

Broadhurst's personal attack on Glubb makes surprising reading. Earlier in their careers there had been a close friendship between the two men but in the years of Broadhurst's retirement – he left the Arab Legion in 1948 – he came to disagree with Glubb's continued presence in Jordan. Much of what he wrote in this personal letter to Peake seems to have been prompted by his irritation with the publicity surrounding Glubb's dismissal but there was also a good deal of ire in what he had to say. 'He neither gave nor won affection', was one hostile comment; 'he had absolutely no personal authority', another – but beneath the rancour it is still possible to understand his main criticism. According to

Broadhurst's line of thought, Glubb still harked back to the old days in Jordan; he longed to renew the simple relationships with the desert dwellers and he failed to understand the brasher, more confident, cosmopolitan and educated Arabs. Also, having been particularly close to Abdullah, he still had access to the court in Amman and claimed that the Foreign Office ignored the constant scheming to get rid of Glubb and misunderstood the strength of Jordanian national feeling. For all concerned Broadhurst thought it would have been less painful had Glubb left Jordan when Hussein first broached the subject in October 1955.

The last weeks of 1955 were dominated by rioting in Amman and elsewhere and a hard-pressed Arab Legion had to take to the streets to restore order, a task for which they had not been properly trained – on 8 January 1956, Lieutenant-Colonel Patrick Lloyd, Royal Artillery, was shot and killed by a sniper while quelling a demonstration at Zerqa. With the country uneasy, 1956 was dawning with all the ingredients for further unrest. The mood was set in an article in the *Daily Herald* on 23 January written by the experienced foreign correspondent Basil Davidson. Having spoken to the government, to Glubb and to opposition leaders, Davidson came to the conclusion that Jordan was on the brink of collapse and was only kept in check by Glubb's mailed fist:

General John Bagot Glubb is in fact the most unpopular man in Jordan. He is feared and hated but the fault is not his own. The fault is with the policy which London now orders him to carry out. This policy comes dangerously near to one of outright military dictatorship.

Jordan, nominally independent, is really in Glubb's hands. Behind the warm blue eyes and the bushy white moustache of Jordan's otherwise congenial dictator, there sits a steel-hard mind that is entirely devoted to duty as Glubb sees it.

Wearily, the Foreign Office asked Amman for their views

and Duke replied that Davidson had spent much of his time talking to Suliman Naboulsi, the leader of the extremist Nationalist-Socialist party and that he was only repeating the Egyptian propaganda message. However, in a revealing aside, Duke also claimed that 'even moderate people, who strongly support the British connection, are now saying that Glubb is a survivor of a former epoch, that he knows too much, and that it is time for him to go'.[36] Like most senior government officials, Duke disliked press comment, especially when it came from an influential journalist like Davidson who had served with Tito's partisans in Yugoslavia during the war and was well known in military and diplomatic circles. He warned London, therefore, that press coverage of the current position in Jordan could only be damaging to Britain's interests if it continued to promote Glubb as a dictator or the power behind the throne.

By so doing, of course, the *Daily Herald* had reiterated the message that was coming out loud and clear from Cairo radio. Throughout February Egyptian propaganda reached a crescendo, perversely at a time when Glubb's relationship with the king had improved slightly, due to the Arab Legion's handling of the riots. On 15 February the Voice of the Arabs claimed that the presence of Glubb and other British officers was undermining Arab nationalism; the next day the same radio station reported that Hussein was on the point of sacking Glubb, 'the symbol of imperialism in the Arab world'; the theme was repeated the following day with renewed allegations that Glubb had betrayed the Palestinians at Ramle and Lydda in 1948 and that he was little more than a covert agent of Zionist imperialism. Other attacks, in newspapers like *Al Gumhouria* and *Al Ahram*, urged the people of Jordan to take matters into their own hands and evict the British from their homelands, otherwise 'thousands of British officers' would arrive to subjugate them.

Although Duke and Shuckburgh had been temporarily relieved by the evidence of a better understanding between Glubb and Hussein, they were by no means certain that it would last. Duke was well aware that Glubb's seeming omniscience on things Jordanian did not recommend itself to the king and that, with the best will in the world, Glubb's days as the main prop of British policy were numbered. Accordingly, at the beginning of February, he recommended that immediate thought should be given to finding a successor, preferably a tried and tested soldier who could be exposed to conditions in Jordan in order to win the king's confidence. As he explained to the Foreign Office, the experience with Dalgleish showed that Hussein was not keen on new faces and that it was important to get a suitable candidate into position soon 'in case a sudden crisis makes Glubb's resignation an earlier possibility than we now imagine or hope'. Who this paragon might be, Duke could not suggest, but he offered the hope that, like Glubb, he would be a larger-than-life public figure:

> Legends are made easily and live long in this part of the world. We suggest, therefore, that it would be of far greater assistance to us here, and to the British connection in general, to have a living legend as Commander of the Legion rather than someone who might be hard working but would not inspire the same sort of loyalty or catch the imagination as a colourful personality with plenty of drive and enthusiasm (though he would need some patience as well).[37]

Amongst other qualifications, Duke hoped that the candidate would have, like Glubb, 'a first-class personality and considerable personal charm ... [and be] not too reserved in manner or at all pompous, with all due respect'. Clearly, Glubb's would be a hard act to follow and Duke acknowledged that it would be impossible to find anyone who possessed his range of experience in the Arab world. The Foreign Office agreed and minuted hopefully that the more forcefully the Jordanian government resisted the Egyptian propaganda, the longer they would be prepared to hold on to Glubb's services. It was to be a forlorn hope.

Hussein probably took the final decision to sack Glubb on 29 February 1956, the day before the order was carried out, but there is little doubt that the idea had been building up in his mind throughout the winter. One of Hussein's principal worries was that, if the Egyptians succeeded in undermining the loyalty of the Arab Legion, his own position could be under threat and Jordan subjected to the possibility of a military coup. This was by no means a wild fear as events were to prove in the following year when Ali Abu Nowar was at the centre of a plot to overthrow Hussein. It was foiled by the king's tenacity of purpose and by the loyal support of the Bedouin elements within the Jordanian Army.

Hussein had also been told by his aides that Glubb had been encouraging Bedouin officers to disseminate to their people in the villages the advantages to Jordan of the Baghdad Pact, an accusation that was reiterated by the prime minister in later discussions with Duke.[38] While Glubb always claimed that he had never given any such orders, he fully supported the idea of Jordan joining the pact as a bulwark against Egyptian and Saudi threats, and he would not have been human had he not encouraged some of his officers to do likewise. However, added to press reports in British magazines like *Picture Post* which hailed Glubb as the uncrowned king of Jordan, Hussein had ample reason to believe that Glubb was a parallel ruler not always pursuing policies which were consistent with those of his own government.

On the military side, too, Hussein believed that Glubb had blundered by underestimating the stocks of ammunition needed by Jordan to maintain her defences, a matter of some concern after the deficiencies exposed in the 1948 war. In fact, since then, the Arab Legion had built up its reserves to allow for thirty days' expenditure at British Army contact rates and in 1955 had received ammunition worth £210,000 from Middle East Land Forces. The only deficiencies were in signal cartridges and smoke shells.[39] All this was well enough known and the relevant paperwork was available for the king's inspection but Glubb believed later that the figures were misunderstood, thus leading to Hussein's belief that there were serious shortages, not of practice shells but of real shells. 'They were naturally shocked at the idea that the commander of the army, threatened by an invasion, had provided only coloured lights and smoke with which to repel the enemy.'[40] This contradictory information only served to weaken Glubb's position and it soon became common knowledge in court circles that the king was about to act: certainly, Dalgleish remembers the aides talking freely about the possibility and after taking his own leave at the palace he was told by Ali Abu Nowar that Glubb would be the next to go.

When the sacking came, it was brutal, to the point and it was made clear that there would be no reversal of the decision. On 29 February Glubb had an audience with the king to finalise arrangements for a visit to Arab Legion positions at Hebron which had been planned for 10 March. After 'a particularly pleasant and congenial interview' he returned home and, later that night, received a telephone message from Ali Abu Nowar who asked him to be in Amman no later than midday – Glubb was due to inspect the 1st Armoured Car Regiment, an all-Bedouin formation, at Zerqa on 1 March. While Glubb was absent from the capital the first steps were taken to dismiss him from office. Shortly before noon Hussein arrived at the prime minister's office and handed Samir Rifai an order, written in his own hand, dismissing Glubb, Brigadier W.M. Hutton, the Legion's Chief of Staff, and Colonel Sir Neville Coghill, the Director of Intelligence. The king said that he expected his government to comply with his wishes and then left, leaving the Head of the Royal Diwan to represent his interests. Ironically, Glubb just missed seeing the king: as he drove back to his office from Zerqa he noticed Hussein's car outside the prime minister's office.

Samir Rifai immediately summoned the Council of Ministers, read them the king's order and said that there were three possible courses of action: to comply with the decision, to ignore it or to remonstrate with Hussein on the grounds that it could cause trouble within the Arab Legion. Although the ministers were inclined to accept the decision without further ado, Samir Rifai won a short reprieve by proposing that the matter should be discussed with Duke – thereby unwittingly demonstrating the client relationship with Britain. At first Duke thought that Hussein's decision might be the result of 'a brainstorm' and, as he told London in an 'incredulous' telegram, he warned the prime minister that Glubb's dismissal could plunge the country into chaos.

> I said that in my view, for the Government to carry out the King's orders without protesting would be a grave shirking of responsibility. The Legion itself might be divided and start fighting whether the orders were carried out or not. The Prime Minister recognised this danger since presumably the King had made sure of support in the Army before he passed the order, and he might even forcibly remove Glubb and the two British officers if his orders were not obeyed. Finally, I said that subject to Glubb's own views I still thought the Government had a duty to remonstrate with the King, particularly as he had not even given any reasons for his orders and, if he remained obdurate, to resign. That would at least put the responsibility squarely on the King.[41]

It was to no avail. Four hours later, at 6.34 p.m., he told London that, in accordance with Hussein's order, Glubb had been summarily dismissed. Meanwhile attempts would be made to limit the damage by suggesting that Glubb had merely gone to Cyprus for a short spell of leave.

However, Glubb refused to take part in the subterfuge: in his eyes the break had to be final as it had been made perfectly clear to him that his services were no longer required. Early that afternoon Samir Rifai had summoned him to his private office where, accompanied by the defence minister, he informed Glubb of the King's decision:

'I dare say it's only a temporary phase,' said Sameer

457

Pasha [*sic*]. 'Perhaps in a few days we'll all be welcoming you back. I've been Prime Minister several times, then I have been dismissed, and now I'm back again.'

'That may apply to politicians,' I [Glubb] said, smiling, 'but I don't think it can apply to me.'[42]

And so it proved: the government had held firm and Glubb must leave immediately, within two hours, for he feared demonstrations once the news broke, but Glubb won a stay of execution and it was agreed that he would leave early the next morning.

All that remained was to pick up some personal belongings from his office and to return home to begin the awful task of packing what possessions he could and to make preparations for the rest to follow on after him. It goes without saying that the decision came as a rude shock, but Rosemary remembers that the task of packing helped to dull the realisation that this was the end of a chapter in their lives. Charles Duke called round with news of the frantic diplomatic attempts that were being made to retrieve the situation but found Glubb resigned to his fate and anxious only to be gone as his position had been made untenable by the king's obvious lack of confidence in him. Other visitors followed, Arab Legion officers from Zerqa, some of them in tears and angrily swearing revenge. To his credit, Glubb reminded them all that they were soldiers under orders and that under no circumstances were they to be disloyal to King Hussein. The saddest farewells were reserved for his Bedouin bodyguards – as Glubb admitted, without them he would have been an easy target for an assassin's bullet.

After a few hours of uneasy sleep, the Glubbs and their children made their way to the airport, accompanied by the defence minister and the Head of the Royal Diwan. No British officers were allowed to be present – their telephone lines had been cut – and only the Dukes were there to bid Glubb farewell. At the airport he was presented with a formal signed photograph of the king thanking him for his past services and wishing him well for the future. There was little more to say – Rosemary asked the Dukes to look after a pet gazelle that had graced her garden in Amman – it had been raining and there was a chill wind, a sorry end, thought Glubb, for his twenty-six years of service to a country in which he had hoped to live out his days:

> As the aircraft rose into the air, I could see the city of Amman below us. I had first seen Amman in 1924, when I arrived on a camel, having ridden across five hundred miles of desert from Baghdad. Then it was a little village. Now it was a city of a quarter of a million inhabitants ... We swung to the west as we passed over Damascus, leaving the snowy crest of Mount Hermon on our left. Soon we skimmed over the ridges of Lebanon, splodged with patches of snow, and headed for the calm blue Mediterranean. Fascinated, I watched the Arab coast fade into the blue mist.[43]

It was not just Jordan that they were leaving behind. In addition to the pet gazelle, the Glubbs had to dispose of Rosemary's private aviary as well as twenty sheep and three ponies and a welter of unwanted household goods. Most of the better pieces of furniture were packed up for shipping back to Britain but the birds and the beasts had to remain in Jordan. Three weeks after the Glubb's departure the sheep and the household items were auctioned off – many Jordanians expressed surprise at Glubb's modest possessions – and the ponies were given to the Arab Legion. On Glubb's orders the birds were presented to the Crown Prince of Iraq but this offer was turned down and the collection was broken up. Eventually, the costs of dealing with Glubb's effects and transporting them back to Britain were deducted from his gratuities: even in the midst of the furore occasioned by his sudden departure, the embassy in Amman kept a careful note of all the charges raised by Glubb and his family.

Although he was not aware of it at the time, he was never

to return to Jordan. Little did he know, too, that his sacking was not just a personal misfortune, but a watershed in Britain's relationship with the Arab peoples of the Middle East. As the Royal Jordanian Air Force Dove aircraft made its way towards Cyprus, the reports of Glubb's sudden departure were about to become headline news all over the world and he had suddenly become a very important person indeed.

14

Imperial Twilight

Glubb's abrupt dismissal came as a nasty slap in the face to the British government: in 1956 there was still enough imperial spirit left in Whitehall for such peremptory treatment from a client state to be considered a personal insult. Duke said as much when he sought an audience with Hussein and reminded him that it hardly seemed 'worthy treatment to dismiss him [Glubb] suddenly like a pilfering houseservant'. Throughout the afternoon and evening of 1 March Duke had worked long and hard in an attempt to retrieve the situation. His only reward had been the audience with the king but, as he told London, Hussein was adamant that the decision could not be reversed and that he was well within his rights to sack a member of his own armed services. It was not a hasty decision, he reminded Duke, but one which he had been forced to take for sound reasons:

> He went on to say that he had discovered grave deficiencies of equipment and stores for the Arab Legion, particularly of ammunition. He also said that there was serious discontent among the officers which had been remedied by the new postings of officers to positions they were fitted to hold. He added that he had also been fighting Egyptian propaganda attacks on Glubb but, from 'the other side' (presumably from Glubb), there had been no cooperation.
>
> He had been upset by constant articles in the Press, even in England, representing Glubb as everything that

461

mattered in Jordan. He concluded by saying that he had felt bound to do what he considered essential for the preservation and honour of the kingdom, and if he had not acted as he had, he feared a much worse situation might have developed. He had sensed danger and had had to act promptly to remove it.[1]

The ammunition shortage had obviously been the trigger but the real reason for the dismissal lay in the king's belief that Glubb was out of step with Jordan's needs and out of date with current military thinking and that his continued presence in the Arab Legion was causing disharmony amongst the office corps and working against the country's interests. Glubb had been warned about these shortcomings, as had the Foreign Office through Shuckburgh, but as no notice had been taken, Hussein had been forced to take this positive, though no doubt unwelcome, step. Once the immediate anger had died down, he hoped that there would be a swift return to the previously cordial relationship. Duke ended his report by saying that Hussein was confident and smiling throughout the interview.

The same could not be said of the British government's reaction to the news which was received with a mixture of alarm, dismay and anger. Eden's first response was one of ill-disguised irritation and, amidst the flurry of telegrams exchanged between London and Amman, he insisted on sending a rap over the knuckles to Hussein, advising him that the decision to sack Glubb had caused deep resentment and that he could not 'foretell its final consequences upon the relations between our two countries'.[2] Rather like a head-master writing a bad school report, Eden ended his telegram with the hope that the king would see sense, withdraw his decision and submit to the British way of thinking. It was hardly the most tactful of messages but, fortunately perhaps, Duke was unable to deliver it until midnight on 2 March and by then, as he told London, Hussein was quite unmoved by its contents.

Both Eden and Hussein had their reasons for adopting a tough stance. The Jordanian king had acted for the good of his country and, with the support of Ali Abu Nowar and his uncle Sharif Nasser bin Jameel, he clearly felt that he was well within his rights to oust Glubb. Besides, his decision had won him a new popularity in the Arab world. From Cairo the Voice of the Arabs poured out congratulations for his firm action in 'exterminating' the British influences in the Arab Legion and hailed him as a true friend of the Arab cause. Similar messages came from Lebanon and Syria whose national press claimed that the king's decisiveness would be welcomed by every patriotic Arab and that the next step would be the reopening of talks with Nasser to re-equip the Arab Legion as an all-Arab army. At the same time, the Jordanian press blamed Glubb for failing to develop the Arab Legion and in one newspaper, *Al Jihad*, it was claimed that his removal would have a cleansing affect on the nation.

The man [Glubb] is now in the hands of history and history never pardons those who tear up the unity of a whole nation. As we express our gratitude to Al Hussein we should not forget the government and its Prime Minister, who have added another credit to their magnificent deeds by meeting national claims. In return for their good deeds we should stand together with this wise Government and support it to achieve its glorious objective.[3]

The most surprising response came from Nasser himself who took the opportunity to rub salt into British wounds by mischievously congratulating Selwyn Lloyd for being a party to the move at a time when Glubb was one of the obstacles to a rapprochement between Egypt and Britain. The British Foreign Secretary was in Cairo at the time and he was greatly taken aback and discomfited by Nasser's suggestion that there had been any British complicity in the decision to topple Glubb.

On the contrary, it was generally supposed in Foreign Office circles that although Nasser himself did not force Hussein's hand, through the use of propaganda and the influence of friends at court in Amman, he had to take a share of the blame for what had happened. Throughout February, on a daily basis, the Voice of the Arabs had forecast Glubb's demise and had kept up a barrage of abuse criticising Britain's influence over Jordan. Although it was not decisive and was only one of the factors involved in the moves to sack Glubb, the constant propaganda did help to create an atmosphere in which Hussein's decision became inevitable. Also, the Glubb incident appeared to many in the Arab world to be part of Nasser's grand strategy, for it was no secret that he wanted to extend his influence into Jordan and to gain control over the Arab Legion by funding it directly from Cairo. Hussein has always insisted that he was not influenced by Nasser, but that was how it was seen by those Arab leaders friendly to Nasser, who regarded Glubb's sacking as a major diplomatic victory for the Egyptian leader and one that strengthened his position in the Middle East. At the same time, it was also regarded as a humiliation for Britain.

Initially, that was how Eden regarded the incident from Britain's point of view and his anger led him to place the blame firmly on Nasser whom he had come to regard as a latter-day Mussolini. At one point during the long weekend of discussions which followed, he asked his advisers to prepare plans for the reoccupation of the Suez Canal Zone in an attempt to retrieve British prestige – the first hint of the sorry events which would lead to the Suez crisis later in the year.

There were solid grounds for Eden's alarm. British pride had been dented and his first reaction was to hit back at Nasser, whom he blamed, and to seek some form of retribution from Hussein; given the mortification of Glubb's hasty removal, this was a justifiable point of view during the first troubled hours as the news was assimilated. Certainly, that was how the British press reported the situation on Saturday

3 March when the headlines and leading articles were heavy with demands for British reaction. The most popular demand was for the freezing of the Arab Legion's subsidy of £8.75 million for the coming year, a proposal which had already been bruited by the Foreign Office. While this was a popular threat, *The Times* preached a caution in its Saturday leader: by all means threaten the withdrawal of the subsidy as a means of showing British displeasure, it advised, but remember the need to maintain Britain's long-standing relationship with Jordan:

> The shabby treatment meted out by the Jordanian government to a British officer who has served Jordan well is not in itself sufficient reason for abandoning the attempt to maintain stability in that country. However, it would be illogical to go on supporting a force that is intended for use in local Middle Eastern adventures or to become entirely an accessory to Russia in arming Arab against Jews.[4]

By then, that had more or less become Eden's point of view – he shared the Foreign Office fear, expressed by Duke and others, that the Arab Legion could fall under Soviet influence – but once the first shock had worn off, calmer counsels prevailed at Chequers for by the Sunday (4 March) Glubb had arrived back in Britain and went to see the Prime Minister there. Glubb's unruffled interpretation of the events in Jordan was a decisive factor in bringing Eden round to the policy of preserving at all costs the relationship with the young king. He was also interviewed by Shuckburgh who remembered that Glubb 'made a most noble impression – no harsh words against the King of Jordan, and a real understanding of the boy's desire to get rid of him, Glubb, who was always preventing him from doing foolish things'. Instead, Glubb advised:

> It would not be right to come down on Jordan like a ton of bricks. Take what they say at its face value; they want to

remain friends. Do not pull out, do not cut the subsidy (you cannot reduce it). Stop sending telegrams and let the dust settle down![5]

This was also the course of action recommended by Duke in Amman. Having faced stonewalling tactics about Glubb's dismissal, the British Ambassador came round to the view that the king was seriously minded to preserve his friendship with Britain and that he wanted the Glubb incident to be forgotten. During a further meeting on 3 March Hussein had asked for the anti-Jordanian tone of the BBC's foreign service broadcasts to be toned down as 'if it continued Jordan would be bound to reply and he thought that no good purpose would be served by starting an exchange of recriminations on the wireless'.[6] Duke replied that he would pass on the request to London but the king should expect British anger for the manner in which he had acted. To avoid future confrontation, Duke suggested that Hussein should make a clear statement on Jordanian Radio explaining why he had decided to sack Glubb and the other two British officers. This was duly broadcast that night at 9 p.m. by which time relative calm had returned to the country after the dancing in the streets and other celebrations which had greeted the first announcement.

After the first feelings of outrage, composure had also returned to the sixty-four British officers still serving in the Legion. All had been stunned by the news and further shocks were to follow when the majority were themselves removed from their commands; although upset, their training and discipline stood firm and they helped to carry out Glubb's orders that there should be no demonstrations on his behalf. Hussein had admitted to Duke that he feared a counter-coup, especially from the Bedouin elements of the Legion who worshipped Glubb but, although provoked, these too remained loyal to the king.

With the country returning to normal, Duke felt that the time was ripe to look once more at British policy and to start mending fences:

On further reflection I wonder if our regard for General Glubb's great personal qualities and services in Jordan and resentment at the ignoble manner of his dismissal have not led us to take a more tragic view than is justified of the significance of this episode for Anglo-Jordan relations generally ... I believe it may well be true that the Jordanians had built up Glubb to almost supernatural stature and were genuinely terrified of him, thinking it was he himself who represented British power and in tackling him they felt they were taking on Great Britain. Yet it was only Glubb they were determined to get rid of – not the British generally and certainly not British help and friendship ... We must not allow our indignation at Glubb's treatment to cause us to assume too hastily that the whole basis for mutual confidence and friendship has been destroyed.[7]

In other words, Glubb was to be cut adrift and allowed to go his own way, freed from the shackles of being Britain's senior and perhaps out-of-date representative in Jordan, a move that would give the Foreign Office a fresh negotiating point. Thus, the arabisation of the Arab Legion became a *fait accompli* – in a matter of hours instead of the years which Glubb had forecast. Brigadier Raadi Ennab was promoted to major-general and took Glubb's place as Chief of Staff; three months later, he was succeeded by Ali Abu Nowar, one of the main instigators of Glubb's removal. All this was recognised as inevitable by the Foreign Office who feared unpleasant consequences if British officers remained in command. As Hussein had warned Shuckburgh the previous autumn, he was unhappy about Glubb's presence as head of the Legion and he was irritated by his 'hasten slowly' approach to the promotion of Arab officers. Although Duke's attitude to Glubb strikes a slightly dismissive note – at the same time the British press and much of the government were expressing their dismay at Hussein's treatment of a well-known British subject – he had in fact found a temporary solution to the impasse. At that stage Hussein and his government did not want a complete break with Britain and as yet they had no wish to surrender the treaty obligations – but they did want to remove Glubb's all-pervasive shadow from their lives.

The Foreign Office was inclined to agree with the assessment – Shuckburgh talked about seeing 'a glimmer of hope' – but the change of direction did not do any favours to Anthony Eden who was under pressure to make a positive statement about British intentions in the House of Commons. His own backbenchers expected him to act with firmness by introducing measures to protect British interests and to rap Hussein over the knuckles for his action. The Labour Opposition had also demanded a debate on the subject and this was set for 7 March, too soon for Eden to reveal that he was attempting to find a rapprochement with the Jordanians. By then Eden was convinced that Hussein's position was under threat from Nasser and that he required staunch British support to meet it. Glubb said as much in a letter to *The Times*, condemning the mood of hysteria which had greeted his dismissal:

> I cannot avoid the impression that it would be a serious political error to 'get tough' with Jordan at this stage. Armed coercion is out of the question, and suddenly to cut off the subsidy would either destroy Jordan or force the King into the arms of friends who would almost certainly ruin him.
>
> I feel strongly that such irrevocable action should not be taken under the influence of resentment.[8]

The trouble was that Eden could not reveal his tactics without endangering the negotiations and, unable to say anything positive, he gave a miserably anodyne performance during the House of Commons debate. His biographer, Robert Rhodes James, admitted that it was one of Eden's worst-ever speeches and that coupled with Britain's humiliation and his own growing impatience with Nasser, Glubb's dismissal was a small but important 'milestone on the road to Suez'.

In the midst of all the diplomatic uproar, Glubb had displayed his customary sang-froid. Rosemary admitted later that this was partly due to the state of shock and partly because they were simply swept along by the tide of events after their rapid departure from Jordan. Having arrived in Cyprus, they were then booked on to a regular Viscount flight to London which was due to arrive at Heathrow on the Saturday evening, 3 March, at 5.40 p.m. At the airport an enormous crowd of journalists awaited them, anxious to interview the man of the moment: it could have been unnerving but a former Arab Legion artillery officer, Brigadier Robert Elliot, had gone to Heathrow to greet his old boss and with the help of the police was able to smuggle the Glubbs out of the terminal. A posse of reporters gave chase as they drove towards the Elliots' home in Camberley, however, and Glubb was forced to stop and give an impromptu press conference in a roadside pub. Had it not been for the intervention of the Elliots the Glubbs would have had a far rougher homecoming, for, astonishingly, the Foreign Office seems not to have made any arrangements to welcome him: instead, the kindly offer of accommodation at Camberley meant that the Glubbs had a sanctuary for those first exhausting days at home.

That Sunday he visited the Foreign Office and Chequers to brief Eden and to explain his belief that the king was not to be blamed for sacking him; and on the following day came the news that he was to be knighted, a wonderful morale-booster, according to Rosemary, and one that gave Glubb a great deal of personal pleasure and satisfaction. He was formally knighted by the Queen a few days later, on 9 March, and the photograph of him outside Buckingham Palace is one of the happiest and most relaxed of his many portraits. He was also much in demand to discuss the Middle East with various parliamentary groups and other interested private societies and his message was always the same: continue supporting Jordan to prevent the possibility of the Soviets gaining a toehold in the country, put pressure on Israel to adjust the frontier for the sake of the Palestinian refugees and counter Egyptian propaganda by building a powerful pro-British transmitter in Jordan. Above all, he insisted that no blame whatsoever should be attached to Hussein who was well within his rights to get rid of an older man with whom he was no longer in sympathy.

By then the government had decided to respond to the new situation in Jordan by gradually withdrawing the remaining British officers from their executive commands in Jordan, a move which the Foreign Office hoped would further the cause of eventual reconciliation. While the British government was not anxious to weaken its links with the headquarters of the Arab Legion, it recognised that it was impossible to retain the officers in executive positions and that it would be sensible to comply with the Jordanian requests. (Bob Melville was also removed from his post as liaison officer in London.) In their places a temporary training team was established under the direction of Lieutenant-Colonel E.V.M. Strickland and the subsidy remained intact – both moves were recommended by the Chiefs of Staff committee which acknowledged the truth of some of Hussein's strictures about the Arab Legion's capabilities. The good sense of the government's decision to allow Jordan a breathing space was proved later in March when Hussein refused to go to Cairo to discuss the new political situation with Nasser and then turned down a joint Egyptian and Saudi Arabian offer to fund the Arab Legion. By then, too, Jordan was no longer a front-page story and had been replaced by other more pressing items – the plan to imprison Archbishop Makarios in Cyprus, the breaking of the world air speed record by a British Fairey Delta aircraft, the forthcoming visit of the Soviet leaders Bulganin and Khrushchev and the shakiness of Eden's own position as Prime Minister.

In the midst of all the various excitements, the Glubbs had to make arrangements to settle down in England, for it was obvious that there could be no return to Jordan, at least for the time being. Accommodation had to be found while the search for a house began in earnest and for a while they rented rooms at Brooklands Farm, South Godstone in Surrey. Then, that summer, they bought a large house with extensive gardens at Mayfield in Sussex, not far away from his parents' former home at Pembury in Kent. Built as a 'country cottage' by the architect Romaine Walker, West Wood St Dunstan was probably too large and needed too much done to it to be entirely suitable, but it was relatively inexpensive, and the Glubbs liked it for the many original Tudor features which the architect had collected and incorporated into the house's design.

The children had to be educated too. Godfrey, now officially known as Faris, would soon be going to Oxford and the others had to complete their educations at boarding school. With the expenditure required for the purchase and renovation of the house and the costs of meeting the children's education, Glubb suddenly realised that he was in financial difficulty. Although he was hardly an extravagant man, he was exceptionally generous and many Jordanians had been the recipients of his largesse – and Rosemary had run the small school for orphans in Amman. Now he was without a regular income and had to depend on a pension whose conditions were far from generous. During the heady period of his homecoming, financial matters could be safely ignored and, as he admitted, he was not yet hard up: as the weeks passed and the question of his pension remained unanswered, he began to fret.

The only British obligation to him was an annual pension of £728, rising to £800, which represented the sum due to him for his service in Palestine. He had also been paid a gratuity of £1,100 for his service in the Royal Engineers between 1915 and 1927 and he was due to receive a gratuity of £2,406 from the Arab Legion plus a further £2,453 on the termination of his employment. This gave him a total of

£5,939 from which the Foreign Office had deducted £1,100 for the expenses in transporting the Glubbs and all their possessions from Amman. This left him with a lump sum of £4,859 and the annual pension of £728, a financial settlement which Glubb – and his many supporters – felt was far from satisfactory, especially as the British government had made much of the fact that he had been the main prop of British policy in Jordan.

In some desperation, Glubb wrote to the Foreign Office whose head, Sir Ivone Kirkpatrick, granted him an interview on 29 May to discuss the problem in greater detail. After a difficult and somewhat embarrassing meeting, Kirkpatrick agreed that Glubb's case should be handled as if he were a lieutenant-general in the British Army; that is, he should receive a lump sum of £3,900 together with an annual pension of £1,300. As Glubb had already received the three gratuity payments, the main need was to bring the pension payments up to the necessary level by increasing them by £500 a year.[9] Initial inquiries revealed that Glubb was due to receive a small Arab Legion pension of £225 a year but the question of the additional £275 became a political football which was kicked between London and Amman as the British and Jordanian governments argued about which country should be responsible for funding the pension requirements.

By the end of June the British Treasury had made it clear that the money would not come from their own resources, a decision which put the matter back in the hands of the Foreign Office and the Jordanian government. For Glubb it was hardly an edifying process but for his family's sake he was forced to maintain pressure on the Foreign Office to do something positive on his behalf. Some of the files from that period remain closed in the Public Records Office but from those which are available it is impossible to ignore the feeling of irritation amongst Foreign Office officials as each new argument arrived from Glubb's hands. Without ever saying so, Kirkpatrick and his officials obviously believed that the continued wrangling over the annual payment of £275 was bad form and that it ill behoved senior army officers and diplomats to be involved in such unseemly matters. For example, in response to a query from Lord Strang, a former Foreign Office head, Kirkpatrick said that while he was sympathetic and agreed that the funds available did not provide Glubb 'with much in the way of fat living in these inflationary days', the general seemed to be a difficult man to please:

> But I should tell you in confidence that Glubb sometimes gives the impression of an old Rip Van Winkle, and I am inclined to think that if I had been in King Hussein's place, I might also have got rid of him.[10]

Only a year previously, the Foreign Office had based its policies in Jordan more or less entirely on Glubb's continued presence there, yet here was the permanent under-secretary describing this prop as a Rip Van Winkle, an elderly survivor from the distant past. The feelings of indifference to Glubb's plight permeated the Foreign Office's Middle East Department throughout the summer and it was not until the end of August that the matter was settled by King Hussein who recommended a payment of £5,000 to honour an earlier Jordanian claim that Glubb would 'live in comfort for the rest of his life'. As the Foreign Office considered that only £3,230 would be required to fund an annual pension of £275, Kirkpatrick felt that Glubb had done well and that the matter could be safely closed:

> I expect you will have already considered using part of this sum to increase your Jordanian pension by the desired amount, thus bridging the gap of which we spoke.[11]

A subsequent memo on the subject recommended that Kirkpatrick should seek an early meeting with Glubb to tell him privately that 'we need do no more for the General'. With the question of the pension settled, it was felt that any possibility of Glubb using his grievances to stir up a press campaign had finally receded – a fear which had unsettled some officials, quite unnecessarily. There had also been some concern that Glubb might have taken up the question directly with the Jordanian government, or even with King Hussein, and would thereby reopen the whole problem of the British administration of the subsidy for the coming year. Both worries were entirely groundless as the Foreign Office should have realised, given their earlier comments about Glubb's probity and the strength of his loyalty to British interests.

At the time it was suggested by some of the sacked British officers of the Arab Legion that Glubb could have done more to help them with their own pensions and gratuities, but this criticism does not bear examination. Glubb always linked his own requests to the plight of the officers who had formerly been in the service of the Arab Legion but was finally told that the responsibility for such matters lay with Amman. He also enlisted the support of Field Marshal Templer who expressed his concern to the Foreign Office that the contract officers might be left without suitable financial recompense – but to no avail. As Glubb's career harked back to the days of the mandate in Palestine – astonishingly, he still had 320 days leave to his credit – he was a special case, but as far as he was able to do so, he kept up the pressure for the British government to do something positive for his former officers. Unfortunately for all concerned, the Foreign Office's attitude remained one of polite regret that they could not do more.

A similar lack of generosity clouded the Foreign Office's treatment of Glubb's requests for suitable employment. Still physically fit and still tolerably young – he was only fifty-nine – Glubb felt that his experience and knowledge of Middle Eastern affairs could be put at the service of the British government and he said as much in a letter to Selwyn Lloyd at the beginning of May:

My whole life has been passed in the public service. There

is an enormous amount of engrossing work I should like to do in England. For example, I am most interested in Arabic (and even African) students here, and it seems to me that to do something for them would be an important public service. I should also like to help in a long-term plan to get across a better picture of Britain and what she stands for to the Arab world, and possibly to other Eastern countries.

I should also like to get suitable English works published in Arabia. (All the bookshops are full of books by Karl Marx, Lenin and Co. in Arabic.)

But all the activities are unpaid. I have a wife and four young children. I cannot go on living on capital.[12]

The letter was passed round the Foreign Office and the Treasury for comment but the reply came back that Glubb was too old for employment by the Civil Service and the Middle East Department stated quite firmly that they could not imagine him 'in any sort of Foreign Office information or allied job'.[13] There was a vague proposal that the British Council might find him employment but nothing came of it and the final suggestion was that a place might be found for him in the Middle East Centre at St Antony's College, Oxford. Nothing more was done for Glubb at the time as the general feeling within the Foreign Office was that he could quite easily earn a living from writing and lecturing. And so it proved.

For the first time in forty years of public service Glubb found that he had time on his hands and that, instead of brooding on what might have been he could return to the love of writing which had emerged after the Second World War. His first book, *The Story of the Arab Legion*, had appeared in the summer of 1948, at the height of the confrontation with Israel. The coincidence had not been lost on the reviewers, many of whom searched in vain for some political significance within its pages. In fact, Glubb had very little to say about the Palestine problem even though he acknowledged that it had affected both Transjordan and his own career. Instead, he concentrated on the desert-dwelling Bedouin people and wrote about their lives with an intimate and sympathetic understanding. Some of the finest passages in the book deal with the intricacies of Bedouin social life, the long rides across the desert, the intensity of shared friendships and the stories and poetry which punctuated the hospitality in the black tents at the end of the day.

These descriptions provide the book with its main inspiration and it can stand on equal terms with any other classic account of the Arabian deserts and their people; indeed, throughout the book, Glubb showed an unerring eye for the changes of mood, climate and landscape which sweep across the desert scene. For some travellers the desert was a huge impersonal arena in which they had to struggle to prevent their own truths and moral definitions blurring into meaninglessness. Not so Glubb. Faced by a country and a climate that were physically and emotionally overwhelming, he had fallen back on the inner certainties of his own faith. In other words, he had refused to imitate the lives of the Bedouin who lived there, for all that he adopted their manners, speech and dress – attributes which made other Europeans believe that he was 'more Arab than the Arabs'. Rather, he maintained a solid and deep core of Englishness and an inner certainty in his own beliefs which were slowly evolving to an intimate sense of love for all things and all people. Often the emotion would come upon him unexpectedly when a simple piece of kindness was transformed to an act of grace:

> How often, in early days, have I leaned wearily on the front of my camel saddle, with aching back after days of riding and dreary nights without light or fire, and with only a cold piece of Arab bread for dinner for fear that the lighting of a fire might bring raiders. Then suddenly I have seen the look-out man come racing down from the top of the hillock where he had been in observation, shouting: 'Good news! A host for the night! I have seen houses!'[14]

476

In time Glubb was to refine that sense of gnosis to a belief that love was an act of will, an extension of God's presence and the greatest and most simple power for good known to man. Glubb also long maintained that he had first understood the meaning of life while living in the barren places of the world where existence had been reduced to a bare simplicity of purpose.

Encouraged by the success of the first book Hodder and Stoughton had persuaded Glubb to continue the story of the Arab Legion and to write about its exploits between 1946 and 1956, the year of his dismissal. They had ample reason to have faith in the project as Glubb was a well-known personality whose views on the Middle East and the Arab world were taken seriously. Within days of his return to England in March 1956 the *Daily Mail* had paid him £6,000 for the serialisation of his story – one reason, perhaps, for the Foreign Office's unwillingness to help him find employment – and he was much in demand as a speaker and commentator on current affairs. However, the resulting book, *A Soldier with the Arabs*, was something of a disappointment, for all that it sold well and received kind reviews. Although it provided an accurate and well-told account of the fighting with Israel in 1948, the chapters dealing with recent events were more restrained. Obviously, he could not be entirely candid about events which had just taken place or about personalities still living, but he seemed to be driven by a need to promote Britain's special relationship with Jordan and at the same time to say nothing untoward about Israel, by the end of 1956 a British ally in the Suez campaign against Egypt. Even the title was non-committal, suggesting that Glubb was not wholly at ease with the project and had turned his back on the full-blooded commitment which suffused the earlier volume.

Fortunately, the passion returned in *War in the Desert* which is a superb account of his adventures in southern Iraq in the 1920s. Published in 1960, this is an excellent history in which political and military analysis gel perfectly with Glubb's knowledge of the area and his feelings of love and respect for the desert tribes. It also deserves its reputation as a classic of military writing for the author's clear-headed and diligently expressed understanding that nobody could control Arabs better than the Arabs themselves and that the Bedouin people were therefore the key to the prevention of inter-tribal warfare. By arming and training the tribes, Glubb gave them self-confidence, self-respect and a sense of purpose at a time when the British imperial instinct was to control and direct.

It was not just the writing of books that sustained Glubb during the years of his retirement from public life. He emerged as a well-respected public speaker and through the Foyle's Agency he embarked on regular lecture tours around the country, addressing Rotary Clubs, schools and other organisations for the fee of twenty guineas (£21) plus expenses. It was a time-consuming and frequently exhausting occupation but, with Rosemary accompanying him, he turned the chore into a holiday and they were able to visit parts of Britain they had never seen before because of his years of absence abroad. He attracted large crowds, too. In October 1956 over 2,500 people turned up to hear him talk about the Middle East in Edinburgh's Usher Hall – after the lecture he was presented with the Royal Scottish Geographical Society's Livingstone Medal for his 'outstanding services in the cause of progress and stability in the Arab world'. As a result of his popularity in Scotland, in 1958 the students of St Andrew's University invited him to stand for the post of Rector, a largely honorary appointment, but in the ensuing election he lost out to the Conservative politician Lord Boothby.

Given Glubb's success as a speaker and his reputation as a soldier-historian, it was hardly surprising that the lure of the United States soon beckoned. This was in the halcyon days of American author tours, before they were devalued by the television promotional circus, and Glubb made a considerable part of his income from taking part in them. In all, he visited America twelve times and, after initially making use of the services of an agency, he made his own arrangements from the contacts he had made. He visited the universities of Yale and

Harvard in 1966 where he made a great impression on his hosts as a conscientious and entertaining speaker who was able to get across his arguments succinctly and often humorously. As Zionism was an important force in American domestic politics he could have met with noisy opposition for his views on Israel whose growing military power he believed to be a threat to the stability of the Middle East. However, his lack of pomposity and his genuine humility in presenting his arguments disarmed his critics, although at the beginning of his first-ever visit his agency attempted to persuade him to issue a conciliatory statement praising Israel and its policies. This, of course, he refused to do.

Not all of Glubb's literary works were military histories. He also wrote a number of books on the Arab world in spite of his publisher's fears that a general lack of interest in the Middle East would lead to low sales. However, Glubb remembered that as a young man in Iraq he had been appalled by his own ignorance of the area's history and he was now determined to put that failing to rights for future generations. The result was a dozen readable and entertaining books which have few academic pretensions but, wearing their author's learning and experience lightly, provide a useful introduction to the whole sweep of Arab history from the golden age of the caliphs to the present day. In books like *The Empire of the Arabs* and *The Great Arab Conquests*, both published in 1963, he is particularly incisive about the great period of Arab expansion from the eighth century onwards.

As books on the Middle East became more popular and more widely available in the 1970s some of Glubb's points of view seemed to be somewhat out of date and conservative, or lacking the passion of a singular argument. Judging from the voluminous notes he wrote, not just for his own books, but also for his own benefit as a means of clearing his mind, he was extremely careful about what he included in a book and what he left out. Reading his cautious views on the state of the modern Arab world or his always sensible analyses of the Palestinian problem, it is to be regretted that he did not give vent to the passion he displayed, for example, in a private note about the lot of his beloved Bedouins. Written late in life, it is worth quoting in full to understand Glubb's depth of feeling on a subject which was so close to his heart:

It would appear inevitable that, sooner or later, the Bedouin will intermingle with the settled population and be infected by them with the resentments and inferiority complexes of our hate-ridden world. Perhaps the more enterprising will abandon the desert life and disappear into the cities as mechanics or merchants or into the settled areas as farmers, losing thereby the characteristics of their nomad culture.

In so far as there is in the breeding of sheep an economic reason for nomadism, some tribesmen will remain nomads, still remaining hardy and virile as they are obliged to be by their way of life. But they will contribute a backwater of their Middle East culture, unnoticed by the great ones of the earth.

At various places along the fringes of the great Arabian deserts sordid little communities are to be seen, consisting of people still living in little ragged tents in the slums of cities. Soon the heavy black tent of the nomad degenerates first into a frayed and ragged strip of goat hair and into two or three old corn sacks vaguely stitched together. Dirty women sit in the dust while even dirtier children waylay passing tourists to beg for coppers.

'I know the Bedouins, a dirty lot of cowards. The only language they understand is a beating,' said an American Jewish gentleman to me after paying a visit to Israel. There is in reality little of the Bedouin about these filthy slum-dwellers, harried by the police and sanitary inspector. In spite of the contempt of this modern imperialistic age, though, perhaps their ancestors many centuries back may once have been nomads. The tent, though perhaps innocent of sanitary arrangements, presupposes a nomadic existence. In the slums of industrial cities, it becomes an offence and a humiliation.

May none of the descendants of the free men I knew ever fall to these depths of vileness![15]

This was a far cry from the bucolic scenes of his youth when wilderness was paradise and the Bedouin seemed to be nature's aristocrats. Given the industrialisation of the Arabian deserts, first through the increased exploitation of oil and then through the construction of modern means of communication, they could not have remained unsullied for ever, but Glubb had been saddened by reports, from friends and television, which spoke of the sorry lot of the Bedouin people caught up in urban society or, worse still, in the Palestinian refugee camps on the West Bank. He had argued that such a fate might befall them in his lecture to the Royal Central Asian Society in 1938 when he argued that the introduction of foreign capital would be the ruin of the desert tribesmen (see Chapter 7), but, in truth, he too had to share some of the responsibility for what had happened in more recent times. By pacifying the Bedouin people and channelling their martial instincts into the service of their country, he undoubtedly did Jordan a service and provided the Hashemite family with a loyal bulwark against Arab nationalism, but, inevitably, the regimentation of the desert tribes changed their way of life. True, many continued to live a nomadic existence, and still do so;* but the mould had been broken and it was impossible for them to return to the fierce independence of earlier times when they roamed the deserts largely unmolested by the nations whose lands they traversed.

However, it has to be admitted that, had Glubb not encouraged the Bedouin tribesmen to join the Arab Legion,

---

*During the build-up to the war to oust Saddam Hussein's forces from Kuwait in 1991, the author visited a British armoured regiment in the northern Saudi Arabian desert. Nearby was a Bedouin encampment equipped with modern American camper vehicles and pick-up trucks for their racing camels.

their transmogrification would have been more painful. Even by the 1930s, when Glubb first arrived in Transjordan, tribal raiding into Saudi Arabia and Iraq was threatening to turn the tribes into a class of outlaw, fit only to be put down: it was one of the conditions of British support that he put a stop to inter-tribal raiding. Instead of punishing them, Glubb had harnessed their latent soldierly virtues and put them into the service of Britain's imperial interests, just as Pitt had done to the Scottish Highlanders whose depredations had tormented successive governments during the eighteenth century.

By the end of the 1950s, though, such considerations mattered little, for the British relationship with Jordan had changed out of all recognition. In the aftermath of Glubb's departure many of the old links which marked Jordan's subservient position disappeared overnight. The Arab Legion became the Jordan Arab Army and there was rapid promotion for many Arab officers who took the place of their superiors from the British Army. In June Ali Abu Nowar became Chief of Staff, thereby taking another huge step along the path which would lead him to eventual confrontation with Hussein. Elections were held in October that same year, bringing to power the same Suliman Nabulsi (Suleiman Naboulsi) who had so bent the ear of the British journalist Basil Davidson and persuaded him to write an anti-Glubb article in the *Daily Herald*. Naboulsi, a West Bank lawyer, soon forged ties with Ali Abu Nowar to bring about the kind of connection between the government and the armed forces which Glubb had long feared.

To begin with, though, the relationship with Britain remained sound enough. This was largely due to the British government's refusal to cut the Arab Legion's subsidy and abrogate the treaty, as many of their backbenchers wanted them to do. Once the fury about Hussein's precipitate decision had died down, it was possible to see that he had not acted illegally and that if the protests continued it would appear to the rest of the Arab world that Britain had been attempting to rule Jordan by means of the treaty relationship.

This was allied to a growing feeling that support for Glubb could also damage British interests because in some Arab minds he was regarded as the main instrument in attempting to force Jordan to join the Baghdad Pact. Besides, a reaction had set in and Glubb's virtues, promoted so heavily by the Foreign Office only a few months earlier, were being called into question. Selwyn Lloyd admitted as much when he told Philip Ingress Bell, a Conservative backbencher, that although he admired Glubb, he felt that his views were long out of date:

> The Foreign Office gave him complete confidence and unbounded support for his work in Jordan. Whatever his virtues, however, he completely failed to realise what was happening in Jordan and to foresee what was coming to him. We have sought since his return to pin him down to what should in practice be done. He has remained very vague.[16]

The main problem was what to do with the Arab Legion which had been synonymous with Glubb's tenure of office. It had also been the framework around which British influence and support had been built and a decision had to be taken about its future relationship with Britain. The War Office had already pointed out that without it Britain no longer had a force in the Levant available in certain circumstances to support British interests in the region and that the army would have to consider increasing the strength of its airborne forces to make good the loss. Clearly, without the presence of Glubb and the other British loan officers it would be untenable to continue paying the subsidy but the Foreign Office was not at all keen to see the Jordanian forces fall under the influence of Saudi Arabia or Egypt should either country take over the financial responsibility. As a short-term stop-gap, the Foreign Office stepped up its efforts to persuade Iraq to provide funds and thereby lure Jordan into the Baghdad Pact.[17]

These were only temporary measures, suitable for the

confused summer months of 1956 when Britain was anxious
to prevent Jordan falling under the influence of Egypt. In the
longer term, both governments realised that the old cosy
treaty arrangements could not continue and it was with some
relief on both sides that Nabulsi began the process of
abrogating the treaty in October 1956 – it was officially terminated on 14 March 1957 and the British subsidy came to an
end. Even if Naboulsi had not made the move it is unlikely that
Jordan's friendship with Britain would have survived the
strains of the ill-starred Suez affair of October and November
1956. Following the nationalisation of the Suez Canal by
Egypt on 26 July, Britain had exerted diplomatic pressure on
Nasser to turn the canal into an international trade route, but
while those negotiations were taking place, Israel attacked
Egypt across the Sinai desert on 29 October as part of a pre-
arranged French plan. An Anglo-French ultimatum to both
countries to stop fighting was accepted by Israel but not by
Egypt, thus giving Britain and France the pretext to start
bombing Egyptian airfields two days later. Airborne forces
landed on 5 November with the main attack going in the
following day amidst a good deal of tactical confusion. International pressure, principally from the United States and the
Soviet Union, put an end to the fiasco but evidence of British
collusion with Israel in instigating the attack on Egypt soured
the long-standing relationship with Hussein. Strickland's
training mission, which had been established after Glubb's
departure, was ordered to leave and Saudi Arabian and
Syrian forces were given leave to enter Jordan. Fortunately
for Hussein, Nasser refused his offer of military support, but
in the aftermath of the affair Hussein began to look to the
Arab world for support and in January 1957 the Arab Solidarity Agreement provided Jordan with an annual subsidy of
£12.5 million which was to be paid by Saudi Arabia, Egypt
and Syria.

During the course of the following winter, Hussein found
himself increasingly at odds with Nabulsi whose left-wing
politics seemed to be leaving Jordan open to the possibility of

Soviet infiltration. Matters came to a head on 10 April 1957 when Hussein sacked the government and formed a new administration under the leadership of the veteran Said el-Mufti. It was then that Ali Abu Nowar made his move by urging the king that he would have to accept the armed forces' candidate or face the consequences – this was the confrontation which Glubb had always feared might happen if the Legion involved itself in politics. However, the loyalty of the Bedouin elements in the army, particularly the 1st Armoured Car Regiment, saved Hussein; the attempted coup failed, Ali Abu Nowar was exposed and disgraced and sent to live in exile in Egypt. For the time being, the king had regained his authority and one good result of his tenacity was the American decision to take over the responsibility for funding Jordan: it was a timely move, for only Saudi Arabia had honoured the terms of the Arab Solidarity Agreement,.

Even though the Americans had taken over the funding and arming of Jordan's armed forces, it was not quite the end of the British connection. In the tense days which followed the bloody coup which swept King Feisal from power in Iraq in July 1958, Britain sent airborne troops and aircraft to Amman to protect Hussein and his crown. When they left later in the year, having successfully completed their mission, Strickland was reappointed military adviser and Jock Dalgleish returned as air adviser. The appointment of both men and the ready assistance given by the Royal Air Force and the 16th Parachute Brigade helped to repair fences with Hussein, but Britain could no longer return to the old client relationship with Jordan which Glubb believed should be the cornerstone of her policy in the Middle East. Hussein had emerged as a world ruler in his own right and, besides, in Britain itself colonialism was becoming a dead letter, unpopular with most politicians and the majority of the people.

Although Glubb accepted that there could be no turning back to the old days, he regretted the termination of the treaty relationship as he had always believed that British support was Jordan's only hope for the future. Not that he ever wanted to return to the country in spite of several requests from Hussein to do so. 'I have never gone back since 1956, mainly for Jordan's own good,' he told a journalist in 1967. 'For I am sure that my return would only stir up trouble for King Hussein with Nasser. I can just hear him taunting: "Ho, ho, here's your imperialist friend back again . . ." Then I must admit that it would be too painful for me to go back after what happened. I just could not turn the dagger in my own wound.'[18]

By then, though, Glubb had made his peace with King Hussein. The first contact had been made in November 1957 shortly after Glubb had presented the king with a copy of A Soldier with the Arabs and Hussein replied to say that he thought highly of it. When he visited London a few months later the two men were allowed to meet and Glubb reported back to the Foreign Office that the audience had been 'extremely cordial', ironically, the very words he had used to describe his last meeting with Hussein on the day before he was sacked. Before the visit, the Foreign Office had decided to omit Glubb's name from the invitation list in case his presence might be thought to have any political significance.[19] Those fears notwithstanding, Hussein went out of his way to make light of the breach that was supposed to exist and very soon a warm relationship grew up between the two men and their families. Whenever he was in London the king always made a point of contacting Glubb, and, each Christmas, greetings, together with a photograph of the royal family, would be sent to the Glubbs.

A further indication of King Hussein's generosity of spirit and his willingness to forget the past came in 1967 after his country's disastrous war with Israel. As a result of Israel's blitzkrieg the Jordanian land and air forces were completely crushed during a forty-eight-hour period of heavy fighting, and Jordan was forced to surrender the West Bank. One reason for the defeat was the deployment of the army in forward defensive positions and the unwillingness of local commanders to retreat or retire towards the high ground away from the frontier with Israel. Had they followed Glubb's tactics of mobile defence they might have stood a better chance, a possibility conceded by Hussein when he visited Glubb later in the year and admitted that the Pasha's policy had, after all, been correct. It was a generous gesture, made by one soldier to another.

As time passed and Glubb's name began to slip into history, he was less in demand as a pundit on Middle Eastern matters; indeed, his book *Syria, Lebanon and Jordan* was made cruelly out of date when it appeared in 1967 at the same time as the Six Day War between the Arabs and the Israelis. By then Glubb was regarded as something of a museum-piece, a soldier-historian whose exploits belonged to Britain's imperial past in the deserts of Arabia. Even his name, Glubb Pasha, had an old-fashioned, exotic ring, even though he himself was proud of the fact that he was the last British subject to have been awarded the title by the Hashemite family. (His friends invariably referred to him as 'the Pasha'.) Whenever he was interviewed he was 'Glubb Pasha' and journalists would often fall back on the idea that he was a latter-day Lawrence of Arabia – and the conceit stuck. In fact, it had never been far away from him.

The novelist Robin Maugham had made the connection in 1941 while visiting Glubb's headquarters at Zerqa to discuss the possibility of forming small units of Arab soldiers to stay behind the enemy lines should the Germans invade in strength in Syria. He was accompanied by Dr Ernest Altounyan who had known Lawrence during the days of the Arab Revolt and was then serving with the Arab Legion. Born in Aleppo, the son of an Armenian father and a Scots mother, Altounyan had been educated at Rugby and Cambridge before taking a medical degree, and had served with the Royal Army Medical Corps during the First World War. A somewhat shadowy figure who worked for British military intelligence under a number of guises, he had first met Lawrence at the Karkamis excavations in Syria and had remained a lifelong friend and admirer. He had every reason to consider Lawrence to be a more remarkable man than Glubb, yet when Maugham asked him who was the greater of the two, he had no hesitation in saying 'this one' as they drew up outside Glubb's headquarters.[20]

A few weeks later, and from a slightly different perspective, Brigadier Kingstone had feared that Glubb might be a Lawrence figure who outstripped him in rank and authority and was anxious to exert his own command before his mobile column set off to relieve Habbaniyah. Like many other regular officers of his generation he remembered Lawrence as a temporary officer and gentleman whose scallywagging guerrilla war amongst the desert Arabs was considered to be beyond the pale. When Kingstone saw the flowing robes and long hair of Glubb's Desert Patrol he feared the worst, for many officers of his age and outlook disliked the habit of wearing native dress which they believed smacked of ostentation or cleverness – both cardinal sins in an officer. John Hackett also saw the connection but he believed that Glubb understood the Arabs better than Lawrence ever did and that 'Glubb was so much of what Lawrence was built up to be, and in fact was not'.[21]

This is very much to the point for, although there are similarities in the careers and lives of both men, Glubb was a very different creature from Lawrence. For a start, he was chary of courting publicity, whereas Lawrence's habit of 'backing into the limelight' helped to create a legend around his life and exploits in the desert. Indeed, so deeply engrained were many of the myths that the real facts of Lawrence's existence are difficult to decipher and he remained a riddle, even to those who knew him reasonably well. Some of the incidents in his life were pure fabrications, despite the fact that he had experienced enough adventure to make such deceits unnecessary and it seems likely that he created the legend both to protect his inner self and to surround himself with an aura of mystery. None of these strictures applies to Glubb who remained a curious mixture of shyness and certitude, a man who preferred to keep his innermost feelings firmly in check. As Hackett implied, Glubb had no need to embellish his achievements, whereas Lawrence was driven to elaborate them or, for different reasons, to obscure them.

Both men handled their success in different ways, too. By all accounts, Lawrence did not object when fellow British officers started referring to him as 'Lawrence of Arabia' in 1917 and both during and after the war he loved being photographed in the flowing white robes and head-dress which lent a sense of glamour and chivalric intent to his desert campaign. On the other hand, Glubb remained the more down-to-earth 'Pasha' who was usually photographed wearing standard British Army-style uniform with a red and blue forage cap or the red and white checked *shamagh* of the Desert Patrol. As a young man in the Iraqi desert he had worn Arab dress for a while – he grew to dislike the photograph of himself which survives from that period – but this was traditional Bedouin dress and not the Sharifian robes adopted by Lawrence. Never a dressy man, such ostentation would have been anathema to Glubb and it is indicative of his lack of worldliness in such matters that he raised no objections when the War Office asked him not to wear Arab Legion uniform on public occasions in Britain after his retirement.

Where the two men find the closest point of connection is in their shared experience of desert warfare, Lawrence's during the Arab Revolt and Glubb's in the pacification of the Iraqi border tribes in the 1920s. Just as Lawrence had secured the tribal harmony of Feisal's army and turned it into a useful military instrument which tied down Turkish forces between Damascus and Medina, so too did Glubb realise the importance of treating the Bedouin as soldiers, instilling in them basic discipline and providing them with reasonable equipment. By so doing, both men flew in the face of received British military opinion which regarded the Bedouin as slipshod allies, more interested in gaining plunder than winning battles.

Although Glubb's forces were engaged in battles that were

489

little more than running skirmishes along the Iraq–Nejd border, his ability to harness the fighting qualities of the Bedouin was no less remarkable than Lawrence's handling of Feisal's army during the right-flank attack on Damascus in 1918. In that respect both men understood the importance of guerrilla warfare in support of conventional operations and realised that the best people to fight were those who lived in, and understood, the terrain. This was especially true of Glubb's handling of the Arab Legion in support of the allied operations in Iraq and Syria in 1941.

It is also true that Glubb was one of that small band of British soldiers and administrators who regarded their service, in some small measure, as repayment of the moral debt for Britain's betrayal of the Arab cause after the First World War. Glubb not only grew to love the Bedouin people but rejoiced in the life he led with them, although he never over-romanticised them as Lawrence did in *Seven Pillars of Wisdom*. In other words, he accepted them for what they were and not what he wanted them to be. In time this respect for the Bedouin led to a distrust of the town-based Arabs – an antipathy shared by Lawrence – and colleagues like Broad-hurst were left to complain that one of the reasons for Glubb's downfall was his inability to come to terms with the younger generation of Arab nationalists. This refusal to take them seriously strikes a discordant note in the career of a man who believed ultimately in the palliative power of love in human relationships but it would be wrong to describe his feelings as simple xenophobia. While it is probably true that his dislike had much to do with the British imperial prefer-ence for straightforward martial races, the attitude can also be explained by Glubb's – and Lawrence's – background and upbringing. In their day, cleverness was frowned upon in military circles and any hint of it had to be extirpated. Outspoken or voluble young men of whatever race or creed were considered suspect, especially if their point of view was nationalistic, and as Glubb persistently made clear, this was a political concept which he believed had been introduced from Europe to the detriment of the Arab people.

There are other connections between Glubb and Lawrence – both men had the misfortune to be described as 'the uncrowned king of Arabia', both wrote extensively of their experiences in the Arab world, both were physically short and, because they knew and understood Arab culture and society, both men were respected in Foreign Office circles at a time when British politicians understood little about the Middle East. For all their love and knowledge of Arabia, it was also their lot to be branded as pro-Zionist imperial lackeys by later generations of Arabs who held them to be partially responsible for the problem of Palestine and its refugees – Lawrence for his betrayal of the Hashemite leaders and Glubb for not taking a more aggressive stance towards the new state of Israel. Such an accusation is easy enough to make and, as instruments of British policy, both men are implicated, but it is difficult to see how either could be blamed directly for the events which followed the Balfour Declaration of 1917.

History was not kind either to the two Hashemite kingdoms which Lawrence helped to bring into being and in whose service Glubb rose to fame. In 1958 Feisal was butchered and Iraq underwent a series of bloody coups which eventually brought the dictator Saddam Hussein to power; and although Jordan survived the disastrous Six Day War in 1967 and the resultant loss of the West Bank, the Palestinian refugee problem remains an ever-present factor in the country's political life, as King Hussein has found to his cost. Against such a tumultuous background, Glubb's belief that British influence could be a power for the good of the Middle East, itself a reiteration of Lawrence's own benevolent imperialism, sounds like a hollow echo from a distant age.

And yet, it would be wrong to end on such a bleak note. Glubb neither claimed that he was an important factor in British Middle Eastern policy nor did he think that he was a significant influence in Jordanian affairs, but that was little more than personal modesty. From the Second World War onwards he was the personification of British authority in Amman and he held together the long and honourable relationship between London and the Hashemite royal family which had been entered into all those years ago by Lawrence. He was also a key player in helping to direct Abdullah's policy in 1948 and his Arab Legion fought the Israelis to a standstill at Latrun which remains the only substantial victory by an Arab army over opposing Israeli forces. Time and time again, the Foreign Office referred to Glubb as the prop on which their policies stood or fell, and Glubb's own papers and reports were frequently revised and incorporated into British strategy – for all that some members of the department were frequently exasperated by statements which they felt to be exaggerated or alarmist. Also, there is no clearer indication of his concern for British interests than the care, attention and foresight he brought to the development of the Arab Legion during and after the Second World War. As the Foreign Office acknowledged after his dismissal, everything depended on his command of the Legion because 'in effect, Her Majesty's Government's support, working through the Legion, has underpinned the social, financial and political structure of Jordan'.[22] Or, as Templer put it after his last visit to Amman, 'for the peasant and the tribesman in Jordan, Glubb Pasha is still more than the government'.[23]

Eventually, the impossibility of serving both Britain and Jordan was to be one of the reasons for his downfall but, in the history of Britain's relationships with the countries of the Middle East, he remains one of the few British imperial servants who succeeded in explaining Arab ways to the West and in interpreting British policies to his hosts. This was particularly true of his service in Iraq where very few Westerners were interested in, or even cared about, life in the apparent wastes of the desert. It also holds good for his career in Jordan where he was one of the cornerstones of the British administration which helped to establish Abdullah's authority. And as a man, with all the strengths and frailties of human nature, he loved and respected the people whom he served – together with Rosemary, the Glubbs became a byword for hospitality and Christian kindness amongst many of the poor and the dispossessed in Jordan. That is no bad epitaph.

Epilogue

In 1971, while lecturing in the United States at Troy State University in Alabama, Glubb suffered a number of fainting fits and had to be flown back to Britain where Rosemary took charge and arranged for him to be seen by a heart specialist. As a result, he was fitted with a heart pacemaker at the National Heart Hospital in London; there were several problems with the original instrument and Glubb had to endure a number of uncomfortable journeys between Mayfield and London before the problem was finally solved. However, it was not just a physical trauma: while lying in his hospital bed he experienced a moment of such spiritual intensity that it transformed forever many of his preconceptions about his personal worth:

> As I lay wondering if I was at any moment going to meet God, I thought to myself, 'What is there in all your life which you can plead in your favour?' I received an overwhelming impression that only acts done for love were of any value whatever. This was not a conversion – I had always read religious books and led, to the best of my ability, a moral life. But it was a loud gong, a megaphone shouting, 'Your present standard isn't good enough! You will not make the grade!'
>
> My self-sufficiency was shattered. I had perhaps been a trifle self-satisfied with my 'successful career'. Suddenly I realised that the whole thing was dirty rags. Only a

complete dedication would do. I can never be thankful enough for that illness.[1]

One result of this overwhelming feeling of benevolence and love towards his fellow men – always there but never coherently expressed – was the publication of Glubb's *The Way of Love* in 1974 and its sequel, *A Purpose for Living*, in 1980. Both books are reflections on the relationship between man and mankind, and between man and God, and both are remarkable for the sense of 'revelation' which he brings to the Christian way of life. Unusually for a man who had spent most of his life soldiering, Glubb also reached the conclusion that the sanctity of human existence is an essential ingredient of Christian faith. Instead of seeing this as a contradiction of his own values, however, it led him back to a long-held belief that military service contained many of the elements of Christian chivalry. As a soldier, Glubb's battles had never been particularly bloody although he saw his share of the carnage on the Western Front and had been sickened by the depredations of the Ikhwan in southern Iraq, but these instances had been driven by hate, the opposite of love. Glubb argued that it was possible to marry the ideals of duty and honour to his belief that love lay at the heart of the Christian life, just as Thomas à Kempis and other mystics had done before him. It sounds simplistic but Glubb's musings on the spiritual life are filled with a quiet passion and intensity of conviction which helped to make his books extremely popular by giving inspiration to his fellow Christians.

Another result of this new spiritual determination was a subtle change in his personality. Always outgoing and friendly in the company of family and friends, with a sense of fun never far away, he became more solitary in the last years of his life and was given to lengthy periods of silence and introspection. It was almost as if he had to withdraw temporarily from the world to discover the inner strength with which to write the final accounts of his career and to understand his deeply held beliefs. During this period, in 1975, he discovered his diaries from the First World War, written in a bundle of old exercise books which had long ago been consigned to his vast collection of personal papers. They were published in book form under the title *Into Battle* and were immediately hailed as a major contribution to the literature of the First World War. Written from Glubb's first-hand experiences as a young man caught up in total warfare, they possess a vividness and honesty which provide a highly personal account of that much-chronicled conflict. This is war seen from the junior officer's point of view; it is not a book about heroes but about ordinary soldiers facing up to the discomfort, fear and boredom of trench warfare, armed only with loyalty, discipline and a sense of common decency. A sequel, *Arabian Adventures*, was less successful, simply because the best material had already been published in his earlier account of his experiences in Iraq, *War in the Desert*.

In his retirement Glubb never became a member of important public committees for their own sake, but he did enjoy involving himself in the pastoral work of the Church of England. For many years he was President of the Deanery Association of the Church of England's Children Society and he took much pleasure from his work as Church Warden in the Church of St Dunstan in Mayfield. When the vicar at the time, Donald Carter, came to be interviewed in 1966 he admitted that the prospect of working with a high-ranking soldier had worried him but he was immediately put at ease by Glubb's courtesy and consideration. When asked by friends if he ever felt intimidated by having a general as Church Warden, Carter always replied, 'Not a bit. He's been used to being in authority himself, he's the first to recognise authority in others.'[3]

As a committed Christian, Glubb did not himself fear death but he had been much saddened by his mother's passing in 1962. A grand old lady, full of years and quaint Irish stories, she left Jordan in the wake of her son's departure and eventually settled in Troutstream Hall, a home for retired missionaries in Rickmansworth. Glubb's sister, Gwenda, still lived abroad, at Amarousion in Greece. By the early 1960s, when she was well into her sixties, she gave up her yacht but remained a doughty traveller, often driving back to Britain in her Dormobile or Citroen Deux Chevaux. She died on 27 May 1990, only a few days short of her ninety-sixth birthday.

Glubb himself died in 1986 after a long illness which he had borne with his customary fortitude and courage. In the last months of his life he had been plagued by cataracts which made reading difficult and he turned instead to the solace of prayer. Often during that difficult time Rosemary would see him tying knots in his handkerchief and would ask him what he wanted to remember. 'To remind me to pray without ceasing,' was the invariable reply. By then he was a very sick man. Two years earlier, in 1984, he had been diagnosed as suffering from aplastic anaemia, a condition which normally requires bone marrow transplants but his age made such an operation impossible. Instead he was given regular blood transfusions but they became increasingly ineffective and during the winter of 1985–6 it was obvious that he was terminally ill. Naomi took responsibility for nursing him at home, where he died on Monday 17 March 1986.

His passing was noted by fulsome obituaries which paid tribute to his life of service to Britain's interests in the Middle East and mentioned the earth-shattering events of March 1956 when he seemed to stand at the heart of the world's affairs. One of his last visitors had been Queen Noor of Jordan, King Hussein's American-born fourth wife, and it was entirely fitting that Hussein himself should provide the eulogy at the service of thanksgiving for the life of Lieutenant-General Sir John Bagot Glubb, KCB, CMG, DSO, OBE, MC which was held in Westminster Abbey on Thursday 17 April 1986. After praising Glubb's meritorious service and devotion to Jordan, Hussein turned to the man himself:

A soldier, a statesman, a public figure and author of remarkable qualities, he belonged to a unique generation of outstanding men who dedicated their entire lives to the establishment of a genuine understanding, deep friendship and mutual respect between the United Kingdom and the Hashemite Kingdom of Jordan, which have since not only survived the turbulence and vicissitudes of a dazzlingly changing world, but which have grown into an exemplary relationship between friendly states in every way ...

... He was a down-to-earth soldier, with a heart, a simple style of life and impeccable integrity, who performed quietly and unassumingly the duties entrusted to him by his second country, Jordan, at a crucial moment in its history and development.[3]

It was an eloquent and moving address to 'the man, the friend, the advisor' whom King Hussein wished to honour and it was appropriate that he should end with the thought that Glubb's memory would 'always be associated with the loftiest qualities a man could be endowed with in his lifetime'. The presence of the king in Westminster Abbey was also a reflection of the fact that, despite the ever-changing shifts of emphasis in Middle Eastern politics, there was still an understanding between the Hashemite Royal Family and the government of the United Kingdom. More than any other tribute, that would have pleased Glubb.

A reserved and self-sufficient man, Glubb was that old-fashioned hybrid, a soldier who was also a scholar, a warrior who was also a man of God and a diplomat who was also on the side of the weak, the humble and the poor. As King Hussein noted in his eulogy, the requirements of the times forced Glubb to play down his role in world affairs yet he remains one of the key figures in the history of British involvement in the politics of the Middle East.

Bibliography

The majority of Glubb's private papers have been deposited in the library of the Middle East Centre, St Antony's College, Oxford. After acquisition they were loosely arranged and filed according to their main areas of interest. Other collections consulted in the Middle East Centre were the papers of H. St John Philby, J.B. Slade-Baker and Sir Edward Spears.

The main primary sources consulted are held by the Public Record Office, Kew:

AIR 8	Chief of Air Staff's Papers
AIR 23	RAF Overseas Commands
AIR 24	RAF Operations Record Books
CAB 128	Cabinet Meetings
CO 730	Colonial Office: Iraq Correspondence
CO 733	Colonial Office: Middle East Correspondence
CO 831	Colonial Office: Transjordan Corespondence
FO 371	Foreign Office: General Political Correspondence
FO 800	Foreign Secretary's Correspondence
PREM 8	Prime Minister's Correspondence
WO 95	War Office: War Diaries

The only lengthy recorded interview with Glubb is held by the Department of Sound Records, Imperial War Museum, in its *Middle East: British Military Personnel* section. Other interviews consulted were those of Sir John Hackett, Denis

Ingram Newman, D.J.E. O'Flynn, and E.H. Tinker. The Museum also holds the papers of Peake Pasha.

Glubb's published books are:

The Story of the Arab Legion, Hodder & Stoughton, London, 1948

A Soldier with the Arabs, Hodder & Stoughton, London, 1957

Britain and the Arabs, Hodder & Stoughton, London, 1959

War in the Desert, Hodder & Stoughton, London, 1960

The Empire of the Arabs, Hodder & Stoughton, London, 1963

The Great Arab Conquests, Hodder & Stoughton, London, 1963

The Course of Empire, Hodder & Stoughton, London, 1965

The Lost Centuries 1145–1453, Hodder & Stoughton, London, 1967

The Middle East Crisis: A Personal Interpretation, Hodder & Stoughton, London, 1967, rev.ed., 1969

The Mixture of Races in the Eastern Arab Countries, Blackwell, Oxford, 1967

Syria, Lebanon and Jordan, Thames & Hudson, London, 1967

A Short History of the Arab Peoples, Hodder & Stoughton, London, 1969, rev. ed., 1978

The Life and Times of Muhammad, Hodder & Stoughton, London, 1970

Peace in the Holy Land: An Historical Analysis of the Palestine Problem, Hodder & Stoughton, London 1971

Soldiers of Fortune: The Story of the Mamelukes, Hodder & Stoughton, London, 1973

The Way of Love: Lessons from a Long Life, Hodder & Stoughton, London, 1974

Haroon Al Rasheed and the Great Abbasids, Hodder & Stoughton, London, 1976

Into Battle: A Soldier's Diary of the Great War, Cassell, London 1978

Arabian Adventures: Ten Joyful Years of Service, Cassell, London, 1978

500

The Fate of Empires and *Search for Survival*, William Blackwood, Edinburgh, 1978

The Changing Scenes of Life, Quartet, London, 1983

A Short History of the Glubb Family, privately printed, 1983

Secondary sources

Abdallah (King Abdullah of Jordan), *My Memories Completed*, Longman, London, 1978

Bar-Joseph, Uri, *The Best of Enemies: Israel and Transjordan in the War of 1948*, Frank Cass, London, 1987

Bell, Gawain, *Shadows on the Sand*, C. Hurst, London, 1983

Ben-Gurion, David, *Talks with Arab Leaders*, Keter Books, Jerusalem, 1972

Bowra, C.M., *Memories*, Weidenfeld and Nicolson, London, 1966

Brown, Malcolm, *Tommy Goes to War*, J.M. Dent, London, 1978

Brown, Malcolm, and Cave, Julia, *A Touch of Genius: The Life of T.E. Lawrence*, J.M. Dent, London, 1988

Buckley, Christopher, *Five Ventures*, HMSO, London, 1954

Collins, Larry, and Lapierre, Dominique, *O Jerusalem!*, Weidenfeld and Nicolson, London, 1972

Dann, Uriel, *King Hussein and the Challenge of Arab Radicalism*, Oxford University Press, Oxford, 1989

Dann, Uriel, *Studies in the History of Transjordan*, Special Studies in the Middle East, Westview Press, Boulder and London, 1984

De Chair, Somerset, *The Golden Carpet*, Faber and Faber, London, 1943

Eden, Anthony, *Full Circle*, Cassell, London, 1960

El-Edroos, S.A., *The Hashemite Arab Army*, Publishing Committee, Amman, 1980

Foot, Hugh, *A Start in Freedom*, Hodder & Stoughton, London, 1966

Fromkin, David, *A Peace to End All Peace: Creating the Modern Middle East, 1914–1922*, André Deutsch, London, 1989

Furlonge, Geoffrey, *Palestine is My Country*, John Murray, London, 1969

Gaunson, A.B., *The Anglo-French Clash in Lebanon and Syria*, Macmillan, London, 1987

Gilbert, Martin, *Churchill: The Stricken World*, Vol. IV, Heinemann, London, 1975

Gilbert, Martin, *Churchill: The Prophet of Truth*, Vol. V, Heinemann, London, 1977

Gilbert, Martin, Companion Volumes to Volumes IV and V of *Churchill*, Heinemann, London, 1978

Gilbert, *Churchill: A Life*, Heineman, London, 1991

Graves, Philip (ed.), *Memoirs of King Abdullah*, Cape, London, 1950

Heikal, Mohamad, *Cutting the Lion's Tail: Suez through Egyptian Eyes*, André Deutsch, London, 1986

Herzog, Chaim, *The Arab–Israeli Wars*, Arms and Armour Press, London, rev.ed., 1984

Horne, Alistair, *Macmillan, 1894–1956*, Vol. I, Macmillan, London, 1988

Hourani, Albert, *A History of the Arab Peoples*, Faber and Faber, London, 1991

Husain (King Hussein of Jordan), *Uneasy Lies the Head*, Heinemann, London, 1978

James, Lawrence, *The Golden Warrior: The Life and Legend of Lawrence of Arabia*, Weidenfeld and Nicolson, London, 1990

James, Robert Rhodes, *Anthony Eden*, Cape, London, 1986

Jarvis, C.S., *Arab Command: The Biography of Lt-Col. F.G. Peake*, Hutchinson, London, 1942

Kimche, Jon and David, *Both Sides of the Hill*, Secker and Warburg, London, 1960

Kirkbride, Alec, *A Crackle of Thorns*, John Murray, London, 1956

Koury, Philip S., *Syria and the French Mandate*, Princeton University Press, Princeton, 1987

Lacouture, Jean, *De Gaulle, The Rebel*, Collins Harvill, London, 1990

Lapping, Brian, *End of Empire*, Granada, London, 1985

Lias, Godfrey, *Glubb's Legion*, Evans, London, 1956

Louis, W.R., *The British Empire in the Middle East 1945–1951*, Oxford University Press, Oxford, 1984

Lucas, W. Scott, *Divided We Stand: Britain, the US and the Suez Crisis*, John Curtis/Hodder and Stoughton, London, 1991

Lunt, James, *Glubb Pasha*, Collins, London, 1984

Lunt, James, *Hussein of Jordan: A Political Biography*, Macmillan, London, 1989

Macmillan, Harold, *Tides of Fortune*, Macmillan, London, 1969

Macmillan, Harold, *Oxford Before the Deluge*, Macmillan, London, 1984

Mansfield, Peter, *A History of the Middle East*, Viking, London, 1991

Mason, Philip, *The Men Who Ruled India*, Vol. II, Cape, London, 1954

Mason, Philip, *A Matter of Honour: An Account of the Indian Army, Its Officers and Men*, Macmillan, London, 1974

Mockler, Anthony, *Our Enemies the French: Being An Account of the War fought between the French and the British*, Leo Cooper, London, 1976

Morris, James, *Farewell the Trumpets: An Imperial Retreat*, Faber and Faber, London, 1978

Nutting, Antony, *No End of a Lesson*, Constable, London, 1967

O'Ballance, Edgar, *The Arab–Israeli War*, Faber and Faber, London, 1948

Omissi, David E., *Air Power and Colonial Control: The Royal Air Force 1919–1939*, Manchester University Press, Manchester and New York, 1990

Pappe, Ilan, *Britain and the Arab–Israeli Conflict*, Macmillan, London, 1988

Playfair, I.S.O., and others, *History of the Second World War: The Mediterranean and Middle East*, Vol. II, HMSO, London, 1956

Shlaim, Avi, *Collusion Across the Jordan*, Oxford University Press, Oxford, 1988

Shuckburgh, Evelyn, *Descent to Suez: Diaries 1951–1956*, Weidenfeld and Nicolson, London, 1986

Silverfarb, Daniel, *Britain's Informal Empire in the Middle East: A Case Study of Iraq*, Oxford University Press, Oxford, 1986

Sluglett, Peter, *Britain in Iraq 1924–1932*, Ithaca Press, London, 1976

Sparrow, Gerald, *Husain of Jordan*, Harrap, London, 1960

Stark, Freya, *East is West*, John Murray, London, 1945

Stark, Freya, *Dust in the Lion's Paw*, John Murray, London, 1961

Sykes, Christopher, *Crossroads to Israel*, Indiana University Press, Bloomington, 1973

Thesiger, Wilfred, *Arabian Sands*, Longman, London, 1959

Towle, Philip Anthony, *Pilots and Rebels: The Use of Aircraft in Unconventional Warfare*, Brasseys, London, 1989

Trevelyan, Humphrey, *The Middle East in Revolution*, Macmillan, London, 1970

Vatikiotis, P.J., *Politics and the Military in Jordan: A Study of the Arab Legion*, Frank Cass, London, 1967

Wilson, Jeremy, *Lawrence of Arabia: The Authorised Biography*, Heinemann, London, 1989

Wilson, Mary C., *Abdullah, Britain and the Making of Jordan*, Cambridge University Press, Cambridge, 1987

Yardley, Michael, *Backing into the Limelight: A Biography of T.E. Lawrence*, Harrap, London, 1985

Young, Peter, *Bedouin Command*, Harrap, London, 1956

Ziegler, Philip, *Mountbatten*, Collins, London, 1985

Notes

Full references to the books cited in the Notes are contained in the Bibliography.

Chapter 1: A Boyish Education (pages 7–32)
1. Glubb, *A Short History of the Glubb Family*, p. 80.
2. Mason, *A Matter of Honour: An Account of the Indian Army, Its Officers and Men*, p. 174.
3. *Short History*, p. 17.
4. ibid., p. 23.
5. ibid., p. 30.
6. Glubb, *Into Battle: A Soldier's Diary of the Great War*, p. 195.
7. *Short History*, p. 33.
8. ibid., p. 43.
9. Glubb, *Arabian Adventures: Ten Years of Joyful Service*, p. 5.
10. Cheltenham College Magazine, 1982, pp. 11–13.
11. ibid.
12. Bowra, *Memories*, p. 36.
13. Morgan, *Cheltenham College: The First Hundred Years*, p. 125.
14. Cheltenham College Magazine, op.cit.
15. *Into Battle*, p. 6.
16. *Arabian Adventures*, p. 6.
17. ibid., p. 7.
18. ibid., pp. 7–8.
19. *Into Battle*, p. 7.

Chapter 2: A Subaltern's War (pages 33–64)
1. *Arabian Adventures*, p. 9.
2. ibid., p. 1.
3. *Into Battle*, p. 7.
4. *Into Battle*, p. 23.
5. War diary, 7th Field Company Royal Engineers, 28 November 1915, WO 95/2821.
6. *Into Battle*, p. 28.

7. E.W. Cotton, quoted in Brown, *Tommy Goes to War*, p. 71.
8. *Into Battle*, p. 31.
9. ibid., p. 32.
10. ibid., p. 34.
11. War diary, February 1916, op. cit.
12. *Into Battle*, p. 44.
13. ibid., pp. 67–68.
14. ibid., p. 86.
15. Glubb, *The Changing Scenes of Life*, pp. 43–4.
16. *Into Battle*, pp. 104–5.
17. *Changing Scenes of Life*, p. 35.
18. *Into Battle*, p. 62.
19. ibid., p. 73.
20. ibid., p. 90.
21. ibid., p. 175.
22. ibid., p. 139.
23. ibid., p. 186.
24. ibid., p. 188.
25. ibid., p. 193.
26. ibid., p. 219.
27. War diary, 11 November 1918, op.cit.

Chapter 3: To the Deserts Wild (pages 65–103)
1. *Short History*, pp. 47–8.
2. *Into Battle*, p. 223.
3. Interview with Lieutenant-General Sir John Bagot Glubb, *Middle East: British Military Personnel*, Department of Sound Archives, Imperial War Museum (IWM), Accession 004410/06.
4. Glubb, diary note, undated, March 1921?, Glubb Papers, Iraq Box 2.
5. *Arabian Adventures*, p. 15.
6. ibid., p. 16.
7. Gilbert, *Churchill: The Stricken World*, p. 217.
8. Air Intelligence in Iraq, 1 December 1929, AIR 2/1196.
9. Address of Farewell from the Indians at Hinaidi Cantonment, April 1922, Glubb Papers, Iraq Box 2.
10. *Arabian Adventures*, p. 49.
11. ibid., p. 51.
12. Intelligence Report from Ramadi, 5 February 1923, Glubb Papers, Iraq Box 2.
13. Glubb, *War in the Desert*, p. 94.
14. Glubb, 'The Pacification of the Iraq Deserts', undated, June 1923?, Glubb Papers, Iraq Box 3.
15. Glubb to H. St John Philby, 7 March 1924, Glubb Papers, Iraq Box 3.
16. Glubb, 'The Desert 1923 – Appreciation by J.B.G.', December 1923, Glubb Papers, Iraq Box 2.
17. Morris, *Farewell the Trumpets: An Imperial Retreat*, p. 250.
18. 'The Desert 1923', op.cit.
19. *Arabian Adventures*, p. 114.
20. ibid., p. 117.
21. Operations Record Book, Air Headquarters Baghdad, December 1923, AIR 24/818.

Chapter 4: Sowing the Wind (pages 104–30)
1. *Arabian Adventures*, pp. 131–2.
2. ibid., p. 129.
3. Glubb, Notes on meetings of Nejd sub-committee, 14 May 1928, Glubb Papers, Iraq Box 2.
4. Glubb to H. St John Philby, 7 March 1924, op.cit.
5. Glubb, 'The Iraq–Nejd Frontier', undated, Glubb Papers, Iraq Box 2.
6. *Arabian Adventures*, p. 135.
7. Air Staff Headquarters memoranda, 1928, AIR 23/796–807.
8. *War in the Desert*, p. 132.
9. British Military Expenditure in Iraq, 1921–1928, January 1929, AIR 8/45.
10. Salmond, 'The Fuller Deployment of Air Power in Imperial Defences', November 1929, AIR 8/45/173534.
11. Various correspondence between High Commissioner and Colonial Office, CO 730/125–140.
12. Bullock, 'Notes on Substitution', Talk to Parliamentary Navy and Air Committee, 21 June 1932, AIR 8/72.
13. Mason, *The Men Who Ruled India*, Vol. II, p. 211.
14. *Arabian Adventures*, p. 168.
15. Glubb to Dobbs, 15 January 1929, CO 730/140/8.
16. Glubb, 'Notes on the Causes which make it essential to establish a permanent administration in the Desert', Glubb to Dobbs, 12 June 1930, CO 730/140/8.
17. Air Headquarters Baghdad, memorandum, 22 June 1928, CO 730/136/5.
18. 'The Iraq–Nejd Frontier', op.cit.

Chapter 5: War on the Frontier (pages 131–64)
1. Dobbs to Ibn Saud, undated, November 1927, CO 730/125/1.
2. Ibn Saud to Dobbs, undated, November 1927, ibid.
3. *War in the Desert*, op.cit., p. 127.
4. *Al-Istiqlal*, undated, March 1928.
5. 'Notes on the Causes', op.cit.
6. Glubb, 'Notes on the Southern Desert Force', undated, summer 1928, Glubb Papers, Iraq Box 2.
7. Glubb to Cornwallis, 30 July 1928, Glubb Papers, Iraq Box 2.
8. Glubb, diary note, undated, April 1928, Glubb Papers, Iraq Box 3.
9. Glubb, diary note, 17 May 1928, Glubb Papers, Iraq Box 3; *War in the Desert*, p. 214.
10. Glubb to Cornwallis, 30 July 1928, op.cit.
11. 'Notes on Substitution', op.cit.
12. *War in the Desert*, p. 240.
13. ibid., p. 241,
14. ibid., p. 245.
15. James, *The Golden Warrior: The Life and Legend of Lawrence of Arabia*, pp. 292–3.
16. *War in the Desert*, p. 255.
17. Interview with John Bagot Glubb, IWM, op.cit.
18. Glubb to Cornwallis, undated, February 1930, Glubb Papers, Iraq Box 3.
19. *War in the Desert*, p. 344.
20. Interview with John Bagot Glubb, IWM, op.cit.
21. Dobbs to Colonial Office, undated, summer 1930, Glubb Papers, Iraq Box 3.

22. 'Visit of the Secretary of State for the Colonies to Iraq', 11 May 1925, CO 730/89/23835.
23. 'Notes on Substitution', op.cit.

Chapter 6: Desert Patrol (pages 165–97)
1. Correspondence and notes in CO 831/11/1–11/6.
2. Macmillan, Oxford Before the Deluge, pp. 27–8.
3. Changing Scenes of Life, p. 108.
4. Peake, note for autobiography, undated, 1940 (?), Peake Papers, IWM 78/73/2.
5. Broadhurst to Peake, 27 March 1956, Peake Papers, IWM 78/73/3.
6. Dann, Studies in the History of Transjordan, p. 22.
7. Glubb, The Story of the Arab Legion, p. 77.
8. ibid., p. 78.
9. Glubb, 'Memorandum on the Situation on the Southern Frontier', 11 December 1930, CO 831/11/1.
10. ibid.
11. ibid.
12. Peake to Cox, 24 December 1930, ibid.
13. Shuckburgh to Chancellor, 18 February 1931, ibid.
14. Chancellor to Shuckburgh, 3 March 1931, CO 831/11/2.
15. Changing Scenes of Life, p. 105.
16. ibid.
17. Interview with General Sir John Hackett, Middle East: British Military Personnel, IWM 004527/05, op.cit.
18. Interview with Brigadier E.H. Tinker, IWM 00493/03, op.cit.
19. The Story of the Arab Legion, pp. 82–83.
20. Glubb, Monthly Report, July 1933, CO 831/23/15.
21. Morris, Farewell the Trumpets, p. 264.
22. Glubb to Kirkbride, 19 August 1931, CO 831/11/5.
23. Kirkbride, A Crackle of Thorns, p. 63.
24. ibid., p. 65.
25. ibid., pp. 67–8.
26. The Story of the Arab Legion, p. 98.
27. Glubb, Monthly Report, March 1933, CO 831/23/13.
28. Vatikiotis, Politics and the Military in Jordan: A Study of the Arab Legion, p. 73.
29. Peake, unpublished autobiography (typescript), chapter XIII, IWM 78/73/2.
30. 'Books on the Desert', private Colonial Office file on Kenneth Williams, CO 831/31/15.
31. The Story of the Arab Legion, p. 208.
32. Interview with Denis Ingram Newman, Middle East: British Military Personnel, IWM 004472/06, op.cit.
33. Changing Scenes of Life, p. 110.
34. Author's interview with Rosemary, Lady Glubb.

Chapter 7: Arab Soldier (pages 198–232)
1. Glubb to Kirkbride, 29 January 1934, 'Events in the Southern Desert', CO 831/29/1.
2. Wilson, King Abdullah, Britain and the Making of Jordan, p. 104.
3. Memorandum by Shuckburgh, 2 February 1931, CO 733/197.

4. ibid.
5. Glubb, 'The Transjordanian Arab Tribes', *Journal of the Royal Central Asian Society*, vol. 25, 1938, p. 458.
6. Official communiqué from H.M.'s Diwan, 24 February 1933, CO 831/21.
7. Sykes, *Crossroads to Israel*, p. 168.
8. *The Story of the Arab Legion*, pp. 227–8.
9. ibid., p. 229.
10. ibid.
11. Glubb, Monthly Report, May 1936, CO 831/37/3.
12. ibid.
13. Glubb to Kirkbride, July 1937, CO 831/41/11.
14. Glubb, Monthly Report, June 1936, CO 831/37/3.
15. Glubb, Monthly Report, December 1937, CO 831/46/9.
16. Cox to Wauchope, 6 July 1937, CO 831/7/3.
17. *The Story of the Arab Legion*, p. 234.
18. William Hickey Diary, *Daily Express*, 23 March 1938.
19. Jarvis, *Arab Command: The Biography of Lt-Col F.G. Peake*, p. 62.
20. *The Story of the Arab Legion*, p. 234.
21. Interview with General Sir John Hackett, IWM, op.cit.
22. *Report by the Royal Commission on Palestine* (Peel Commission), Cmnd 5479, 1936–7, p. 375.
23. Palestine Report, Preliminary Departmental Comments, 23 June 1937, FO 371/2808.
24. Glubb, Monthly Report, March 1939, CO 831/51/10.
25. Glubb, Monthly Report, April 1939, ibid.
26. ibid.
27. *The Story of the Arab Legion*, p. 239.
28. ibid., p. 242.
29. ibid.
30. MacMichael to Macdonald, 29 August 1938, 'Arab Legion: Vacancies for Officer Commanding, Second-in-Command and O/C Desert', CO 831/49/15.
31. ibid.
32. MacMichael to Colonial Office, 23 September 1938, ibid.
33. MacMichael to Macdonald, 13 January 1939, 'Arab Legion: Vacancies for CO, Second-in-Command', CO 831/53//8.
34. Confidential note on Glubb's appointment, 21 January 1939, ibid.
35. Glubb, *A Soldier with the Arabs*, p. 19.

Chapter 8: Battle Honours: Iraq 1941 (pages 233–65)
1. Glubb, 'Arab Legion History', report for the Colonial Office, undated, summer 1939, CO 831/54/14.
2. MacMichael to Macdonald, 20 January 1940, 'Arab Legion Reserve', CO 831/56/7.
3. Interview with John Bagot Glubb, IWM, op.cit.
4. MacMichael to Lord Lloyd, 30 September 1940, Administration Reports for 1940, CO 831/55/7.
5. Glubb, Monthly Report, June 1939, CO 831/51/10.
6. Glubb, Monthly Report, September 1939, ibid.
7. ibid.

8. ibid.
9. Gilbert, *Churchill: The Stricken World*, p. 524.
10. Dann, *Studies in the History of Transjordan*, pp. 117–9.
11. Kirkbride to MacMichael, 20 July 1942, 'War Reactions in Transjordan', CO 831/59/16.
12. Abdullah to MacMichael, 5 March 1942, ibid.
13. MacMichael to Colonial Office, 14 July 1942, ibid.
14. Glubb, Monthly Report, October 1939, CO 831/51/10.
15. Glubb, 'A Report on the Role played by the Arab Legion in connection with the Recent Operations in Iraq', 10 June 1941, Glubb Papers, Transjordan Box 4.
16. *The Story of the Arab Legion*, p. 257.
17. Glubb to Somerset de Chair, 31 December 1942, Glubb Papers, Transjordan Box 5.
18. 'Report on the Role played by the Arab Legion', op.cit.
19. De Chair, *The Golden Carpet*, p. 18.
20. 'Report on the Role played by the Arab Legion', op.cit.
21. Glubb to de Chair, op.cit.
22. 'Report on the Role played by the Arab Legion', op.cit.
23. *The Story of the Arab Legion*, p. 298.
24. 'Report on the Role played by the Arab Legion', op.cit.
25. *The Story of the Arab Legion*, p. 302.
26. 'Report on the Role played by the Arab Legion', op.cit.
27. Glubb, 'A Further Note on the Peace Terms in the Middle East', undated, 1943, Glubb Papers, Transjordan Box 8.

Chapter 9: 'Our Joint Enterprise in the Levant' (pages 266–302)
1. Glubb, 'A Note on a visit to Damascus', 27–29 November 1941, CO 831/58/12.
2. Glubb, 'Periodic Report on Transjordan', 1 February–31 May 1942, Glubb Papers, Transjordan Box 4.
3. 'Further Note on the Peace Terms in the Middle East', op.cit.
4. ME 0 40 26, 8 July 1940, CAB 95/1.
5. Kirkbride, *Crackle of Thorns*, p. 147.
6. *The Story of the Arab Legion*, p. 307.
7. Glubb, 'A Note on the Future of the Arab Legion', undated, 1945, Glubb Papers, Transjordan Box 8.
8. *The Story of the Arab Legion*, p. 344.
9. Playfair, *History of the Second World War: The Mediterranean and Middle East*, vol. II, p. 200.
10. Gilbert, *Churchill: A Life*, p. 698.
11. Lacouture, *De Gaulle, The Rebel*, p. 301.
12. *The Story of the Arab Legion*, p. 311.
13. ibid., p. 322.
14. Bell, *Shadows on the Sand*, p. 138.
15. Lyttelton to Wilson, 28 August 1941, quoted in Gauson, *The Anglo-French Clash in Lebanon and Syria*, p. 75.
16. 'Note on a Visit to Damascus', op.cit.
17. Interview with John Bagot Glubb, IWM, op.cit.
18. Vatikiotis, *Politics and the Military in Jordan*, pp. 77.

19. Foot, *A Start in Freedom*, pp. 76–7.
20. T.E. Lawrence, 'Twenty-Seven Articles', *Arab Bulletin*, August 1917.
21. Bell, *Shadows on the Sand*, p. 142.
22. Author's interview with John Salmon.
23. Glubb, 'Note on Arab Politeness', 30 December 1944, Glubb Papers, Transjordan Box 5.
24. Glubb, notes on 'Security Briefing HQ 9th Army', 17 January 1941, Glubb Papers, Transjordan Box 8.
25. *A Soldier with the Arabs* p. 47.
26. Interview with John Bagot Glubb, IWM, op.cit.
27. Kirkbride to Colonial Office, 8 February 1944, Glubb Papers, Transjordan Box 8.
28. Glubb, 'Note on the Arab Legion', for Paiforce Headquarters Monthly Newsletter, undated, 1944, Glubb Papers, Transjordan Box 5.

Chapter 10: Abdullah's Man (pages 303–39)
1. Glubb, 'Note on the Future of the Arab Legion', op.cit.
2. 'Purchase of Transport for the Arab Legion', June 1946, FO 371/52930.
3. Minute by J.S. Bennett, 13 June 1941, CO 831/59/6.
4. 'Periodic Report', op.cit.
5. ibid.
6. Glubb, 'A Note on the Possible Political Results of Disbanding the Arab Legion Infantry Companies', June 1946, FO 371/52930.
7. Foreign Office memorandum, May 1946, FO 371/52935.
8. Foreign Office to Kirkbride, 13 December 1946, FO 371/52932.
9. Kirkbride to Bevin, 24 September 1946, FO 371/52936.
10. Glubb to Cunningham, 27 May 1946, FO 371/52931.
11. Barker to Cunningham, 19 August 1946, ibid.
12. Cunningham to Colonial Office, 8 June 1946, FO 371/52930.
13. 'Disposition of Arab Legion', October 1946, FO 371/52932.
14. Minute by G.W. Furlonge, undated, October 1946, FO 371/52931.
15. Arab Legion Quarterly Historical Report, September 1946, WO 261/535.
16. Glubb, 'British Officers for the Arab Legion', undated, September 1946, FO 371/52930.
17. Stanley Unwin to Glubb, 7 October 1942, Glubb Papers, Transjordan Box 3.
18. Colonial Office memorandum, 'The Story of the Arab Legion', 11 September 1947, FO 371/52930.
19. *A Soldier with the Arabs*, p. 190.
20. CIA to Foreign Office, 18 August 1948, FO 371/68831.
21. *A Soldier with the Arabs*, p. 67.
22. 'Note on the Future of the Arab Legion', op.cit.
23. *A Soldier with the Arabs*, p. 44.
24. Glubb, 'Rhymes on the Report of the Anglo-American Commission', undated, 1946, Glubb Papers, Transjordan Box 8.
25. Glubb, 'The Ideal Solution for Palestine', private note, undated, 1946, Glubb Papers, ibid.
26. 'Appreciation by the Chiefs of Staff of the Minimum Size which could be contemplated for the Arab Legion in our own interests', December 1947, FO 371/68827.
27. Cunningham to Foreign Office, 9 March 1948, FO 371/68828.

28. Kirkbride to Foreign Office, November 1947, FO 371/62194.
29. The idea that Abdullah was working independently of the Foreign Office was first advanced by Jon and David Kimche in their book *Both Sides of the Hill.* Jon Kimche, a journalist, launched a personal attack on Glubb in *Italia Sozialista,* 25 May 1948.
30. Foreign Office minute of a meeting to discuss the future organisation of the Arab Legion, 6 January 1948, FO 371/68827.
31. H.J. Beeley, minute on Transjordanian plans to seize part of Palestine, 6 January 1948, FO 371/68364.
32. ibid.
33. 'Future Organisation of the Arab Legion', op.cit.
34. 'Note on the Future of the Arab Legion', op.cit.
35. 'Brief conversation with Trans-Jordan's Prime Minister on Palestine', 6 February 1948, FO 371/68367.
36. *A Soldier with the Arabs,* p. 63.
37. Official minute of the meeting as contained in Bevin to Kirkbride, 9 February 1948, FO 371/68836.
38. 'Transjordan – A Possible Forecast of Events in Palestine', Record of a Conversation between Brigadier Glubb Pasha and DMI War Office, 30 January 1948, FO 371/68369.

Chapter 11: The First Arab–Israeli War (pages 340–76)
1. *A Soldier with the Arabs,* p. 81.
2. Kirkbride to Foreign Office, 13 May 1948, FO 371/68854.
3. 'Transjordan – A Possible Forecast of Events in Palestine', op.cit.
4. Herzog, *The Arab–Israeli Wars,* p. 24.
5. Abdel Rahman Azzam to King Abdullah, 15 April 1948, copied from Foreign Office to Amman, FO 371/68852.
6. 'Equipment passed to Arab Legion from Palestine', May 1948, FO 371/68828.
7. Major-General James Lunt, letter to *The Times,* 4 October 1990.
8. Herzog, *The Arab–Israeli Wars,* p. 101.
9. *A Soldier with the Arabs,* p. 101.
10. ibid., p. 98.
11. Bevin to Alexander, 13 May 1948, FO 800/477.
12. Alexander to Bevin, 27 April 1948, FO 371/68853.
13. Listowel to Bevin, 18 May 1948, ibid.
14. Foreign Office to Kirkbride, 7 May 1948, ibid.
15. Kirkbride to Foreign Office, 13 May 1948, FO 371/68854.
16. Foreign Office to Kirkbride, 29 May 1948, ibid.
17. Major-General J.E.C. McCandlish to Foreign Office, 12 May 1948, FO 371/68853.
18. *A Soldier with the Arabs,* p. 118.
19. Kirkbride to Foreign Office, 19 May 1948, FO 371/68829.
20. *A Soldier with the Arabs,* p. 128.
21. Herzog, *The Arab–Israeli Wars,* p. 65.
22. Foreign Office to US Secretary of State, 24 May 1948, FO 371/68830.
23. Bevin to Kirkbride, 24 May 1948, FO 800/488.
24. Glubb, 'The Fighting in Jerusalem, May 1948', undated, 1973 (?) Glubb Papers, Transjordan Box 5.
25. *A Soldier with the Arabs,* pp. 162–3.

26. Glubb, 'The Trans-Jordan Situation', 12 August 1948, FO 371/68822.
27. ibid.
28. Foreign Office minute, 14 August 1948, FO 371/68832.
29. Pirie-Gordon to Foreign Office, 25 July 1948, FO 371/68822.

Chapter 12: The Divided Peace (pages 377–418)
1. 'The Trans-Jordan Situation', op.cit.
2. ibid.
3. Abdullah to Bevin, copied in Foreign Office to Amman, 21 August 1948, FO 371/68831.
4. ibid.
5. ibid.
6. 'Size and Shape of the Arab Legion for 1949–50', note by the War Office, 27 December 1948, FO 371/68832.
7. Foreign Office minute, 25 August 1948, FO 371/68822.
8. 'The Trans-Jordan Situation', op.cit.
9. *A Soldier with the Arabs*, p. 181.
10. ibid., p. 183.
11. Glubb to Goldie, 21 October 1948, quoted in Lunt, *Glubb Pasha*, p. 154.
12. Glubb, 'Trans-Jordan and Palestine', 5 October 1948, FO 371/68842.
13. Kirkbride to Foreign Office, 21 October 1948, FO 371/68864.
14. Interview with John Bagot Glubb, IWM, op.cit.
15. ibid.
16. 'Size and Shape of the Arab Legion for 1949–50', op.cit.
17. C-in-C MELF to War Office, 16 August 1948, FO 371/68832.
18. 'Size and Shape of the Arab Legion for 1950/51', note by the War Office, 21 January 1950, FO 371/82752.
19. Foreign Office minute, 25 August 1949, FO 371/68822.
20. Glubb, 'A Note on the Need for a Longer Term Plan for the Arab Legion', 23 May 1950, FO 371/82752.
21. Glubb to Robertson, 17 May 1951, FO 371/91820.
22. Foreign Office to Amman, 9 December 1952, FO 371/98887.
23. Foreign Office minute, 22 April 1949, FO 371/75295.
24. Interview with General Sir John Hackett, IWM, op.cit.
25. Amman to Foreign Office, 3 April 1952, FO 371/75295.
26. Glubb to Foreign Ofice, 9 May 1949, FO 371/75295
27. Lawrence Grisewold, 'Glubb Interview', *Palestine Post*, 6 July 1949, passed to Foreign Office from Amman, 22 July 1949, ibid.
28. 'Glubb's views on the Disposal of the Arab Areas of Palestine', Kirkbride to Foreign Office, 30 September 1948, FO 371/68642.
29. Kirkbride, 'Annual Report on the Hashemite Kingdom of Jordan for 1951', FO 371/98836.
30. Kirkbride to Foreign Office, 21 October 1948, FO 371/68864.
31. Gamel Abdel Nasser, quoted in Ben-Gurion, *Talks with Arab Leaders*, p. 298.
32. Glubb, 'A Note on the Situation in Jordan', 1 July 1952, FO 371/98861.
33. Lieutenant-Colonel H.B. Calvert, War Office memorandum to Foreign Office, 8 September 1949, FO 371/75298.
34. Kirkbride to Foreign Office, 8 December 1950, FO 371/82751.
35. 'Arab Legion Finances 1953/54', note by Foreign Office, 13 August 1952, FO 371/98882.

36. Robertson to Glubb, 24 October 1952, FO 371/98886.
37. Collins and Lapierre, *O Jerusalem!*, p. 197.
38. Author's interview with Colonel Robert Melville.
39. 'A Note on the Need for a Longer Term Plan for the Arab Legion', op.cit.
40. Foreign Office to Amman, 23 September 1953, FO 371/104925.
41. Lunt, *Glubb Pasha*, p. 178.

Chapter 13: Farewell to Arms (pages 419–60)
1. Glubb, 'Jordan and Egypt', 17 December 1953, FO 371/110925.
2. Duke to Shuckburgh, 6 July 1954, FO 371/110928.
3. Foreign Office minute on Glubb to Foreign Office, 29 December 1955, FO 371/121540.
4. Glubb, Notes on Disloyal Jordanian Officers, undated, July 1956 (?), Glubb Papers, Transjordan Box 8.
5. Foreign Office to Amman, 29 September 1955, FO 371/115713.
6. Amman to Foreign Office, 3 November 1955, FO 371/115684.
7. Glubb to Foreign Office, 28 November 1955, FO 371/115532.
8. Glubb, 'Need for Increases to Arab Legion as a result of Russian Penetration in Egypt', 30 October 1955, FO 371/115682.
9. Glubb to Robertson, 24 October 1952, FO 371/98886.
10. Foreign Office minute on General Templer's visit to Jordan, June 1955, FO 371/115681.
11. Glubb to Foreign Office, 5 January 1955, FO 371/115670.
12. Minute on Templer's Visit, op.cit.
13. Glubb to Melville, 3 October 1955, FO 371/115670.
14. Shuckburgh, *Descent to Suez: Diaries 1951–1956*, p. 262.
15. ibid., p. 304.
16. Macmillan, *Tides of Fortune*, p. 653.
17. Statement issued by 'Group of Jordanian Free Officers engaged in the National Struggle', November 1955, FO 371/1156894.
18. Amman to Foreign Office, 12 January 1956, FO 371/121491.
19. Glubb to Templer, 2 February 1956, FO 371/12156.
20. Duke to Foreign Office, 29 February 1956, ibid.
21. Brief for Foreign Secretary, 'Cairo Propaganda Attacks on General Glubb', 28 February 1956, FO 371/121560.
22. Minutes of Conservative Parliamentary Foreign Affairs Committee, 22 March 1956, FO 371/121544.
23. Lunt, *Hussein of Jordan: A Political Biography*, p. 18.
24. *A Soldier with the Arabs*, p. 396.
25. Amman to Foreign Office, 29 September 1955, FO 371/115713.
26. Wing Commander Jock Dalgleish, private memoir.
27. Foreign Office minute of meeting with Glubb, 11 August 1954, FO 371/110928.
28. Duke to Shuckburgh, 6 October 1955, FO 371/115683.
29. ibid.
30. Shuckburgh to Duke, 5 November 1955, ibid.
31. Duke to Shuckburgh, 6 October 1955, ibid.
32. *A Soldier with the Arabs*, p. 366.
33. Beirut to Foreign Office, 1 May 1956, FO 371/121560.
34. Currie to Selwyn Lloyd, 7 January 1956, FO 371/121491.

35. Broadhurst to Peake, 27 March 1956, op.cit.
36. Amman to Foreign Office, 23 January 1956, FO 371/121560.
37. Duke to Rose, 1 February 1956, ibid.
38. Amman to Foreign Office, 3 March 1956, FO 371/121541.
39. Amman to Foreign Office, 5 March 1956, FO 371/121564.
40. *A Soldier with the Arabs*, p. 425.
41. Duke to Foreign Office, 1 March 1956, FO 371/121540.
42. *A Soldier with the Arabs*, p. 423.
43. ibid., p. 428.

Chapter 14: Imperial Twilight (pages 461–93)
1. Duke to Foreign Office, 1 March 1956, FO 800/724.
2. Eden to Amman, 1 March 1956, ibid.
3. *Al Jihad*, 3 March 1956, passed from Amman to Foreign Office, 3 March 1956, FO 371/121541.
4. *The Times*, 3 March 1956.
5. Shuckburgh, *Descent to Suez*, p. 342.
6. Duke to Foreign Office, 3 March 1956, FO 371/121541.
7. Duke to Foreign Office, 5 March 1956, ibid.
8. Glubb, Letter to *The Times*, 9 March 1956.
9. Sir Ivone Kirkpatrick, minute of meeting with Glubb, 29 May 1956, FO 371/121549.
10. Kirkpatrick to Lord Strang, undated, June 1956, ibid.
11. Kirkpatrick to Glubb, 20 September 1956, FO 371/121551.
12. Glubb to Selwyn Lloyd, 1 May 1956, FO 371/121547.
13. Foreign Office memorandum for Selwyn Lloyd, 11 May 1956, ibid.
14. *The Story of the Arab Legion*, p. 139.
15. Glubb, personal note on the fate of the Bedouin, undated, Glubb Papers, Transjordan Box 8.
16. Selwyn Lloyd to P. Ingress Bell, 24 June 1957, FO 371/127941.
17. Duke, 'Assessment of Arab Legion's Present Position', 28 May 1956, FO 371/121565; Antony Nutting to Eden, 5 March 1956, FO 800/734.
18. James Wightman, 'The Double Anguish of Glubb Pasha', *Scottish Sunday Express*, 11 June 1967.
19. Foreign Office minute, undated, March 1958, FO 371/142155.
20. Robin Maugham, 'The Desert God who ended on the Scrapheap', *People*, 22 March 1970.
21. Interview with General Sir John Hackett, IWM, op.cit.
22. 'Assessment of Arab Legion's Present Position', op.cit.
23. 'Memoir of Arab Legion', February 1956, FO 371/115682.

Epilogue (pages 494–98)
1. Glubb, *The Way of Love*, pp. 60–61.
2. Canon Donald Carter, address at Glubb's funeral, St Dunstan's Church, Mayfield, March 1986.
3. His Majesty The King of the Hashemite Kingdom of Jordan, 'A Eulogy of a Memorable Man, John Bagot Glubb', Westminster Abbey, 17 April 1986.

Index

☐	The Boer War	Thomas Pakenham	£9.99
☐	The Scramble for Africa	Thomas Pakenham	£9.99
☐	The Caged Lion	William Manchester	£7.99
☐	The Last Lion	William Manchester	£10.99
☐	The Bloody Game	Paul Fussell	£9.99
☐	The Washing of the Spears	Donald Morris	£8.99

Abacus now offers an exciting range of quality titles by both established and new authors. All of the books in this series are available from:

Little, Brown and Company (UK) Limited,
P.O. Box 11,
Falmouth,
Cornwall TR10 9EN.

Alternatively you may fax your order to the above address.
Fax No. 0326 376423.

Payments can be made as follows: cheque, postal order (payable to Little, Brown and Company) or by credit cards, Visa/Access. Do not send cash or currency. UK customers and B.F.P.O. please allow £1.00 for postage and packing for the first book, plus 50p for the second book, plus 30p for each additional book up to a maximum charge of £3.00 (7 books plus).

Overseas customers including Ireland, please allow £2.00 for the first book plus £1.00 for the second book, plus 50p for each additional book.

NAME (Block Letters) ....

....

ADDRESS ....

....

....

☐ I enclose my remittance for _____

☐ I wish to pay by Access/Visa Card

Number ☐☐☐☐☐☐☐☐☐☐☐☐☐☐☐☐

Card Expiry Date ☐☐☐☐